SPECULATIVE ENTERPRISE

Speculative Enterprise

*Public Theaters and Financial Markets
in London, 1688–1763*

MATTIE BURKERT

UNIVERSITY OF VIRGINIA PRESS
Charlottesville and London

University of Virginia Press
© 2021 by the Rector and Visitors of the University of Virginia
All rights reserved
Printed in the United States of America on acid-free paper

First published 2021

9 8 7 6 5 4 3 2 1

Library of Congress Cataloging-in-Publication Data

Names: Burkert, Mattie, author.
Title: Speculative enterprise : public theaters and financial markets in London, 1688–1763 / Mattie Burkert.
Description: Charlottesville : University of Virginia Press, 2021. | Includes bibliographical references and index.
Identifiers: LCCN 2020051345 (print) | LCCN 2020051346 (ebook) | ISBN 9780813945958 (hardcover) | ISBN 9780813945965 (paperback) | ISBN 9780813945972 (ebook)
Subjects: LCSH: Theater—England—London—History—18th century. | Theatrical companies—England—London—History—18th century. | Theater—Economic aspects—England—London. | London (England)—Economic conditions—18th century. | Great Britain—Economic conditions—18th century.
Classification: LCC PN2596.L6 B835 2021 (print) | LCC PN2596.L6 (ebook) | DDC 792.09421—dc23
LC record available at https://lccn.loc.gov/2020051345
LC ebook record available at https://lccn.loc.gov/2020051346

Cover art: The Lottery, William Hogarth, after 1724 (The Metropolitan Museum of Art, New York; www.metmuseum.org); *Whitehall Evening Post* 383, February 25, 1721, 3 (Harry Ransom Center, The University of Texas at Austin)

For John and Mina

CONTENTS

Acknowledgments ix

Introduction: The Theater-Finance Nexus 1

Part I. The Great Recoinage (1695–1698)

1. "Virtue Is as Much Debased as Our Money":
   Generic and Economic Instability in *Love's Last Shift* 23
2. Recoining the Repertory: Prologues, Epilogues, and Crisis 45

Interlude (1700–1720)

3. Women at the Theater-Finance Nexus: Susanna Centlivre
   as Playwright-Adventurer 79

Part II. The South Sea Bubble (1720–1722)

4. Defrauding the Public: Spectacle and Speculation
   in Steele's *Theatre* and *The Conscious Lovers* 123
5. "His Title, Not His Play, We Set to Sale": Literary Property
   in the Aftermath of the South Sea Bubble 156

Coda: The Theater-Finance Nexus in Later
   Eighteenth-Century London 185

Notes 199
Bibliography 233
Index 263

ACKNOWLEDGMENTS

At the outset of a book about debt, risk, and contingency, it seems fitting to thank the many individuals and institutions that have invested in this very speculative project over the years.

My doctoral dissertation, on which this book is based, was supported by a Mellon/ACLS Dissertation Completion Fellowship, as well as the Department of English, the Graduate School, and the Office of the Vice Chancellor for Research and Graduate Education at the University of Wisconsin–Madison, with funding from the Wisconsin Alumni Research Foundation. Subsequent archival research and writing was supported by the Department of English and a generous grant from the Center for Women and Gender (now the Center for Intersectional Gender Studies and Research) at Utah State University. In its final stages, the book benefited from a publication subvention grant from the Oregon Center for the Humanities and the College of Arts and Sciences at the University of Oregon. I owe a debt of gratitude to the archivists and staff at the British Library, the Folger Shakespeare Library, the V&A Archives, and the National Archives of the United Kingdom, where I conducted research for this project. My thanks extend to the institutions that allowed me to use images of items from their collections: the British Library, the Harry Ransom Center at the University of Texas at Austin, and the Metropolitan Museum of Art in New York. I am also grateful to the University of Chicago Press for allowing me to reproduce, as part of chapter 1 of this book, material previously published in *Modern Philology*, vol. 114 (© 2016 by the University of Chicago; all rights reserved).

I am deeply grateful to my editor, Angie Hogan, for her enthusiastic encouragement of this project, and to Leslie Tingle, Ellen Satrom, Jason Coleman, Emily K. Grandstaff, and all the staff at the University of Virginia

Press for their incredible energy, expertise, and professionalism in shepherding this work from manuscript to book. Particular thanks go to two reviewers—John O'Brien and one who remains anonymous to me—who took the time to offer rigorous feedback that made this an inestimably better work of scholarship.

I also wish to express my gratitude to the many mentors and colleagues who have helped to bring this book into existence. Karen Britland provided unflagging support for this work and continues to serve as a model of scholarly generosity. She, along with Mark Vareschi, Theresa Kelley, Kristina Straub, and Thomas Broman, guided the doctoral research that eventually became this book. Other formative input during that time came from Robin Valenza, David Loewenstein, Michael Witmore, Aparna Dharwadker, Katherine Lanning, Victor Lenthe, Laini Kavaloski, Theresa Ngyuen, and Mary Fiorenza. After my arrival at Utah State University, my colleagues Christine Cooper-Rompato, Lynne McNeill, Felipe Valencia, and Phebe Jensen offered generative responses to early versions of chapter 3. Jane Wessel, Chelsea Philips, and Leah Benedict were a font of insight, accountability, and camaraderie throughout the revision process. Tita Chico, Rebecca Shapiro, Emily Friedman, Kate Ozment, and Carrie Shanafelt created supportive spaces for daily work in the last stages of manuscript preparation, during which time Camille Sleight provided invaluable assistance.

My family and friends were an inexhaustible source of encouragement, love, and perspective throughout this lengthy process; my deepest thanks go to Phil Burkert; Susan and Rory Pople; Hannah Corcoran; Cas, Sandy, and Sarah Karczewski; Lauren Hock; Leah Misemer; Rachel Herzl-Betz; Faina Polt; and Jessie Gurd. Finally, it is to John, my loudest cheerleader and toughest critic—and to Mina, who came into being alongside these pages—that I dedicate this work.

SPECULATIVE ENTERPRISE

• INTRODUCTION •

The Theater-Finance Nexus

As a symphony of music plays, the curtain rises, revealing a stage set with two wheels of fortune—round drums over six feet tall fitted with an elaborate set of doors, locks, and cranks. The goddesses of fortune and justice, Fortuna and Astrea, descend from above in golden chariots and deliver grand orations on the mysteries of destiny, fate, and chance.[1] Finally, the long-awaited moment arrives: over 1.5 million numbered ticket stubs, one corresponding with each lottery ticket sold, are placed inside one of the enormous wheels. One thousand winning "benefit" tickets labeled with prize amounts from £1 to £1,000 are placed inside the other wheel, along with a number of "blanks" indicating no prize.[2] A young boy turns the crank of the first wheel, rotating the contents; he reaches within, draws a ticket, and reads out the number, which matches a ticket held by someone in the crowd gathered around the stage. A boy at the other wheel turns its crank, unlocks one of its doors, and summons forth the adventurer's fate.[3]

The date is October 18, 1698, and the occasion is the first day of drawings for the Wheel of Fortune lottery at the Theatre Royal in Dorset Garden, a venue normally used for semi-operas and other spectacular entertainments. At a moment of intense competition among lotteries, this one was exceptionally successful, due to the unusually low cost of entry—each ticket cost only a penny—and because the extravagance of the drawing itself was advertised months in advance.[4] This performance illustrates vividly the profound material and figural links between the theater and financial markets in London around the turn of the eighteenth century. These connections persisted beyond the moment of the Wheel of Fortune, as a c. 1724

FIGURE 1. *The Lottery*, William Hogarth, after 1724. (The Metropolitan Museum of Art, New York; www.metmuseum.org)

satirical engraving by William Hogarth demonstrates (fig. 1). In his image *The Lottery*, the goddesses Fortune and Wantonness stand onstage and draw tickets from drums like those used for the 1698 lottery. The entire image is framed by curtains, further emphasizing the theatricality of the scene. The audience, made up of allegorical figures like Hope, Fear, Suspence, Folly, and Misfortune, is overseen by National Credit on a pedestal, a reminder that the lotteries were intimately tied to the operations of public finance that underpinned England's development as a global fiscal and military power.

This book turns to the period of "financial revolution" that followed the Revolution of 1688 in England.[5] In the decades following William and Mary's ascent to the throne, England saw the widespread adoption of credit-based currencies, securities markets, boom-bust cycles, speculative bubbles, insurance schemes, and lotteries, as well as the formalization of the national debt. While the story of England's transition to financial capitalism is a familiar one, however, the centrality of the public theater to this story has been overlooked. London's public playhouses played a key role in debates over new financial instruments and institutions and their broader cultural ramifications. Performances engaged with financial concerns at the level of plot, characterization, and language, addressing audience members as economic subjects within complex webs of interdependence and conflict. As a site of cultural recycling, the repertory theater was uniquely positioned to intervene in financial debates, which often hinged on the relationship of England's present to its economic past. Revivals and adaptations of Tudor and early Stuart plays drew attention to the experience of markets a century earlier, while new plays self-consciously reworked inherited tropes and genres to meet the needs of the day.[6] In engaging with dramatic tradition in these ways, the theater complicated both nostalgic visions of England's precapitalist past and uncritical celebrations of its fiscal modernity.[7]

The link between theatrical and financial markets was material as well as conceptual: the economics of the theater was significantly reshaped during this period. The public playhouses struggled to accommodate the changing tastes of audiences, which were reconfigured by changing class structures and gender roles. In this shifting and competitive environment, theaters repeatedly merged and split, testing out innovations from the worlds of trade and finance as they tried to survive. Observers recognized these shifts and articulated a sense of the theater as a form of mass culture that operated according to the rules of the market, increasingly speculative and dependent on public opinion. Drury Lane and Exchange Alley became connected sites in conversations about who determined value in London's increasingly crowded and diverse public spheres; about the growing power of self-proclaimed experts to shape public opinion; and about the abstraction of commodities as objects of market speculation. Contemporaries expressed concern that the new norms of the market penetrated the production of artistic objects, affecting the compensation and status of cultural workers—playwrights, actors, managers, and critics—as well as the forms plays took. These concerns found voice in the wider media landscape of the theater: in dramatic criticism and in the pages of the periodical press, producers and consumers of theatrical media reveled in and agonized over the theater's embeddedness within speculative market structures. In doing so they highlighted the often-abstract ties between the value of commodities and the publics that determined their value.

To say that theater and finance were "speculative enterprises" during this period is to underline the dynamics of risk, chance, and anticipation that defined investment in either market. In economic usage the term "speculation" has two distinct but related meanings: "The action or practice of buying and selling goods, land, stocks and shares, etc., in order to profit by the rise or fall in the market value, as distinct from regular trading or investment," on the one hand; and "engagement in any business enterprise or transaction of a venturesome or risky nature, but offering the chance of great or unusual gain," on the other.[8] To trade based on one's beliefs about future prices is intrinsically hazardous but carries the possibility of gains commensurate to that exposure—a possibility that attracted investors to the theater as well as to ventures like the Wheel of Fortune lottery and the South Sea scheme of 1720, which promised outlandish returns on modest outlays. Furthermore, the term "speculative," associated with abstraction and conjecture, suggests the dependence of this new financial order on operations of imagination like those cultivated by dramatic entertainment. As Jean-Christophe Agnew argues in his influential *Worlds Apart: The Market and the Theater in Anglo-American Thought, 1550–1750* (1986), the concurrent rise of capitalist market structures and public theater is no mere coincidence. Rather, Agnew insists, these realms are bound by "special and often implicit conditions of belief and accountability" and by a concern with the representation of increasingly invisible and depersonalized value.[9]

Building on Agnew's account, this study traces the figurative relay between financial and theatrical markets and explores how they produced a discursive space for debating the operations of speculative investment, the power of the rising middling classes, and the growing ability of public opinion to affect commodity values and shape institutions. I argue that this discursive space, which I call the "theater-finance nexus," was central to understandings of London's emergent public spheres and to debates about their possibilities and risks. This project is not merely a study of the tropology of economics in dramatic materials, nor is it a straightforward history of playhouse finances; rather, it offers a new understanding of a discursive object that emerged in response to the structural parallels and shared contradictions of public formation in the playhouses and coffeehouses of London. At a moment when the formal discipline of political economy was in its infancy, the theater provided a discourse zone for understanding complex economic systems—one that stressed the contingency and potential irrationality of markets, rather than quantification and reason.[10]

Furthermore, as the Wheel of Fortune entertainment and Hogarth's engraving suggest, gender was central to these debates. In the published epilogue to the Dorset Garden drawing, Fortuna—played by Miss Porter, an adolescent actress known for her delivery of sexually suggestive prologues and epilogues at the theater in Lincoln's Inn Fields—compares her limited stock of prizes to the number of sexual favors one woman can bestow.[11] In doing so she participates in a broader feminization of speculative financial behavior, associated with the seductive, fickle, and unstable goddesses of Fortune, Credit, and Luxury.[12] Women's increased involvement in financial markets prompted anxieties about the emasculating influence of commodification and speculation. At the same time, the theater was a sphere in which women were actively involved as actresses, playwrights, investors, and managers; as such, it provided a model for thinking about what it meant for women to operate in public.

This book contends that the conceptual nexus of theater and finance was vital to eighteenth-century economic, political, and social thought. Yet the theater and its media landscape have been understudied as sites for the transmission of public knowledge, hopes, and fears about emergent financial structures in the long eighteenth century. While economic historians have long relied on pamphlets and treatises as barometers of public opinion about Britain's changing financial system, literary scholars have tended to focus on poetry, satire, and the novel to understand the imaginative representation of markets.[13] The theater is a rich site for investigation of cultural attitudes toward economics for several reasons. First, the British theater has always been a for-profit enterprise; unlike many poetic and prose forms, it was never imagined to stand above market forces. Second, the theater of the Restoration and eighteenth century brought together people of different social classes in a public venue.[14] Indeed, theater—not the novel—was the form of literary entertainment most central to public life in eighteenth-century London.[15] And third, contemporaries were deeply attuned to parallels between the intangibility of credit-based financial markets and the ephemerality of performance. Writers of the period registered the fact that credit, like performance, seemed phantasmal yet produced powerful real-world effects.[16]

This book draws new attention to the relationship between financial markets and the theater of the long eighteenth century. At the same time, it contributes to ongoing efforts to bring together economic and literary history. Since the 1970s "New Economic Criticism" has fused the cultural materialism of Marxist literary theory with the philosophical and linguistic interests of poststructuralism to reflect on interrelations between economics and literature.[17] Scholars in this tradition investigate the historical and formal relationships between economic structures such as indebtedness, exchange, and speculation, on the one hand, and the guiding logics of literary and cultural texts on the other. They also attend to the economics of literary production, including the status of literary commodities, literature as intellectual property, and the professionalization of authorship.[18] My own study necessarily touches on these subjects, even as it draws attention to a new locus of inquiry: the theater-finance nexus of seventeenth- and eighteenth-century England.

This book also draws on a robust body of work focused on the interplay of economics and the early modern stage.[19] These studies, however, tend to end their inquiries with the late seventeenth century; relatively little scholarship takes up the material and figural relationships between theatrical and financial markets after the Restoration. While theater historians have engaged closely with the business of the theater itself in the later period, and while critics of dramatic literature have pointed out the presence of economic figures and discourses in eighteenth-century play texts, the sustained interactions between finance and theater as topics of public debate have gone largely unremarked.[20] One notable exception, John O'Brien's *Harlequin Britain* (2004), argues that the theater served as a symbol of Britain's economic and political modernity, provoking anxieties about the rise of mass culture and the vulnerability of the nascent public sphere to commercial interests. While O'Brien traces the ways that cultural phenomena respond to and reflect developments in markets, however, I seek to bring a new attention to the mutual influence of these two spheres, which developed in tandem and formed a conceptual nexus that enabled powerful theorizations of publicity.

Any account of the emergence and operations of publics must engage in debates that remain profoundly influenced by Jürgen Habermas's account of the "bourgeois public sphere," a virtual space in which private people came together to debate matters of common concern and to hold authorities accountable. For Habermas and his followers, the coffeehouses and periodical press of London at the turn of the eighteenth century were central to the development of this virtual space. While Habermas acknowledges that the Enlightenment bourgeois public sphere failed to achieve the universality to which it pretended—being, for instance, far more open to men and property owners than to women and laborers—he holds it up as a standard of discourse from which his own moment has fallen. In his account, twentieth-century mass media and culture industries have weakened the ability of critical public debate to hold institutions to account; in an era of corporatized media, it is increasingly easy for the wealthy and powerful to promote their own interests and nearly impossible for those without capital to intervene.[21]

Feminist theorists have long objected to Habermas's ideal of rational-critical debate, pointing out that its protocols exclude members of groups culturally marked as irrational, including women and ethnic or racial minorities.[22] More recently, queer theorist Michael Warner has developed a rich theory of counterpublics: publics defined in tension to the larger public, operating according to different protocols of debate from those of the bourgeois public sphere.[23] Mass culture and consumer culture are not the evil for Warner that they are for Habermas; rather, they have the potential to be counterpublic-forming because they controvert the notion of rationality as the defining feature of public life. Mass culture—understood as a field of shared media experiences in which individuals' desires and identifications are shaped in self-aware relation to consumer society—undermines the notion that anyone operates objectively or rationally. In forcing individuals to confront the ways their desires are shaped by media and commodification, mass culture calls into being a "mass-public subject" that was "unanticipated within the classical bourgeois public sphere."[24] Media scholars have tended to view the intimate relationship between the public sphere and consumerism as a product of twentieth-century mass media like radio, television, and film. What I argue, however, is that the mass-public subject was very much a felt reality in long-eighteenth-century England. At the very moment when the bourgeois public sphere and rational-critical debate were adumbrated in periodicals like Joseph Addison and Richard Steele's *Spectator*, so too was the supposedly irrational mass public shaped by its consumption of commoditized media.[25]

This prehistory has gone unremarked in part because historians of the public sphere have focused insistently on print media, paying limited attention to the role of the theater in generating and sustaining the public sphere. Warner himself views print as the "imaginary reference point of the public" in the eighteenth century, a focus that prevents him from viewing how his own theories are anticipated in the theatrical mass culture of the earlier period.[26] Taking the playhouse, rather than the coffeehouse, as the paradigmatic space of early modern public formation makes it possible to see how a public domain might openly flaunt, rather than suppress, its relationship to the market. The theater positions audience members not as rational, liberal, bourgeois subjects participating in reasoned debate about matters of shared concern but instead as economic and embodied subjects who operate in complex networks, dependent on and in conflict with the interests of others. Plays themselves dramatize these complicated and conflictual relations, while prologues, epilogues, advertisements, and reviews address theatergoers as consumers deciding what performances are worth paying to attend. The public addressed in the theater is the mass subject, the consumer of mass culture openly influenced by market imperatives and by operations of power.

Following Warner, I find that this kind of mass culture and mass subjectivity had the potential to give voice to new forms of collective interest, creating space for those who had been excluded from participation in the implicitly white, masculine, propertied bourgeois public sphere. At the same time, observers like Steele sounded the alarm about the more frightening potentials of publics and counterpublics: the tyranny of the majority, the assault on enlightened rationality by market forces, and the cooptation of the public interest by highly capitalized private interests. Throughout this study I examine materials that mark Londoners' growing awareness that the rational-critical bourgeois public sphere existed alongside, even interpenetrated, a consumerist and irrational mass public that had the potential to coerce or to be coopted. But in both finance and theater—two realms whose relationship to the masses was being reconfigured at the same moment—they also sensed the potential for this energetic space to exceed the control of any one particular interest. In sum, today's debates about mass publicity and mass culture have their roots in concerns articulated in the long eighteenth century, a fact that becomes evident when we attend to the theater-finance nexus.[27]

Importantly, the theatrical public I analyze throughout this book is a mediated one, constructed and maintained through circulating media. As performance studies has shown, the special nature of a live event is part of what makes the theater a privileged arena for experiencing and theorizing public life.[28] Yet the boundaries of the "public" sensed in the eighteenth-century theater extended beyond the crowd at one night's show, spilling out into a wider media landscape: published prologues and epilogues; advertisements for performances and for printed plays; celebrity anecdotes and gossip; and reviews and criticism. In foregrounding the mediated nature of the theatrical public sphere—a mediation that helped bring the theater-finance nexus into being by placing economic and entertainment news into regular contact in the periodical press—this book contributes to the recent methodological turn towards intermedial studies of theater.[29] Recognizing the intermediality of eighteenth-century theater requires a sharper understanding of those artifacts previously considered ancillary to "the drama"—cast lists, title pages, songs, playbills, and the like.[30] Whereas these documents have often been used to register the bare facts of theater history, this study takes seriously the sophisticated cultural work they did as they engaged with financial developments, and it emphasizes the unique window these materials provide onto the public's immediate responses to theatrical events and controversies. The media environment surrounding the playhouse was a vibrant space of interaction and debate, as crucial to the construction of the theatrical public sphere as performance itself. For that reason, the chapters of this book open out from discussions of selected plays to engage with a variety of archival materials from across the London mediascape.

While my focus is on the late seventeenth and early eighteenth centuries, any study of theater—a medium that endlessly recycles itself—must attend to continuity as much as change. While different from the prewar theater in many ways—including the presence of women on the stage and the use of elaborate scenery—the Restoration and eighteenth-century theater inherited and adapted the texts and traditions of Elizabethan and early Stuart drama. Likewise, the developments of the financial revolution represent an intensification and acceleration of England's transition to financial capitalism, but they cannot be understood apart from a longer history of agrarian and mercantile capitalism extending back generations. In order to grasp the material and historical conditions under which the theater-finance nexus developed, it is necessary first to trace the interrelated histories of London's public theaters and its financial sector from the late sixteenth through the seventeenth century. During this period the playhouses and the stock market developed parallel institutional structures, as the theaters increasingly came to resemble joint-stock trading companies and to be tied up in the operations of the stock market.

Under Elizabeth I and James I, England witnessed several interrelated economic developments that together laid the groundwork for later events.

Population growth and urbanization produced a rapid expansion of commercial activity. Widespread currency shortages, exacerbated by criminal clipping and counterfeiting of the coinage, pushed financial transactions away from cash and towards credit.[31] The early seventeenth century also witnessed the beginnings of state-sponsored international speculative trade; the most important development in this area was the chartering of the East India Company in 1600. It is to this moment that many historians trace the beginnings of English political economy, as government officials and intellectuals attempted to articulate the fundamentals of an economic system undergoing significant reconfiguration.[32]

As more of the population followed commerce by moving towards cities, the traveling playing companies settled down in London, renting out theaters on a temporary basis. Although these companies were sponsored by monarchs and nobles, they were typically managed internally by a member of the acting troupe.[33] Drama during this period reflected the economic upheaval of the time. For instance, as the credit system took hold, individuals' financial well-being was increasingly based on social assessments of their character—one possible reason why plays from the sixteenth and early seventeenth century are so preoccupied with the difficulty of reliably gauging another person's trustworthiness.[34]

A credit system based on interpersonal exchanges and debt was insufficient to deal with the larger challenges facing England's economy, however. The demands of financing England's participation in the Thirty Years' War (1618–48) and in the first three Anglo-Dutch Wars (1652–54, 1665–67, 1672–74) made it clear that the government needed access to large-scale, transferable credit instruments to support trade and military expenditures.[35] During the English civil wars (1642–51) and Interregnum (1649–60), goldsmith bankers and scriveners became increasingly prominent, lending to Oliver Cromwell's government and dealing in credit instruments including bills of exchange, checks, and promissory notes. On his accession, Charles II also relied on credit to invest in projects such as the improvement of the Royal Navy and the reconstruction of London following the Great Fire—strengthening the power of goldsmith bankers and deepening the relationship between the crown and the financial sector.[36] A critical event in Restoration economic and cultural history was the Stop of the Exchequer, Charles II's 1672 decision to suspend interest payments on half of the state's debt, which caused a run on the banks and diminished the crown's credit. The Great Stop drew public attention to the fact that the monarch could not be held truly accountable for his or her debts, prompting demands for a national banking system in which Parliament would hold the national debt.[37] This system would not be realized, however, until after the Revolution Settlement.

The Restoration of the Stuart monarchy also brought with it the reopening of the public playhouses, which had been shuttered during the Interregnum due to Puritan antitheatrical sentiment.[38] Charles II changed the theatrical landscape dramatically, however, when he granted patents to two courtiers, Thomas Killigrew and William Davenant, to establish playing companies of a new kind.[39] As Judith Milhous explains, the Restoration patentees had an "absolutely unprecedented" legal authority to operate a theatrical monopoly and to pass it on to their heirs and assigns. While they retained the formal designation as the King's and the Duke's companies and were obligated to pay the Master of Revels to license their scripts, they otherwise had autonomous power over the selection of plays, the hiring and firing of actors, admission prices, and—importantly—the construction of new theaters.[40] Rather than operating out of the existing playhouses, both chose first to convert tennis courts and then to construct new buildings at Dorset Garden and Drury Lane that could accommodate more sophisticated scenery and machinery.[41] The companies were now firmly associated with the theaters where they played.[42]

These patent theaters experimented with new legal and financial models that pushed the boundaries of royal control. While Charles II had created two patents meant to be transferred to Killigrew and Davenant's heirs and assigns in perpetuity, in practice the patents made it possible for interest in the theaters' operations to be purchased, traded, mortgaged, and subdivided into smaller and smaller pieces. As O'Brien puts it: "If to the monarch the patents were a means of institutionalizing his traditional role as supervisor of entertainment, to the managers they were the conditions of the London stage's becoming a money-making cartel."[43] A kind of stock and derivatives market developed around the theater patents and around the real estate that they allowed the companies to develop. For example, the King's and Duke's companies sold building shares to raise capital for construction of the Dorset Garden and Drury Lane playhouses. Initially, the companies paid building shareholders a regular fee, much like rent; later these shareholders received a percentage of acting company profits. The building shares were transferable and did not convey any managing or decision-making power in the company, and as such, they had an ambiguous relationship to the equity and power located in the patent.[44] In addition to these building shares, the companies also distributed profit shares, which worked quite differently. In Davenant's company, for example, the company was divided into twenty shares, of which approximately half were held by members of the Davenant family and by investors; these shares conveyed a financial interest in the underlying patent. The remaining shares, which carried a right to a portion of the company's profits but not to any part of the patent, were held by the leading actors in the company.[45]

The story of the patent theaters after 1670 is one of constant legal battles and corporate intrigue. The King's Company in particular, plagued by Thomas Killigrew's mismanagement and recovering from a devastating 1672 fire, struggled throughout the 1670s. Eventually, Charles Davenant and Charles Killigrew agreed to merge their fathers' theaters in 1682. The new United Company, operating under Davenant's patent, held a monopoly on licensed theater in London for over a decade. The company fell under the control of lawyer Christopher Rich and courtier Thomas Skipwith in 1687 when Alexander Davenant—who had purchased the patent from his brother using money borrowed from Rich and Skipwith—fell behind on his payments and fled to the Canary Islands.[46] The new owner-managers' first move was to buy out the actors' shares. Jocelyn Powell explains that this allowed them to lower the actors' salaries, which was "the quickest way of reducing the charges of performances and getting more money for the shareholder."[47] Resisting what they saw as Rich's exploitative business practices, a group of veteran actors under the leadership of Thomas Betterton defected in spring 1695, acquiring a license from the Lord Chamberlain to operate a rival theatrical cooperative at Lincoln's Inn Fields.[48] Rejecting the kind of profiteering they saw in Rich's behavior, the actors distributed shares amongst themselves by a majority vote and forbade the participation of outside investors.[49]

As this history illustrates, from the earliest days of the Restoration—when the interests of the nobility held the most sway in the theaters—the patent companies were fundamentally dependent on and beholden to shareholders, including not only members of the company but also outside investors. They were speculative enterprises, underwritten by the government but entrenched in a new financial system that moved according to the mysterious forces of public opinion; as a result, they experimented constantly with new methods of raising money. By the 1720s, Judith Milhous notes, "theatre had grown . . . so large and potentially profitable that it was possible to divorce daily operations from ownership almost entirely and to speculate in ownership as a separate commodity."[50] Over the early decades of the eighteenth century, building on market practices originating in the sixteenth and seventeenth centuries, the public theaters became a major financial engine. Like the joint-stock trading companies underpinning England's overseas trade, the patent theaters of the early eighteenth century were financial operations licensed and backed by the government in which private investors could "adventure" for a profit.

Over the same period that the theater was becoming an increasingly speculative market, England's financial system was becoming more dependent on credit and novel financial instruments. With the Revolution Settlement, Parliament not only replaced King James II with William and Mary; it also placed strict limits on the crown's finances and took over responsibility for funding the military.[51] In 1694 the Bank of England was founded to absorb the national debt, formalizing the notion that the nation had its own credit identity separate from that of the monarch.[52] At the same time, other innovations made their way onto the London financial scene: the treasury began experimenting with new ways to raise money, such as lotteries; a sophisticated securities market developed, leading to a rise in stockbroking and stockjobbing; and a boom in patents and joint-stock companies produced a speculative environment that led Daniel Defoe to call the 1690s "The Projecting Age."[53] Many of these trading companies purchased portions of the national debt in exchange for monopolistic trading privileges, further blurring the lines between public and private finance.

Meanwhile, Exchange Alley operatives were among those changing the makeup of the theatrical audience. While Restoration theaters were somewhat socially and economically diverse, scholars generally agree that the patent theaters of the 1660s and '70s reflected the influence and tastes of King Charles II and his court.[54] During the reigns of William and Mary (1689–1702) and later Anne (1702–14), the association between the theater and crown was severely weakened, with royal patronage resuming in a meaningful way only with the Hanoverian accession in 1714. Under these conditions, and as citizens and traders gained both disposable income and cultural power in the post-1688 era, audiences appear to have become more dominated by the "middling sort," who influenced theatrical offerings through their cheers, jeers, and riots, as well as through published commentary and criticism.[55] Felicity Nussbaum argues that the increasing heterogeneity of audiences, combined with their active (even disruptive) engagement with the performers onstage, produced a "democratizing effect," albeit one that depended on the continued visibility rather than the eradication of class distinctions.[56] In the decades around the turn of the eighteenth century, audiences were frequently represented as mixed—nowhere more so than in prologues and epilogues that anatomized audiences by gender, social class, and occupation, as I discuss in chapter 2. Theater managers found themselves speculating on the kinds of plays that would be most likely to bring in both wealthy patrons who would fill the expensive boxes and more modest patrons who would fill the expansive pit.[57] While it is virtually impossible to ascertain the actual class makeup of theatrical audiences at this time, contemporary accounts record a sense that the class-based perspectives of nonelites were having a growing influence on the repertory. In this way the theater emblematized broader competition between classes at a time when the balance of political, economic, and cultural power was perceived to be shifting.

These changes were brought into particular focus during moments of financial crisis, which were frequent in the early eighteenth century, as the financial sector became increasingly entwined with all areas of the economy.[58] Such upheavals are fruitful loci for literary and cultural analysis, as David A. Zimmerman has observed, because they "incite explosive battles over the market's conceptualizations, its forms and functions, and its social meanings."[59] For that reason, this book is divided into two parts, each structured around a significant financial crisis. "Part 1: The Great Recoinage" examines the currency depreciation of the mid-1690s and its relationship to concurrent debates about dramatic genres and taste—debates precipitated by the breakup of a longstanding theatrical monopoly and the rival companies' ensuing competition for spectators. As suggested above, the problem of currency depreciation stretched back at least into the sixteenth century, but it took on new urgency with the foundation of the Bank of England in 1694. The bank emblematized the transition of wealth and power from land to the cash/credit nexus; while the monarch, who had previously owned the nation's debt, could claim all of England as his collateral, the bank's credit rested on its reserves of silver coin. This uncertainty and the financial pressures of the Nine Years' War (1688–97) led to a crisis of confidence in the mid-1690s that heightened anxiety over long-standing issues of counterfeiting and clipping. A Parliamentary showdown over the nature of monetary value resulted in a full recall and reissue of the nation's silver coin. Because the amount of real silver in circulation was so much lower than its face value, Parliament's controversial decision to undertake a full-value recoinage worsened the shortage of money. Nonetheless, supporters of the plan hoped that reminting the nation's coin at face value would restore faith in the Bank of England, providing long-term economic stability that would make up for short-term hardship.

Chapter 1, "'Virtue Is as Much Debased as Our Money': Generic and Economic Instability in *Love's Last Shift*," centers on the 1696 comedy that marked future poet laureate Colley Cibber's authorial debut. *Love's Last Shift* is often viewed by critics as an early sentimental comedy. While aristocratic social satire had dominated Restoration comedy, this new, gentler, reform-minded comedy was perceived as a vehicle for ascendant middling-class mores. A close examination of the play's financial themes, however, reveals its self-conscious exploration of the changing function of comedy in post-1688 society. Cibber figures the repurposing of inherited genres through metaphors of recoinage and speculative investment, highlighting the cyclical nature of financial and dramatic change alike. Ultimately, he unmasks both dramatic and economic reforms of his day as symptoms of a broader cultural obsession with novelty.

Chapter 2, "Recoining the Repertory: Prologues, Epilogues, and Crisis," situates Cibber's play within broader debates over the interrelated dynamics of theatrical and financial markets, as represented by dozens of dramatic prologues and epilogues printed between 1695 and 1697. These pieces used the conceptual nexus of finance and theater to theorize the relationship between value and public opinion; the potential of speculation as a source of innovation and risk; and the growing power of middling-class professionals, who brought a spirit of entrepreneurialism and self-promotion to spheres of influence that had long been dominated by patronage and the upper classes. The mid-1690s saw numerous topical performance pieces reflecting on the competition between the Patent Company at the Theatre Royal Drury Lane, which had previously held a monopoly on public theater in London, and the new Actor's Company at Lincoln's Inn Fields. This rivalry was insistently staged in generational terms, as the young and inexperienced actors who remained with the old company battled the venerable but aging troupe at the new company. Stage orations from Drury Lane touted the Patent Company's adaptations of Tudor and Stuart drama, which were figured as a kind of recoined currency. These freshly minted plays were imagined to be restoring the repertory to an earlier standard of value while simultaneously incorporating novel features that—like the new milled edges on coins—could make recycled drama "current." While some prologues and epilogues celebrated the innovation produced by competition, others questioned whether England's cultural heritage should be driven by competition for audiences and the profit motive. These pieces exposed the vulnerability of cultural and financial markets alike to manipulation by new kinds of self-proclaimed experts—whether financial professionals or theater critics—who had the power to fabricate value and guide the energies of public opinion in order to promote their own selfish interests. Prologues and epilogues could perform this cultural work because they mined what I show to be a widespread and commonly understood relation between theatrical and financial markets as sites of contest within emergent public spheres. The dialogic forms of the prologue and epilogue, delivered in conversation with the audience, were exemplary for their notice of competing voices and for their dramatization of public dissent as well as consensus.

The concerns expressed in prologues and epilogues of the 1690s reached a fever pitch during the 1720s with the speculative investment scheme and marketwide boom and bust known collectively today as the South Sea Bubble. Chapter 3, "Women at the Theater-Finance Nexus: Susanna Centlivre as Playwright-Adventurer," bridges the period between the recoinage of the 1690s and the South Sea Bubble of 1720 by tracing the career of Centlivre, who wrote sixteen plays and several afterpieces between 1700 and 1722. Well known in her time for comedies like *The Gamester* (1705) and *The Busie Body* (1709) that remained in repertory for over a century after her death, Centlivre is today recognized for her dramatic engagement with Whig political and economic ideologies and for her placement of those ideas in conversation with discourses of women's rights. A number of critics have explored how Centlivre's dramatic works represent economically charged sites—from the private gambling table to the raucous stock exchange to the public theater itself—as having the ability to bring men and women together on equal footing or to perpetuate gendered exclusion. In this chapter I broaden the focus to examine how Centlivre's own participation in the theatrical and print markets enacts and complicates the ideas set forth in her plays, including *The Gamester, The Busie Body, The Basset*

Table (1705), and *A Bold Stroke for a Wife* (1718), as well as in her poem *A Woman's Case* (1720). Her actions as an economic agent, I argue, demonstrate the potential of the commercial theater to function as a privileged sphere where women could work around the regular channels of political and economic participation from which they were excluded. At the same time, Centlivre's works expose the double edge of speculative financial and theatrical markets: while capable of opening up new forms of agency for women like herself, these sites were also susceptible to become vehicles for private interests to overtake the public good.

Centlivre's work reflects key shifts in the debates taking place at the theater-finance nexus over the course of her career—shifts precipitated by the South Sea Bubble of 1720. Building on concerns about the growing power of middling-class people that had circulated since the 1690s, dramatic texts and theatrical media of the 1720s expressed new fears: that economic and cultural elites might pretend to middling-class values in order to coopt the growing power of the public sphere; that the public might devolve into a mindless mob, squandering its social capital in favor of immediate sensual gratification; and that predatory elites might in fact promote such unruly crowd behavior, cultivating habits of mind that could lead to a more docile and less critical or politically powerful public. These debates were given voice in the periodical press, which became an increasingly influential force in the early decades of the eighteenth century. As the newspapers delved into financial news with greater detail and urgency, they also began including regular advertisements and reviews for theatrical performances. While the two chapters in "Part 2: The South Sea Bubble" continue to reflect on dramatic texts in performance, then, they also consider the periodical press that was increasingly central to the theater-finance nexus. In the newspapers and on stage, I show, representations of the South Sea crisis enabled new explorations of the power and vulnerability of the mass public.

Chapter 4, "Defrauding the Public: Spectacle and Speculation in Steele's *Theatre* and *The Conscious Lovers*," examines a periodical by Richard Steele, former *Spectator* author, playwright, and theater patentee. In the *Theatre*'s twenty-eight issues, Steele foretells the downfall of the South Sea Company at the height of public optimism, linking the investment scheme to the Royal Academy of Music's speculative funding of an Italian opera house in London. Both companies figure the dark side of the public sphere, harnessing the imaginative power of spectacle and speculation to direct the irrational energies of public opinion and exploiting the middling classes to advance the interests of a wealthy few. Placing the *Theatre* in conversation with Steele's popular and influential play *The Conscious Lovers* (1722), I offer a new reading of the character Indiana as a figure for the South Sea Company's risky trade in the West Indies—not, as she is often understood, for the operations of the East India Company. This link enriches our understanding of the play's critique of the precarious joint-stock trading companies that undergirded England's colonial trade and their troubling ability to blur the lines between the agendas of the old elite and the emergent middling classes.

Chapter 5, "'His Title, Not His Play, We Set to Sale': Literary Property in the Aftermath of the South Sea Bubble," returns to the prolific Colley Cibber, whose 1721 comedy *The Refusal* centers on the family of a fictional South Sea Company director, Sir Gilbert Wrangle. Contrary to the conventional view of Sir Gilbert as a vehicle for Cibber's promarket ideology, I read him as a figure representing the elite who have coopted the optimism of the masses for their own purposes—a critique that aligns with those articulated by Cibber's colleague Steele. While exposing the dishonesty of Sir Gilbert, however, *The Refusal* spreads blame more widely, representing the investing and spectating publics not as naïve dupes, but as willing participants in what they recognized to be an exploitive project. Cibber's commentary on the South Sea crisis was reframed in deeply ironic ways, however, by his play's publicity and reception. In a series of advertisements, bookseller Edmund Curll and newspaper editor Nathaniel Mist cast *The Refusal* as plagiarism. These advertisements interacted with surrounding financial news on the pages of London periodicals to portray theatrical adaptation as another form of fabricated value, building a complex web of similarities among the South Sea scheme, the business of stage adaptation, and the cutthroat world of publishing.[60] These connections were latent in the public imagination, I find, and activated by the financial themes of *The Refusal*.

I conclude with a coda that looks ahead to the Half-Price Riots of 1763 in order to examine the continued and shifting relationship of the theater-finance nexus to broader debates about public formation over the course of the eighteenth century. The riots in question occurred in response to the suspension of the longstanding discount on admissions to shows after the third act of the mainpiece (which was often followed by additional entertainments). In response to this threat, theatergoers mounted carefully choreographed destructions of playhouse property and successfully compelled the managers to maintain half-price admissions. As I argue, these protesters framed their right to be part of the theatrical public sphere in terms of their economic agency within the highly speculative theatrical market, which was opposed to the traditional property rights claimed by theater patentees and shareholders. Examining media coverage of the riots, this coda reveals how the theater became a proving ground for wider theories about the nature of the public and its relationship to competing forms of economic agency.

Taken together, these chapters reveal how the theater-finance nexus took shape in the late seventeenth century and facilitated, in the following decades, the emergence of a new and newly self-conscious mass public. In other words, this not merely the story of the emergence of the theater-finance nexus as such; it is the story of the forms of public relations that were enabled, identified, and theorized at that nexus and that we are able to see when we attend to this discursive space. It is the story of how public opinion—often linked conceptually by contemporaries to the interests and values of the middling classes—coalesced as a significant economic and cultural force in the final decades of the seventeenth century; how this powerful force was understood, by the 1720s, to be vulnerable to exploitation by the elite; and how these debates over the nature of publicity enabled, by mid-century, the development of new counterpublics. The speculative theatrical and financial enterprises of the 1720s realized the worst fears expressed in the 1690s about the commodification and commercialization of public life; yet, counterintuitively, the outcome of these struggles was not merely the entrenchment of elite power in the guise of popular will. Instead, the classed and gendered counterpublics that took shape within the fundamentally commercial relations of the entertainment industry theorized and practiced new forms of participation in public life that were available to nonelites. That is, the very features of the theater that mirrored financial markets and alarmed contemporaries—its hyper-commercialism, its dependence on a fragile and volatile collective opinion, its accessibility to members of different classes and genders, and its ability to circumvent processes of rational-critical debate in which cultural elites held the advantage—were the features that allowed counterpublics to emerge there and enabled the playhouse to provide an alternative to the coffeehouse as the locus of economic and political debate.

Across the moments of economic upheaval examined here, it becomes clear that financial capitalism exists in a state of perpetual crisis, its continuation dependent on an ongoing myth of novelty. Each crisis is experienced as configuring new and unprecedented relationships between individuals, publics, and institutions.[61] As an embodied repository of cultural memory, theater and its media landscape have a privileged ability to undermine this myth, uncovering links between seemingly disparate historical moments and persons. This study performs a parallel act of recovery—revealing affinities between financial crises and their representations across time and showing how these crises continue to highlight the same questions they have always raised about materiality and abstraction, mystification and criminality, and the vital and simultaneously dangerous power of collective imagination.

PART I

The Great Recoinage
(1695–1698)

• 1 •

"Virtue Is as Much Debased as Our Money"

Generic and Economic Instability in Love's Last Shift

This chapter explores a genre at the heart of the theater-finance nexus: stage comedy. From the sixteenth century, comedy was understood as the dramatic genre that best lent itself to commentary on the present. The prologue to Ben Jonson's *Every Man in His Humour* (1598) promises: "But deedes, and language, such as men doe use: / And persons, such as *Comedie* would chuse, / When she would shew an Image of the times, / And sport with humane follies, not with crimes."[1] In John Dryden's *Of Dramatick Poesy* (1668), Neander describes "the nature of Comedy" as "the imitation of common persons and ordinary speaking," as opposed to the elevated subject matter of tragedy.[2] From the Elizabethan age through the Restoration and into the eighteenth century, such theories prevailed: comedy should concern itself with ordinary life in the present, leaving tragedy to represent historical settings and matters of state. Because of this contemporary focus, comedy was often the genre that thematized economic developments most insistently; the city comedy of the Jacobean period, with its emphasis on money and credit culture, is a case in point.[3]

It makes sense, then, that the comedies of the 1690s reflect the rapidly changing economic conditions that followed the Revolution Settlement. The events of 1688–89 not only represented a fundamental change in the way the nation's finances were handled; they also coincided with and, in some ways, precipitated an economic crisis that immediately affected ordinary people's lives. William and Mary's war on France required increased taxes, led to shipping blockades that hurt trade, and contributed to the currency crisis that provoked a major recoinage in the mid-1690s. During this period a series of bad harvests also produced food shortages, so that, as Brodie Waddell has argued, "people in every corner of the country felt the pinch of hardship for much of William III's reign."[4] This acute awareness of economic difficulty naturally made its way into comedies of the day.

At the same time, stage comedy was in transition during the 1690s, moving away from the rakish, witty, aristocratic romps of the Restoration period and toward the moralistic, middling-class, domestic plots that would dominate the eighteenth century. One play often seen as marking this transition to the sentimental is Colley Cibber's (1671–1757) *Love's Last Shift; or, The Fool in Fashion*.[5] Following its successful 1696 premiere at the Theatre Royal in Drury Lane, Cibber's playwriting debut inspired a hit sequel—John Vanbrugh's *The Relapse* (1697)—and entered the repertory, where it remained for decades. Despite early audiences' appreciation for *Love's Last Shift*, however, modern critics have shown less enthusiasm. Throughout most of the twentieth century, literary scholars—influenced, perhaps, by Alexander Pope's portrait of Cibber as the Prince of Dulness in *The Dunciad in Four Books* (1743)[6]—lambasted the play for its generic unevenness, accusing Cibber of demonstrating insincerity and opportunism in the attempt to suture a reform plot onto a sex comedy that would satisfy both aristocratic and middling-class audiences.[7]

The play's popularity stemmed, in part, from the fact that it offered a new variation on the reform plot that had long been a feature of drama.[8] It centers on a rake, Loveless, who returns to London after a decade and hears that the wife he abandoned in England, Amanda, is dead. This rumor turns out not to be true, and in a virtuous twist on the conventional bed trick, Amanda disguises herself as a prostitute in order to seduce him back to faithfulness. Once he realizes that his long-suffering wife is a worthwhile lover and that his roving was driven by a misguided desire for novelty, Loveless delivers a lengthy speech expressing regret for his behavior and pledging to be faithful in the future. Unlike most of his rakish predecessors—Willmore of Aphra Behn's *The Rover* (1677), for example—Loveless appears to reform wholeheartedly and sincerely. While many critics have seen Loveless's conversion as too abrupt to be convincing, others have argued that the play was likely less uneven on the stage than it appears on the page.[9]

Yet even among its earliest audiences, there were those who registered the play's ambiguities and moments of incoherence. A theater critic noted in 1699 that "[t]he Plot indeed seems to be new, as it is surprising and *admirable*;

but some of the Criticks will have it founded on a very great improbability, viz. on *Loveless*'s not knowing his Wife."[10] Here, I aim to offer a more satisfying explanation for the formal inconsistency that has struck audiences and readers from the beginning. I argue that *Love's Last Shift* deliberately exposes the incompatibility of the moralistic reform movements of the 1690s with the inherited plotlines and character types of the repertory. This formal disjunction, often read as a sign of Cibber's opportunism, in fact allows him to theorize the social and cultural changes taking place at the end of the seventeenth century. Specifically, Cibber explores issues of historical continuity and change through the metaphor of financial innovation in order to ask whether his society is actually progressing or merely papering over deep historical problems. Ultimately, Cibber suggests that the cultural obsession with reform (of financial institutions, of public morality, of dramatic genres) may be seen as a backlash against Restoration values, but it may also be seen as playing to a less virtuous impulse—namely, the enthusiasm for novelty pervading London society. Cibber's play undercuts the optimistic rhetoric circulating at this time by raising the possibility that the turn toward virtue is just another fashion. Without denying the real political and social changes taking place in England in the 1690s or the role of Cibber's generation in ushering in and embracing those changes, I aim to show that Cibber's play is more critical of the discourse of novelty surrounding financial, commercial, and cultural innovation than previously recognized.

The problems of novelty that Cibber raises reflect a central preoccupation in London in the 1690s. J. S. Peters has identified a "general cultural anxiety about the new" in this period, affecting everything from the "new science" and the battle between the Ancients and the Moderns, to the debates surrounding new financial structures, to the growing appetite for news and the rise of the periodical press. While some met the rapid economic, social, and cultural changes taking place at the end of the century with enthusiasm, others, like Dryden and Jonathan Swift, questioned the value as well as the very possibility of novelty.[11] I locate Cibber's play within this complex of ambivalence about the new. As I read it, the play engages with the possibility that novelty is illusory, and it does so specifically by exploring the parallels between two arenas in which newness is a potentially false source of value: financial and theatrical markets.

Love's Last Shift develops the problem of novelty through two principal financial motifs, which in turn speak to the economics of the theater. One motif is that of coins and bullion—an immediately pressing concern, as the play was written and performed while England's debased metal currency was being collected and reminted. The first section of this chapter focuses on how *Love's Last Shift* brings together the depreciation crisis of the mid-1690s with the transition from license to virtue. The play repeatedly uses the tropes of bullion and specie as metaphors for virtue—the signature value of the more humane or moralistic comedy beginning to gain prominence at this moment—and entertains the question of whether their worth is constant or fluctuates with changing tides of public opinion. By extension, the play likens the recoinage of a devalued currency to the reformation of social mores and cultural forms, including dramatic genres. Through the metaphor of recoinage, Cibber shows how both economic and cultural metamorphosis require the base materials of the past to be melted down and milled into something new for the present, a process that exposes the contingent and historically situated nature of value.

The second section focuses on the motif of speculative investment, as practiced by the foppish Sir Novelty Fashion. The late seventeenth century witnessed an explosion in "projects"—speculative ventures to raise money for public improvements, inventions, lotteries, and the like through complex investment schemes. In his 1697 financial treatise *An Essay Upon Projects*, Daniel Defoe claimed that he and his contemporaries were living in an unprecedented moment, insisting that "the past Ages have never come up to the degree of Projecting and Inventing . . . which we see this Age arriv'd to."[12] This sense of newness was not unique to Defoe; joint-stock companies and speculative financial instruments had existed for decades, yet many printed materials of the period emphasized the novelty of market structures and practices that seemed to have emerged suddenly. Cibber's play, however, challenges this sense of projects as inventive. Sir Novelty Fashion uses speculative investment both to create new clothing trends and to revive old ones; in addition, he artificially inflates his former mistress's "stock" when he buys her off at the end of the play. Sir Novelty profits from cycling faded fashions and lovers back around in the guise of the latest thing, suggesting that speculative investment, like recoinage, is simply a way of making the old appear new.

The third section of this chapter examines how Cibber's play links its core insight about financial markets to the dynamics of the theatrical market. Just as the recoinage troubles the relationship between the base materials of the past and the refashionings of the present, the reform of dramatic genres turns out to be a superficial facelift of an established structure, designed to meet the public's insatiable demand for novelty. Cibber foregrounds the generic unevenness of his play in order to reveal the tension between the licentiousness of inherited genres and tropes and contemporary attempts to reform the theater.[13] The play invites audiences to recognize its virtue as a pretense. In doing so, it suggests that playwrights who attempt to accommodate the conflicting desires of audiences are forced to give the repertory an illusory sheen of morality. The supposedly virtuous new strains of comedy and tragedy attract audiences who are obsessed not with moral reform but with the new.

One way Cibber highlights his play's uneasy relationship to the repertory and theatrical tradition is through the figure of the fop, a stock character type that he adapts to new ends. Cibber encourages the audience to think of Sir Novelty Fashion as a figure who represents not only the investor but also, relatedly, the playwright. Cibber wrote the part of Sir Novelty for himself and played the role in *Love's Last Shift* as well as in later plays.[14] In performance, then, the fop investor and the playwright were linked by the body of the actor, but in the text they are also connected through numerous metadramatic references that tie Sir Novelty's profitable revivals of old fashions to the activities of the professional playwright. While critics have disagreed about whether Cibber ushered in or simply catered to the rise of sentimental comedy, the play itself troubles this false dichotomy as it reveals the overlap between shaping and aping trends.

My goal in reassessing this particular play is not merely to contribute to ongoing efforts to extricate Cibber's work from the legacy of scorn exhibited in much twentieth-century criticism, although that is a worthwhile endeavor.[15] Rather, my examination of *Love's Last Shift* serves as a case study that introduces the methodological approach I take throughout the rest of this book, which moves beyond conventional literary analyses of economic motifs in dramatic texts in order to better understand how theater professionals and audiences alike engaged with historically specific market dynamics—and how this engagement allowed them to develop a new discursive object, the theater-finance nexus. Other critics who have noted the financial terminology and imagery in *Love's Last Shift* have tended to reproduce familiar arguments about the economics of marriage and the increasing moralism of the rising middling classes. For instance, Laurie Finke interprets the play's alignment of feminine virtue with money as a largely conventional treatment of women's role as vehicles of property exchange, imposing modern assumptions about supply and demand onto a fundamentally different situation: "When chastity becomes a commodity, its worth, like that of all commodities, increases in proportion to its unavailability... just as an overabundance of currency debases its value."[16] Yet England did not experience an "overabundance of currency" at any point in the early modern period, especially not in the 1690s. In bypassing the play's specific historical context, scholars like Finke have painted an incomplete picture of how Cibber engaged with financial and cultural change. This chapter attempts to offer a more textured account of how contemporaries understood the relationship between the events now known as England's "financial revolution" and contemporaneous changes in public morality and taste.

In order to write a play that was so deeply engaged with the complex dynamics of currency and stock markets, Cibber had to count on sophisticated audiences who were highly attuned to financial developments. This play therefore serves as evidence that the theater was a public sphere in which financial developments were debated just as hotly as they were in coffeehouses and the periodical press. Cultural histories of finance, such as those by Anne Murphy and Carl Wennerlind, have examined public attitudes toward these events largely through analyses of pamphlets and treatises; yet drama provided another medium for engaging with these changes, one that was more amenable to ambiguity. *Love's Last Shift* illustrates how two key features of dramatic literature and performance in this period—its dialogism, which allowed competing voices to be heard, and its playful metatheatricality, which promoted self-reflexivity—enabled dramatic engagements with financial developments to accommodate a degree of nuance seldom found in print polemics. Orienting our understanding of this moment through drama and theater can therefore offer new insights into the broader conceptual exchanges that took place between economic, moral, and cultural reforms in the wake of the Revolution of 1688.

Recoinage

Love's Last Shift debuted during an economic crisis that lasted the better part of a decade and resulted in a near-total recoinage of England's silver currency. I begin this section with an overview of the factors that led to the recoinage and the immediate financial and political consequences of that decision. I then examine several moments in the play that make reference to the recoinage as a way of engaging with issues of value, stability, and change. Cibber repeatedly links coin and virtue throughout the play in order to demonstrate how value, both financial and moral, fluctuates over time in relation to public opinion.

The causes of the so-called Great Recoinage were multiple, including longstanding practices of clipping and counterfeiting, the economic impacts of the Nine Years' War (1688–97), and the formation of the Bank of England (1694). Silver coins had been debased for decades by clippers who shaved metal off the edges and melted down the gold or silver shavings to sell as bullion abroad. The pressures of the Nine Years' War on international markets worsened these longstanding problems and heightened public awareness of them. To fund the king's troops on the Continent, silver pounds were sold for bills of exchange that the army could then redeem for foreign currency. As the international markets became flooded with the English pound, it became a weaker currency, and its exchange rate fell in relation to bullion. Because the price of silver on the markets was rising while the value of the pound was fixed by law, it became even more advantageous for goldsmith bankers to send silver overseas.[17] In time, this illegal export of clipped silver led to a crisis of confidence in England's currency. By 1695 the silver content of circulating coins had fallen to less than 50 percent of face value; as the public began to mistrust the pound, the gold guinea gained preference. In mid-1695 the price of the guinea rose 40 percent to thirty shillings. This rising price of gold at home and silver on the international market created arbitrage opportunities for goldsmiths, who sold silver abroad for gold and then sold the gold to the mint at a profit. As a result, at the same time that the supply of small-denomination silver coins in England was dwindling and their value was becoming increasingly suspect, the supply of high-value gold coins began increasing.[18]

A consensus developed that England's silver coins needed to be reminted, but the logistics presented a problem. Because the amount of real silver in the circulating currency supply was so much less than its face value, a full-value recoinage would worsen the shortage of money by reducing the number of coins in circulation. The alternative proposed by Secretary of the Treasury William Lowndes was to recoin so that the silver content of each coin would be 80 percent of its face value. After a much-publicized debate carried out in person and in printed pamphlets, Parliament authorized a full-value recoinage.[19] The process of collecting and reminting the nation's silver specie began in 1696.[20]

The monetary crisis was predictably worsened by the decision. As clipped coins were taken out of circulation, the already-insufficient money supply dwindled and public confidence sank. The recoinage also created problems for the newly established Bank of England, which was backed by the pound sterling. As the bank's depositors lost faith in the English pound, they also lost faith in bank stocks, which eventually led to a bank run in May 1696.[21] The effects of this series of events, which economic historian Charles Larkin refers to as "one of the first 'modern' economic crises,"[22] were felt keenly not only by merchants, stockjobbers, and goldsmiths but by Londoners of every class. A London correspondent of the Duke of Beaufort wrote on May 5, 1696, that, due to the lack of circulating coin in the city "the common people begin to grow a little mutinous."[23] *Love's Last Shift*, which debuted in the same month that the Recoinage Act was passed and took effect, reflects public concern over the value of money. The play returns again and again to the fact that gold coins are overvalued while silver coins are debased, highlighting the destabilizing effects of their changing value relative to one another. As such, the text of *Love's Last Shift* provides a unique window onto perceptions of these economic events as they unfolded, helping to fill something of a gap in the existing economic histories that focus primarily on the printed debates.

The play's interest in monetary worth is signaled in its opening scene, which evokes both the shortage of silver change and the inflated value of gold coins. When Young Worthy gives Loveless's man Snap a guinea, the servant seems shocked at receiving such a large coin, exclaiming, "Bless my eye sight, a Guinea—Sir!" When Loveless later asks Young Worthy, "[C]an'st not thou lend me the fellow to that same Guinea you gave my Man[?]" Young Worthy obliges, saying, "[T]here 'tis, and all I have." This remark suggests the distinct possibility that Young Worthy's seeming generosity results from the fact that he does not have smaller denominations on hand. After Young Worthy exits, Loveless rejoices at receiving a guinea and exults in the lavish evening's entertainment it will afford him: "[H]ere's that will provide us of a Dinner and a brace of Whores into the bargain, at least as Guinea's and Whores goe now."[24] This remark establishes the play's obsession with the falling value of women, but it would also have had a more immediate resonance for audiences at early performances of *Love's Last Shift:* Loveless's remark would have served as a reminder of the skyrocketing value of the guinea, which was at its peak during the recoinage crisis. The exchange between Loveless and Young Worthy reflects a local phenomenon—the increasing price of gold in shillings—that, according to historian George Caffentzis, was largely responsible for precipitating the public's awareness of the English government's inability to stabilize its currency in relation to the value of bullion on the international market.[25]

In his 1721 collected works, Cibber added a footnote to Loveless's line about "Guinea's and Whores," the only footnote in the entire play; it reads, "Guineas went then at 30 s."[26] By 1721 a guinea was worth just 21 shillings. Cibber's addition of the footnote to that collection indicates that he considered the inflationary conditions of the 1690s an important context for understanding the exchange between Loveless and Snap—important enough to clarify for readers two decades later. After that date the guinea footnote continued to appear in editions of the play, and it persists today in anthologies that include *Love's Last Shift.*[27] In Blackwell's *Restoration Drama: An Anthology* (2000), the footnote is merely identified as "Cibber's own note," but the date is not indicated and no other explanation is offered for the allusion.[28] Like the majority of the references to the financial situation of the mid-1690s that occur throughout the play, it has been largely unexamined; as a result, a dimension of the play's social and economic commentary has been lost. In order to recover Cibber's engagement with financial markets in the play, this section takes up two more moments in which Cibber draws on the resources of comedy—in particular the genre's interest in gender and the economics of marriage—in order to portray currency as a commodity whose fluctuating value signifies the underlying instability of the economy and of society more broadly.[29]

The link established by Loveless between women's virtue and money is reinforced by Young Worthy at the end of act 1. He declares his intent to woo Narcissa not for the "strange *Chimæra's* call'd Virtues" but for far more practical reasons: "[H]er 1000 l. a year, and that's the Loadstone that attracts my heart." He concludes the scene with a tidy triplet: "Women are changed from what they were of old: / Therefore let Lovers still this Maxim hold, / *She's only worth that brings her weight in Gold*" (18). Women's dowries and their moral worth are represented as interchangeable, the gold standing in the place of the faded virtue. This seems like a straightforward bit of nostalgia (women are no longer as virtuous as they once were) followed by rakish opportunism (therefore I'll marry for money instead). However, Young Worthy's neat aphorism is complicated by the fact established in the first scene: gold's value is subject to inflation.

The formulaic equation of gold and virtue is further complicated throughout the rest of the play, which repeatedly interrogates changing social mores in London. In act 3 Loveless, who has been abroad at least since 1688, asks Young Worthy how sexual manners have changed in the last decade: "[H]ark ye Friend, are the Women as tame and civil as they were before I left the Town? Can they Endure the Smell of Tobacco, or Vouchsafe a Man a Word with a Dirty Cravat on?" Young Worthy assures him, "Ay, that they will; for Keeping is almost out of Fashion: so that now an Honest Fellow with a Promising Back need not fear a Nights lodging for Bare Goodfellowship." Young Worthy's statement suggests that the sexual economy of London has become more egalitarian since the Revolution: whereas during the decades following the Restoration, women could be kept as mistresses by fashionable gentlemen, now they can no longer command the same rates and have begun coupling with less polished men. Loveless is surprised that any "Honest Fellow" can now receive favors without having to pay the upkeep of a mistress, as he assumes that women will not have sex if there is no financial benefit to it: "If Whoring be so poorly encourag'd, methinks the Women shou'd turn honest in their own Defence." Loveless assumes that all individuals are motivated by profit and that women might withhold their favors as a form of economic self-protection. However, Young Worthy insists that women remain available despite the decline of keeping: "Faith I don't find there's a Whore the less for it; the Pleasure of Fornication is still the same; all the Difference is, Lewdness is not so Barefac'd, as heretofore" (43). In Young Worthy's view, then, London society of the 1690s is as driven by libido as that of the Restoration; however, illicit pleasures have become private sins rather than public transactions. Here as elsewhere the play suggests that people are as much subject to their interests, passions, and inclinations as ever, despite the emergence of a new desire to be perceived as virtuous and reasonable.

Although Young Worthy begins the conversation by stating that "keeping" has gone out of fashion in favor of less public prostitution—implying that society is, at least on the surface, behaving according to more virtuous principles—he goes on to argue that virtue is in fact less widespread than it was previously: "Virtue is as much debased as our Money; for Maidenheads are as scarce as our Mill'd Half-crowns; and Faith, *Dei gratia* is as hard to be found in a Girl of Sixteen, as round the Brims of an Old Shilling" (43). This statement, which seems to contradict Young Worthy's earlier remarks about the continuity of vice from the Restoration to the present, must be understood within the specific context of the recoinage crisis. The decline of virtue is compared to the degradation of the currency: just as an "Old Shilling," a hammered silver coin from the reign of Elizabeth or James I, would have had "Dei gratia" (by the grace of God) clipped or merely rubbed off of its edges, young women too lack God's grace due to overuse.[30] In contrast to these hammered coins, whose rough edges made them easier to clip without detection, the "Mill'd Half-crowns" to which Young Worthy refers were silver coins minted after 1663, whose edges were ridged to make them harder to clip or counterfeit. Milling was an imperfect solution due to the technological limitations of the mint's equipment, but the textured edges of coins were clearly symbolic of the government's increased attention to and scrutiny of its currency.[31] However, because milled coins could not be surreptitiously clipped, they were simply melted down to bullion by arbitragers and sent out of the monetary supply entirely. According to Young Worthy, the recently milled silver coins, like "Maidenheads," are a relatively "scarce" presence on the streets of London. The contrast between the clipped old coin and the milled new one in this image serves to highlight the fact that clipping actually helped keep coins in the money supply; efforts to shore up the integrity of the coinage were self-defeating and milled coins made themselves scarce.

Young Worthy's statements, taken together, express nostalgia only to undercut it: the show of virtue, like shiny new milled coins, represents the present generation's attempts to cover up unsavory realities without understanding their root cause. As he sees it, women no longer whore in public—"Lewdness is not so Barefac'd, as heretofore"—but they have not stopped fornicating. In Young Worthy's view, the falling-off of public displays of license, like new milling technologies, is a superficial solution to the debasement of public life. *Love's Last Shift* thus exposes the tension between the value assigned to coins by the government and the value of the metals they contain: long imagined to be a stable repository of value, precious metals were increasingly understood as inflatable commodities subject to market fluctuations. By aligning this concern with questions of gender and morality, the play suggests that newly fashionable performances of virtue do not necessarily reflect an increase in women's intrinsic value.

The present generation may have elevated virtue and coined a seemingly more impervious currency, but its belief in the integrity of these efforts is ultimately self-deluding.

The play imagines the recoinage as a parallel to the reform movements sweeping London in the 1690s, a connection that other contemporaries of Cibber's also drew. John Evelyn, for instance, repeatedly referred in his diary to the proposed recoinage as a "reform" of the currency. In his entry for December 22, 1695, he noted: "The Parliament wondrous Intent on ways to Reforme the Coine"; on January 12, 1696, around the time *Love's Last Shift* debuted, Evelyn registered the "Greate confusion & distraction" among the people "by reason of the clip'd mony & the difficulty found in reforming it"; and a few weeks later, on February 2, he once again remarked, "The Parliament intent on reforming the Coine."[32] The notion of the recoinage as a "reform"—the same word used by groups such as the Society for the Reformation of Manners, crusaders for public morality in 1690s England— suggests the imaginative link between these attempts to solve longstanding perceived problems with the nation's currency and with its moral values.[33] Cibber works with this link and questions the extent to which supposed improvements in the economy and public life represent fundamental changes. Furthermore, Evelyn's diary provides evidence of the public furor over the recoinage, which he frequently describes as confusion, discontentment, and disorder, and for which he alternately blames the impotency of the mint and the dishonesty of goldsmiths and bankers.[34] As a record of its time, Evelyn's diary provides evidence that the play's concern with coinage and its questions of value would have been immediately relevant to audiences. Indeed, Cibber seems to have counted on the theatergoing public having a working understanding of clipping, counterfeiting, milling, and arbitrage; being aware of the wild fluctuations in the relative value of gold and silver coins; and keeping abreast of ongoing debates over whether the value of metallic currencies was intrinsic or socially constructed.

The play's attention to the mutable value of specie creates the impression that coins, made of metals that can be traded as bullion, may not actually be more secure than any other speculative commodity. As references throughout the play to the Bank of England and the goldsmiths remind audiences and readers, currency and the stock exchange were increasingly connected. For instance, Narcissa complains near the end of act 2 that the promiscuous Lady Manlove "has such a Fund of kind Compliance for all young Fellows, whose Love lies dead upon their hands, that she has been as great a Hindrance to us Vertuous Women, as ever the Bank of England was to City Gold-Smiths." Lady Manlove attracts young men away from less sexually available rivals like Narcissa, just as the bank used attractive interest rates to undercut the goldsmith bankers as the middlemen of public finance. Young Worthy rejoins: "The Reason of that is Madam, because you Vertuous Ladies pay no Interest: I must confess the Principal, our Health is a little securer with you" (32). Although she is more generous with "Interest" (sexual favors) than her competitors, then, Lady Manlove is unable to secure their principal (the health they enter into the engagement with) because of her likely venereal disease. Lady Manlove, like the Bank of England, offers short-term gain but with high volatility; one runs a higher risk of losing one's deposit with the new bank than with the goldsmiths. This moment is intimately connected to the play's concern with coinage, since it was in part the instability of currency that made the pound-backed Bank of England a risky depository. *Love's Last Shift* precedes the bank run by several months, but it reflects the public's growing skepticism regarding the bank's trustworthiness. Just as the bank had difficulty backing investors' principal because of the debasement of the coin, Lady Manlove is unable to secure her lovers' health because of the erosion of her virtue. This complex allusion once more aligns virtue and coinage, showing how both are unstable repositories of value, subject to fluctuations of public trust and opinion.

The volatility of specie and the rise of institutions like the Bank of England led the nation to rely increasingly on credit-backed financial instruments throughout the eighteenth century. Although the recoinage is often seen as the last stand of bullionism, Carl Wennerlind makes a compelling case for thinking of it as an important part of the shift to credit. According to Wennerlind, the push for a full-value recoinage was designed to ensure faith in the Bank of England, which was backed by silver coin, and thus to allow public credit in the form of bank stocks to remain the engine of state finance.[35] The idea was that the recoined currency would enable credit to fill the gap in the money supply over the long term, while simultaneously increasing acceptance of the new regime. The connections between speculative investment and the recoinage, including their interarticulations within the developing systems of public finance, were not lost on the London public. The next section examines how *Love's Last Shift* explores the shared assumptions undergirding the two systems. Cibber draws viewers' attention to a central tension animating both currency and stock markets: on the one hand, coins and commodities are imagined to have an immutable value; on the other, their value is actually driven by public opinion, which prizes novelty first and foremost. The recoinage taps into the desire both for intrinsic worth and for innovation by using a reform to create something new that is restored to its old standard, now able to pass for the value that was always essential to it. Likewise, as the next section will explore, the speculative investor must understand the power of public opinion to shape the value of commodities, even as he works to obscure that power and to make contingent commodity values appear inherent.

Investment

International markets and speculative trading practices were already developing across Europe and in England before the 1690s. Joint-stock companies such as the Dutch and British East India companies began operating in the early decades of the seventeenth century; at the same time, a securities market developed as derivatives (financial instruments that derive their value from that of underlying assets) were used to speculate on food and other commodities.[36] As speculation and investment became more complex, the goldsmith bankers of London developed expertise that allowed them to understand and direct the flow of capital between domestic and international markets.[37] Thus, the seeds for the stock market and credit economy in England were sown well before the 1690s.

However, the combination of several factors led to an explosion in investment at the end of the century. In 1687 the discovery of sunken treasure in the Caribbean increased speculation in similar expeditions.[38] After William and Mary came to the throne and went to war with France, investment in war technologies increased; at the same time, international shipping became riskier and slower, leading funds that would normally have been invested in overseas trade to be diverted to finance.[39] These factors contributed, beginning in 1689, to a boom in patents on new inventions, licenses for banking and lottery projects, and the like.[40] The immediate spurs to speculation interacted with a nascent capital market to produce what Defoe called the "Projecting Age."[41]

The public became increasingly fascinated by the potential for gain through risk, a fascination on which the government capitalized to fund the Nine Years' War. Parliament raised millions through the sale of lottery tickets and annuities.[42] To make it possible for people of modest means to participate in these ventures, speculators bought large numbers of tickets and sold low-priced shares in them. This not only enabled broader swaths of the public to join in the excitement but also made it possible for gamblers to buy shares in several different tickets and maximize their odds of winning.[43] As Londoners were gripped by what we might think of as an early speculative mania, they, like Defoe, tended to imagine that they were living in an unprecedented era. According to P. G. M. Dickson, although "the big increase in the market after 1688 was built on existing foundations," many "contemporaries were so impressed by the swift-moving events in which they were caught up that they tended to ignore this, and to treat the market as a new phenomenon."[44] Sir Novelty Fashion, the fop of *Love's Last Shift*, embodies this fascination with speculation but also complicates audiences' perception of the newness of this behavior. The character's investment practices draw attention to the complex relationship between novelty and recycling within the stock and commodities markets. In addition, the play's self-conscious variation on the fop character type highlights its relationship to the repertory and positions theater as a speculative market where seeming innovations may fail or succeed unpredictably. As with coins and the standards of virtue they represent throughout the play, Sir Novelty's presence suggests that the value of commodities and plays alike depends on the public believing in their (often simulated) newness.

Sir Novelty, like previous Restoration fops, is absurd in part because of his obsession with fashion. His description of this interest, however, is unique in the parallel it draws between trend-setting and speculative investment. He explains at length how he has begun wearing a new kind of trimming in order to support the ribbon weavers of London, who have suffered during the mourning period for Queen Mary—a time of limited sartorial extravagance and therefore a hardship for producers of ornament. The fashion Sir Novelty promotes is "pretty well for second Mourning," and he professes that his goal is "to set the poor Rogues up again, by recommending this sort of Trimming." Here, Sir Novelty seems like a mere commodities speculator, a private trader. However, his investments are quickly linked to the operations of public finance. Sir Novelty boasts that he was offered a massive bribe "as a Gratuity to encourage it [the trend]" but offered his services for free instead, "being too well acquainted with the consequence of taking a Bribe, in a National concern!" (20–21). Sir Novelty likely refers to the corruption scandal that surrounded the East India Company in 1695, when it was revealed that the company had paid bribes to members of Parliament in order to win a renewal of its charter in 1693 without substantially breaking up its monopoly.[45] Sir Novelty's reference is significant when considering fashion as an analogy for investment behavior. In the mid-1690s, techniques of finance that had previously been associated only with speculative projecting were beginning to be used in public finance. This passage highlights the new intimate relationship between speculation and national well-being, as in the case of the Bank of England subscription being used to underwrite the national debt, as well as showing the vulnerability of this system to corruption. In the figure of Sir Novelty, the relationship is miniaturized and trivialized: he invests in a fashion trend and considers it a national concern because it affects the way people dress in mourning for the Queen. Yet the comment evokes the increasingly close relationship between private speculative behavior and public finance.

Clothing is not the only market sector Sir Novelty manipulates, however. He also responds to the debased commodity value of women that so vexes characters like Young Worthy. After spurning his mistress Flareit and eliciting her wrath, Sir Novelty offers her a new lover and a hundred pounds per year for life in exchange for his freedom. Elder Worthy chides him: "Methinks, *Sir Novelty,* you were a little too extravagant in your Settlement, considering how the price of Women is fallen." Again, the idea is that women are less valuable than they were in the past—not a given at this point in the play, when this nostalgic myth has been repeatedly called into question. Sir Novelty responds that he deliberately overpaid Flareit to reinflate the value of women: "Therefore I did it—to be the first man shou'd raise their price: For the Devil take me, but the Women of the Town now come down so low" (96). Sir Novelty believes, along with Young Worthy, that women are debased, but unlike Worthy he thinks that they can be improved by basing their worth on credit. His solution, representative of the shift from bullionism to credit-based financial structures, parallels the motif of recoinage as a solution that relies on public acceptance of increased face value. As I have shown, the play frequently figures women as coins whose intrinsic value is in question despite their superficially virtuous appearance; here, women are speculative commodities that can be inflated. Women are thus a crucial link that connects the operations of credit and coin in the play; they reveal the instability of any financial instrument, the value of which is necessarily based on public consensus. Sir Novelty's "raising" of his mistress is also a low-plot version of the narrative of improvement and reform represented by Loveless and Amanda: Sir Novelty espouses a kind of optimistic belief that the fallen ladies of London may be redeemed. Sir Novelty's version of improvement is superficial and fundamentally unstable, however; it relies on the manipulation of stock values rather than the raising of commodities' (or women's) intrinsic worth (or virtue).

Scholars have recognized Sir Novelty as a kind of projector, investing money on the speculation that his innovation will catch on and benefit his own and the public's fortunes. Kristina Straub and Susan Staves have shown how fops like Sir Novelty are loci for considering issues of consumption and public display.[46] Laura Rosenthal has argued that Sir Novelty's account of his assistance to the ribbon weavers "crudely exposes economic relations, foregrounding the potential irrationality of the market itself" and invoking "the deeper threat of male economic hysteria" identified by J. G. A. Pocock.[47] Yet these accounts do not attend to one of the most striking features of Sir Novelty's speculations: the fashions he promotes are not strictly novel. When the fop first appears in act 1, Elder Worthy describes him to the other characters: "I can't say he's a Slave to every New Fashion, for he pretends to be the Master of it, and is ever reviving some Old, or advanceing some New Piece of Foppery" (9). This sentiment is echoed by Sir Novelty himself in cataloging the fashions he has pioneered: "[T]he Cravat-string, the Garter, the Sword-knot, the Centurine, the Bardash, the Steinkirk, the large Button, the long Sleeve, the Plume, and full Peruque, were all created, cry'd down, or revived by me; in a word Madam, there has never been any thing particularly taking, or agreeable for these ten Years past, but your humble Servant was the Author of it" (28). Both Elder Worthy and Sir Novelty himself describe his business in terms of "reviving" old fashions at least as often as he creates new ones. Sir Novelty's investments do more than just suggest the irrationality of financial capitalism; they also figure the circularity of the market—its appeal to public desire for novelty to simulate value and spur investment. Given the link forged within the play between Sir Novelty's speculations in fashion and his actual participation in both public and private financial markets, his character comes to represent the circularity of market trends more broadly, as well as the tenuous, socially determined value of speculative financial instruments.

Theatrical Markets

Sir Novelty himself is a kind of revived fashion, an old commodity made new. While critics have disagreed about whether Sir Novelty is kinder than previous fops or more vicious, central to the action or peripheral, they tend to agree that he is a descendant of many other fops in the repertory including Le Beau, Sir Courtly Nice, and most significantly, Sir Fopling Flutter from George Etherege's *The Man of Mode* (1676).[48] Lois Potter points out that Etherege's best-known play was "Cibber's favourite model."[49] While *The Man of Mode* was not an especially popular play in the 1690s, contemporaries easily recognized the resemblance between Sir Novelty and Sir Fopling. One remarked in 1699 that "the Characters of *Sir Novelty, Snap, Narcissa*, and *the Elder Worthy*, seem to be good Copies of *Sir Fopling, Jerry* in *Love for Love*, *Setter* in the *Old Batchelor*, &c. Of *Melantha* in *Marriage Alamode*, &c. and *Vain-love* in the *Old Batchelor*."[50] As Potter has shown, however, Sir Novelty deviates from Sir Fopling in his more direct romantic involvement with women and his increased "nonchalance" in the face of his lover's passion.[51] Cibber reworked the Restoration's Sir Fopling as a less foolish figure, but the references and parallels to the earlier play emphasize the through-line and suggest that the playwright, like Sir Novelty himself, is as much in the business of revival as invention.

The figure of the fop overlaps with that of the playwright throughout *Love's Last Shift*. For instance, Sir Novelty announces his intention to write a play revolving around a fop whose elegant dress masks his lack of refinement: "[M]y Chiefest Character shall be a down-right *English Booby*, that affects to be a Beau, without either Genius, or Foreign Education" (39). It is nearly impossible to ignore the similarity between the play Sir Novelty plans to write and the one in which he appears, nor can one fail to notice that the character he describes is much like himself. This metadramatic moment is intensified by the fact that Cibber wrote the part of Sir Novelty for himself: the fop and the writer shared a physical body onstage during the play's early runs. The analogies between the fop, the investor, and the playwright are worked out at length in the prologue to *Love's Last Shift*, which imaginatively links these roles in terms of their middling-class status. According to the prologue, fops are malleable and must learn their airs through hard work: "Ev'n Folly has its Growth: Few Fools are made, / You Drudge, and Sweat for't, as it were a Trade" (A6, lines 19–20). Being a fop is a form of labor, despite the fop's careful affectation of leisure. Similarly, the inexperienced playwright must be taught to anticipate and satisfy the audience's desires and tastes: "By Gentle Lessons you [the audience] your Joys improve, / And Mold her [the playwright's] Awkward Passion into Love" (A6, lines 17–18). New playwrights and foppish fools, like young wives, are trained up in their occupations over time. Whereas playwrights and fops alike were often portrayed as aristocratic during the years immediately following the Restoration, both are envisioned here as apprentices to a trade, a distinctly middling-class role.

The prologue also compares the playwright to a speculator who invests in overseas ventures without capital: "Nor need our Young one Dread a Shipwreck here; / Who Trades without a Stock has nought to fear" (A6, lines 5–6). The young and inexperienced writer is imagined as having little to lose because he has not yet established his reputation. Like the playwright-as-fop, the playwright-as-investor begins from nothing and must build up his career in a risky environment. As the image of the first-time playwright bleeds into those of fops and speculators, inviting comparisons between the three roles, we can see the sinew that connects Sir Novelty's foppishness to his identity as an investor: the speculator, the man of fashion, and the theater professional all must engage in a balancing act between anticipating and acceding to invisible market forces. The savvy investor or fop appears to lead by closely following the latest trends.

His adaptation of the fop type is not the only way that Cibber positions his play as a response to the Restoration repertory. Loveless left London before the Revolution, which makes him a kind of figure for Restoration culture—a rake stuck in time who needs to be updated for the new era. Similarly, Narcissa mocks the aging Mrs. Holdout as "A thing that won't believe her self out of date, though she was a Known Woman at the Restauration"; Young Worthy calls her "one that is proud of being an Original of Fashionable Fornication, and values her self mightily for being one of the first Mistresses that ever kept her Coach publickly in *England*" (46–47). Aparna Gollapudi interprets this as the moment when the ghost of Nell Gwynn is laughed off-stage, and certainly it positions Restoration bawdiness as a formerly cutting-edge sensibility that now seems old-fashioned.[52] Narcissa later comments on the difficulty of restructuring English tastes to match new social and political conditions: "[C]onsidering what dull Souls our Nation are: I find 'tis an harder matter to reform their Manners than their Government, or Religion." Elder Worthy, more optimistic, declares, "Since the One has been so happily

Accomplish'd, I know no reason why we should despair of the Other" (46). The play here explicitly announces its intentions to reform the audience's tastes, and it follows up in the epilogue by drawing attention to the fifth-act conversion as the mechanism of change.

More than any other part of *Love's Last Shift*, the epilogue highlights Cibber's attempt to bridge the bawdy comedic tastes of wealthy theatergoers and the moralistic leanings of increasingly middling-class spectators. It explicitly breaks down the audience by class and gender and describes the likely reactions of each group to the climactic fifth-act reform. First, the "Kind Citty-Gentlemen" (i.e., the merchants and tradesmen) will appreciate the play because it does not feature any cit-cuckolding and instead mocks the fashionable fops who threaten their marriages. Rakes may be displeased by Loveless's decision to relinquish the pleasures of bawdry, but the speaker, a young woman, reminds them that the playwright is "Lewd for above four Acts, Gentlemen!" (B1, line 16). She explains that the anomalously virtuous fifth act is designed for the women in the audience:

> For Faith he [the playwright] knew, when once he'd chang'd his Fortune,
> And reform'd his Vice, 'twas Time—to drop the Curtain.
> Four Acts for your Course Pallats was design'd
> But Then the Ladies Last is more refin'd,
> They for *Amanda*'s sake will sure be Kind.
> Pray let this Figure once your pitty move,
> Can you resist the Pleading God of Love![53]
> In vain my Pray'rs the other Sex pursue,
> Vnless your Conquering smiles their stubborn hearts subdue.
>   (B1, lines 17–25)

Spectators are invited to emulate Amanda's triumph over Loveless's wanderings, using their "Conquering smiles" to "subdue" the "stubborn hearts" of men who prefer more rakish entertainment. In other words, the women in the audience are called on to use their charms to reform the men's taste in theater, just as they have seen Amanda use hers to reform Loveless's sexual vices.

If the implication is that men's taste in drama can be reformed according to the same principles Amanda uses to win back her husband, then it is important to remember she does not simply use her physical beauty or winning personality to coax him back to their marriage; rather, she fools him into believing that spending the night with her will be a new experience. He becomes a faithful husband not by choice but through the seductive allure of the familiar wrapped in a veneer of novelty. Current scholarly attempts to defend Cibber's characterization by saying that the conversion works better on the stage than on the page might be missing the point; as evidenced by the epilogue's self-awareness about the play's generic unevenness, the reform is not supposed to be entirely convincing. Just as women, metaphorically linked to debased coins or fallen stocks, try to stabilize their volatile value through newly fashionable performances of virtue, perhaps Amanda produces a similarly superficial inflationary situation in "reforming" Loveless. Likewise, the epilogue touts the play's ability to deliver the reforms the audience claims to want, even as it suggests that the public's new interest in virtue is merely another face of the fetishization of novelty.

Love's Last Shift leaves open the question of whether a conversion that works by operating on established tastes and habits—here, the need for variety, whether sexual or theatrical—actually enacts a change in disposition.[54] By likening critical members of the audience to Loveless, Cibber implies that his play is an attempt to seduce them into more virtuous ways by combining the rakish elements of past pleasures with the illusion of novelty. Rather than indicating insincerity, then, the epilogue is Cibber's attempt to engage metatheatrically with changing tastes; he asks his audience to consider how they, like Loveless, might overvalue the new. By extension, the play asks whether the playwright merely appeals to audiences' desire for novelty in his seeming "reform" of the Restoration sex comedy. Like Amanda contemplating the morality of seducing her husband under false pretenses—"[I]f I Court and Conquer him, as a Mistress, am not I accessary to his violating the Bonds of Marriage?"—Cibber questions the ethics of appealing to his audience's better angels via their love of novelty (34). In sum, Cibber invites his audience to engage critically with the very cultural shifts that the play is now seen as representing—specifically, the push for more moralistic forms of comedy and the relationship of that generic shift to the growing financial and cultural power of the middling classes in the wake of the Revolution of 1688.

I have argued that *Love's Last Shift* encourages audiences to think critically about the apparent novelty of emergent cultural and economic forms. Cibber's play implicitly links coinage, stocks, fashions, entertainment, and morality, showing how the public's desire for innovation inflates the perceived value of a range of publicly traded goods. Like the financial motifs throughout the play, the epilogue's commentary on the fifth-act conversion highlights the contradictions inherent in the process of recycling inherited forms while appealing to current tastes. The topicality, dialogism, and self-referentiality of stage comedy allow Cibber to draw links between a variety of permutations of the rage for novelty reshaping public life in London at the end of the seventeenth century. In bringing attention to the overvaluation of novelty in a range of economic and cultural arenas, Cibber alerts audience members to the power they have as participants in the construction of public opinion, but he also warns them of the ease with which they may be deluded.

Love's Last Shift exemplifies the ways that drama from this period engaged its audiences in debates about changing economic conditions, prompting spectators to view themselves as agents within complex financial systems. It suggests the importance of studying the theater as a public sphere that invited forms of financial and political engagement distinct from those exhibited in coffeehouses and the periodical press. The next chapter will sketch the contours of the larger debates into which Cibber's play entered by examining a variety of prologues and epilogues from the 1694–95 and 1695–96 seasons. These pieces reveal that the analogy Cibber draws between the recoinage and theatrical adaptation was not an uncommon one and that this metaphorical association acted as a vehicle for a wide range of positions on the proper relationship of the present to the past. Cibber's play took its cues from the broader theater-finance nexus, in which the economic and cultural upheaval of the 1690s produced a flurry of commentary on the interrelated dynamics of financial and theatrical markets.

• 2 •

Recoining the Repertory

Prologues, Epilogues, and Crisis

The previous chapter showed how Colley Cibber's *Love's Last Shift* figures the changing function of comedy in post-1688 society through metaphors of recoinage and speculative investment, raising along the way broader concerns about the power and fallibility of public opinion. In this chapter I situate Cibber's play within a larger debate over market operations in 1690s London by exploring the deployment of similar analogies in prologues and epilogues of the 1695–96 and 1696–97 theater seasons. While Cibber's play represents the public as dangerously in thrall to novelty, that obsession is represented as part of a general zeitgeist, the fault of no one group or institution in particular. A broader view of prologues and epilogues performed around the same time, however, reveals a multitude of attempts to identify more precisely the agents who steered and guided public opinion, as well as efforts to blame the public more forcefully for its gullibility.

The prologues and epilogues examined in this chapter were composed, performed, and printed during the most acute phase of the recoinage; equally important, this moment also witnessed the breakup of the theater monopoly held by the United Company since 1682. During the 1694–95 season, longstanding tensions between the actors and manager Christopher Rich came to a head. These tensions largely revolved around the actors' perception of Rich as a greedy and controlling leader, willing to sacrifice his employees' interests to those of his shareholders. Following a series of unsuccessful talks, veteran actor Thomas Betterton and a group of fifteen fellow players that included Edward Kynaston, Elizabeth Barry, and Anne Bracegirdle seceded to open their own new theater in Lincoln's Inn Fields.

After the public mourning for the death of Queen Mary in December, the season resumed in April 1695, with two companies, rather than one, staging offerings on any given night. Betterton's troupe, which included nearly all the star performers of the time, became known as the Actors' Company, while Rich's players were referred to as the Patent Company.

Following the Actors' Rebellion, then, Londoners found themselves with a choice of theater companies for the first time in more than a decade. There was, however, an important difference from the duopoly of the 1660s and '70s. While the Duke's and King's companies had retained exclusive, government-sanctioned rights to perform specific plays by Shakespeare, Jonson, Fletcher, and the like, the post-1695 companies each had access to the entire repertory. They responded by mounting rival productions of staples like *Hamlet* but found that this technique simply divided audiences, who scrambled between the houses to get the full comparative effect.[1] The managers were forced to turn to novelty to gain the upper hand, and new plays proliferated. The author of *A Comparison between the Two Stages* (1702) reviews 160 new plays (not including revivals) staged between 1695 and 1702.[2] Even the theatrical pieces themselves admit that the glut of new offerings was overwhelming: the prologue to *Pausanias, The Betrayer of His Country* (performed around April 1696 at Drury Lane) begins, "New Plays have been so frequent, all this Season; / We must believe You'r tir'd, and you have Reason."[3]

Debate about the theatrical rift and ensuing rivalry was staged in insistently financial terms, as writers of the time used the theatrical duopoly to support quite different arguments about the role government should play in regulating market competition. This link was enabled by the similarities between the structures of the Restoration and eighteenth-century theaters and those of the joint-stock ventures that represented England's trade interests abroad. It may also have been inspired by a historical coincidence: in 1695, as the Actors' Rebellion took its stand against corrupt leadership enabled by the state-sanctioned monopoly over an entire commercial sector, investors were learning about underhanded dealings at the East India Company. They responded by putting pressure on Parliament to break up the company's monopoly on trade to the East by backing a rival New East India Company. In April 1695—the same month that the New Theater opened at Lincoln's Inn Fields—John Evelyn noted in his diary: "Sir T Cooke discovers what prodigious Bribes have ben given by some of the E. India Company [out] of the stock, which makes an extraordinary Clamor."⁴ The East India Company fought to maintain its monopoly through corrosive government influence, even as Betterton and his crew successfully created the same kind of duopoly many investors hoped to see in the East India trade. This parallel is reflected in *A Comparison between the Two Stages* as well as in Cibber's autobiography, *An Apology for the Life of Colley Cibber* (1740). Both texts connect the theatrical duopoly and the two East India companies in order to conceptualize the value of government-sanctioned monopolies.

The author of *A Comparison* argues that the innovation driven by competition is detrimental to art: poetry "never was at so low an Ebb, and yet the Stages were never so delug'd: I am sure you can't name me five Plays that have indur'd six Days acting, for fifty that were damn'd in three." The author attributes this decline in quality to the split of the theaters seven years previously, which "made way for a multitude of young Writers, some of whom had nothing else to subsist on but their Pens."⁵ The rise of "scribblers" is as much at play in theater criticism as in Augustan satire of the print market as a whole in the wake of the lapsed Licensing Act; drama and criticism, like other forms of writing, were perceived as being produced at unprecedented rates but to the detriment of quality. The author of *A Comparison* also complains about the rising ticket prices inflicted by the struggling companies and compares the two theater companies to the rival East India companies, whose competition is seen as laying waste to the market sector for which they fight: "'[T]is the Profit of the Stage that makes so many Scribblers, and surfeits the Town with new Eighteen-penny Plays. This and the freedom of two Stages have serv'd Poetry, just as the two Companies did the Indian Trade, they have reduc'd almost to nothing."⁶ In other words, the author does not see the two companies suffering from their competition with one another; instead, he sees them as colluding to inundate the public with low-quality material at ever steeper prices.

When Cibber draws a similar analogy between the theaters and the trading companies in his autobiography decades later, he does so with a very different aim. In his *Apology* he recalls the early years of the rivalry, consistently describing the theaters in terms equally fitting to a joint-stock trading company. For instance, Cibber describes how, prior to 1695, the United Company was primarily a money-making venture for its backers:

> [T]he united Patentees impos'd their own Terms, upon the Actors; for the Profits of acting were then divided into twenty Shares, ten of which went to the Proprietors, and the other Moiety to the principal Actors, in such Sub-divisions as their different Merit might pretend to. These Shares of the Patentees were promiscuously sold out to Mony-making Persons, call'd Adventurers, who, tho' utterly ignorant of Theatrical Affairs, were still admitted to a proportionate Vote in the Management of them; all particular Encouragements to Actors were by them, of Consequence, look'd upon as so many Sums deducted from their private Dividends.[7]

Cibber attributes much of the abuse inflicted on the actors in the United Company to the lack of competition in the absence of a rival theater—"One only Theatre" was "in Possession of the whole Town." The shareholders did not only control the playhouse; they controlled the entire "Town," that is, the people who come to see plays. For these profit-minded shareholders ("Adventurers," the same name given to speculative investors in overseas trade), actors were merely financial burdens that cut into the bottom line. Like the author of *A Comparison*, Cibber expresses anxiety about what happens when the theater operates like a joint-stock company, but he has no nostalgia for the monopoly system. Instead, he sees the economic competition between the two companies as a way to ensure fair labor conditions by providing workers multiple venues in which to ply their trade. For actors and playwrights, in an environment where the profit motive is so strong, he insists that a duopoly is preferable to a monopoly.

Of course, the economic conditions of the theater did not map neatly onto those of the East India trade. However, the fact that the breakup of the theaters in 1695 could be seen retroactively (in 1702 and again in 1740) as a parallel to the establishment of the rival New East India Company illustrates the extent to which the theater had become a site of imaginative engagement with financial institutions. The emergence of a new company tapped into the moment's obsession with commercial entrepreneurship and innovation—"projecting," as well as recoinage and financial reform. The parallels between the theatrical and trade monopolies enabled contemporaries to test the possible results of various courses of action and to advance theories about the dynamics of nascent capitalist structures. At stake in the two texts above is the question of whether the theater is fundamentally an artistic and cultural institution or a commercial undertaking. Is it more important to structure the theater in a way that promotes the best possible art, allows the greatest number of potentially playgoers to purchase tickets, most enriches the managers and shareholders, or ensures the best possible working conditions for employees? In framing such questions in relation to financial markets, these texts raise larger questions about what kind of public the audience constitutes: Is it a rational and discerning body passing ethical and aesthetic judgment on theatrical productions? Or does the theatergoing public exist in a fundamentally commercial relation to art and ideas?

In the tumultuous years following the breakup of the United Company, during which time the English economy was being rapidly reconfigured, prologues and epilogues were a crucial site of topical commentary and debate. These pieces frequently treated the theatrical market as a laboratory for understanding how financial markets might behave, and vice-versa. The recoinage crisis, in particular, offered up a set of tropes that proved malleable and suggestive enough to permeate the topical performance pieces of the day. Below, I argue that these representations of the currency shortage and crisis, while intriguing in themselves, have broader implications for the imaginative convergence of the financial and theatrical spheres. Reading these pieces reveals previously unrecognized forms of debate over the overlapping struggles of the middling classes for control over institutions once governed by the crown and the elite: public finance and the theater.

The pieces I examine in this chapter explore dynamics of scarcity, abundance, and value—dynamics very much at play during a moment that saw both a shortage of silver coins and a glut of inflated gold currency—in a theatrical market that struggled financially at the same time that it became saturated by new and newly revived plays. Ultimately, these prologues and epilogues express both anxiety and approval toward the new attitudes and mechanisms governing both the theater and finance, including speculation, entrepreneurialism, and public opinion. They highlight how joint-stock trading companies, upstart theaters, novel stage spectacles, dramatic revivals, and the recoinage itself are all, in a sense, "projects" that tout novelty even as they evoke and recode the past. These pieces explore many of the same topics and concerns as *Love's Last Shift*, discussed in chapter 1, but they examine a wider range of theatrical innovations taking place in the 1690s—not only the reform of stage comedy to accommodate increasingly moralistic social norms but also the introduction of new songs, dances, and subplots to revived plays and the rise of experimental forms like semi-opera and pantomime. Across London's financial and cultural institutions, as the field of commodities becomes more crowded, the relative value of those commodities becomes ever harder for ordinary people to assess. Is this company's stock a worthwhile investment? Will the experience of seeing this new play be worth the price of admission? In response to the increasing competition across financial and cultural markets, new classes of self-appointed experts—critics, stockjobbers, bankers—emerged to manage public opinion. The pieces I examine in this chapter offer differing visions of the role of those experts vis-à-vis the wider public.

Prologues and epilogues are inherently dialogic forms that illuminate the importance of the theater as a space of debate; as such, they provide an under-utilized archive that helps to establish the contours of the theater-finance nexus. I begin by establishing the historical and formal characteristics of prologues and epilogues that make them an important site for financial and cultural debates. I then examine a selection of pieces from the 1695–96 and 1696–97 seasons that engage with the recoinage and other concurrent economic developments, highlighting the divergent uses to which they put the same financial tropes. I conclude by focusing on a single piece—the prologue to *The Sham Lawyer; or, The Lucky Extravagant* (performed in May 1697 at Drury Lane)—that unites the various threads I trace throughout the larger archive of performance pieces from the period. These threads include the parallel shortages of both dramatic wit and coin; the tense relationship between the playing companies and the increasingly discerning audiences on which they depended for their financial survival; the rise of a younger generation of playwrights who drew on and adapted the dramatic tradition in complex ways; and the changing landscape of theatrical entertainment, with its growing dependence on spectacle. In giving voice to competing views of the theatrical marketplace, the *Sham Lawyer* prologue exemplifies the ability of the theater-finance nexus to produce richly contrasting visions of London's public spheres.

The Archive

Prologues and epilogues have long served theater historians as material evidence of performance history; in this chapter I consider the cultural work they did in engaging with economic and financial developments. In doing so I contribute to a growing body of scholarship that rejects the longstanding view of these pieces as merely ancillary to the mainpiece and instead takes early modern prologues, epilogues, and other framing performance elements seriously as objects of analysis.[8]

Diana Solomon identifies 1,570 extant prologues and epilogues from the period 1660–1714—a remarkably large and rich body of literature.[9] Prologues and epilogues are an especially valuable archive for the final decade of the seventeenth century, a period for which performance records are limited.[10] Pierre Danchin, who edited the six-volume reference work *The Prologues and Epilogues of the Restoration, 1660–1700*, points out that the number of extant stage orations balloons after 1690 compared to the previous three decades.[11] Danchin attributes this spike in part to the split of the United Company, as the rivalry between the two companies played out largely in the topical orations at the beginnings and ends of performances as well as in printed versions of those pieces.[12] Prologues and epilogues became longer and more elaborate as each theater used them to draw audiences to its own side of the conflict.

Furthermore, prologues and epilogues are a rich and valuable archive for this volatile period because, as a form, they offer an important window onto public feeling around current events. Whereas plays—even topical comedies like *Love's Last Shift*—were often intended to maintain their relevance across several weeks, months, or years, a prologue or epilogue might only be performed on one or two nights, its survival beyond that point dependent on its inclusion in the printed text. The timeliness of these pieces means that they provide valuable insights into public opinion about economic shifts at specific moments in time, exposing the degree to which the theater was responsive to financial developments.[13] This intense topicality also allows prologues and epilogues to mediate between past and present, using contemporary references to update old plays for the current moment. Paulina Kewes notes that head- and tailpieces were often used to highlight the sources of a play, particularly if it was adapted from a well-known writer like Fletcher or Shakespeare whose fame might be a selling point early in the play's run.[14] Daniel Ennis and Judith Slagle go further, arguing that prologues and epilogues to revivals were an "essential rhetorical glue whereby eighteenth-century audiences were attached to seventeenth-century scripts."[15] The very topicality of these pieces allowed them to suture the past to the present for which they stood.

Not only are prologues and epilogues well-positioned to comment on broad economic conditions at a particular moment; they also perform important work as marketing devices within the economic system of the theater itself. These pieces encode the playhouse's commercial relationship to its publics by framing audiences' expectations around a mainpiece, justifying the expense of their tickets, and imploring them to speak well of the play to potential attendees of future performances. Prologues and epilogues frequently foreground the economic interdependence of playwrights, actors, theater managers, critics, and audiences, positioning spectators within a network of highly commercialized relations. By placing broader financial themes and references into dialog with such explorations of the economics of the theater, these pieces draw links between the financial and entertainment industries, exploring the overlapping practices of public-making that occurred in these different spaces. The rest of this section details the various ways these framing pieces participate in and refer to the economic dynamics of the theater.

Across the seventeenth and eighteenth centuries, prologues frequently previewed the play to come and begged for the audience's patience, while epilogues apologized for any defects in the play and requested the audience's applause—a device called the "plaudite."[16] The framing orations' often apologetic and defensive tone is more than rhetorical. It reflects their very real material function: to elicit the applause necessary to ensure the success and survival of the play. As Tiffany Stern explains, stage orations from the Elizabethan period onward were temporary pieces designed for the first few performances of the play.[17] From the late sixteenth through the eighteenth century, first-day tickets cost more than admission for other days because those who paid to be in attendance at the premiere were purchasing entry into "a highly ritualized theatrical moment"—the judgment, represented by the audience's response at the end of the first performance, that determined whether the play would be performed again and whether parts would be cut or otherwise changed to better appeal to spectators.[18] Because of this function, prologues and epilogues were typically reserved for new plays and revivals and may have been dropped once the author's benefit was reached on the third day.[19] Perhaps as an extension of their role in ensuring the financial success of playwright and playing company alike, many of these pieces came to reflect more self-consciously on the material conditions of producing and consuming plays, as in the famous prologue to Shakespeare's *Henry V*.[20]

Although the basic material and rhetorical function of prologues and epilogues remained largely stable from the late sixteenth through the eighteenth century, the forms did change over time. One major shift was in the range of personae used to deliver these orations. The Elizabethan prologue speaker was highly conventionalized: a stand-in for the author, he wore a long black cloak, a beard, and a laurel wreath, making him appear, as Stern puts it, "something between a beggar and a scholar." The other common speaker was the "armed prologue," who came onstage dressed for battle in anticipation of the audience's attack. Epilogues could be delivered by one of these two figures or by a character from the play.[21] Originally, conventionalized prologue and epilogue roles were held by young actors, often those who were making the transition from women's to men's roles.[22] After the Restoration, however, these pieces were increasingly delivered by celebrity actors, as prologues and epilogues became a desirable venue for performers seeking to raise their public profiles. Players more often spoke the pieces as themselves rather than as conventionalized figures or as their characters in the play.[23] As such, the pieces became increasingly tied to marketing the plays within a developing celebrity culture where individual actors were commodified and packaged according to audience desires.

Prologues and epilogues also provided a site for negotiating relationships of authority and obligation among writers, actors, and audiences. They were sometimes written by the author of the play, but just as often by another party—a writer connected to the playhouse, a friend of the playwright's, or even an actor within the company. These pieces frequently reflect a real tension between the interests of the actors and the playhouse on the one hand, and those of the writer they purport to assist on the other; as Stern argues, these pieces allowed a theater to distance itself from the playwright if the play looked to be unsuccessful.[24] Actors performing *in propria persona* might complain about the source material they had to work with, or playwrights might complain about the low quality of the performers charged with realizing their scripts.

These tensions can be explained, in part, by the increasingly entrepreneurial culture of theatrical authorship in the period. Not only were the playhouses like joint-stock ventures, but playwrights themselves were becoming more like speculative investors entangled in a competitive market with high-risk, high-reward opportunities. While many dramatists before the Interregnum had been connected to a single company—receiving regular payment in exchange for a certain number of new scripts, revisions, prologues, and epilogues per year—Restoration and eighteenth-century theater managers increasingly paid playwrights a retainer guaranteeing first right of refusal for new scripts. Under this system, the sale of scripts no longer afforded writers any fee: contracted writers kept their retainer, while amateurs simply gave their script to the company in the hopes of it reaching a third-day benefit. At the same time, authors gained the right to publish their play texts, which had been the exclusive prerogative of the playing companies prior to the civil wars. They used prefaces and dedicatory epistles to solicit additional patronage from the wealthy and powerful—not necessarily material support, as had been more common in the earlier period, but rather influence in the playhouse, high attendance on the benefit day, loosened censorship, or the promise of a court performance.[25] As Kewes puts it:

> The later seventeenth-century playwright was no longer an employee of the company, as most of the pre-Commonwealth playwrights had been, but an entrepreneur and an investor of sorts. Although his or her long-term income from the theatre may not have been as stable over the years as that of the early seventeenth-century professionals, the author's potential profit from any one play could well have exceeded theirs.... The loss of what we would today call job security was compensated for by an unprecedented opportunity for speculative investment of one's talent, time, and skill in the hope of earning an equally unprecedented financial return.[26]

This dynamic undoubtedly affected the tensions on display in prologues and epilogues of the period: although the playhouse and the playwright should, in theory, have been on the same side, each was gauging the risk factors the other brought to the arrangement. Alliances became more strategic and less based on loyalty, as attested to by the frequent (and sometimes repeated) movement of actors and playwrights between the two companies. J. S. Peters notes that scribblers—professional writers, especially inexperienced ones—came to be seen like bankers: social upstarts in newly powerful trades that depended on credit and speculation.[27]

In addition to encoding tensions between playwrights and playing companies, prologues and epilogues also triangulated the relationship between the producers of culture and their publics—critics, ordinary playgoers, and everyone in between. Douglas Bruster and Robert Weimann see the prologue and epilogue as "proto-contractual" forms that negotiated the exchange "between what was offered on stages and what, before the show began, was paid for."[28] The company offered a specific kind and amount of entertainment in return for the audience's money and applause. Rivka Swenson has shown how some prologues attempted to enlist audiences to the playwright's side, creating an alliance against critics as well as audience members who might disrupt performances.[29] Given the delicate economic interests at play, it may appear strange that one of the most enduring conceits throughout this period was the "railing" or "huffing" prologue or epilogue, a piece in which the speaker criticized the spectators' lack of taste or judgment, occasionally singling out specific groups for particular satire. But huffing served to acknowledge the audience's cultural and economic power and, as Paul McCallum has shown, was a complex activity that walked a fine and strategic line between flattery and insult.[30]

As this overview indicates, the limited scholarship on prologues and epilogues recognizes two sets of features: their intense topicality and their role in mediating between historical moments; and their triangulation of authors, actors, and audiences in a complex network of social and economic relations. The convergence of these features makes these pieces especially rich objects for my analysis of the theater-finance nexus.[31] This chapter examines how prologues' and epilogues' reflections on the workings of theatrical markets were used to theorize and engage imaginatively with financial market forces within the specific context of the turbulent years 1695–97. I choose to treat these framing pieces as an archive separate from the mainpieces with which they appeared, not to deny the very real relationship many of them had to the larger performance events in which they were first received but because there is considerable evidence that they were often written and circulated separately.[32] I argue that these pieces' topicality, their status as a marketing devices, and their role as intermediaries between the repertory and the moment of performance allows them to play a key role in conversations about what it means for cultural markets to operate according to the same rules as financial markets. As such, prologues and epilogues are central to the development of a mass public that experiences itself as having a commercial relationship to entertainment—the beginnings of what, following Michael Warner, I understand as mass culture.

Figuring Change

The mid- to late 1690s were a time of crisis not only in the public theaters of London but also in the economy. As detailed in chapter 1, the recoinage that began in 1696 made silver pounds painfully scarce and inflated the value of the gold guinea. As the price of gold vis-à-vis the pound sterling rose, the public became increasingly aware of the gap between the legally decreed value of the coinage and its purchasing power. As a result, Londoners became cognizant of the complex interplay of abundance, dearth, and speculation that affected the value of money. Specie's supposedly "intrinsic" worth, guaranteed by the crown and the mint, was no match for the actions of clippers, counterfeiters, and arbitragers nor for the forces of public faith and skepticism at work in its valuation.[33] This interplay of wealth and scarcity is repeatedly evoked in prologues and epilogues, which use the recoinage crisis to figure the debasement of "true" dramatic wit as it interacts with an oversupply of new and revived plays as well as to mark the oversupply of critics who transformed the definition of wit to suit their own ends.

A typical example of the wit/money analogy can be found in the epilogue to Robert Gould's *The Rival Sisters*, performed at Drury Lane around October 1695. The epilogue, written by Thomas D'Urfey and delivered by John Verbruggen, imagines the young playwright's fear of the critical wits in the pit. It further reflects on how the stage has changed for the worse as playwrights and critics alike have begun springing up in large numbers. The speaker quips:

> Ah! Sirs—if this be call'd the Golden Age,
> I fear it will prove fatal to the Stage:
> For now of Wit and Gold w'ave such strange store,
> That the excess of it does make us Poor:
> Ev'n in the midst of Plenty we shall fall.
> Criticks and Clippers have undone us all.[34]

Just as clippers have depleted the silver supply, indirectly contributing to the oversupply and overvaluation of the gold guinea, critics "clip" at new plays and flood the literary market with their opinions. True dramatic wit is scarce and debased, like the pound sterling, while the new, false wit of critics abounds, its oversupply producing no true abundance. Critics and clippers alike wield a nefarious influence on the market, enriching themselves at the expense of the wider economies in which they operate.

The speaker goes on to lament an idealized past in which audience members did not aspire to be wits and when playwrights did not come from every social rank:

> In former Times, when we were at no Charge,
> When Wit was narrow, and Half-Crown was large,
> When Cit in Cloak came pleas'd to see our Whims,
> And brought Queen *Bess*'s Shillings broad as his Hat brims;
> Then was a glorious thriving Time for Players[.] (lines 26–30)

Leaving aside the obvious contradictions with certain historical facts—that the scarcity of money had plagued the English economy since at least Elizabeth's reign, that clipping had been going on for the better part of a century, and that earlier playwrights (especially Jonson) had also complained about audiences' critical disposition—it is obvious that these lines express nostalgia for an era when coins were larger and wit belonged to a more "narrow" group of people. In this imagined past audiences were a "dull Crowd" (line 31) as willing to laugh at bear-baiting as at comedies; they did not engage in a competition of wits with theater professionals but acted as passive consumers of plays and other entertainments. As the verse continues, the rise of critics and wits in the pits slides into the emergence of new playwrights from all ranks of society: "Thro' all degrees of Men starts up a Bard, / The Beau, the Cit, the Lawyer—and the Lord" (lines 36–37). This social leveling, in turn, creates a glut of unsuccessful plays:

> Above twice fifty Plays each Year are made,
> And of twice fifty Plays scarce five are Play'd.
> Strange Paradox! No Age did e'er let loose
> So many Wits, or so much Gold produce,
> Yet we want both for necessary use. (lines 38–42)

Just as high-value gold guineas are abundant but do not fit the day-to-day needs of ordinary Londoners making small purchases, the proliferation of aspiring wits fails to outfit the stage with high-quality plays that can attract audiences on several successive evenings. The theatrical market, like the broader economy, is crushed under a superabundance of useless wealth as self-appointed experts manipulate value for their own gain.

At the end of the epilogue, the speaker returns to his initial focus on the plethora of wits in the pit. He addresses his final lines to those who intend to criticize the players: "[T]ho' you come prepar'd to use us ill, / Change but your Money, and y'are welcome still" (lines 44–45). These lines reflect the ultimate reality that the theater is at the mercy of its audience, in need of the coins they pay for their tickets. Despite the speaker's grandstanding against the presumptions of would-be critics, he and his fellow actors are materially dependent upon the wits' good will and that of the wider public whose opinions the wits might influence. The piece as a whole establishes a figurative analogy between the dearth/abundance paradox and the phenomenon of social leveling, both in the theater and in the larger economy. It suggests that the collapse of old social, economic, and aesthetic hierarchies creates a situation in which value is difficult to determine. Under William, as the war rages against France and new financial institutions spring up to support it, middling-class merchants and tradesmen are gaining new kinds of power to control the nation's future, even as a centuries-old currency appears to have suddenly lost its value. Similarly, following the split of the theaters, new kinds of economic competition have created space for the ascendency of wits—both critics and playwrights—from the middling ranks. Yet the increased competition and production does not result in an improvement in quality; instead, most new plays, like most new financial projects, fail miserably. In the world of this epilogue, at least, newer is not always better.

The wit/money analogy became commonplace over the course of the recoinage crisis, and as in the case of the epilogue to *The Rival Sisters*, it frequently served to turn the lens on the critics, implicating them in the very cultural and artistic degradation they delighted in blaming on theater professionals. In an epilogue to John Dryden Jr.'s *The Husband His Own Cuckold*, performed at Lincoln's Inn Fields around June 1696, speaker Anne Bracegirdle accuses the critics of finding ridiculous costumes funnier than verbal humor: "You laugh not, Gallants, as by proof appears, / At what his Beauship says, but what he wears."[35] The critics, she suggests, encourage playwrights to produce this kind of low comedy rather than a comedy rich in linguistic play and social commentary.

Bracegirdle continues: "The Truth on 't is, the Payment of the Pit / Is like for like, Clipt Money for Clipt Wit."[36] That is, the critics have bought their tickets with debased money and therefore deserve the debased wit they have purchased.

Similarly, the prologue to *The City Bride* (performed at Lincoln's Inn Fields around March 1696) asks the audience to "lend" the speaker its applause:

> And if I ne're repay it, 'tis no more,
> Than many of you Sparks have done before:
> With this distinction, that you ran indebt,
> For want of Money, we for want of Wit.
> In vain I plead! a Man as soon may get
> Mill'd Silver, as one favour from the Pit.[37]

Just as the young men ("Sparks") lack money to pay their debts, the playhouse lacks witty fare for audiences. Money is compared not only to wit but also to the critics' "favour," with the implication that both are in equally short supply. The prologue ends by asking the audience to let the play "pass" as they do the "present coin," turning a blind eye to the fact that the poet's "Allay runs not so fine" as might be wished.[38] In other words, like a coin that passes at face value despite containing less than the indicated amount of precious metal, this play should earn more applause than its actual contents deserve. By drawing attention to the audience members' own debts and to the ways they ignore the debasement of the currency, the speaker implicates audiences in the playhouse's failure to produce value, suggesting that they are complicit in allowing commercial value to become increasingly unmoored from intrinsic worth. The speaker demands that the audience support the playhouse just as they do other institutions that run on credit and broken promises, from the Bank of England to local shopkeepers. As such, this piece reinforces a vision of the interconnected financial situations of all those in the actual and virtual public space of the theater.

Likewise, a topical epilogue to Aphra Behn's *The Younger Brother*, performed at Drury Lane around February 1696, invites the audience to judge the play but asks them to "be kind," reminding them the money they have paid today will only be worth half of its face value to the theater once it is sent off to the mint to be recoined:

> For to our Cost (alas [sic] we soon shall find,
> Perhaps not half the mony ye design'd
> Consider, Sirs, it goes to be refin'd.
> And since in all Exchanges 'tis a notion,
> For what ye take to be in due proportion,
> So may we justly hope no wrong is done ye,
> If ye have par of Wit, for par of Mony.[39]

The audience has paid for the entertainment with coins that will soon be remilled to reflect their actual metal content. By offloading these coins, on which they would have lost money, the audience has in effect enjoyed a half-price show. Even if they only receive half as much wit as they paid for at the face value of their tickets, the speaker argues, they have really received "par of Wit" for the true metallic value of their money. The financial suffering of the playhouse is once again deployed to silence critics, emphasizing the complicity of all audience members in exploiting the theater and urging them not to inflict further harm through harsh reviews.

Another prologue addresses the analogy between criticism and the financial world, but it takes a distinctly darker tone. The anonymous *Timoleon*, which may or may not actually have been performed, dates to February or March 1697, the nadir of the economic depression. Its prologue begins by noting that poets and players alike are struggling to survive, but it blames the dire state of the theater on the growing body of aspiring scribblers whose plays give the actors very little with which to work. The companies "Labour" at great "Expence" but without "Gains," claims the speaker.[40] The piece moves quickly into a catalog of dishonest professionals who work only for personal profit: the ambitious churchman, the lawyer, and of course, "the griping Usurer" who

> his Coffer fills,
> Instead of Gold, with Tallies and Bank-bills.
> Starving the Soldier, whil'st he buys his Pay,
> Decrying Credit, only that he may,
> Restore to Morrow what he has damn'd to Day.[41]

The speaker expresses disapproval of the credit economy filling the void left by an unreliable currency, suggesting that this credit-based system is most advantageous for dishonest middling-class professionals. The newly powerful men of trade and finance who wield influence in the English economy are hypocrites: they manipulate public opinion for and against particular financial instruments, creating conditions under which they can—in today's idiom—buy low and sell high. The terms "restore" and "damn'd" evoke the language of theatrical criticism, beginning to suggest a parallel between these hypocritical usurers and the critics who plague the theater.

As the prologue continues, it further develops the analogy, while simultaneously suggesting that the economic conditions of the theater are quite different from those of the business world. Critics, like the lawyers and usurers described above, attempt to make a profit from others' labor without producing anything of value themselves:

> If they can't Judge, yet they can Damn a Play:
> Not those from *Tom*'s alone, but every Cit,
> With scru'd up Face, cries, *Damme, where's the Wit?*
> From weighing Plums and Sugar, has pretence
> To hold the Scales and Balances of Sence.[42]

While these lines draw a parallel between the predation of critics and those of the other professions discussed above, they also point to a fundamental difference between the financial and theatrical markets: plays are not the same kind of things as "Plums and Sugar." In turning theater critics and pretending to be wits, City merchants mistake their experience weighing commodities in their shops for an ability to weigh sense. Furthermore, there are echoes between this portrait and that of the usurer who cries down credit only to revive it tomorrow. These lines suggest an arbitrary manipulation of public opinion for personal gain. The echo of "damn'd," "Damn" and "Damme" links these portraits of different kinds of hypocrites, aligning the developing financial sector, the ordinary merchant, and the pit-dwelling critic in a nexus of crass, self-serving upstarts.

This prologue ultimately rejects the equation of wit or dramatic art with other commodities and displaces accusations of commercialism, insisting that the theater, unlike other sectors of London's economy, does not reward empty simulacra of value. Those who attempt to treat the theater like a speculative financial market are castigated; yet the fact that the prologue can so easily imagine each sphere in terms of the other suggests the inescapability of market logic for the theaters. With two houses to choose from, audiences could be easily swayed. If the critics damned the play at one house, theatergoers could throng to the other, much like investors moving their capital into the latest joint-stock venture based on a rumor overheard in a coffeehouse. The emergence of critics as arbiters and manipulators of public opinion was in some ways as inevitable as the emergence of a class of brokers, stockjobbers, and goldsmith bankers who claimed arcane knowledge in order to control the movement of capital. Across the theater-finance nexus, this piece shows, new types of experts were asserting themselves, attempting to harness the growing power of public opinion in the unruly spaces created by newly fluid market structures.

Dramatic Experiments

The economic difficulties facing London society in the mid-1690s would have created challenges for the theaters under any circumstances, as cash-poor individuals cut back on nonessentials like play tickets. As a case in point, the preface to *The Unhappy Kindness,* performed around July 1696 at Drury Lane, explicitly blames the play's poor initial attendance on "the Scarcity of Money" during the summer and expresses hope that the play will fare better in the winter.[43] The struggle to attract audiences was intensified in the newly competitive environment created by the breakup of the United Company. Under this perfect storm of conditions, it became harder than ever for either of the rival companies to fill the house on any given night.

The theaters realized that they needed new strategies to draw spectators. Kathryn Lowerre articulates the dilemma that faced the companies: "At the turn of the eighteenth century, the London theaters were engaged in an elaborate balancing act: offering audiences both generic familiarity and novelty. If new productions were too formulaic, they might not please. If they were too experimental, they also ran the risk of a quick dismissal. Audiences enjoyed moments within productions which operated on multiple levels—rewarding and challenging an audience's theatrical knowledge."[44] While the theatrical tradition after 1695 was a continuation in important ways of what came before, then, innovation was a key survival tactic for the rival theaters. Novelty took many forms: generic experimentation in mainpieces; a greater emphasis on music, dancing, and spectacle; and the development of new hybrid entertainment forms like semi-opera and pantomime. Other critics have explored how print criticism of the period reflected on the companies' experiments with dramatic and theatrical experience, but I wish to shift focus to prologues and epilogues, which provide a different perspective on these developments.[45] I find that prologues and epilogues foregrounded the tense relationship between dramatic tradition—often personified by John Fletcher—and new forms of entertainment that placed music, dancing, and spectacle, rather than language, at the center. While print criticism often took an antiquarian or nostalgic view of the stage, promoting a sense of a national literary tradition that was being violated by the rise of nonverbal performance elements, prologues and epilogues engaged in a more openended exploration of the ways that economic conditions shaped dramatic form and mediated contemporary theater's relationship to its inheritance.

In the aftermath of the United Company's split, the Actors' Company at Lincoln's Inn Fields attempted to stake a claim to theatrical tradition by touting the venerability of its celebrity performers, several of whom had been known to the public since the early days of the Restoration. The author of *A Comparison between the Two Stages* recalls that the strategy initially worked, putting the Patent Company at Drury Lane at a disadvantage: "'Twas strange that the general defection of the old Actors which left *Drury-lane,* and the fondness which the better sort shew'd for 'em at the opening of their *New-house,* and indeed the Novelty it self, had not quite destroy'd those few young ones that remain'd behind."[46] Betterton's crew benefitted from the "Novelty" of their "*New-house,*" despite being "old Actors"—that is, they reaped the advantage of experience as well as that of seeming fresh and unfamiliar. To combat the Actors' Company's claims on novelty, the Patent Company began using prologues and epilogues to market itself as a group of fresh-faced upstarts, in opposition to the aging troupe at Lincoln's Inn Fields. The actors drew attention to their youth by figuring themselves as "Birds just fledg'd in th' Nest" and by having child actresses deliver salacious prologues and epilogues centered on their youth and budding sexuality.[47] Furthermore, in several framing pieces, the Drury Lane company claimed to be enlivening the repertory through its adaptations, revivals, and experiments with spectacle. By updating their dramatic inheritance according to current trends in music, dancing, and special effects, the young actors turned the tables on their rivals, finding their own way to claim the best of both antiquity and novelty.

The Patent Company's framing orations developed an association between the actors' youth and their dependence on the theatrical tradition. This was especially the case with revivals of plays by Francis Beaumont and

John Fletcher. For instance, in the prologue to Elkanah Settle's alteration of *Philaster, or, Love Lies a-Bleeding*, performed around December 1695, Hildebrand Horden declares: "We safely fight behind great *Fletcher*'s Shield / That good old Play *Philaster* ne're can fail, / But we Young Actors how shall we prevail?"[48] He refers to the actors at Lincoln's Inn Fields as "The Elder Heroes of the other Stage" but reminds audience members that Betterton and his company "[w]ere Striplings once of our young Beardless Age" and asks them to be patient with the young players during their "Tryal-Year."[49] In this case, the venerability of both the Fletcher play and the actors of the other company are contrasted to the youth and inexperience of Rich's actors.

A more antagonistic relationship is established in the apparatus to *Bonduca, or, the British Heroine*, which debuted at Drury Lane in September 1695 and was based on Fletcher's *The Tragedie of Bonduca* (1611). In the preface George Powell attempts a tenuous balance between familiarity and novelty, calling the play "a Fabrick of Antiquity" but insisting that an anonymous adapter has contributed "several Alterations, besides the two First Acts New Writ."[50] The prologue to the play begins by evoking the antiquity of the play as well, referring to Fletcher as "the great Dead" asleep "i' th' Laurel Bed," and calling on "His proud *Bonduca*" to awaken.[51] The prologue quickly switches gears, however, leaving Fletcher to sleep and reminding the audience that the theaters are at war in the present: "We've bus'ness with the Living, not the Dead" (line 6). It goes on to tout the young company's "Growing Spring" as an advantage over the "Fading Autumn" at the other theater (line 17), and it insists that Drury Lane is better equipped to accommodate the public's new desire for spectacle:

> Yet we'ave the Advantage, a Fairer Light,
> Our Nobler *Theatre's*. Nay we are bringing
> Machines, Scenes, Opera's, Musick, Dancing, Singing;
> Translated from the Chiller, Bleaker *Strand*
> To your sweet *Covent-Garden's* Warmer Land. (lines 19–23)

In other words, Rich's company is updating the venerable old plays of the early Stuart period for new tastes, adding music and dancing that is missing from the originals.

In the lines that follow, Betterton's company is likewise portrayed as distinguished but out-of-date: "To us, Young Players, then let some Smiles fall: / Let not their dear Antiquities sweep all. / Antiquity on a Stage? Oh

Fye! 'tis Idle" (lines 24–26). Going so far as to describe the rivals as "Old, Decrepid, Wither'd," the prologue concludes by petitioning the audience: "To th' Young your Love, to th' old your Reverence pay" (lines 29, 36). Here, the "old" to whom "Reverence" should be paid is ambiguous: Is it the elder company at Lincoln's Inn Fields, or the dead "Bard" from the beginning of the piece? If the latter, these closing lines suggest that a revival of an old play by young actors should incite both love and reverence. At the same time, their ambiguity holds open the comparison between the old play and the old company, aligning the young players with the fresh "Alterations" and new spectacles that have been added to the play. This piece ultimately advances the argument that the Patent Company's youth puts it in the unique position to adapt the repertory to current tastes, including the vogue for visual and musical spectacle.

The generational conflict between the companies at Lincoln's Inn Fields and Drury Lane had a complex relationship to nostalgia for "ancient" plays and the perceived need to keep them fresh. Yet not everyone agreed that updating repertory plays with spectacular elements was a culturally useful activity. Some saw the new emphasis on music, dancing, and effects as merely a way of appealing to the tastes of the masses. Whereas the Patent Company used prologues and epilogues to make a case for adaptation, the character Critic in *A Comparison between the Two Stages* lambasts the Actors' Company for the same. He dismisses Betterton's plays as being "but alterations of other Men's Plays new dipt, and christen'd with other Names," giving the example that *The Vintner Trick'd* is merely John Marston's *The Dutch Courtesan* under a new title.[52] Likewise, the innovations that Rich's company touted in the prologue to *Bonduca* were not universally celebrated; critics considered such diversions a weak compensation for the lack of "sense" in modern plays. For instance, Edward Filmer's preface to *The Unnatural Brother*, performed around December 1696 or January 1697 at Lincoln's Inn Fields, attributes the play's failure on stage to the fact that it was "too grave for the Age," featuring no trendy comedic underplot to counterbalance the high tragic plot.[53] Filmer insists that he intended to appeal to discerning viewers rather than the "rabble," but he laments that aesthetic tastes have become degraded in all echelons of society: "I find that even our men of Sense, have been so long entertained with the gaudy, glaring splendor of our Operas, that nothing now can please their eyes, but what dazels 'em: And that their ears have, of late, been so well belabour'd with Drums, Kettle-Drums, Trumpets, and Hautboys, that they are almost become deaf to Sense, or any thing else, convey'd to 'em in a less Noise, than those their darling Consorts generally are."[54] Filmer thus associates the "dazel" of new musical entertainments and operas with a decline of "Sense," evoking a conventional opposition between intellectual sense and the pleasure of the senses. In paratexts like these that appear alongside printed texts of plays, the rise of spectacle is straightforwardly attributed to society's declining tastes.

A prologue to Edward Ravenscroft's *The Anatomist* (performed around November 1696 at Lincoln's Inn Fields) similarly pits substance against spectacle, but it pays closer attention to the relationship between the rise of new forms of entertainment and the changing economic conditions of the theater. The speaker, Betterton, begins by rejecting any hope the audience might have for "Pageant Decoration" but assures them that the play has plenty of novelty: "Yet is our Entertainment odd and new / We've in our Show the First of Cuckolds too: / And what we call a Masque some will allow / To be an Op'ra, as the World goes now."[55] The qualifying phrases "some will allow" and "as the World goes now" suggest skepticism towards the use of the fashionable label of "Op'ra" to describe an old-fashioned "Masque," and the speaker insists that "we" (the acting company) still adhere to the old terminology.[56] Yet in deference to changing tastes, Betterton acquiesces reluctantly to audience preferences. He uses the promise of something like an opera to keep them in their seats for the "odd and new" show—actually an adaptation of a French farce, Noël Lebreton de Hauteroche's *Crispin Médecin*. Betterton goes on to express nostalgia for a time when drama had more substance and plays more staying power:

> Once Song and Dance cou'd buoy up want of Thinking,
> But now those Bladders can't prevent its Sinking:
> Plays grow so heavy, that those helps are vain;
> Three times they sink, and never rise again.[57]

These lines express a conventional complaint that new plays no longer survive for more than three nights (a truism in prologues and epilogues of this period, despite the fact that several plays enjoyed longer runs). Here, though, the nostalgia is a bit different from Filmer's: instead of longing for a time when sense rather than spectacle ruled the stage, this prologue laments that song and dance can no longer compensate for a lack of poetic skill the way they used to. These lines suggest that the players—unlike certain playwrights and critics—are less nostalgic for an era of masterful dramatic art than for a time when the theater was financially stable.

The prologue to *The Anatomist* eventually reveals its satiric target as the Drury Lane company's recent failed opera, *Brutus of Alba*:

> Well, if our Neighbours the Precedence claim,
> For good dull Stuff we'll not dispute with them.
> Our Medley is perhaps as much too light,
> But let it pass—We don't take Money yet by weight.[58]

These lines change the meaning of the preceding ones, showing that the "want of Thinking" that cannot be "buoy[ed] up" by music and dancing is symptomatic of *Brutus* in particular, more than theater in general. The prologue here entertains the possibility that *The Anatomist* is just as "dull" and "light" as *Brutus*, meaning that it is just as lacking in sense, but asks the audience to let it pass just as they do their dull, light coins. The government only accepts coins by weight at this moment, but the theater promises to take coins at face value and asks for similar leniency from the audience. Much like the 1696 epilogue to *The Younger Brother* discussed above, in which the audience is reminded that they have paid for their tickets with degraded currency, here the light coinage works as a metaphor for the audience's acceptance of "light" entertainments. At the mint and in the theater, the value of a public institution's offerings is fundamentally at the mercy of public opinion; it is the public's faith in or desire for a commodity that determines whether that commodity can circulate.

The prologue to Filmer's *The Unnatural Brother* (the preface to which is discussed above) simultaneously invokes and rejects the nostalgia that accompanies the wit/money metaphor, again linking its critique of economic nostalgia to debates around the increasingly spectacular nature of entertainment. The prologue begins: "Bless'd were those happy daies, if ever any, / When Poets flow'd with Wit, and you with Money."[59] Immediately, the phrase "if ever any" casts doubt on the idea of an idealized past in which wit and money were abundant. The speaker continues: "But now, both Wit and Money run so low, / They're at the poorest Ebb they e're can know, / This Clipt, that dwindled into Farce and Show" (lines 3–5). The speaker imagines the turn to spectacle as the source of wit's debasement—a debasement attributed, in many of the other pieces discussed above, to the rise of wits and critics in the pit. These lines can be compared with the prologue to *The Anatomist*, which, as we have seen, cast "Song and Dance" as ways to "buoy up want of Thinking," partial and temporary solutions to, rather than causes of, the problem. Both pieces see plays that lack substance as light coins whose metallic content falls short of their face value. Here, changes in theatrical form represent the degradation rather than the recirculation of drama. This approach is starkly unlike that taken by Colley Cibber, whose *Love's Last Shift* imagines the recoinage as a figure for generic change—a way of melting down the materials of the past, extracting their core value, and reshaping them into something that works in the present. It also differs from the approach taken by Drury Lane's Patent Company at this time (where Cibber was an actor and where *Love's Last Shift* was staged), which was largely to figure spectacle as a way of updating the repertory for current tastes.

The prologue to *The Unnatural Brother* goes on to suggest a difference between the debasement of dramatic wit and that of silver money:

> As for our Coin, the Wisdom of the State,
> May stop our ruine and prevent our Fate;
> What will not pass by Tale, may pass by Weight.
> But who can our corrupted Wit restore,
> And make that Currant as it was before? (lines 6–10)

The state can mend the currency: by weighing coins and redeeming their metallic content, the mint can restore the coins whose face value ("Tale") is inaccurate. However, no such procedure can be applied to the stage's "corrupted Wit." The speaker explains that plays may conceal their value from a cursory inspection:

> O! could we but with equal Balance sit,
> And by the nicest scruples weigh our Wit,
> How many pieces good, and fair to sight,
> Would yet be found by many Grains too light?" (lines 11–14)

While many of the prologues and epilogues of this season imagine the theater in terms of financial institutions and emphasize the intimate, troubled relationship between the various economic agents who coexist in the space of the theater, this piece suggests that the playhouse is what Agnew calls a "world apart," a zone that remains out of reach of the government's regulatory efforts. As such, it is arguably even more subject to public opinion than the coinage, because no outside authority can step in if the masses lead the theater's values astray. The prologues' and epilogues' treatment of the rise of spectacle as an acquiescence to audience tastes reveals a sense that the public's power over the market has become excessive and that the elite have lost their power to control institutions like the theater.

Recoining the Repertory: The Prologue to *The Sham Lawyer*

Like other prologues to Fletcher adaptations discussed above, the prologue to *The Sham Lawyer; or, The Lucky Extravagant* reflects on how that giant of the repertory was updated and recycled to meet current needs. Performed in May 1697 at Drury Lane, *The Sham Lawyer*—attributed to James Drake—was an adaptation and amalgamation of two Fletcher plays: *Wit without Money* and *The Spanish Curate* (which Fletcher cowrote with Philip Massinger). This adaptation's prologue brings together several tropes and themes that run throughout the topical orations of this period: the parallel shortages of wit and coin; the friction between the theatrical companies and the increasingly critical audiences on which they depended; the rise of a new generation of playwrights who reworked their dramatic inheritance in complex ways; and the theaters' increasing dependence on novel musical and visual spectacles to draw in audiences, even to revivals of old plays that did not originally include spectacular elements. In joining these threads, the piece reveals their conceptual entanglements.

The prologue begins by invoking the well-worn analogy between the dire state of currency and dramatic art:

> As want of Coin did store of Banks beget;
> So Poets swarm upon this Dearth of Wit.
> And as those Banks, when ready Cash grew scant,
> Excus'd non-payments by the publick want:
> Ill Poets so, when you on them reflect,
> Their proper Faults upon the Times reject.[60]

Here, the overabundance of new playwrights is compared not to the inflated value and supply of gold as in the pieces above but rather to the plethora of new financial institutions springing up to offer credit instruments that can fill the void left by the discredited currency. The banks, like the writers, "swarm upon" the public's need, suggesting predation or exploitation. Yet both bankers and poets fail to meet the public demand, and they even blame the public for their own failures. The Bank of England had been unable to handle the credit crunch of the previous spring, and Parliament had stopped payment on annuities and lottery tickets, decimating people's faith in the ability of public financial institutions to honor their debts. These lines suggest that just as the banks blame larger economic conditions for their own failures, so too do bad writers attribute the failure of their plays to the competition between the theaters, the public's degraded taste, or the scarcity of money. In both cases, those responsible for the declining condition of public life use circular logic to blame that very condition for their own inability to solve it.

The next lines shift the metaphor, likening failed writers to bankrupts rather than to the banks, a change in figuration that works precisely because financial institutions were seen as exhibiting the same material and moral deficits as debtors:

> Shoals of damn'd Play-wrights in our Pits are found
> Like Brother Bankrupts for each other bound;
> Who, sinking first themselves beneath the Test,
> With joint Endeavour strive to damn the rest:
> And, having fail'd to satisfie the Town,
> Turn Levellers and cry all credit down. (lines 7–12)

The location of the "damn'd Play-wrights" in the pit not only evokes Dante's *Inferno*, but also draws on the commonplace that the wits writing failed plays are the same ones writing the criticism that harms the stage, thereby inflicting a double wound on the playhouses. Once a bankrupt wit's own play fails, he begins writing criticism that ensures the failure of his "Brother" poets. The notion that these unsuccessful playwrights are like insolvent borrowers who "cry all credit down" in order to destroy the system they have abused is reminiscent of the prologue to *Timoleon* examined above. The prologue to *The Sham Lawyer* makes explicit what was implicit in the earlier example: critics who damn plays, it claims, are playing a game with the theater like risk takers do with the financial system. They mount a disingenuous criticism of current conditions only to manipulate public opinion, which they may reverse just as easily tomorrow if it benefits them personally. In both economic and theatrical markets, laborers and consumers alike are at the mercy of a new class of self-proclaimed experts who ultimately serve themselves rather than the public.

The critics are not the only ones responsible for this situation, however; the next lines of the prologue draw attention to the complacency of audiences who passively accept whatever is on offer:

> Fools, French-men, Players, fill the crouded Pit,
> Those sworn Confederates to write down Wit.
> Instead of Manly sense, and strong writ Plays,
> They bring you *Harlequin,* and *Opera's.*
> They let you thus, like Children, have your will.
> Knowing how fond you are of Rattles still. (lines 13–18)

The "strong writ Plays"—plays that emphasize the literary and dramatic art of plot, characterization, and dialog—are being replaced by "*Harlequin,* and *Opera's,*" mere toys in comparison. Whereas the writers of old-fashioned drama possess "Manly sense," audiences who enjoy these new musical entertainments are "like Children." Although the agents of this unfortunate change are still the "Fools, French-men, Players," and other aspiring wits of the "crouded Pit," the audience is clearly implicated in this shift. At this moment, then, the prologue begins to do exactly what it earlier accused failed poets of doing: it places at least some of the blame for the decline of theater on debased public tastes.

The prologue goes on to lament the losses the theater has suffered as a result of the false wits' superficial offerings:

> These Practices on us have brought such Ills,
> That half our Customers protest our Bills;
> And our Receipts of late to less amount
> Than formerly by double Bank discount. (lines 19–22)

Now, the theater itself is like a bank that issues "Bills," a term that evokes playbills as well as bills of exchange. Just as the Bank of England might discount its bills—making them less expensive and therefore attractive enough to overcome public mistrust in the bank's paper credit—the theater also takes in lower "Receipts" as it loses the public's trust. The theater, like the bank, depends on public confidence to function.

In the course of these lines, the hack playwrights slip metaphorically from banks to bankrupts crying down credit, and the theater itself is figured as a bank. The fluidity of the metaphor reveals not only the difficulty of mapping the theatrical economy directly onto English financial markets but also the richness and polyvalence of the imaginative connections available. The financial metaphors continue with the introduction of the novice playwright, who, like Cibber in the prologue to *Love's Last Shift*, is compared to a fledgling investor:

> Our young Beginner, fearing this to day.
> Offers Security for his first Play.
> To raise his Stock he wise provision made,
> Of a rich Partner to support the Trade:
> Whose visible Estate, and Credit yet
> Make his Bills current through the Land of Wit.
> Which upon sight, if any doubt be made
> In specie shall in new mill'd Wit be paid. (lines 23–30)

The young author of *The Sham Lawyer* has "raise[d] his Stock" by taking on an established investing partner: John Fletcher. Like the inexperienced company at Drury Lane claiming to "safely fight behind great Fletcher's Shield" in the prologue to *Philaster*, here another member of the younger generation of theater practitioners finds shelter in this major Jacobean playwright's shadow.

Fletcher, like some perfect marriage of the Bank of England and its rival Land Bank (backed not by silver, but by mortgages), has wealth both in his "Estate" and in his "Credit," which "Make his Bills current throughout the Land of Wit." Not only are Fletcher's bills—unlike those of the theater in the lines above—"current," meaning they will be accepted anywhere; they are also redeemable for currency, "specie" to be paid "upon sight." Fletcher is even better than the banks, because he pays ready money on demand. The significance of this statement is twofold: first, mounting a Fletcher play is profitable for the theaters; and second, his established wealth can generate "new mill'd Wit." The emphasis is on the freshness and wholeness of what can be produced from his estate, not on the venerability of some ancient, unsullied Elizabethan coins.

The lines that follow expand on this notion by revealing that the young playwright has, in fact, recoined Fletcher:

> For like our Mints, our Scribler has made bold,
> To make all new by melting down the Old.
> Nor can you blame him, if he has the Skill,
> But to maintain the Ancient Standard still;
> For, what he finds in weight deficient grown.
> He will make good with Bullion of his own. (lines 31–36)

In this metaphor adaptation works in precisely the same way as the recoinage: the materials of past generations, which have "deficient grown," undergo a process of "melting down" and being supplemented with new "Bullion" in order to return them to "the Ancient Standard." These lines make the case that the values of the past can be kept alive only if they are augmented with new materials; they can only remain current if revived. At the same time, the playwright still aspires to the "Ancient Standard." This point is important because the prologue has previously identified some innovations, such as pantomime, as superficial solutions to the theater's woes. Only certain forms of novelty, then, work according to the successful logic of recoinage.

In keeping with the notion of updating the old to hold it to its own standards, the prologue implicitly promises that the play will appeal to the new values audiences bring to the playhouse—specifically, middling-class virtues and a softening of Restoration-era satire. There is, however, one group upon which the playwright has failed to turn his satirical lens, perhaps mistakenly:

> And yet the Fool did the whole City spare.
> Like running Traders thus he does begin,
> By courteous dealing first to draw you in.
> If to his word this time you find him just,
> It may encourage you to greater Trust.
> Next time perhaps alone He'l [sic] undertake,
> And by your Favours in your Debts may break. (lines 43–49)

The prologue considers the writer a "Fool" for sparing "the whole City," a term that refers to the London financial sector with its merchants, tradesmen, investors, and bankers. Cit-cuckolding, a common element in earlier drama, will not be found in this adaptation. The prologue further suggests that the playwright's light dealing with the City is a deliberate choice, designed to spark interest in his new venture: like stockjobbers or "running

Traders," he begins by "courteous dealing" with prospective investors. In other words, he appeals to middling-class audiences who have it within their power to support his future endeavors, hoping to "encourage" them "to greater Trust" so that they will underwrite his further efforts. The final lines promise that his next play might be an original one, written "alone"—i.e., without his business partner Fletcher—if the audience will lend him their "Favours," or applause. Ultimately he hopes to be in the audience's debt, a speculator collecting others' funds and investing them in the large, risky project of his theatrical career.

The figuration of the playwright as a speculator recalls the prologue and epilogue to *Love's Last Shift* discussed in chapter 1. Here, however, the figure reflects not only the playwright's middling-class occupation and the entrepreneurial, risk-taking disposition it requires, but also indicates the very real presence of middling-class audiences and their power as financial supporters of a highly speculative joint-stock endeavor: the public theater. While the ideals of the earlier Stuart theater, as exemplified by Fletcher, are worth preserving and aspiring to, such an undertaking is impossible without the support of the new class of theatergoers who have new expectations regarding the role of satire, virtue, and didacticism in entertainment. These expectations are worth appealing to because they are fundamentally compatible with tradition, capable of being blended in an alloy with the base materials of the repertory. Harlequinades and operas, on the other hand, are false, faddish solutions to the theater's growing pains at this tumultuous moment. While this piece offers a clear solution, however, it is also haunted by the possibility that Jacobean ideals may not survive the demands of new class of theatergoers if those spectators' tastes cannot be channeled correctly. The tidiness of the concluding lines does little to smooth the rapid and unsettling reconfigurations of the financial metaphors early in the piece, which above all suggest the uneasy relationships among the multiple, competing agents in London's emerging and overlapping publics.

This piece relates in important ways to trends that can be seen across the prologues and epilogues of the 1695–96 and 1696–97 seasons. As young writers and actors arrived on the stage to replace the Restoration-era giants represented by the Actors' Company, they saw themselves not only bringing new expectations (such as the desire for music and spectacle) but also reviving prewar values in their rejection of Restoration bawdry and hard satire. Echoing Cibber's insight in *Love's Last Shift*—that many forms of novelty are really acts of recycling—the *Sham Lawyer*'s prologue draws attention to the tensions and contradictions inherent in the process of reforming the dramatic tradition. Like the recoinage, the reshaping of the theater in the 1690s sought to restore drama to an earlier standard while also introducing new features and forms that, like milled edges on coins, made drama "current." Furthermore, as in the case of the recoinage, the changes in the theater were associated with the growing financial and cultural power of the expanding middling classes. The tension in the figuring of revivals and adaptations stemmed from the fundamental disjunction between the way some members of these classes saw themselves (as being capable of restoring fundamental English values that had become corrupted by the upper classes, for example) and the way others saw them (as radically destabilizing and displacing existing hierarchies and standards). If some stage orations from this period display anxiety around speculation, entrepreneurialism, and public opinion, others—like the prologue to *The Sham Lawyer*—express optimism about the influence of young, middling-class people on the theater, both as practitioners and as audience members.

This chapter has largely focused on how prologues and epilogues used a specific economic phenomenon, the recoinage crisis, to reflect on the dynamics of the entertainment industry. However, the resonance that these pieces established between theatrical and financial markets was one that went far beyond a single financial crisis in the public imagination. The economic developments taking place in the mid-1690s provided an imaginative lens for the rival theaters to think through the new market dynamics they were forced to negotiate in the face of massive pressures, both internal and external to the theater. The figurative link between financial and theatrical markets was a plastic one, deployed to consider multiple issues from a variety of perspectives. As we have seen, these pieces used the conceptual nexus of finance and theater to theorize the relationship between value and public opinion, the possibilities of speculation as a source of innovation or risk, and the growing power of the middling classes, which brought a spirit of entrepreneurialism to spheres of influence that had been dominated by patronage and the upper classes.

At the same time, these texts complicate our usual scholarly narratives about the rise of middling-class values. The heterogeneity of the pieces examined here attests to the contention and debate within the middling classes about which values were worth promoting, as well as about the extent to which the broader public, as opposed to the economic elite, should control institutions and determine value. After all, most of the people writing and performing these pieces were theater professionals, not aristocrats, yet they do not speak with one voice. Some are critical of innovation and spectacle, while others embrace it. Drawing on a widespread and commonly understood correlation between theaters and financial markets as large, government-backed enterprises reliant on public trust to operate, many of these pieces celebrate (or at least appeal to) the public's unprecedented power over the success and failure of institutions. Others suggest that dramatic art suffers under the conditions of speculative finance, in which self-interested opinion makers—speculators on the one hand, and critics on the other—fabricate value by manipulating the public. At the same time, and perhaps ironically, these head- and tailpieces are themselves attempts to steer public sentiment; that is, they harness the same forces of expertise and influence that they critique. In this sense, prologues and epilogues offer an alternative site of cultural negotiation and authority, one that should be examined alongside documents like financial treatises and dramatic criticism that are the focus of so much scholarship. The dialogic forms of the prologue and epilogue, delivered in conversation with the audience and, as we have seen, in conversation with other such stage orations, are exemplary for their notice of competing voices and their dramatization of public dissent as well as consensus.

Interlude
(1700–1720)

• 3 •

Women at the Theater-Finance Nexus

Susanna Centlivre as Playwright-Adventurer

The first two chapters of this book have examined the interactions between theater and finance in the 1690s, a time of significant change both in England's financial system and in its public theaters. Plays, prologues, epilogues, and dramatic criticism from this decade attest to the conceptual relay between the financial and theatrical spheres. As I have shown, economic events like the recoinage and the establishment of the Bank of England resonated in complex ways with cultural events like the Actors' Rebellion and the reestablishment of a theatrical duopoly. Over the two decades that followed, as the credit economy grew, debt and speculation came to play an increasingly prominent role in the English economy. Public finance became ever more entwined with commercial enterprises in ways that witnesses found both exciting and disturbing. The culmination of these developments, and the next major event in England's economic history, was the South Sea Bubble of 1720, which will be the focus of subsequent chapters.[1]

Here, I take up the two decades between the financial revolution of the 1690s and the bubble of 1720. These years were notable not only in economic but also theatrical history, as the management and financial structures of the leading companies changed almost yearly. This chapter examines the events of this tumultuous period through the career of playwright Susanna Centlivre (c. 1669–1723), who had sixteen plays and an afterpiece staged between 1700 and 1722.[2] As I will show, Centlivre's career reflects the changing stakes of debates in the theater-finance nexus during this significant transitional period. Her early plays reflect thematically on the pleasures and perils of risk taking even as her efforts to market these plays and bring about their success epitomize the new ideal of the entrepreneurial playwright represented in the prologues and epilogues of the 1690s. Like those prologues and epilogues, Centlivre's plays engage at a metatheatrical level with contemporary debates about playhouse finances, exposing the increasing mystification of market operations and the tensions these operations fostered between the public good and private self-interest. Furthermore, Centlivre was explicitly interested in how speculative market structures allowed her, as a middling-class woman writer, to gain access to economic and cultural spheres of influence long off-limits to members of her gender and social class.

In her own lifetime Centlivre was "minor celebrity" who drew notice in periodicals including the *Tatler*, the *Female Tatler*, and the *Lover*, and whose portrait was advertised for sale in the London papers.[3] A well-known Whig reported to hold raucous parties on King George I's birthday, she was a regular target of Tory satirists, appearing as one of the two "slip-shod Muses" in Alexander Pope's *Dunciad* and as "the *Cook's Wife* in *Buckingham Court*" in one of his attacks on publisher Edmund Curll.[4] She is frequently identified with the character Phoebe Clinket in Pope, John Gay, and John Arbuthnot's play *Three Hours after Marriage* (1717) and as the mantua-maker-cum-procuress in Delarivier Manley's *New Atalantis*.[5] Beyond these political attacks, she appears regularly in antifeminist satires—grouped, for example, with Mary Pix and Catherine Trotter in the anonymous *A Letter from the Dead Thomas Brown to the Living Heraclitus* (1704) and with Manley and Aphra Behn in John Duncombe's *Feminiad* (1754).[6] Her contributions to epistolary collections, her occasional poems, and the prologues and epilogues written to her plays by various colleagues suggest that she moved in literary circles with Abel Boyer, Nicholas Rowe, George Farquhar, Jane Wiseman, Sarah Fyge Egerton, Richard Steele, and Anthony Hammond; literary anecdotes from the period provide evidence of her friendship with actress and theatrical entrepreneur Anne Oldfield and her possible involvement in a social circle involving Daniel Defoe and Eliza Haywood.[7] From 1719 onward dubious accounts of her life—rife with contradictory information, fairy-tale features, and elements of the picaresque—routinely crop up in catalogs of dramatists. These tales invoke, variously, her family's political exile during the English civil wars, her early loss of her parents, her wicked stepmother, her escape from home, her rumored love affairs and multiple marriages, her travels with a company of strolling players, her cross-dressed adventures at university, her captivation of husband Joseph Centlivre while performing in breeches, her squabbles with the actors in London, her supposed borrowings from and dependence on men writers in her circle, and her proud display of extravagant gifts from powerful patrons. As such, these salacious and often contradictory accounts attest to her early biographers' difficulty reconciling Centlivre's gender and apparently modest origins with the fact that she was clearly educated, openly political, and wildly successful.[8] A significant figure in the cultural world of Augustan London, Centlivre wrote plays that remained in the theatrical repertories for over a century.[9] Yet after the mid-nineteenth century, her work lapsed into obscurity as literary and dramatic canons were formed that largely excluded women writers.[10]

Most recent scholarship on Centlivre has concerned her engagement with Whig political philosophy. Building on Pocock's suggestion that the mobility of property opened up room for women's economic agency, numerous studies have examined how Centlivre represents the feminist potential of commercial society as an alternative to the institutions of civil society, as well as how her plays reveal the limits of Lockean contract theory for women.[11] This chapter broadens the focus; in addition to exploring how Centlivre used her writing to engage in debates about the gendered dynamics of England's changing financial system, I show how her own actions as an economic agent reflected and responded to those dynamics. Several critics have shown that Centlivre's plays, which are often highly metatheatrical, draw attention to performance as means for women to exert their agency where it is otherwise constrained.[12] Here, I insist that it is not only through acting that the theater initiated new possibilities for women but also through the highly speculative dynamics of theatrical finance. Centlivre's actions as an economic agent, I argue, highlight the commercial theater's ability to function as a privileged sphere in which women could circumvent the ordinary channels of economic participation from which they were normally excluded. In turning to Centlivre's hitherto unexplored commentaries on and navigations of theatrical markets, I reveal that it was not simply (as Pocock would have it) the abstraction of financial instruments or the recognition of women as contractual agents that allowed Centlivre to thrive in this space; rather, her success hinged on her recognition of the contingency and irrationality of the theatrical market.

While Centlivre embraced speculation and risk in her negotiations of gender, authorship, and celebrity, however, she also expressed significant concerns about the very forms of economic behavior in which she herself engaged. A close analysis of her later works reveals that Centlivre became increasingly critical of the vulnerability of speculative financial markets—both those that underpinned the theatrical public sphere and those undergirding England's fiscal-military enterprises—to private interests willing to subvert the public good. Just as the prologues and epilogues examined in chapter 2 expressed concern that the democratizing tendencies of speculative markets could become a cover for elite power to sustain itself, Centlivre grew wary over the course of her career that class- and gender-based power could be entrenched in new ways by the very institutions that enabled and sustained her unusual success as a woman writer of modest origins. Centlivre, then, was both an enthusiastic participant in and an incisive critic of the developments in speculative markets between the revolutionary events of the 1690s and the sobering Bubble year of 1720.

As I trace Centlivre's engagement with theatrical finance and markets more generally, however, I do not wish to reproduce all-too-common assumptions about Centlivre's status as a "mere" businesswoman or commercial playwright. As Jacky Bratton points out, the feminist critics who rediscovered Centlivre in the late twentieth century were so eager to reclaim her work as "literary" that they attempted to downplay her engagement with the business of the theater. As a result, they tended to reinforce a gendered dichotomy: on the one hand, the masculinist discourse of literary aesthetics, solitary genius, and self-conscious difficulty passed down by Romantic-era critics like Coleridge; and on the other, the figure of the commercial theater, so often devalued as a feminized, collaborative, and popular art form.[13] In order to do justice to Centlivre's work without enacting what Bratton calls "a hegemonic move upon the theatre," I take up her call to attend to Centlivre's intertheatricality—that is, her work's interdependence with the network of practices, performers, music, dancing, and audience desires that shaped an evening at the theater and the life of a performance text.[14] In doing so, I aim to explore how Centlivre drew on the resources of both the stage and the page to negotiate her place as a woman within broader economic and cultural systems.

The first section of this chapter examines how Centlivre's first hit play, *The Gamester*, and its companion piece, *The Basset Table*, intervened in public debates over theatrical finance around the time of their debut in 1705. It further argues that Centlivre's choice to take these closely related plays to two different theaters reflected an embrace of risk that existed in tension with the plays' critique of gambling and broader complexes of speculative behavior. The second section extends this discussion of Centlivre's marketing strategies by focusing on her biggest success during her own lifetime, *The Busie Body* (1709). I argue that the play's Incognita figure provides a window onto Centlivre's own practices of authorial masking and unmasking, which allowed her to capitalize on otherwise damaging rumors and controversies around her status as a woman writer. The third section further complicates our understanding of Centlivre's engagement with speculative market practices by exposing her play *A Bold Stroke for a Wife* (1718) and her poem *A Woman's Case* (1720) as previously unrecognized critiques of the South Sea Company. I argue that these texts demonstrate Centlivre's increasing ambivalence about the entanglement of Britain's public credit with speculative trading ventures, and I suggest that her poem, ostensibly a request for company shares, was in fact a successful ploy for economic support from the House of Hanover. More than a mere acquiescence to old styles of royal patronage, however, the poem's interaction with Centlivre's stage career positions the theater as an alternative speculative economy—one in which women could clear a profit by applying techniques of risk assessment and management similar to those used in the world of joint-stock finance, while circumventing the structures that excluded them, in many cases, from full participation in that world.

1705: *The Gamester* and *The Basset Table*

Centlivre's plays *The Gamester* and *The Basset Table* both premiered in 1705, and both center on the social ills of gambling.[15] The former concerns itself with the predominantly masculine space of the public dice table, the latter with mixed-gender card games in a private home. It is in some ways intuitive to read these representations of gambling as figurative engagements with speculative financial behavior more generally. As Jesse Molesworth points out, eighteenth-century observers like William Hogarth viewed gambling as part of a larger mania for risk-taking behaviors, alongside the lotteries and the stock markets. For many at the time, speculation—whether in joint-stock trading ventures or in games of chance—was thought to be driven primarily by greed.[16] Centlivre, like many of her contemporaries, seems to have viewed the gaming table as a microcosm of broader economic trends and behaviors in her society, and many scholars have examined these plays as reflections on broader changes in England's financial system, class structure, and gendered order at the beginning of the eighteenth century.[17] In this section, I wish to shift attention to how they intervened in debates swirling around theatrical markets in particular at the moment of their debut. As I will show, Centlivre's commentary on the speculative dynamics of playhouse finance goes beyond conventional condemnations of risk taking as simply imprudent or greedy; instead, her plays acknowledge the pleasures and opportunities speculation affords to the individual, while at the same time drawing attention the important ways in which this type of behavior can disrupt local economies and exacerbate social inequality.

Both *The Gamester* and *The Basset Table* invite the viewer to consider gambling and theatergoing as analogous, morally ambiguous forms of entertainment. In *The Gamester*, the titular gamester Valere mocks his father Sir Thomas's prudishness, predicting that "now will he rail as heartily against Gaming, as the Whigs against Plays."[18] Similarly, in *The Basset Table*, moralist Lady Lucy and *bon vivante* Lady Reveller debate whether playgoing or gambling is more detrimental to women's reputations.[19] Moments like these invite viewers to think about the plays' investigations of gambling—its moral and economic consequences as well as its effects on public life—as having implications for the theater, another arena of arguably harmless yet ethically suspect diversion in which the new rules of the market had begun to pervade social interactions.

Indeed, from the earliest publicity for *The Gamester*, audiences were encouraged to think of the play in connection with issues of economic competition between the theaters. The prologue and epilogue to *The Gamester* were printed on February 3, 1705, in the *Diverting Post*, a source of theatrical commentary and gossip that regularly published news on the economics of the playhouses. The prologue reads at first as a conventional appeal for audience sympathy and loyalty during a period of competition, developing an extended metaphor of the players at Lincoln's Inn Fields as the neglected wife to the Town. The epilogue offers a more direct reflection on the themes of the accompanying play, including a lengthy commentary on the evils of gaming, which is presented as a vicious cycle of predatory behavior in which "Vultures" exploit an innocent "Bubble," who in turn becomes a "Sharper" himself.[20] Suddenly, and without transition, the epilogue then returns to the discussion of theatrical competition begun in the prologue, lamenting that the players, "like old Mistresses," are unable to keep the Town's attention, unable even to "bribe" audiences with music and dance; the actors at Lincoln's Inn Fields are left "Like *Tantalus,* 'midst Plenty, thus to starve." The lines bring the issues of gambling and predation from the epilogue into conversation with those of theatrical competition raised originally in the prologue. While the prologue and epilogue were not written by Centlivre, they clearly take their cues from the plot and themes of her play, and they reinforce the implicit analogy between gambling and theatrical finance evident in the text of *The Gamester*. In this prologue and epilogue, as in the play itself, the theatrical marketplace is at risk of becoming a zero-sum game like the dice table, where one person's (or playing company's) prosperity comes at the cost of the other's ruin.

As this prologue and epilogue begin to suggest, *The Gamester*'s commentary on speculation and risk is tied closely to the specific dynamics of competition between the theaters in 1705 and to a particular set of debates about theatrical finance that swirled in the press that year. For the decade following the Actors' Rebellion of 1695, roughly the same managerial arrangement had stood in the London theaters: Christopher Rich managed the Patent Company, which performed at Drury Lane and Dorset Garden under patents deriving from those granted to William Davenant and Thomas Killigrew following the Restoration, while the company at Lincoln's Inn Fields, managed by Thomas Betterton, operated under an acting license.[21] It was widely understood that neither company was financially healthy, and in 1705 rumors of a merger began to circulate. The possibility of a reunited company, combined with the opening of the new Queen's Theatre in the Haymarket, prompted intense scrutiny of perceived financial malfeasance at both houses, as I will show. This scrutiny, in turn, sparked debate over the appropriate balance between the private interest needed to promote investment in cultural activity and the public's right to demand accountability and transparency.

Managers at both houses were perceived as keeping profits to themselves, depriving actors, vendors, and shareholders alike of their fair share. In continuing to operate under the now forty-year-old patents, Rich's company was obliged to make dividend payments to holders of renters' shares in the properties as well as acting or "adventurers' shares," which represented portions of the company's profits from performances. Evidence from Chancery Court lawsuits and the daily papers suggests, however, that he made no such payments during the years following the 1695 loss of the monopoly, claiming that there were no profits from which to pay dividends.[22] And Rich was not the only manager suspected of misdealing and profiteering. The dedication to an unacted play titled *The Lunatick,* printed around March 1705, addresses the "rulers" of Lincoln's Inn Fields (Betterton, along with Anne Bracegirdle and Elizabeth Barry) and cautions them to consider what they will give up by accepting a union:

> There will be no more Clandestine Sharing betwixt You without the rest; no more private Accounts, and Double Books; no more paying Debts half a score times over out of the Publick Stock, yet never paying them in reality at all. There will be no more sinking Three Hundred and fifty Pounds at a time in the Money repaid on a famous Singer's Account, but never accounted for to the rest of the Sharers; no more stopping all the Pay of the Under Actors on Subscription-Nights, when You were allowed forty or fifty Pound a Night for the House, besides the Benefit of the Galleries; no more sinking the Court-Money into Your own Pockets, and letting the Sallary People and Under Sharers Starve without Pay; no more taking Benefit-Days in the best Season of the Year, and Dunning the Quality for Guinea-Tickets to help out the Defects of all the other above-named Perquisites; no fifty Shillings per Week for scowring Old Lace, nor burning it, and selling the Product for private Advantage; no Twenty Shillings a Day House-Rent; no sharing Profits with the Poetasters.[23]

The writer accuses the management of cheating shareholders, vendors, and wage laborers in order to line their own pockets and those of the top performers and playwrights. The "private Advantage" pursued by the greedy managers (along with the singers and poetasters they prop up) is contrasted with the "Publick Stock," as the passage assembles a public that includes "the Sharers," "Court-Money" and "the Quality" alongside "Sallary People," "Under Sharers," and "Under Actors." In essence, the writer evokes the specter of a creative-managerial class that funnels the wealth of the upper classes into its own pockets, disrupting the imagined flow of money from the wealthy to the lower classes.

Amidst this fray, John Vanbrugh and William Congreve opened the Queen's Theatre in the Haymarket in April 1705. The building was financed using subscription money largely from noble patrons, a process that was followed avidly and represented as a speculative "project" in the papers. The *Diverting Post*, for example, announced in October 1704 that the theater, "built by the Subscription Money of most of our Nobility," was nearing completion, and the paper published a satirical poem: "On the Projectors of the New Play-House in the Hay-Market" the following April.[24] When Betterton's company moved there in early 1705 to try out the new space, commentators expressed optimism that Vanbrugh would use his elite backers' funds to promote the public good. For instance, *The Post-Boy Robb'd of His Mail* (1706), attributed to Drury Lane prompter Charles Gildon, includes a letter promising a tell-all about the establishment of the Queen's Theatre. The letter acknowledges the accusation that Christopher Rich, perhaps bowing to shareholder pressure, has put profits above the public good: "The *Play-house* having been granted to private Hands, nothing was minded but private Advantages."[25] The writer goes on to explain, however, that such corruption is the logical result of treating the right to perform plays as a piece of speculative property: "By Sale this Patent comes into the Hands of those who know even less than the first Possessors of it[.] . . . Money purchas'd the Business, and therefore the Business must be made to bring in the Money into the Purchaser's Pockets" (343). This text represents Vanbrugh's Haymarket project as an opportunity to break the cycle of profiteering and exploitation, restoring the theater to its former glory. According to the writer, at the inception of the Queen's Theatre,

> Men of Sense were in hopes, that a Poet had publick Spirit enough to regard only the Publick Good of those who upheld the Diversion by their Writing, or their Acting, which might have brought the Stage soon to its antient Lustre, and gain'd him more Credit (and perhaps all things consider'd) not less Money. If he had call'd in many Men of Learning, and Art, into the Management, and sought no farther Advantage from the Business that cost him little, than others equally qualify'd, except a Reimbursement of what he had really expended more than the Subscriptions. Thus he wou'd have enlarg'd his Reputation, and made Friends of all the Men of Sense, Wit and Poetry, present, and to come; and wou'd have persuaded the World, that he was not so unpoetical a Lover of only his own sordid Interest, as to mind nothing else. (343–44)

Again, the "publick Spirit" and "Public Good" are abstract values that could be supported by the wealth of elite investors; as the conditional verbs of this fantasy suggest, however, these high aspirations are ultimately circumvented by the greed of entrepreneurs who, unsatisfied with merely recouping their costs, inevitably pursue profit and "sordid" individual interest.

The writer goes on to describe Vanbrugh's attempt to realize the long-rumored union of all the actors of both major companies to perform together at the Haymarket. This union was often debated in terms of its effect on shareholders; indeed, in one of his own missives to the Lord Chamberlain, Vanbrugh argued that a union would make it harder for Rich to conceal profits from his investors.[26] The writer of *The Post-Boy Robb'd*, who expresses skepticism about Rich's management of the patent in the passage above, also opposes Vanbrugh's scheme because it is directly "contrary to the Pleasure and Will of his Benefactors, who gave him their Subscriptions to keep up two Companies" (344). He then encloses Vanbrugh's proposal to the Lord Chamberlain on July 19, 1705, as well as Rich's answer, both of which are preoccupied with what will happen to the Drury Lane shareholders if such a union occurs. While Vanbrugh claims that profits from the United Company will be distributed proportionally to those who previously held shares in the patent, Rich insists that the proposed union will result in the effective dissolution of the patent, thereby compromising "divers Marriages, Settlements, Morgages, Contracts, and the Support of many Families" (346). Rich's response insinuates that Vanbrugh's proposal is not, as he suggests, a win-win for investors in both the old Patent Company and the new theater in the Haymarket, but rather a reallocation of limited resources: "If I shall now be depriv'd of reaping the Benefit of such my Labour and Charges, what must the Effect be, but the undoings of my self, and of the Interests of those engag'd with me, to raise great Estates to Mr. *Vanbrugh*, and a few others, on our Ruins?" (346). This letter represents theatrical finance as a densely interconnected web of domestic and public economies; in doing so, it echoes the dedication to *The Lunatick* discussed above, which imagined a flow of wealth between elite investors and the lowest-paid workers disrupted by the greed of a creative-managerial class. Here, it is Vanbrugh rather than Betterton who accrues "great Estates" to a few confederates at the expense of all others. Rich's warning of this wealth built "on our Ruins" suggests that such profiteering can transform the economy from one in which individuals' fortunes are harmoniously intertwined (an investor's marriage settlement bolstered by a successful run of a new play, for instance) into a competitive game in which one person's fortune is another's ruin.

A printed petition by the actors at Drury Lane from this period deploys similar arguments to urge the Lord Chamberlain to deny the proposed merger, evoking the financial harm that will come to the actors' families: "[A]n Union of the *two Companies* cannot be without great Prejudice, if not utter *Ruine*, to them and their Numerous Families."[27] Furthermore, the actors insist that such a unification would run counter "to the intention of the Nobility and Gentry, who Subscrib'd to the Building of a New Theatre, and to the frequent Encouragements given by them for the support of two Houses."[28] In other words, a union would violate the interests of the subscribers, who contributed their money in hopes of having more entertainment options, not fewer. It is interesting that the actors seem to have formed an alliance with Rich on this issue, as their resentment of his management was notorious.[29] Indeed, the petition's insistence that the actors are "fully Content with the Terms and Conditions under which they now Act" after years of highly public friction with Rich raises the possibility that the players may have been compelled to allow their names to be included as a condition of continued employment.[30] Nonetheless, the petition creates the appearance of a united front; as in *The Post-Boy Robb'd of His Mail*, the workers and the elite are represented as being unified against the perceived threat of greedy entrepreneurs pursuing private interest.

Centlivre's *The Gamester* reflects and responds to these public debates over the changing management and investment structures in the theaters. Act 3 in particular dramatizes the complex interrelations among economic agents, evoking the network of domestic and personal finances surrounding the theaters. As the act begins, Valere stands in possession of a large sum of money following a successful night of gambling. When his creditors call on him for payment of his overdue debts, Valere—hoping to stake his winnings once again the coming evening—pretends not to have any cash. The milliner, Mrs. Topknot, explains that her daughter is soon to be married, "but the small Fortune we design for her, must be paid down upon the Nail—therefore, Sir, I intreat you to help me to my Money, if possible." Valere insists "upon honour" that he is unable to pay the longstanding debt; even when Mrs. Topknot asks for a partial payment of ten guineas, he claims not to have five. Next, the tailor Galloon makes his case: "[M]y Wife is ready to

Lye in—and Coals are very dear—and Journey mens Wages must be paid." Yet Valere again refuses.[31] The audience member who knows that Valere has over five hundred guineas on hand might be discomfited by his refusal to pay such relatively small debts, upon which depend marriage contracts and childbed accommodations. As Anderson observes, Valere's debts "constrain the lives of men and women who are tied to Valere through larger social networks of power and jeopardize their comic narratives of marriage and reproduction."[32] Importantly, these networks of power and interconnectedness mirror those that were evoked in protests against the unification of the theatrical companies, which were imagined as having the potential to disrupt the domestic finances of actors and shareholders alike.[33]

This scene not only reveals the damage that upper-class gambling inflicts on the entire economy; it also furthers the play's larger commentary on class hierarchies and the archaic sensibilities on which they depend. Valere's untruthful oath "upon honour" reflects his willingness to invoke his privilege as a person of quality and a gentleman as well as the emptiness of the very honor he invokes. The scene therefore echoes and reinforces the servant Hector's biting commentary in act 2; addressing Sir Thomas, he observes: "You may cheat Widows, Orphans, Tradesmen without a Blush—but a Debt of Honour, Sir, must be paid—I cou'd name you some Noblemen that pays no Body—yet a Debt of Honour, Sir, is as sure as their ready Money." Sir Thomas replies: "He that makes no Conscience of wronging the Man—whose Goods have been deliver'd for his use, can have no pretence to Honour—whatever Title he may wear."[34] These moments highlight the double standard whereby only the nobility can evade their debts and only debts between people of quality are honored, while debts to the lower classes go unpaid. High-stakes gambling requires both privilege and a safety net to withstand a loss, and the consequences of irresponsible gambling are not felt by Valere himself. Like the unflattering portraits of Rich and Vanbrugh circulating in the popular press, Valere engages in speculative behavior and then passes along his losses to those further down the social ladder. Centlivre does not simply castigate Valere for his greed—indeed, at times the play seems to elicit empathy for Valere's addiction, and the marriage plot ends happily with his redemption and reform—but her real interest lies in the ways that his economic privilege shields him from the most harmful effects of his behavior while allowing the ripple effects of his actions to damage economically vulnerable members of his network.

Likewise, in *The Basset Table* Lady Lucy rejects Sir James's defense of gaming—"Cards are harmless Bits of Paper"—with an impassioned exposition of its ills: "Cards are harmless Bits of Paper in themselves, yet through them what Mischiefs have been Done? What Orphans Wrong'd? What Tradesmen Ruin'd? . . . Madam's Grandeur must be Upheld—tho' the Baker and Butcher shut up Shop." Sir James does not deny her characterization but insists it applies only to the nobility: "Oh! Your Ladiship wrongs us middling Gentlemen there; to Ruin Tradesmen is the Qualities Prerogative only; and none beneath a Lord can pretend to do't with an Honourable Air."[35] Once again, risky financial behavior transforms an economy of complex interdependence capable of sustaining members at all levels into a game with winners and losers. Those with the most resources are best able to withstand the risks of gambling, not only because their material needs are cared for but also because they have the economic power and privilege to socialize their losses.

Centlivre's representation of the profound interrelatedness of economic agents, paired with her concern over a model of financial interaction in which one person's gain is always another's ruin, places her gaming plays squarely in conversation with debates about the financing of the theaters, from profit sharing at the patent houses to subscriptions at the Haymarket. Yet Centlivre reserves her most biting criticisms for the nobility rather than the middling-class people with whom they mix at the gaming table. Her assessment of the economic and social ramifications of speculation differs from most of the print media coverage of the theater management and shareholders surrounding the 1705 opening of the Haymarket. The coverage, as I have shown, tended to demonize theater managers and entrepreneurs as placing their private interest above a concept of the public good imagined to be shared by the upper and lower classes alike. In that regard, debates about the theater were often invested in an understanding of economic circulation that imagined resources as flowing from higher to lower classes, constructing a common interest under threat from an emergent creative-managerial middle class. This ideology in turn served to naturalize the hierarchical class system. Centlivre exposes members of the nobility for using empty concepts like "honor" to sustain their elite status while at the same time socializing the losses arising from their risky behavior. Her plays serve as a warning to lower- and middling-class audience members not to trust discourses that would align their interests with those of the elite, urging instead an informed and savvy approach to the competitive realms of credit, finance, and speculation.

Centlivre displayed such canny financial agency in her own navigation of the rivalry between the theaters during this turbulent moment. *The Gamester* had a successful first run of at least twelve nights at Lincoln's Inn Fields in February 1705. Betterton's company brought *The Gamester* to the Haymarket later that spring, performing it at the Queen's Theatre on April 27 and May 23, and again after their return to Lincoln's Inn Fields, on October 12 and 19 of the following season. The same company performed *The Gamester* once again on November 19, the day before *The Basset Table* debuted at Drury Lane. The *Daily Courant* for November 19 contains an advertisement for that night's performance of *Arsinoe Queen of Cyprus* at Drury Lane, which concludes, "And to Morrow being Tuesday will be presented a new Comedy, never acted before, call'd, The Basset Table." Immediately following this line is the next advertisement: "At the Queen's Theatre in the Hay-Market, this present Monday, being the 19th of November, will be presented a Comedy, call'd, The Gamester."[36] While neither advertisement mentions the two plays' common authorship, the timing is suggestive; taken together with the fact that the title page to the first edition of *The Basset Table* ascribes the new play to "the Author of the *Gamester*," this sequence of performances suggests that the shared authorship of the two plays was already at least rumored, if not common knowledge.[37] Was Betterton's company betting on audience awareness of the link between the two plays and attempting to capitalize on public anticipation of the new offering at the rival house? Once *The Basset Table* had premiered, the connections would have been even more obvious, as the two plays are strikingly similar in theme and plot structure.

The sequence of performances on November 19 and 20 also illustrates why Centlivre might have chosen to take *The Basset Table*, with its strong connections to *The Gamester*, to Drury Lane. At first it might seem like a strategy to minimize risk, spreading her work across multiple houses to reach a larger potential number of viewers. But in fact, it is a surprising move given that the Lincoln's Inn Fields/Haymarket company had so successfully mounted the earlier play, taking it to at least a twelfth night and continuing to stage the play occasionally beyond the initial run. Like her gamester Valere, staking his winnings rather than pocketing them, Centlivre appears to have taken a massive risk within a highly competitive environment. In positioning her plays as commodities that the two companies could leverage against one another, she gambled on the power of hype and competition to provoke just the kind of behavior exhibited at the Haymarket on November 19.

Centlivre's willingness to engage with the theatrical marketplace in ways that embraced speculation, risk, and competition helped her to succeed during an exceptionally difficult time for playwrights in general, but particularly for women playwrights. As Jay Oney points out, Centlivre was unique among the major women playwrights of her day in that she wrote for both companies—unlike, Mary Pix, for example, who remained loyal to the company at Lincoln's Inn Fields from 1696 onward. And while all of them took advantage of the competition sparked at the opening of the Haymarket to sell new plays for performance during the 1705–6 season, Centlivre was the only one whose theatrical career continued for years to come.[38] The case of *The Basset Table* suggests why. Oney cites a number of examples in which Centlivre moved companies after a play flopped or was rejected at the rival playhouse, but *The Basset Table* is fundamentally different: it demonstrates not simply reactive self-protection but a long-term strategy to play the companies against one another in their desire to acquire her scripts, even creating competition for audiences between her own plays. This strategy would have allowed her to hedge her bets against the possibility of a union between the two companies; if a merger were to occur, her plays might be easier to market to the newly united company if she had recently written roles for players from both houses.

Although *The Basset Table* was less successful, in the end, than *The Gamester*, Centlivre continued to alternate her plays between the patent houses, using moments of reorganization to her advantage. The next section examines how Centlivre took advantage of another turbulent moment in the public theaters in 1709–10. Her work during this time reflects not only on the issues of class-based power and privilege reflected in *The Gamester* and *The Basset Table* but also on questions of gender and the ramifications of new speculative market dynamics for women in particular.

1709–1710: *The Busie Body*

The years immediately following the opening of the Haymarket in 1705 were chaotic in the theaters, and the papers remained riveted on the ongoing financial and interpersonal intrigue. In the winter of 1705–6 Betterton brought his company to the Queen's Theatre, leaving Lincoln's Inn Fields abandoned until 1714. In summer 1706 Vanbrugh transferred management of the new theater to Owen Swiney, who seems to have cut a deal with Christopher Rich: Drury Lane would get the exclusive right to perform music if Rich would send his best actors to the Haymarket.[39] This arrangement was reversed, however, by an order of union by the Lord Chamberlain's office on December 31, 1707, which joined all of the actors at Drury Lane, granted that house the exclusive right to perform plays, and gave the Haymarket a monopoly on opera.[40] The actors, now together at Drury Lane, continued to be unhappy with Rich's management. Their discontentment was well known: in a printed broadside of a prologue from a private performance, they asked benefactor Richard Norton to "Buy out these sorded *Pattent-Masters*, / And make a *Free Gift* of it to the *Actors*."[41] Unbeknownst to Rich, his actors began making secret deals with Swiney to move to the Haymarket, apparently with the Lord Chamberlain's knowledge. On April 30, 1709, the Lord Chamberlain's office ordered Rich not to deduct more than £40 from an actor's benefit night to cover the house's expenses, and on June 6, Rich was silenced for disobeying the order. The following month the actors were given permission to perform plays at the Haymarket on nights when operas were not offered.

As the 1709–10 season began, Drury Lane lay under a silencing order, and the United Company of actors performed plays four nights a week at the Haymarket, which they shared with opera under Swiney's management. In November William Collier secured a license that allowed him to stage plays at the abandoned Drury Lane playhouse, and on November 23, 1709, playgoers could once again choose between two houses.[42] Rich was to have his revenge, however; in June 1710 the actors at Drury Lane staged a violent uprising against Collier. In a letter to Collier manager Aaron Hill describes how a group of leading actors, angered by Hill taking away the joint management responsibilities he had previously delegated to the players, refused to act and even threatened to steal the costumes. Hill, hearing of these events, came to London, where he was confronted and chased away by an armed crowd of actors and theatergoers. Hill claims that Rich passed by during these events and was hailed as the architect of the riot, a suspicion that is echoed in the *Tatler*.[43] Following the uprising the playhouse in Drury Lane was shut for the rest of the summer, and the new season began unusually late in the fall of 1710 due to the uncertainty about how the theaters would be managed moving forward.[44]

It was into the chaos of 1709 that Centlivre brought forth what was to become one of her most popular and enduring plays: *The Busie Body*. As was the case with *The Gamester* and *The Basset Table*, *The Busie Body* seems to have thrived during a moment of intense instability in the theaters. On May 12, 1709, shortly before Rich's silencing, *The Busie Body* premiered at Drury Lane and ran for four consecutive nights, including a third-night benefit for Centlivre on May 14. A 1747 account attributed to John Mottley suggests the actors' initial dislike of the play: Robert Wilks supposedly "threw it [his part] off the Stage into the Pit, and swore that no body would bear to sit to hear such stuff." Audiences' expectations were likewise low: "[T]hose who had heard of it, were told it was a silly thing wrote by a Woman, that the Players had no Opinion of it, and on the first Day there was a very poor House."[45] Certainly, the advertisement for the first night (in the *Daily Courant* for May 12) does not seem to have done the play any favors; much more space is devoted to an upcoming revival of *The Comical Revenge* on May 18, with merely a few lines allocated to that evening's offering. Furthermore, although the notice touts the new play as "Never Acted before," it does not include the note that appeared the subsequent day that the *The Busie Body* was "Written by the Author of a Comedy call'd, The Gamester." If Centlivre's back-catalog was an asset, it was one the management failed to harness until the new play demonstrated potential with audiences.[46]

After this rocky start, the play was performed at least three more times with the same cast during the short time remaining in the season, including another benefit for Centlivre on May 21. By the end of the 1708–9 season, the play had become a clear hit despite its late debut, rumored actor resistance, and lackluster publicity. Although *The Busie Body* had a strong showing at the end of the spring of 1709, however, it would have to wait for the following season to make its biggest impression. The 1747 description of the play's early success continues: "[A] strong Proof of this Play having greatly pleased, was, upon the Company's dividing, and one Part of them going to the *Haymarket*, that it was acted at both Houses together for six Nights running in Opposition to one another; *Pack*, who did it first, playing the part of *Marplot* at *Drury-lane*, and *Dogget* at the same Part in the *Haymarket*."[47] Here, again, the record of advertised performances shows the 1747 account to be exaggerated but supports its essential claims. In October 1709, with the actors united at the Haymarket and Drury Lane dark, the company put on several performances of *The Busie Body*.[48] Strikingly, the advertisements in the *Daily Courant* tout the novelty of the event, starting with the headline "Never Acted there before, By her Majesty's Company of Comedians."[49] Subsequent advertisements echo this claim, touting the play as "Never acted there but once" and "Never Acted there but twice."[50] These advertisements leverage the change in venue from Drury Lane to the Queen's Theatre in the Haymarket as a reason playgoers might wish to attend even if they had already seen the play during its initial run at the end of the previous season. The claim of novelty is striking given that much of the cast remained the same: while the role of Marplot was switched from George Pack to Thomas Doggett, Robert Wilks continued to play Airy, Richard Estcourt to play Gripe, John Mills to play Charles, and Letitia Cross to play Miranda. From October 12 onward the advertisements include a formula that touts the play's novelty in a different way, referring to it not as "a Comedy call'd, The Busie-Body" (as on October 10 and 11), but rather as "the last new Comedy call'd, The Busie-Body." This phrase allows the advertisements to signal that even if the play is a known quantity at this point, it is still the newest ware on offer. Centlivre's play seems to have benefited from the chaotic rearrangement of playing companies, which allowed it to have a kind of second chance at a first run.

After the new company reopened Drury Lane on November 23, one of the first plays they took up was *The Busie Body*, which they performed on November 26 and December 8. The cast was largely new, but Pack reprised the role of Marplot he had played in the initial run in May. Drury Lane continued to mount *The Busie Body*, along with Centlivre's *The Gamester* and her new afterpiece *A Bickerstaff's Burying*, regularly throughout the season. In the spring of 1710 both companies performed *The Busie Body* (Queen's on April 22, and Drury Lane on May 16). While this series of events does not quite rise to the level of *The Busie Body* being "acted at both Houses together for six Nights running in Opposition to one another" as the 1747 account claims, it is still remarkable that both houses laid claim to Centlivre's play simultaneously and performed competing versions of it. The ever-changing configuration of actors, managers, and playhouses created an environment that was toxic for some writers but that enabled productions of *The Busie Body* to claim certain forms of novelty and to benefit from the competition between the rival houses. Centlivre herself played an active role in taking advantage of the upheaval by continuing to vary her offerings between the two companies; for instance, she took *The Man's Bewitch'd* to the Haymarket in December 1709 before offering

A Bickerstaff's Burying to Collier's Drury Lane in March 1710 and *Marplot* (the sequel to *The Busie Body*) to the newly reconfigured Drury Lane management in the fall of 1710.

The plot of *The Busie Body* itself offers some insights into the strategies Centlivre used to drum up excitement about her plays; in particular it helps us see how the interplay of authorial masking and unmasking she practiced at this point in her career was related to her conceptualization of women's place within emergent financial market structures. It lays bare these strategies through its representation of marriage as a speculative financial market not unlike the theater. As lovers Charles and Isabinda plot to thwart the arranged marriage preferred by the latter's controlling father Sir Jealous Traffick, and as Sir George Airy and Miranda contrive to dupe her greedy and lascivious guardian Sir Francis Gripe and access her inheritance, the play draws parallels between the institutions of wardship and arranged marriage that allow English parents and guardians to profit from their daughters. Sir Francis and Sir Jealous treat their dependents as property of which they have a right to dispense, an economic model that the play suggests is outdated in this new era of global trade and speculative finance. Through its twin marriage plots, *The Busie Body* explores how women might extend their agency by capitalizing on the forms of abstraction and ephemerality that characterize these new speculative markets.

The opening scene establishes the play's interest in the economics of marriage and the status of marriageable women as commodities. Sir George asks Charles whether he knows Sir Francis's plans for his ward: "[W]hat do's he intend to do with *Miranda*? Is she to be sold in private? or will he put her up by way of Auction, at who bids most?"[51] Far from critiquing Miranda's treatment as a commodity, however, he makes it clear that he is eager to place his own bid. In the second act Sir Jealous scolds Isabinda for looking out her balcony window, comparing her sexual exposure to commercial availability: "Why don't you write a Bill upon your Forehead, to show Passengers there's something to be Let" (24). Sir Jealous does not disapprove of his daughter being for sale—he himself is arranging for the most profitable match possible, a Spanish merchant—but he reserves the right to define the terms by which her body circulates.

As the women struggle to regain control over their choices of suitor, the play explores how the understanding of women as property within marriage transactions is complicated by the rise of the speculative trade in commodities. At the play's climax Charles disguises himself as the long-awaited Spanish merchant and attempts to marry Isabinda under her father's nose. When Charles is unable to produce the jointure originally promised to Sir Jealous, Sir George, acting as his translator, explains that Charles's worth is wrapped up in overseas trade. Since "[m]oney you know is dangerous returning by Sea," Charles has brought the means to produce the jointure "in Merchandize, Tobacco, Sugars, Spices, Limons, and so forth, which shall be turn'd into Money with all Expedition" (62–63). Sir Jealous accepts his bond in the meantime, taking a signature in place of commodities that stand, in turn, for money he expects to receive eventually. The litany of particular goods seems to convince him of the reality of the nonexistent cargo; insufficiently wary of the risks of speculating on trade ventures, he is cheated of his daughter's jointure. This transaction suggests that marriage is less an exchange of goods than a risky and intangible investment, and Sir Jealous comes across as foolish because he understands commodities to be sure things rather than risks.

In a world in which property has become more mobile and ephemeral, the play suggests, women can position themselves as volatile media of exchange—a potentially dangerous and problematic position, to be sure, but one that they can then exploit to advance their own interests and desires. Miranda, understanding that her father and suitor view her as a piece of property for sale, refigures herself as a speculative investment. In disguise as "Incognita," she speaks with Sir George about his desire to marry Miranda, warning him that women "are the worst Things you can deal in, and damage the soonest; your very Breath destroys 'em, and I fear you'll never see your Return" (11). Like commodities futures, women are imagined as an ephemeral, immaterial, and risky commodity in which to trade. In fact, Miranda seems to make herself even more abstract and ephemeral by disguising herself as Incognita, only allowing Sir George to interact with her fully in that persona and remaining silent when he encounters her as Miranda. The audience knows that Sir George is in love with Incognita's wit and with Miranda's beauty but is unaware that they are the same woman. The split allows Miranda to plan assignations with a freedom she would not ordinarily enjoy. She insists on the secret identity as a form of power she reserves entirely to herself; when Sir George threatens to unmask her, she warns him of the effect it will have on his reputation: "And how will it sound in a Chocolate-House, that Sir George Airy rudely pull'd off a Ladies

Mask, when he had given her his Honour, that he never would, directly or indirectly endeavor to know her till she gave him Leave" (11). Deploying the specter of public opinion, represented by the chocolate house, she reserves to herself the right to circulate in public as Incognita and to control public awareness of her own identity.[52]

Miranda's choice to become Incognita offers a new way to think about Centlivre's own masking and unmasking in publicity around her plays. Like Miranda, Centlivre made herself more desirable as a speculative commodity through selective concealment and revelation of her identity. As Catherine Gallagher has argued, eighteenth-century women writers like Aphra Behn, Delarivier Manley, Charlotte Lennox, Frances Burney, and Maria Edgeworth harnessed the association of the literary marketplace with disembodiment in order to yoke authorship to cultural notions of femininity as "nothingness"—thereby turning their gender into an asset rather than a liability in debates over emerging notions of authorship and intellectual property.[53] While Gallagher does not discuss Centlivre in particular, Michael Gavin has shown how Centlivre's early contributions to epistolary miscellanies played strategically with anonymity and autobiography; by both inviting and rejecting identification with the protagonist of the letters, Gavin shows, Centlivre reflected more broadly on the position of women as both subjects and objects of discourse within debates over gender, morality, and the stage.[54] Building on this work, here I place *The Busie Body* in conversation with press coverage surrounding its debut in order to shed new light on the strategies of revelation and concealment available to women writers navigating the theatrical market—strategies that applied as well to speculative markets more generally.

Centlivre's gender, but not her name, was circulated in publicity for the initial run of *The Busie Body*. The author's gender does seem to have been well known early on in the play's run, even if her identity was not; the *Tatler* for May 14 states: "To Night was acted a Second Time a Comedy call'd, *The Busie Body*: This Play is written by a Lady."[55] By May 24 the *Tatler* was again evoking the author's gender, this time as an explanation for the play's strengths: "On Saturday last was presented, *The Busie Body*, a Comedy, written (as I have heretofore remark'd) by a Woman. The Plot and Incidents of the Play are laid with that Subtilty of Spirit which is peculiar to Females of Wit, and is very seldom well perform'd by those of the other Sex, in whom Craft in Love is an Act of Invention, and not, as with Women, the Effect of Nature and Instinct."⁵⁶ The prologue published with the first edition, and therefore likely performed with the play during its initial run, likewise acknowledges that the author is a woman without naming Centlivre: "Be kind, and bear a Woman's Treat to Night; / Let your Indulgence all her Fears allay, / And none but Woman-Haters damn this Play" (A3v, lines 39–41). Centlivre's status as a woman playwright is discussed at even greater length in the *Female Tatler,* which contains the earliest report of the above-mentioned anecdote about Wilks throwing his part into the pit in front of Centlivre during a rehearsal. The account is juxtaposed with the reflection that "no Woman ever yet turn'd *Poetess,* but lost her *Reputation* by appearing at *Rehearsals.*" While the anecdote is meant to show that "the *Treatment Authors* meet with from the *Play'rs,* is too gross for a *Woman* to bear," the defense of Centlivre's play against Wilks's ill manners and bad judgment is tempered by the strong implication that she has compromised her feminine virtue (and therefore her right to expect better treatment) by working in the theater at all.⁵⁷ This article also provides insight into how contemporaries understood the market mechanics of the theater as a potential set of tools that women playwrights could use to navigate their difficult position; tongue firmly in cheek, the narrator Mrs. Crackenthorpe relates a discussion between herself and her friend Lady Sneak about how they might avoid such a confrontation by offering Wilks all the profits from a play, which would force him to spread rumors of its quality around town.

By the time *The Busie Body* was published—which must have been before its second run in the fall, since the October advertisements notify readers of where the play text is available for purchase—it featured Centlivre's name on both the title page and the dedication. This was clearly a deliberate choice: up to this point in Centlivre's career, she had alternated between publishing anonymously and under her own name. Furthermore, her anonymous works were sometimes touted as the product of an unnamed woman's pen, sometimes associated with her previous works, and other times associated with an author implied to be a man; for example, the prologue to *The Stolen Heiress* (1703) alludes to the playwright in the masculine gender.⁵⁸ Critics often characterize these decisions as reactive. Tanya M. Caldwell, for instance, describes how Centlivre began by publishing under her name before "retreating behind anonymity."⁵⁹ John Wilson Bowyer likewise states that after Centlivre's first play was printed under her name, "she would have to accept varying degrees of anonymity for some years."⁶⁰ Laura Rosenthal acknowledges that it "is not clear that Centlivre always would have had control over whether or not her name appeared on her published plays," but she accords more agency to Centlivre in these decisions, suggesting that "she does, however, seem to have gone through a period when she preferred anonymity."[61] Critics who view Centlivre as passive in this process often point to her dedication to *The Platonick Lady*, in which she complains that the publisher of *Love's Contrivance* made a deliberate decision, without her consent, to disguise her gender in order to raise his own profits. His signing the dedication with "two Letters of a wrong Name," she says, "was the height of Injustice to me, yet his imposing on the Town turn'd to account with him; and thus passing for a Man's, it has been play'd at least a hundred times."[62] She goes on to explain how prejudices against women in the literary marketplace led the bookseller to this course of action: "A Play secretly introduc'd to the House, whilst the Author remains unknown, is approv'd by every Body. . . . But if by chance the Plot's discover'd, and the Brat found Fatherless, immediately it flags in the Opinion of those that extoll'd it before, and the Bookseller falls in his Price, with this Reason only, *It is a Woman's.*" By way of example, she relates a story she heard from the bookseller of *The Gamester* of a "Spark" who saw the play several times before learning that it was by a woman, at which point he "threw down the Book, and put up his Money, saying, he had spent too much after it already, and was sure if the Town had known that, it wou'd never have run ten days."[63] Throughout this dedication, Centlivre's focus remains insistently on the economic disadvantage she faces as a woman in the literary marketplace, as the market value of her wares fluctuates solely in relation to public rumor and opinion about her identity. Yet it is worth noting that the dedication to *The Platonick Lady* is itself unsigned, and the title page ascribes the play only to "the Author of the *Gamester,* and *Love's Contrivance.*" Rather than reading this piece as a straightforward relation of fact, then, it is possible to read it as part of a larger strategy of self-representation.

While the story of how *Love's Contrivance* came to be signed "R. M." may well be true, Centlivre did manage to get her name and gender—sometimes one, sometimes the other, and sometimes both—attached to her plays early on, either in print or in performance advertisements and paratexts, and it is entirely possible that she also played a role in deciding when to withhold that information. This likelihood is strengthened by an advertisement placed in the *Daily Courant* two days after the publication of *Love's Contrivance:*

"Whereas the last New Comedy, call'd, *Love's Contrivance; or, Le Medecin Malgre Luy*, has the two Letters R. M. to the Dedication, This is to give Notice, that the Name of the Author (who for some Reasons is not willing to be known at present) does not begin with those two Letters. The true Name will shortly be made known."[64] The mysterious allusion to the author having "some Reasons" to remain anonymous, combined with the promise of revelation in the near future, suggests that Centlivre chose not to reveal her name in the aftermath of this incident but rather to use it to her advantage, stoking intrigue and interest around her identity. Even if the decision to ascribe the dedication to "R. M." was outside of her control, then, she reclaimed her anonymity as a weapon.[65]

It was only a few years after this controversy that *The Busie Body* was staged anonymously and then printed under Centlivre's name. The character of Miranda/Incognita in that play offers a figure of a woman selectively revealing and concealing her identity in order to strategically control her relationship to a highly speculative market, extending her agency within public spaces where men sought to circulate her as a commodity. Centlivre's deployment of her gender and identity, like the alternation of her plays between competing playhouses, allowed her to harness the volatility of the theatrical and publishing markets to her advantage, helping to overcome some of the disadvantages she faced as a woman. At the same time, as the next section will explore, she became increasingly aware of the potential dangers of these spaces and, in particular, of the ways in which speculative market dynamics might be used to entrench the very elite masculine interests they appeared to destabilize.

1718–1720: *A Bold Stroke for A Wife* and *A Woman's Case*

In the decade following the success of *The Busie Body,* Centlivre continued to flourish amidst tumult in the theaters. In April 1714 her play *The Wonder; or, A Woman Keeps a Secret* enjoyed a successful six-night debut at Drury Lane, now under the control of actor-managers Robert Wilks, Barton Booth, and Colley Cibber. The play was performed there again for the prince on December 16, and when John Rich reopened the playhouse at Lincoln's Inn Fields later that month, he made an apparent attempt to capitalize on its popularity by immediately staging back-to-back performances of *The Gamester* and *The Busie Body* twice within the space of two weeks. On May

5 Drury Lane responded with its own production of *The Busie Body*, and both companies continued to mount rival versions of that play throughout the 1716–17 season. The Drury Lane company scored a coup when they again received Centlivre's newest play, *The Cruel Gift*, in December 1716. Yet just over a year later, in February 1718, Centlivre brought her latest, *A Bold Stroke for a Wife*, to Lincoln's Inn Fields, once again exploiting the intense rivalry between the major playhouses.[66] This section takes up *Bold Stroke*, which, like *The Gamester, The Basset Table*, and *The Busie Body*, responds to contemporary debates about the intersection of speculative finance and theatrical economics, reflecting on the possibilities and perils for women operating at that intersection. Coming late in Centlivre's career, however, this play also sounds the alarm about the dangers of the stock markets and expresses concerns about how the exploitation of others in pursuit of private interest can creep from Exchange Alley into the playhouse.

My interpretation of this play builds on and complicates Misty Anderson's influential formulation of *Bold Stroke* as a statement of Centlivre's growing cynicism about the potential for women to achieve liberty and equality by extending the "egalitarian possibilities of commercial contracts" to the marriage contract—potentials Anderson sees epitomized in Centlivre's 1720 poem *A Woman's Case*, addressed to South Sea Company director Charles Joye.[67] Anderson emphasizes the relative passivity of *Bold Stroke*'s protagonist, Anne Lovely, who depends on Colonel Fainwell to free her from her four guardians through his deft manipulation of legal and financial documents, as well as his navigation of masculinized spaces like the Exchange Alley coffeehouse Jonathan's.[68] While this play and *A Woman's Case* do express hope for and disappointment in women's access to public finance and, by extension, economic self-determination, I contend that they use these gender-based concerns to mount broader critiques of the excesses of financial markets as a whole. Taken together, these texts suggest that a growing culture of exploitation distorts those qualities of speculative enterprise that make it potentially leveling; in doing so, this exploitation compromises the opportunities that have arisen for women and other nonelites in these spaces.

The play's most obvious critique of speculative trade revolves around the character of Tradelove, one of the four guardians Colonel Fainwell must outwit in order to gain the hand (and fortune) of Anne Lovely. While Centlivre was a vocal Whig, her characterization of exchange-broker Tradelove—with his outsized love of the Dutch and his unscrupulous business practices—reflects an excessive and grotesque version of her party's values, one that she reveals as actually undermining rather than supporting England's pursuit of fiscal-military dominance. The tavern keeper Sackbut offers the play's first description of Tradelove as "a Fellow that will out-lie the Devil for the Advantage of Stock and cheat his Father that got him in the Bargain."[69] Freeman, a merchant and friend of Fainwell's, supports Sackbut's account, relating a story of how Tradelove once leapt at the opportunity to engage in insider trading: "I happen'd to have a Letter from a Correspondent two Hours before the News arrived of the *French* King's Death; I communicated it to him; upon which he bought up all the Stock he could, and what with that, and some Wagers he laid, he told me, he had got to the Tune of Five Hundred Pounds" (5). In this anecdote Tradelove exercises the advantage of superior news sources to manipulate the market and profit at others' expense; just as importantly, his behavior mixes speculation and gambling, as his stock trading is augmented with winnings from "Wagers." Here, the zero-sum economy represented in *The Gamester* and *The Basset Table* returns, but this time it has entered the world of finance on which rests England's fortunes in war and trade. The stakes, so to speak, have been raised.

This exchange in the opening scene sets the stage for act 4, which begins in Jonathan's, a raucous scene of stock trading with rapid-fire dialog punctuated by the cries of coffee-boys. As traders strike deals involving South Sea Company and East India Company bonds, lottery tickets, and the cash reserves of the Sword Blade Company, Freeman knowingly passes a piece of false news to Tradelove. He claims that the Spanish are lifting their siege of Cagliari, news that "will be publick" within "two or three Hours" (36). Anticipating an increase in trade that will stimulate the stock market, Tradelove buys a large amount of stock in the South Sea Company, which is most directly implicated in relations with Spain. The other traders open a kind of secondary market, placing bets with one another on whether this news is true; their actions directly mirror the way that Tradelove has just gambled on the veracity of information, reinforcing the implied analogy between stock trading and gambling. When Tradelove later learns that he has been tricked, Freeman blames the false report on "some roguish Stockjobber" who "has done it on purpose to make me lose my Money" (42). Freeman suggests that he repay Tradelove's resulting debts to a visiting Dutch merchant (really Fainwell in disguise) by offering the merchant the right to marry his ward.

While Tradelove knows that his consent alone means little without that of Anne Lovely's other three guardians, he withholds this information from the "merchant" in order to settle the debt as expeditiously as possible. This episode reflects how cheating and misdealing propagate through the economy: when one individual is the victim of a scam, he swindles another in turn to settle his debts and preserve his own interests.

While the scenes involving Tradelove offer the most overt commentary on the stock market, the workings of speculative finance are also evoked in the other guardians' scenes. In act 3 Fainwell attempts to impress the virtuoso Periwinkle by pretending to be a collector of curiosities from around the world, including "an Indian Leaf, which open, will cover an Acre of Land, yet folds up into so little a Compass, you may put it into your Snuff-Box.... [M]ine is but a little one; I have seen some of them that would cover one of the Carribian Islands." In response to this fabulous tale, Periwinkle muses, "I admire our *East India* Company imports none of them, they would certainly find their Account in them" (27). While Periwinkle claims a purely intellectual interest in such curiosities, then, he is clearly aware of their potential as objects of international trade and speculation; his immediate leap to commodify the "Indian Leaf" even suggests the possibility that his real motivation in seeking out curiosities is his own material enrichment.

The foppish Modelove, too, evokes the workings of the markets during his initial interaction with Fainwell. Modelove expresses his love of balls and masquerades, with which Fainwell—in disguise as a French beau—expresses agreement: "I hope the People of Quality in *England* will support that Branch of Pleasure, which was imported with their Peace, and since naturaliz'd by the ingenious Mr. *Heidegger*" (13). The reference is to John James Heidegger, a Swiss immigrant to England who was then the manager of the King's (formerly Queen's) Theatre in the Haymarket and a promoter of masquerade balls there. Modelove is quick to inform Fainwell that he is a financial backer of Heidegger's enterprise: "The Ladies assure me it will become Part of the Constitution,—upon which I subscrib'd an hundred Guineas—it will be of great Service to the Publick, at least to the Company of Surgeons, and the City in general" (13). Like Tradelove, Modelove is an adventurer, backing risky ventures—in this case, subscription masquerades at the Haymarket—based on rumor. His claim that "it will be of great Service to the Publick" echoes arguments that would be made the following year for the establishment of the Royal Academy of Music, also housed in the Haymarket theater after Heidegger suspended operations. Modelove's comment further suggests that such claims are really smokescreens for private interests, including those of the surgeons, who presumably anticipate a robust business in treating sexually transmitted infections. This foreign import ultimately has the effect of transferring money and status from the gentry who support it to the traders in the City. The scenes featuring Periwinkle and Modelove thus work to extend the implications of the Tradelove scenes, showing how the exploitive logic of the stock exchange bleeds into all corners of society, including theatrical finance.

The full implications of this critique are felt in the example of Fainwell himself, a metatheatrical figure who reflects the ways that the excesses of the markets make their way into the theater. Fainwell is a consummate actor, taking on numerous personae over the course of the play as he transforms himself into the kind of suitor who will appeal to each guardian. John O'Brien describes Fainwell as "an avatar of the new, protean individual said to have been called for by the emergence of capitalism," his triumph a reflection of Centlivre's promarket Whiggism; Rebecca Tierney-Hynes and Al Coppola likewise view Fainwell as a vehicle for Centlivre's defense of what Pocock would call "the new economic man" against charges of effeminacy and weakness.[70] Interpretations such as these are complicated, however, by the fact that Fainwell is also very much complicit in the exploitive behaviors highlighted above. While Tradelove is placed under scrutiny for his willingness to cheat others out of their assets, Fainwell spends the entire play tricking the guardians into signing away their rights to refuse Anne Lovely's potential suitors. He does so by using Freeman's connections and credit—his reputation with Tradelove, specifically—which lends credibility to his false news of the lifted siege. His disguises are augmented by an "Equipage of *India*" (7) provided by one of Freeman's associates recently returned from the West Indies (and therefore likely associated with the slave-trading South Sea Company). The "Equipage" includes not only the clothing and accoutrements necessary to impress Modelove but also three servants described in racialized terms: "[Y]ou shall have his Servants; there's a Black, a Tawny-Moor, and a *Frenchman*" (6). Fainwell in effect benefits from the spoils of overseas trade and shows his willingness to participate in the objectification and exchange of foreign people as though they were commodities.

Likewise, Fainwell is complicit in the guardians' treatment of Anne as a piece of property that can be traded, signed away, or even abstracted as a financial instrument and used to settle other debts. Tradelove is quite explicit about Anne's usefulness as an instrument of exchange, declaring, "Who the Devil would be a Guardian, / *If when Cash runs low, our Coffers t'enlarge, / We can't, like other Stocks, transfer our Charge?*" (43). Later, Periwinkle mocks Tradelove for trading Anne, exclaiming, "[W]hat did you look upon her as part of your Stock?" (66)—which is, of course, precisely the case. Similarly, when Modelove summons Tradelove and Periwinkle early in the play and asks their intentions regarding Ann Lovely, he demands of Tradelove: "Must she be sent to the *Indies* for a Venture?" (21), a possibility echoed later when Anne rejects Tradelove's hopes of marrying her to a Dutch merchant, protesting that such a man would send her "for a Venture" (53). Yet for all that Tradelove comes under scrutiny and ridicule for treating Anne as a tradable commodity or security, it is impossible to ignore the fact that Fainwell does the same. He undertakes most of his plot without Anne's knowledge or explicit support, based only on a previous acquaintance at Bath. He assumes, based on their earlier conversations, that she will consent, but his alacrity for disguises and lies seems just as much a sign of his need to take thrilling risks and to claim victory over competing interests.[71] He states the logic of his conquest in the first scene, declaring that "he that runs the Risque, deserves the Fair" (7). His assertion that extravagant rewards are the compensation for taking risks at which others might balk is a sentiment with which any trader in Jonathan's might agree. These lines further position Anne Lovely as a prize to be won, her own opinion a secondary consideration. Fainwell's heady mix of exuberant disguise with risky and exploitive behavior wins over the audience, but the play also leaves room for unease around his treatment of Anne and the guardians on his way to victory, suggesting the dangers for women when the exploitive excesses of the stock exchange make their way into the world of performance and theater. Women, already conceptualized as property in so many ways, risk being caught up in speculative markets not as agents (as in *The Busie Body*), but as media of exchange.

In Centlivre's own case, the record of advertisements for her plays displays a similar ambiguity: Was she always engaging in calculated risks, playing the rival theaters against one another as they competed for her latest plays? Or was she sometimes merely the medium through which they undercut one another, an instrument in their competition for audiences and profits? This tension cuts to the heart of Centlivre's activities as what might be called a playwright-adventurer: she was critical of the predatory elements of speculative finance, yet it was the speculative nature of theatrical markets that she exploited in order to succeed. Financial markets and, to an even greater extent, theatrical markets opened up to women in new ways, not only because of women's ability to enter into contracts—an ability Centlivre exposes as limited through figures like Anne Lovely—and not only through the mechanism of performance, but also through the embrace of abstraction and risk. Centlivre took advantage of this speculative environment even as she demonstrated an awareness of its pitfalls and problems.

Centlivre's most explicit exploration of this tension is found in her poem *A Woman's Case: In an Epistle to Charles Joye, Esq; Deputy-Governer of the South Sea* (1720), which represents an ostensible request for South Sea stock from Joye in exchange for her longstanding loyalty to the Whig party. While recognizing the poem's cheeky sense of humor, critics have consistently read it as a sincere request for a kind of financial recognition regularly received by Centlivre's Tory men counterparts. In contrast, I read the poem as a critique of the South Sea Company and its ties to the Tory party, and I argue that Centlivre in fact uses the poem to provoke support from the House of Hanover for her theatrical offerings. In order to understand how Centlivre's poem reflects both her embrace of and concerns about speculative finance, it is worth pausing to understand the events to which it responds: the lead-up to the South Sea Bubble of 1720.

The South Sea Company was created to contain the fallout from the "Loss of the City" in 1710, a showdown between Queen Anne and the City financial sector over payment of short-term military bonds. Concerned that the new Tory ministry and Parliament would fail to pay war debts incurred by their Whig predecessors, investors sold off stocks in England's public debt, leading to a credit crunch. In 1711 the Tory Parliament approved a plan by Robert Harley, the newly appointed Chancellor of the Exchequer, to refinance £9 million of unfunded short-term debt as a long-term loan. Holders of military bonds were permitted to exchange those bonds for shares in a new private joint-stock venture, the South Sea Company.[72] The chartering of the new company achieved the dual aims of improving England's credit and creating a Tory counterweight to the Whig-led Bank of England and East India Company.[73]

The company began trading with the Spanish Americas in 1713, following the Treaty of Utrecht, which granted it a monopoly on the slave trade in the West Indies and the Spanish Americas (a monopoly also known as the *Asiento*). In 1718, however, hostilities with Spain resumed, halting the South Sea Company's ventures and forcing it to look for other sources of revenue.[74] In 1719 the company was allowed to restructure another portion of the national debt—the 1710 Lottery Orders and the overdue interest on them—which allowed the company to generate stock value in the absence of trade. As part of the same deal, the company was also empowered to create additional new stock to make a loan to the government. These shares, which had a face value of £100, sold for a market price of £114; since only the £100 per share was earmarked for the government loan, the company kept the remaining £14, thereby increasing its cash flow. The success of this experiment encouraged the directors to try the operation on a larger scale the following year.[75] In January 1720 the company submitted a proposal to engraft over £30 million of public debt represented by previously issued annuities.[76] The deal was approved by Parliament and the Crown, and it went into effect in April amidst giddy predictions that the restructuring agreement would make it possible to pay off the entire national debt in twenty-five years.[77]

In order for the company to make money from this deal, however, the price of South Sea shares had to rise well above their nominal value of £100.[78] To keep prices high, the directors engaged in experimental market manipulations focused on the deferral and abstraction of share values from the company's underlying financial situation. For example, in April they announced that investors would receive a 10 percent dividend, paid out in additional stock, at midsummer; this announcement led share prices to spike in May.[79] They also spaced two types of investment activity across several dates: between April and July three "subscriptions" provided opportunities for holders of government debts to register their intention to exchange their annuities for South Sea shares. Each group of subscribers then had to wait weeks or months for the company to announce the terms of exchange and decide whether they still wanted to move forward with the trade. The annuity exchange was therefore a long, drawn-out process that made it impossible to tell how much of the allowed capital stock had been raised at any given moment. In order to sell shares while the price was high and rising, rather than waiting until they had raised the entire capital stock, the directors also held "money subscriptions," dates when new stock was announced and made available for subscription. (The vehicle of subscription was employed because the actual stock technically could not be sold until the underlying capital had been raised from the exchange of annuities.) By spacing out the subscriptions and money subscriptions over the summer months, the directors promoted an atmosphere of frenzied optimism that severed the market value of stock from the debt-to-equity swaps meant to secure that value. They also obscured the fact that dividends were being paid out of the capital raised from new share issues, since the company had no profits from trade to distribute.[80] As Richard Dale points out, investors were essentially being paid back their own money—the definition of a chain-letter or Ponzi scheme, in which those who buy into a scheme early make money at the expense of those who invest late.[81]

At the height of the speculative mania, according to some calculations, the company's share values totaled about 500 percent of its tangible net assets.[82] The bubble burst in September 1720; from the high-water mark of around £1,000, South Sea stock fell precipitously, ending the year close to £200.[83] In the aftermath of the crash, Parliament passed a bailout called the Act to Restore Publick Credit (1721), which forgave a large portion of the company's debts to the government and redistributed gains realized by earlier subscribers to compensate later subscribers for some of their losses.[84] Following an investigation by the Committee of Secrecy, many directors were forced to forfeit portions of their estates, which were used to repay ruined shareholders; beyond that, some members of the inner circle were expelled from public office, convicted of corruption, and even accused of treason.[85]

One member of the inner circle was Charles Joye, whose guilt was deemed sufficient to compel him to forfeit £35,000 of the £40,000 he made from the scheme.[86] It was to Joye that Centlivre addressed *A Woman's Case*. Published as a fourteen-page pamphlet with "By Mrs. Cent-livre" on the title page, the poem asks Joye to issue the poet stock in the South Sea Company as a reward for her loyalty to the Whig party. There was precedent for Centlivre's request: playwright John Gay had received a gift of £2,000 stock from James Craggs the younger, Secretary of State.[87] According to Susan Staves, Centlivre's poem openly and self-reflectively translates the conventional patronage relationship from the realm of "mystified gift economy into an open commercial market transaction, words in praise in exchange for stock."[88] Anderson points to the portrayal of Joseph Centlivre within the poem as "a nag, a feminized man," as evidence that Centlivre, like the women protagonists of her plays, inverted gender roles and drew power in her marriage from her ability to negotiate financial contracts.[89] O'Brien views the poem's "unhappy domestic scene" as "a testimony to the fact that an abstract political ideal like liberty only goes so far when it is not secured by the material support of property."[90] Each of these interpretations provides valuable insights into Centlivre's exploration of the interrelations of finance, politics, gender, and the literary economy. Yet they leave unchallenged two fundamental assumptions I wish to dispute: first, that the poem is meant to be taken as a loosely accurate reflection of Centlivre's home life; and second, that it is an earnest appeal for South Sea Company stock.[91] If *A Woman's Case* is instead read as a dialog among characters with competing perspectives and interests—a form in which Centlivre, as a dramatist, excelled—it becomes clear that the poem represents a critique of the South Sea Company, not an attempt to elicit a gift of shares.

The poem's staging of competing voices is evident in its structure: it begins with a direct address to Joye recounting the poet's loyalty to the Whig cause; moves through a comedic dispute between Centlivre and her husband about whether she was right to take risks with his career in Queen Anne's kitchen by supporting the electoral prince George at a time when his father's claim to the throne was in dispute; returns to a narration of the poet's unrewarded labors on behalf of her party; ventriloquizes her Tory rivals' mockery of Centlivre's plight; and then returns to the domestic argument, in which Joseph Centlivre demands that his wife appeal to a patron for South Sea shares. The poet concludes with a final promise to Joye that he will find her a loyal panegyrist if he only makes her a gift of stock. The poetic persona is heard both as the narrating voice appealing to Joye and as a speaker in the dialog with her husband; however, of the poem's 219 lines, just 92 are spoken by the poetic speaker and 13 by her character in the dialog. The remaining 114 lines are spoken by the husband (93) and by the chorus of mocking Tories (21). More than half of the poem is given over to voices other than the poet's. This dialogic structure allows Centlivre to introduce critiques of the South Sea scheme that she might not be able to express if the poem were entirely in her own voice.

The poem expresses two main concerns about the South Sea investment scheme: first, that it is a Tory enterprise that has drawn in even Whig investors, essentially tricking prominent Whigs into funding the Tory cause instead of rewarding their own partisans; and second, that its claims to advance the public good are a smokescreen for private interests. Along the way, the poem expresses an awareness of writing as a business undertaking that requires canny navigation of political and economic headwinds and a regret that this is the case; while other characters assume that the poet's primary motivation in writing is to make money, she voices a frustrated desire to be left alone with her muse, a wish that the poem suggests can never be realized.

The poem's first criticism of the South Sea scheme, built throughout the sections in the narrator's voice, is that it has enticed Whig investors to finance a Tory-backed company. The opening lines immediately link the investment scheme of 1720 to the partisan sea change of 1710; punning on her addressee's name, Centlivre claims that she has not been happy in a decade: "Ah Joye! thy Name I never knew, / At least these twice Four Years, and Two."[92] The poet goes on to explain what happened around 1710 to so disquiet her: "Soon after Spouse and I were Chain'd, / At Helm the *Tory* Part reign'd. / The Queen I lov'd, but hated those / Who prov'd themselves my Country's Foes" (1–2). With the Tories in the ascendency, the poet explains, she remained a loyal partisan writer, defying fellow Whig Richard Steele's advice to keep a low profile (2). The allusion to Steele is significant here; if, as I will suggest below, the poem was published around February or March 1720, then Steele would already have begun publishing his periodical the *Theatre* (which I discuss at length in chapter 4). By late February the *Theatre* was engaged in a sustained criticism of the South Sea scheme; it was also, at that point, transparently the product of Steele's hand despite his use of a fictional narrator. The reference to Steele therefore places Centlivre's poem into proximity and conversation with one of the most visible periodical critiques of the South Sea Company's investment scheme in early 1720.

The poet character recalls that when rebuked by her husband for endangering his post as Yeoman of the Mouth in Queen Anne's kitchen, she had assured him that her loyalty would be rewarded upon her party's return to power: "When all the *Whigs* in Post you see, / You'll thank, instead of chiding me" (4). Yet at the time of writing, with Whigs once again "uppermost," she remains unrewarded; unlike Tories, who "kept their Herd in constant Pay" during their time of dominance, the Whigs imagine their cause to be so just that it needs no paid partisans to defend it in the press (4). The poem gives voice to the Tories who mock the poet's situation:

Yet, Madam! are you unprovided?
You, who stickled late and early,
Against the wicked Schemes of H——y [Harley]
. . .
One might have thought this Golden Age,
You'ad left off Writing for the Stage;
And from *South-Sea* got Gold——true *Sterling* (5)

The allusion to the "wicked Schemes of H[arle]y" likely refers to her designation of Robert Harley as a "traitor" in her poem "Upon the Bells Ringing at St. Martins in the Fields, on St. George's Day, 1716, being the Anniversary of Queen Anne's Coronation," printed in the *Flying Post* for May 12, 1716. At that time, Harley had been impeached by the House of Commons for corruption and misconduct in the negotiation of the Treaty of Utrecht, as well as influence peddling during the turnover of the Parliament from the Whigs to the Tories in 1710–11.[93] Centlivre's self-citational allusion raises questions about why she would wish to invest in the brainchild of someone whose "Schemes" she had opposed in the past. Likewise, the suggestion to invest in the "South Sea" instead of writing is placed into the mouths of her rivals, reinforcing the association of that company with the Tory party. The Tory chorus goes on to point out that "*Whigs* in Place have still been known / To help all Parties but their own" and advises her to "Advance your Foes, your Friends ne'er mind; / For whether you do well or ill, / Your Friends, you know, will be—Friends still" (6). These lines reveal Centlivre's acute awareness that investing in the South Sea Company would be a way of supporting her "Foes" and hedging her bets in case they returned to power.

The narrator's husband, like her Tory rivals, assumes that the purpose of her writing is to make money and that investing is a viable alternative form of income. He points out that her predictions of rewards for her loyalty have been proven wrong: "You made me hope the Lord knows what, / When *Whigs* shou'd Rule, of This, and That; / But from your boasted Friends I see / Small Benefit accrues to me" (8). Indeed, he suggests that the Whigs who should be supporting her have spent their money instead on investing in the South Sea scheme: "Nor can my Wages feed your Mouth, / That's sunk into the *Sea* of *South*." Under these circumstances, he issues an ultimatum: "Some Ruler of *South-Sea* implore, / Or see my injur'd Face no more" (9). The poet thus makes it clear that the request she is making is against her own inclination: she would prefer to continue working on her plays and partisan writings but is forced by her husband and by the Whigs' misguided priorities to beg for stock instead. Taken together with the poem's reminder that the South Sea Company is a Tory-backed enterprise, another one of the "wicked Schemes of Harley," this passage makes it clear that Centlivre's appeal for stock in the company is ambivalent if not entirely backhanded.

Centlivre places her most pointed criticism of the South Sea Company, however, into her husband's mouth. The poem reaches its climax with Joseph Centlivre's extended directions to his wife about how she must request a gift of stock and his promises to reward her in turn with marital bliss. When her character interjects that it will be impossible to find a subscription not already reserved for one of the existing stockholders, Joseph replies:

> *South Sea* is meant a Publick Good,
> (Or so we'd have it understood:)
> Then where's the Good, if none must share,
> But such as are grown Wealthy there?
> Must only then the Rich engross,
> The Publick Wealth to Publick Loss?
> They cannot sure be so uncivil,
> Monopolizing—is the Devil. (10–11)

Joseph's faux-innocent speech raises the very possibility he denies: the company's rhetoric of public good barely conceals a scheme for the wealthy to profit from the investing public. A nascent skepticism can be identified here that resonates with Centlivre's experience navigating speculative theatrical markets, in which the exploitive potential of investment schemes was often—as we have seen—masked by claims of public mindedness.

The very fears Centlivre's poem expresses about "the Rich engross[ing] the Publick Wealth to Publick Loss" under the guise of "Publick Good" are realized in the minutes of the Court of Directors of the South Sea Company for 1720, preserved in the British Library. The minutes from the Court's meeting on February 2 record the development of "Explanations Amendments & additions" to proposals sent to the House of Commons on January 27; these changes are designed to "be for the Interest of the Company and best secure the Acceptance thereof."[94] The revised document sent to Parliament and reproduced in the minutes refers repeatedly and insistently to the public interest that would be served by the company's proposed engraftment of the national debt; the directors express their "earnest Desire to contribute their utmost to the reducing and paying off the Publick Debts" (14), offer to make changes to the suggested payment rates and schedule "if this Hon[ora]ble House do think it more for the Interest of the Publick" (15), and agree to make payments to the Exchequer "for the Service of the Publick" (16) on any annuities that are not exchanged for South Sea stock within the agreed upon time frame. The document further insists that "this Company is very sensible that the Prosperity of this Nation does greatly depend upon the discharging the Publick Debts (a motive which induced them to make the first Proposition of this Publick and Beneficial Nature)" (16–17).

While the document submitted to Parliament emphasizes the South Sea Company's public-mindedness and desire to improve public credit, however, records of internal discussions among the directors reflect other interests. On April 21, 1720, for example, they calculate that they can make a "Clear pfitt [profit]" (20) of over £3 million on a single subscription if stock prices rise high enough. Fearing that the scheme may be vulnerable to market manipulations, however, they empower the directors to take any actions that might best serve the company and its profits:

> And for as much as this profit to the Company in the further Execution of the Act does chiefly depend on the price of the Stock and as attempts may be made to Depreciate the stock at the Time of the Execution of the Act. Therefore your Court of Directors do think it may be for the Interest of the Company: and will Enable them to Perfect the Execution of the Act. That your said Court of Directors be Impowered to lend money on the present and to by Increased Capital stock of this Company and to do all such Matters and things as they shall Judge most for the good of the Company. (21)

The public interest has been replaced by the "Interest of the Company"; the public good has been superseded by the "good of the Company." Yet throughout this period the directors are quite conscious about the company's public image; at meetings on May 19, August 12, August 25, September 9, and November 10, they approve advertisements to be placed in daily and weekly papers like the *Daily Courant, Evening Post,* and *Saturday's Gazette,* notifying the public of opportunities to invest in the scheme (27,

36, 39, 44, 49, 70). This strategic use of the newspapers to manipulate public opinion about a project designed to advance the interests of a few private individuals is precisely what the Joseph Centlivre character in *A Woman's Case* imagines of the South Sea Company.

Both Bowyer and Staves note that there is no record of Centlivre receiving any stock in return for her request, but, as I have argued, the poem does not seem designed to elicit the reward for which it purports to ask.[95] Instead, its layers of dialog and irony give voice to serious reservations about the investment scheme as an engine for Tories and the wealthy to engross the wealth of the nation—including unwittingly complicit Whigs—using an emptied-out rhetoric of public good. At the same time, Centlivre herself was a savvy manipulator of the print market to advance her own financial interests, and *A Woman's Case* appears to have alerted her friends in high places of her need for material support. On March 17, 1720, Drury Lane made a last-minute change of plans, bumping an anticipated revival of *Volpone* in favor of a performance of *The Busie Body* by royal command.[96] King George I (r. 1714–27) ordered the players to put on Centlivre's most popular play for her benefit, ensuring that she would take home all the profits after house operating expenses were deducted. The king's abrupt intervention to secure her a benefit is an unusual enough event to suggest a timely external provocation—such as Centlivre's poem, which offers within its opening two pages an account of how she undertook great political and personal risk to dedicate her 1714 play *The Wonder* to George Augustus, Electoral Prince of Hanover, son of the future King George I. She reminds the king of her loyalty at a time when his accession was not yet guaranteed: "To GEORGE of *Wales* I Dedicated, / Tho' then at Court I knew him Hated . . . / Yet spight of *Steele's* Advice I did it; / Nay tho' my Husband's Place forbid it."[97] The abrupt announcement of a command benefit performance of *The Busie Body* on March 17 suggests that the king may have been spurred to action by an awareness that one of the earliest and loudest supporters of the Hanoverian accession was publicly expressing doubt that her loyalty would be recognized or rewarded. It also places the publication of *A Woman's Case* in February or March 1720.[98]

King George was not the only contemporary who seems to have understood *A Woman's Case* as something other than as a straightforward request for shares in the South Sea Company. The poem was reprinted in Dublin as part of a subscription miscellany the following year, after the South Sea

Bubble had burst. It was retitled "Letter from Mrs. C———e, to Mr. Joy, Deputy-Governour of the South-Sea," a title that highlights its topical relevance.[99] The collection features a wide variety of pieces, including other poems that are critical of the South Sea scheme; one of these, "The Bubble," was circulated widely and, although it was published anonymously, is commonly attributed to Jonathan Swift.[100] The speaker of the poem pretends to offer a moral fable about the "young Advent'rer," imagined as a modern Icarus on "Paper-Wings" who falls into "*Southern Seas.*" But whereas a "Moralist" might enjoy explicating this tale to expose the "Rashness of the *Cretan* Youth," the poem's speaker rejects such fables (149–50). Rather, he explains that the young man is the victim of a larger scam, an amateur who falls prey to "DIRECTORS" who "better know their Tools" (150). While acknowledging that the losers in the South Sea investment scheme were complicit with a predatory machine, eager participants in a zero-sum game, the poem places the lion's share of the blame squarely on the exploitive directors of the South Sea Company:

> One Fool may from another win,
> And then get off with Money stor'd;
> But if a *Sharper* once gets in,
> He throws at all, and Sweeps the Board.
> As Fishes on each other prey,
> The Great ones swallowing up the Small;
> So fares it in the *Southern* Sea:
> But Whale-DIRECTORS eat up all. (150–51)

These lines invoke the commonplace analogy between speculative investment and gambling; as in the epilogue to *The Gamester,* this poem emphasizes the fact that gamblers, like investors, profit from one another's losses. Their small-scale rapacity is qualitatively different, however, from the actions of the "*Sharper*"—literally a trickster or cheat—who comes in and "Sweeps the Board," collecting all the other players' money at once. The speaker performs two moves simultaneously, figuring the overarching culture of exploitation while maintaining a fundamental distinction between the scales on which ordinary investors and the South Sea Directors operate. The similarity between behaviors at the top and bottom of the chain does not exonerate those at the top, because their profits are everyone else's losses. The decision to include Centlivre's poem in the same collection as this biting commentary suggests that *A Woman's Case* resonated more strongly as a critique of the South Sea scheme in its own moment than it has for more recent critics.

Despite Centlivre's reservations about the speculative nature of theatrical and literary markets, which she feared would empower private interests rather than promoting the public good, she too played the game. As this chapter has shown, Centlivre understood her plays as speculative goods to which she retained a certain kind of claim, outside of our usual understandings of intellectual or creative ownership.[101] It was not her ability to enter into contracts but her awareness of her plays as commodities—abstracted, subdivided, and speculated on—that allowed her to thrive in this chaotic market and to have her interventions into larger debates about theatrical and public finance staged and read. Centlivre's career thus reveals an alternative ethos of speculative ownership that enriches our understanding of how women could relate to intangible property in the early eighteenth century.

Centlivre's contemporaries seem to have been aware of her knack for leveraging the economic value of her works to advance her career, even from her earliest appearances on the London theatrical scene. A satirical poem titled *The Players Turn'd Academicks* (1703) paints a fictional portrait of Betterton taking his company to Oxford, an occasion that allows the poet to caricature the actors, managers, and playwrights involved in the theaters at the turn of the century. One stanza refers to Centlivre as part of a network of women who exert troubling forms of financial agency:

> The first that took Coach, and had often took—,
> Was the fam'd Mrs. B—with P—x at her A—,[102]
> A Tool of a Scribe, and a Poetress great,
> That was said to *Write* well, because well she could *Treat*,
> And for her sake had written her Husband in *Debt*.
> While *Carrol*, her Sister-Adventurer in Print,
> Took her Leave all in Tears, with a *Curt'sie* and *Squint*,[103]
> And would certainly take the same Journey as she,
> Had she not giv'n away *Medicin Malgre Lui*.[104]

Here, playwright Mary Pix—accused of having driven her husband into debt with her writing career—sits next to Elizabeth Barry, with whom she was known to have a close relationship. Both are accused of sexual availability and even prostitution, a commonplace aspersion cast on women writers and actors in the period. "Carrol"—she would not be named Centlivre until her 1707 marriage—is Pix's "Sister-Adventurer," but she is unable to join the other two women because she has no money, having given away the profits from her play *Love's Contrivance; or, Le Medecin Malgre Lui*. Beyond its bawdy allusions to the doctoring of venereal disease, this line refers to an anecdote that Centlivre had given the £10 she earned from the sale of that play's copyright to the actress Frances Knight; P. B. Anderson suggests that she did so "with the intention of securing an influential friend inside the playhouse."[105] The allusion to what was apparently a well-known transaction between Centlivre and Knight relies on readers to recognize the portrayal of the playwright as willing to trade on her income from published plays in a speculative bid for future access to and success in the theaters. Interestingly, the lines that follow these accuse Barry of both stockjobbing and prostitution. As a whole, then, the poem paints a picture of a network of women playwrights and actors supporting one another to the detriment of their masculine counterparts, revealing that the alternative economic agency the theater provided to women was a topic of debate and concern in the early decades of the eighteenth century.

As this chapter has shown, Centlivre both thematized and took advantage of new speculative market dynamics that allowed her to circumvent economic and civil institutions that excluded women and other nonelites. Likewise, her work built on and responded to concerns that had been raised in the prologues and epilogues of the 1690s about the ways that the democratizing potential of these new market structures could become corrupted. *The Gamester* and *The Basset Table* dramatize the leveling potential of the gaming table and speculative markets more generally for those willing to take risks—as Centlivre did, in using her plays to pit the rival theaters against one another—while also showing how the wealthy could take advantage of their position to socialize the losses they sustained in these spaces. *The Busie Body* revels in the ways that speculative markets destabilized the value of commodities, creating the potential for women to reclaim agency over their public circulation—just as Centlivre did, in selectively revealing and concealing her authorial identity. By the 1720s *A Bold Stroke for a Wife* and *A Woman's Case* reflected Centlivre's growing recognition and rejection of her contemporaries' attempts to define a "public" that included the masses but essentially represented the interests of the wealthy, masculine elite, and she cautioned her audiences to resist such attempts to coopt the power of the many to serve the interests of the few. Centlivre's later texts reflect a key shift in her thinking brought about by the events leading up to the South Sea Bubble, as concerns emerged that the newly powerful middling classes might be manipulated into squandering their social capital in exchange for the pleasures of spectacle and speculation. As the coming chapters will explore, the Bubble year loomed large in the periodical press and on the stage, and representations of the crisis enabled new explorations of the power and vulnerability of the mass public as it operated in both theatrical and financial markets.

PART II

The South Sea Bubble
(1720–1722)

• 4 •

Defrauding the Public

Spectacle and Speculation in Steele's Theatre *and* The Conscious Lovers

The previous chapter examined how playwright Susanna Centlivre simultaneously deployed and critiqued the speculative systems of gain at work in financial and theatrical markets in the early decades of the eighteenth century. As I have argued, the period surrounding the South Sea Bubble prompted a key shift in Centlivre's thinking. While many of her works exhibit varying levels of optimism and concern about the ways that people of different genders and social classes could gain access to speculative markets, her poem *A Woman's Case*, published in 1720, reflects a fear that the masculine elite might actively coopt the very mechanisms that made these markets potentially open and equalizing, crafting investment schemes that would appear to serve the interests of a broad-based public while in fact funneling wealth to a privileged few. This chapter examines a similar dynamic at work in the writings of another theater professional whose thinking was profoundly affected by the events of the Bubble year: prominent journalist, playwright, theater manager, and Member of Parliament Richard Steele (1672–1729). Steele, like Centlivre, gave voice to the concern that elites could use new market structures and dynamics to hijack what appeared to be middling-class sentiments. His writings from this period offer insight into the competing visions of the public sphere available to keen observers of these events; as such, they provide evidence of the changing stakes of debates taking place at the theater-finance nexus during this period.

The first half of this chapter considers the *Theatre*, a short-lived periodical published during the first three months of 1720. In the *Theatre*'s twenty-eight issues, Steele attacks both the South Sea Company and the Royal Academy of Music, a joint-stock company that funded the new Italian opera in London. Steele forges tropological links between the two enterprises, arguing that they prey on the worst aspects of crowd mentality, exploiting the public's desire for spectacle and speculation in order to advance the interests of an elite few. Steele portrays his enemies as threats to the development of the kind of reasonable, well-mannered public sphere he attempts to advance throughout his periodical and dramatic writings. Steele's argument about the parallels between the South Sea scheme and the opera company are carried out not only in the *Theatre's* articles and essays but also in its mock advertisements, which are striking in their use of irony to draw new attention the interworkings of financial and theatrical markets.

The second half of this chapter uses the *Theatre* as a point of entry to reexamine Steele's popular and influential play *The Conscious Lovers* (1722). While this comedy is often seen as part of Steele's project to develop the kind of classical bourgeois public sphere later described by Jürgen Habermas, my analysis challenges the assumption that Steele held such an anodyne vision of the public. Reading the play in the context of the South Sea Bubble and in conversation with the *Theatre*, I argue that *The Conscious Lovers* elicits critical engagement with issues of finance and colonial trade. The romantic union at the heart of the play does more than dramatize the wished-for marriage of the landed and moneyed classes: the happy couple's interactions also shed light on the chaotic underbelly of the joint-stock companies undergirding England's colonial trade. Ultimately, Steele's play explores how the powerful trading companies exploited the hopes and values of the middling classes—as well as the collective power of these people, realized through public opinion—to benefit the wealthy.

In the interrelated texts I examine here, the material and figurative links between theater and finance enable new articulations of the overlapping public spheres of eighteenth-century London. Crucially, it is the crisis surrounding the South Sea Company that brings these issues to the fore.[1] In the debates that sprang up in the theater-finance nexus during the South Sea affair, the intersections of the stock market and the entertainment industry figured the paradoxical power and vulnerability of an emerging middling-class public coming to terms with its own influence over political, financial, and cultural institutions. Then, as now, the Bubble loomed large in collective imagination as a paradigmatic example of two distinct phenomena: the infectious irrationality of crowds and the exploitive nature of speculative finance. In the heady optimism of spring and summer 1720, the panic of that fall, and the disenchantment of the ensuing winter, historians have long seen a case study in either the precipitancy of the masses or the public's vulnerability to the manipulations of a rapacious few.[2]

Interpretations of the significance of the South Sea Bubble pivot on whether investors should have known that the crash was coming. Behavioral economists, who emphasize the psychological dimensions of market participation, argue that investors had ample warning and stayed in the market anyway, behavior that reflects undue optimism and speculative mania rather than rational decision making.[3] Believers in the inherent rationality and self-regulation of markets, on the other hand, counter that investors were acting on the best information available and that the scheme's failure can be attributed either to the fact that it was an unprecedented experiment or to the company directors' deliberate perpetration of a scam on unsuspecting dupes. The former interpretation views the investing public as a mad and irrational crowd, while the latter offers a vision of a rational, yet ignorant and victimized, public.[4] In recent years some economic historians have proposed a middle ground; they see the South Sea affair as a rational bubble in which fundamentally reasonable behavior on the part of some directors and investors coexisted with elements of fraud, naïveté, and "noise trading"— that is, trading based on rumors and unreliable news sources.[5] Within such a model exists the possibility that some investors understood the scheme to be unsustainable and made an informed decision to get in early and cash out when prices were high.[6] According to this final view, the market for South Sea shares arose neither from the irrationality of crowds nor from the victimization of the ignorant masses at the hands of a few predatory directors but rather reflected the pervasion of exploitive impulses throughout the investing public.

All these interpretations of the South Sea scheme are on display in the rich archive of materials that took shape in the theater-finance nexus around 1720. The crisis was understood at the time to be a critical moment in the emergence of publics and continues to be seen as an event that evokes the dark side of the public sphere. This chapter contributes to ongoing attempts to understand imaginative representations of the South Sea affair by tracking the interactions of drama, theater, and the periodical press during the

Bubble and its aftermath.[7] The symbolic dimension of the crisis is important to understand because the actual economic effects of the South Sea Bubble were negligible in contrast to its profound social and political impact; as John Brewer insists, "The actual structure of credit markets was less important than the widespread perception of a crisis fuelled by a well-developed press and the intense public interest."[8] My examination of how the theatrical media landscape interacted with financial news and opinion at this tumultuous moment—a moment when the trustworthiness of institutions and the rationality of the masses were very much in question—reveals how the theater-finance nexus became a site for Londoners like Steele to share their bleakest visions of the relationships between markets and their publics.

The *Theatre*

In January 1720 the *Theatre* entered a crowded field of print periodicals that were strongly and self-reflectively associated with a nebulous "public" making itself felt in political life and in the arts. Julie Stone Peters notes that newspapers were referred to as "the Publick Papers" and "the Public Prints" and observes that they consistently "represented themselves as organs of the public voice."[9] Yet the public did not speak with a single voice. To contemporaries, the public was Janus-faced: enlightened and respectable on the one hand; a monstrous mob on the other.[10] The public prints shaped and responded to both faces. At a time when newspapers were frequently associated with partisanship and unreliability—a legacy of their emergence during the seventeenth-century civil wars and their proliferation during the Exclusion Crisis—writers like Daniel Defoe, Joseph Addison, and Richard Steele put forth periodicals that were explicitly opposed to this kind of disreputable news mongering, claiming to emphasize moral reflection and civil dialog over debate and disagreement.[11]

These "polite" periodicals' self-conscious reflection on and interaction with their audiences has made them an important source for theorizations of eighteenth-century publics. In Habermas's *The Structural Transformation of the Public Sphere* (1962), the account of the bourgeois public sphere relies heavily on the collaborations of Steele and Addison, particularly the *Tatler* (1709–11) and the *Spectator* (1711–12). For Habermas these texts provide evidence of the role of the periodical press and coffeehouse society in the construction of a virtual collective of private individuals with the ability to challenge and even overturn authority through rational-critical debate.[12] Later theorists have taken up the connection, viewing Addison and Steele as founding fathers of the modern conception of the public. Michael Warner, for instance, treats the *Spectator* as an exemplary public-forming text: "It describes its readers as an active public, a critical tribunal. Readers are called on to pass informed and reflective judgment on fashion, taste, manners, and gender relations. The procedure of impersonal discussion gives private matters full public relevance, while allowing the participants in that discussion to have the kind of generality that had formerly been the privilege of the state or the church."[13] Yet recent scholarship has also recognized that what Warner calls the "masculine bourgeois moral urbanity" of Mr. Spectator was not a universally held perspective in Addison and Steele's London; instead, much of the work of their periodicals was prescriptive, imagining an ideal of impersonal discussion and judgment rather than reflecting the reality of coffeehouse society.[14]

Scholarly narratives about Addison and Steele's role in forming and reflecting the eighteenth-century London public sphere have focused insistently on the *Tatler* and *Spectator*. These periodicals, while somewhat heterogeneous in content and tone, generally reflect the writers' optimism about the potential of the press to cultivate a polite, mannered public capable of reasoned judgments. This chapter shifts the discussion to Steele's later effort, the *Theatre*, which reflects a more complex view of the relationship between the individuals who make up the public and the forces that seek to influence their tastes and behaviors. While Mr. Spectator aims to shape his public, the narrator of the *Theatre* is aware of how easily the public is manipulated into collective actions, even when those actions are against its own best interests. The *Theatre*'s vision of London's masses—excitable, irrational, and vulnerable rather than rational, active, and powerful—reflects Steele's understanding of consumer culture and the mass-public subject as emergent formations that represented the dark side of the public sphere.[15]

The *Theatre* was published every Tuesday and Saturday from January 2 to April 5, 1720. Initially a joint publication effort between James Roberts and William Rufus Chetwood, the periodical picked up additional publishers throughout its run, suggesting that it sold fairly well. The degree of popular demand is illustrated by a January 1720 notice in the *Post Boy*: "Whereas Complaint hath been made of the Want of this Paper, occasion'd by their not being regularly dispers'd by the Hawkers," new issues will be available from select booksellers.[16] The *Theatre*'s ongoing success is further attested to by the increased volume of advertisements over the course of its run, evidence that it reached a substantial readership and was therefore a good value for advertisers.

One reason for the periodical's continued visibility and success was the profusion of responses and rebuttals it inspired, such as the *Anti-Theatre*, which was published twice weekly from February through April 1720 with the express purpose of refuting the positions taken in the latest issues of the *Theatre*. Steele's appetite for controversies and rivalries was such a major part of his paper's appeal that when John Nichols compiled and edited the *Theatre* in 1791, he packaged it with the *Anti-Theatre*.[17] Furthermore, the movement of these rivalries between the pages of the periodical and the stage itself is evidenced by an advertisement for a farce titled *The Theatre*: "All in the Characters of the Italian Theatre," performed at Lincoln's Inn Fields on April 22 and 23, 1720, and accompanied by "a new Prologue to the Town by Sir Richard Steele." The fact that this performance was advertised by Drury Lane's rival house—along with the fact that the prologue does not survive in the copious archival collections of Steele's correspondence, drafts, and occasional writings—raises the distinct possibility that it was a topical satire on, rather than an adaptation or reflection of, the periodical.[18]

Indeed, the shifting structure and focus of the *Theatre* itself attests to the gravitational pull of controversy for Steele. The first issue establishes that the periodical will consist mainly of moral essays arranged around the domestic and social life of its fictional narrator, fifty-one-year-old Sir John Edgar.[19] However, Sir John's family and friends disappear early on, their anticipated adventures replaced by extended commentaries on the function of the public theaters, the South Sea Bill moving through Parliament, and the opening of an Italian opera financed by a new joint-stock company, the Royal Academy of Music. John Loftis laments the periodical's divergence from its original intended form, describing it as "a hodge-podge of essays in very different veins, having no inner principle of coherence" except that "they are expressions of Steele's personal interests and preoccupations."[20] Contrary to Loftis, I propose that the *Theatre*'s jarring admixture of subject matter is both deliberate and revealing. Steele portrays the Italian opera as mere spectacle that—like South Sea shares—offers the public amusement but lacks underlying value. Furthermore, Steele draws attention to the parallel financial structures underpinning both the South Sea Company and the Royal Academy of Music. Like the South Sea Company, which was a

Tory counterpart to Whig trading ventures such as the East India Company, the Royal Academy was underwritten by the nobility and positioned to compete with patent theaters like Steele's at Drury Lane. For Steele, both the Royal Academy and the South Sea Company represent the elite cooptation of speculative finance, which stirs the public imagination with the promise of opportunity for the many yet serves the interests of only the few.

My reexamination of the *Theatre* in this chapter takes seriously Steele's intertwining of seemingly divergent aesthetic, social, and cultural issues, which results in part from the paper's genesis at the imaginative and material intersections of theatrical, ministerial, and financial politics. The *Theatre* was to some extent a vehicle for Steele to protest his legal exclusion from the administration of the theater for which he owned the patent. Sometimes referred to as the "governor" of Drury Lane, Steele was the sole holder of a patent that he claimed descended from the original rights given to William Davenant and Thomas Killigrew at the Restoration. The theater's license to act on a day-to-day basis, however, was a separate legal document held jointly by Steele and the managers of Drury Lane: Colley Cibber, Robert Wilks, and Barton Booth. The Drury Lane management found itself in an escalating power struggle with the Lord Chamberlain's office following the Duke of Newcastle's appointment to that post in 1717. The disagreement revolved around the question of authority over the theaters. Newcastle contended that the playhouses were under his office's jurisdiction, and he insisted that the managers must observe longstanding obligations like submitting plays to the Master of Revels for pre-performance licensing. Steele, however, maintained that his patent granted him autonomy, and he and the managers publicly defied Newcastle's attempts to bring them under control. In September 1719 Cibber published an inflammatory dedication to his play *Ximena* celebrating Steele's independent mindedness; in response to this provocation, Newcastle consulted a lawyer about the ambiguous legal status of the theater patent, hoping to weaken Drury Lane's claims to independence.[21]

Concurrent political contentions helped bring the conflict to a head. Newcastle and Steele were on opposite sides of the debate over the controversial Peerage Bill; its defeat in December 1719 was a signal victory for Robert Walpole's opposition faction (which included Steele) and an embarrassment to supporters of the reigning Stanhope-Sunderland ministry (which included Newcastle).[22] Shortly thereafter, Newcastle made his first move, prohibiting Cibber from participating in the operations of the theater as writer, actor, or manager. On January 23, 1720, Drury Lane's acting license was rescinded, effectively suspending performances there despite the fact that the patent to the theater itself was not revoked. Four days later Newcastle issued a new license to Wilks, Cibber, and Booth, leaving off Steele's name. Performances resumed on January 28 with Cibber restored to his former privileges, and in the months that followed, Newcastle attempted to exert greater influence on the selection of plays.[23] Excluded from participating in operations at Drury Lane, Steele vented his spleen in the *Theatre*, where he also vocally denounced the South Sea Bill advocated by the Stanhope-Sunderland ministry and opposed by Walpole's allies.

Beginning in late February 1720, the South Sea Bill becomes one of the main foci of the *Theatre*. Issue 17 (February 27) summarizes key points from Steele's two pamphlets on the matter, *The Crisis of Property* and *A Nation a Family*, insisting that holders of annuities cannot be forced to exchange their holdings for South Sea stock and expressing concern that the arrangement will damage public credit.[24] The issue reflects Steele's cynicism about the motivations behind the bill: "Now the *South-Sea* Proposal of lowering the Interest of Money, will be evidently attended with this Scarcity of it, which will be the Destruction of Trade, and Ruin of the Nation, for the enriching of a few; for, as I said, when the Value of Money is cheap, Bankers will, by the assistance of Paper-Credit, draw it into their own Hands, and by draining the Country of it, render it scarce." While Steele does not accuse the company directors of outright conspiracy to defraud the public, he does insist that the consequences of the scheme will be the "enriching of a few"—the bankers—at the expense of the "Ruin of the Nation."

Theatre 20 (March 8) more pointedly exposes the South Sea Company's illicit operations, insisting that the directors will pay dividends using borrowed money and that the company is buying up its own stock, creating the false appearance of value. Steele calls on the company to open its books so that holders of government debt can make informed decisions about whether to exchange their annuities for shares. "Before the Annuitants subscribe in their Annuities to the *South-Sea* Company, they demand to see the following Accounts fairly stated," he begins, before offering a long list of specific measures of financial health that investors should be able to assess: the gains and losses from the slave trade guaranteed by the *Asiento*, the principle and interest rates of the company's current debts, the payments the company has received from the Exchequer, and so on. If the directors refuse to divulge these numbers, or if the profits are revealed to come from any source other than real trade, then Steele insists that "the Managers of this Stock will be no other in plain *English*, but like the Bank at a Gaming-table, who sit in greater Security, and swallow by insensible degrees the Cash of the unfortunate Adventurers round the Board." Whereas in the earlier issue literal bankers stood to reap a windfall from the South Sea scheme, here the company managers are transformed into the metaphorical bankers of a gambling table, slowly and deliberately preying on "the unfortunate Adventurers" who were foolish enough to risk their cash.

In *Theatre* 22 (March 15) Steele once again insists that the company's value is artificial, pointing out its lack of trade and demanding to know the source of its underlying worth. *Theatre* 24 (March 23) reinforces the disconnection between the company's lack of trade and its rising stock value, and it again insists on the predatory nature of the scheme: "But so long as they [the South Sea Company] have no other Trade but that of Stock-jobbing, it is hard to find whence that Profit can grow; and I fear that no Use will be made of that advanced Price, but the returning at several times large Portions of it, to give the greater Appearance of wonderful Gains, to increase the Price of Stock, for the enriching those who are in the Secret, and to the Ruin of those who are impos'd on by them." Here, Steele rightly predicts that the directors will illegally pay out so-called dividends to early investors using the cash taken in from later investors—creating the illusion of financial well-being in order to inflate stock values artificially and promoting a continued cycle of simulated profit.

Unable to turn the tide of public opinion with such polemical analyses, Steele tried a new tactic in *Theatre* 27 (April 2). The issue consists entirely of a series of detailed calculations of the South Sea Company's underlying stock value under a variety of circumstances as well as a projection of the return on investment expected on a single share at the various proposed interest rates. These meticulous calculations serve to demonstrate that under any number of conditions, investment in the South Sea Company will provide modest, if any, benefits to individual investors, unless the stock price can be forced well above a realistic value—in which case a handful of early investors may benefit and all others suffer. Issue 27 is quite different in content and tone from the other issues of the periodical, its stark rows of sums with minimal commentary presented as self-evident proof of the scheme's fraudulence. This self-evidence is underlined by the brief conclusion: "For the truth of all these Calculations, I appeal to every

'Prentice-boy."²⁵ The only interpretive commentary is provided by the opening and closing quotations. The issue begins with an epigraph from John Denham's poem "Cooper's Hill": "Here, with like haste, though different ways, they run, / Some to undo, and some to be undone." It concludes cryptically with an unattributed quotation from Horace, "*Occupet extremum scabies*. 'MURRAIN take the hindmost.'" The Denham quotation previews the unequal outcomes of the scheme, in which the directors will undo and the investors will be undone; the concluding quotation from Horace takes the idea further, implying that death and disease will catch those who finish last in the race—or, in this case, those who invest too late to cash in.

Throughout the *Theatre*, Steele suggests that excitement about the ill-advised South Sea scheme is a result of the public's susceptibility to distracting spectacle and foreign influence. As I will show, he makes this case by interweaving his critiques of the South Sea Company with satire of the Italian opera being opened in London. Steele's periodical expresses fear that both of these innovations—speculative mania and the craze for opera—give rise to an uncritical public that demands mere amusement. This imagined public's irrationality and sensuality render it passive and therefore vulnerable to the machinations of predatory elites who aim to reshape public finance and public entertainment alike, deluding the masses into acting against their own interests. In order to understand how Steele makes this case, it is necessary first to sketch the history of the establishment of the Royal Academy of Music.

Italian, all-sung opera was first produced in London in 1705 and was immediately successful among the fashionable; however, it was financially unsustainable, and the opera company at the Haymarket suspended its operations in 1717.²⁶ In January 1719 a group of aristocrats petitioned the king to allow the creation of a joint-stock company to finance an opera in London that they imagined would rival those on the Continent. This company, the Royal Academy, was incorporated on May 9 and granted a twenty-one-year royal charter on July 27. The king himself personally pledged the Academy £1,000 per year. In addition, some sixty-four subscribers pledged over £15,000 capital, well in excess of the £10,000 capitalization from fifty subscribers the company was supposed to raise. The original shareholders were largely courtiers and elites, and the Royal Academy was widely seen as a pet project of the crown and nobility.

Nonetheless, the company took its structure from the world of finance rather than that of royal patronage. It had a board of twenty directors elected from among the subscribers, and it was headed by a governor and deputy governor. Subscribers were obligated to pay their pledges incrementally when calls were issued by the board. As these details suggest, the investment and governance mechanisms were quite similar to those of other joint-stock ventures like the South Sea Company. Robert Hume describes the unconventional financial structure as "a peculiar amalgam of royal household appendage and public stock company" and a "strange hybrid designed by the nobility to support their plaything."[27] Thomas McGeary likewise highlights the tensions inherent in the company's structure: "As a profit-oriented opera house open to the paying public, the Royal Academy resembled the commercial opera houses in Hamburg and Venice. Yet because of the royal patent, bounty, and veto and governance by aristocrats who were often court office holders ... there is an element of an opera produced by and for the court and aristocrats, but one without the political or dynastic functions of typical Continental court operas."[28] If the opera was a poor fit for a joint-stock financial structure, why didn't the backers simply support it through more old-fashioned forms of patronage? Hume argues the venture came at a time when speculative investment seemed to be the answer to all problems: "The Royal Academy was launched in the midst of South Sea fever, and this was no coincidence."[29] As a sign of that optimistic "fever," the academy originally anticipated that it would be able to make a 25 percent dividend payout to shareholders.[30] J. Merrill Knapp similarly links the two enterprises, pointing out that two South Sea directors numbered among the academy's subscribers and citing the *Theatre* as evidence that the "association of the 'musical' company with other stock floating ventures was not lost upon perceptive observers."[31] Steele's work in the *Theatre* goes beyond merely associating the South Sea Company and the Royal Academy, however; Steele also exposes the similarities between the two to make a larger case for how the pleasures of speculative markets allow the powerful to prey on the easily deluded and distracted masses.

Many of Steele's critiques of the Royal Academy of Music are grounded in complaints about the opera that were conventional at the time. McGeary glosses the myriad concerns early eighteenth-century Londoners raised about this newly popular form of entertainment: "Literary critics claimed opera was an irrational, sensuous art form, sung in a foreign language that violated verisimilitude and decorum. Dramatists and friends of British theater saw opera and highly paid singers as threats to native talent and dramatic traditions. Social reformers and moralists ... condemned opera as an expensive offspring of luxury that led to vice, sensuality, and effeminacy.... Nationalists objected to the presence of a foreign art on the London stage."[32] Colley Cibber, for instance, reflects in his memoir on how the rise of the Italian opera in London led the two patent companies to begin incorporating more music and dancing into their entertainments to attract crowds that increasingly demanded these elements. He explains that the success of one such hybrid, *The Loves of Mars and Venus*, led to the mounting of more "monstrous Medlies" at both houses, each "outvying, in Expence, like contending Bribes on both sides at an Election, to secure a Majority of the Multitude." He laments that regardless of merit, "the Few will never be a Match for the Many, unless Authority should think fit to interpose, and put down these Poetical Drams, these Gin-shops of the Stage, that intoxicate its Auditors, and dishonour their Understanding."[33] Cibber sees the "intoxicating" effects of semi-operatic entertainment as a cheap ploy to attract "the Multitude," who are simultaneously figured as people of "Understanding" and as victims of false consciousness. For Cibber the apparently democratic processes of public opinion formation—whether with regards to the stage or to a Parliamentary contest—can be coopted by highly capitalized special interests. Ultimately, he appeals to "Authority," imagined here as benevolent, to intercede when the public does not act in its own best interest.

Such critiques were likewise a regular feature of Steele's earlier periodical efforts in the *Tatler* and the *Spectator*, which frequently mocked the Italian opera and the audiences who flocked to it.[34] In the *Theatre* Steele echoes commonplace concerns that the opera corrupts spectators by appealing to their senses rather than their rationality. Steele's intervention in the *Theatre* is novel, however, insofar as he uses these well-worn criticisms of the opera to offer a parallel critique of speculative finance. In linking the operations of the entertainment industry with those of fraudulent financial ventures, Steele develops a broader theory of how publics form and operate and of how they relate to institutions that are dominated by the social and economic elite. Specifically, he draws a causal link between irrational pleasures—whether those of the opera or of speculative investment—and the cultivation of passivity, arguing that the opera and the South Sea scheme alike create mindless masses rather than active, thoughtful participants. In short, Steele insists that a public in thrall to its senses is not only irrational but incapable of self-direction; it acts at the behest of those who control its pleasures, and it is therefore susceptible to self-destructive behaviors willed by those who would see the public sphere compromised and its power to hold institutions accountable weakened.

Steele's most sustained critique of the predatory aesthetics and economics of the opera appears in *Theatre* 18 (March 1) around the same time that his case against the South Sea Company begins to intensify. Steele's distaste for operatic music hinges on a conventional opposition between "sound" and "sense"—the former representing the mindless sensory pleasure of musical entertainment, the latter representing the potential for intellectual and ethical engagement he considers to be inherent in dialog-driven plays. The narrator comments ironically that "pleasures are of late years improved to a most exquisite softness, and the delight of sound has prevailed over the pain of sense," implying that the London public shies away from entertainments that require mental effort. He offers an example of the kind of song that is approved of by "the present refiners of our taste in Music and Poetry." It is a nonsense song, entirely devoid of meaning:

I.

So notwithstanding heretofore
Strait forward by and by
Now everlastingly therefore
Too low and eke too high

II.

Then for almost and also why
Not thus when less so near
Oh! for hereafter quite so nigh
But greatly ever here.

The narrator observes that this piece has been "admirably well set to Musick by a famous *Italian* Master" and is sure to be met with applause, "for it gives no manner of Disturbance to the Head, but merely serves to be added to Sounds proper for the Syllables." The current taste, then, is for verses designed primarily as accompaniments to music rather than as vehicles for meaning; songs need only have stresses and rhymes in the right places to be considered art.

The association of this type of music with Italian influences (i.e., the "famous *Italian* Master") is reinforced by the narrator's assertion that this song is to be approved for the stage by a "Council of Ten" that makes its decisions "according to the Rules and Methods imported by Sir *Politick Wou'dbe*, from the State of *Venice*." A character from Ben Jonson's *Volpone* (1606), which was performed regularly throughout the early eighteenth century, Sir Politick is an English knight living in Venice who is made a fool by his naïve desire for the trappings of Italian sophistication.[35] The evocation of Sir Politick, then, serves as a dig at the English appetite for Italian culture. The joke, however, has darker and more material implications. The very gullibility and naïveté that render Sir Politick susceptible to foreign influence also make him vulnerable to get-rich-quick schemes. Throughout *Volpone* Sir Politick undertakes several ill-advised money-making ventures. His absurd financial projects, however, have their more sinister counterpart in the titular Volpone's manipulations of others for his personal gain.[36] The reference, then, offers a compressed suggestion of how the gullible masses' fascination with foreign sophistication and luxury works through the same channels as their desire for easy riches and how both of these weaknesses make them easy prey.[37] The implication is reinforced by the narrator's assertion that Sir Politick's aesthetic preferences are being taken up by the council precisely because "all great Men know, if you can command absolutely the Toys of little people, you will, by a Parity of Reason, come into the Possession and Direction of the Goods and Chattels of the rest of the World." The "Toys," or nonsense songs and sensory pleasures of the opera, enable the council to exploit the "little people" and thereby gain economic domination over "the rest of the World."

While the reference to *Volpone* begins to suggest the relevance of that play's vision of economic and cultural exploitation for Londoners in 1720, the rest of *Theatre* 18 makes the connection even more explicit. The narrator decries the art of the nonsense song as symptomatic of a culture in which people attempt to make a profit without producing real value:

> If these high Designs were carried on, nonsensical as they are, without Prospect of Gain, there would be still something liberal in them; but they have receiv'd a Tincture of all the Sense, that seems to remain amongst us, the Sense of Profit. But there is a Stock laid in to impose upon the Stupidity of their Admirers; and it is expected that there will be a nightly Succession of Bubbles in Numbers large enough, who will part with their Cash, as well as their Understanding, to support a mechanick and mean Profit rais'd by Gentlemen of Honour and

Quality upon ingenious Arts. Arbitrary Dealings with Performers of both Sexes to bring them to their Prizes, and helping their No-sense or Nonsense of Reason with their No-sense or Nonsense of Conscience, are the Methods by which this lamentable Community of Virtuoso's seem to aim at an Establishment.

The passage is rife with the language of finance—"Stock," "Profit," "Gain," "Cash," and "Bubbles." Steele uses this language to lament that the culture of sense and manners has been replaced by one obsessed with finance, in which profit is made from the "stupidity" of "Bubbles"—gullible individuals who have been tricked into foolhardy investments. Opera-goers voluntarily relinquish sense in favor of "No-sense or Nonsense," entertainment devoid of content or real value, much like a worthless stock that represents no underlying capital. Naïve spectators gladly pay real money for the false value produced by the opera company, parting with "their Cash, as well as their Understanding" in the same move. Worse, in Steele's view, the fraud is being perpetrated by "gentlemen of honour and quality" upon their economic and social inferiors. There is nothing "liberal" in the opera company's empty entertainment because it is a deliberate con on people who know no better. It is at this point that the satirical and fictionalized commentary gives way to a critique more explicitly grounded in current events, as the "Virtuoso's" and their attempted "Establishment" clearly refer to the Royal Academy of Music.

Theatre 18, then, links financial and cultural predation through its concern with the falsified value of opera tickets, which are implicitly linked to valueless stocks. The end of the issue, however, features a notice that extends this concern explicitly to the realm of the stock market. The notice appears directly above the publisher's advertisements, which allows it to evoke visually and contextually the stock-price listings printed in many periodicals of the day. It reads: "Yesterday South-Sea was 174. Opera-Company 83, and a half. No Transfer" (fig. 2). The "Opera-Company" listed here is clearly meant to be the Royal Academy. However, the stock price is facetious: the Royal Academy's shares were not publicly traded, and its share prices were not commonly printed in periodicals—although meetings of its directors and sharers were advertised in the papers, ensuring that Londoners were quite aware of the venture.[38] The phrase "no transfer" was used in stock-price listings at the time to indicate whether shares in one company could be exchanged for shares in another and at what rate. In this case, the phrase "no transfer" is technically

> *An eminent* Turkey Merchant, *and an ingenious Foreigner, do hereby give Notice, That if any Person will discover the Libeller, or Libellers, who has and have falsly and maliciously insinuated in their Writings, that Sir* R——d S——le *is ugly, so as they may be prosecuted by Law, shall have all fitting Encouragements; the said Gentlemen having lost considerable Matches, by reason of the Similitude of their Persons to the said injur'd* Knight.
>
> Yesterday South-Sea was 174. Opera-Company 83, and a half. No Transfer.
>
> ## ADVERTISEMENTS.
>
> This Day is publish'd,
>
> *** A Nation a Family: Being the Sequel of the Crisis of Property: Or a Plan for the Improvement of the South-Sea Proposal. By Sir Richard Steele, Knt. Member of Parliament. To be had at the same Places with this Paper; and at J. Brotherton's at the Black-Bull in Cornhill. Price 6 d.
>
> In a few Days will be Publish'd,
>
> ☨ Loyalty to His Majesty King George: Recommended in Eight Sermons: Preach'd at St. Mary le Savoy. By Richard Synge, Chaplain at Somerset-House. Dedicated to the Duke of Newcastle.

FIGURE 2. Detail from *Theatre* 18, March 1, 1720, verso. (© The British Library Board, Burney Collection 201b)

correct: one could not pay for stock in the South Sea Company using Royal Academy shares, or vice-versa. However, this fact would have been self-evident to readers, who would have been aware that the opera company did not typically feature in stock listings alongside the major trading companies. The gratuitousness of the phrase "no transfer," then, operates to draw attention to the very possibility it forecloses, inviting the reader to imagine what *could* be transferred between the two companies. In that sense, it reinforces and highlights the conceptual transfer Steele has encouraged throughout the issue in his references to Sir Politick Wou'dbe and to the Council of Ten's predation on "Bubbles."

Steele once again lists the price of the opera stock in *Theatre* 20 (March 8), the issue demanding that the South Sea Company open its books to inspection by potential investors. An openly satirical announcement again appears shortly before the publisher's advertisements at the end of the second page: "*At the Rehearsal on* Friday *last, Signior* Nihilini Beneditti *rose half a Note above his Pitch formerly known. Opera Stock from 83 and an half, when he began; at 90 when he ended.*" This advertisement is a barely-veiled reference to a well-known castrato singer, Nicolini (Nicola Grimaldi), but the transformation of his name into "Nihilini" returns to the motif of "no-sense or nonsense," in which entertainment has been evacuated of its intellectual content and therefore of its cultural and financial value.[39] Here, the producer of that entertainment is himself nothing, "nihil," the diminutive ending further reducing his significance. In the opera, Signior Nothing produces no sense, yet he still inflates the opera's stock value. This advertisement, then, mocks the irrationality of stock prices and their tenuous relationship to actual assets, implying that the public's enthusiasm for meaningless spectacle plays a role in the inflationary movements of markets.

The idea that the price of the company's stock could jump 6.5 points in the space of time a performer holds a note is meant, of course, to be absurd. It has its direct parallel, however, in a "Postscript" that appears before the advertisements in *Theatre* 24 (March 22; fig. 3): "*The Stock of the* South-Sea *rose fifty per Cent. in one Hour's Time, which, by the Year, is* 8760 l. *per Cent. and that upon the Whole, forty Millions comes to* 17,520,000,000,000. *I am considering, at this Rate, in what time the Company may purchase the Terraqueous Globe, Gibraltar and Minorca inclusive.*" Again, price movements appear irrational, particularly when compressed into a short period: how could a company double in value in an hour? This kind of up-to-the-minute reporting of stock values was impossible at a time when prices were reported in daily and weekly periodicals rather than on any kind of real-time centralized exchange. Nonetheless, the satirical notice portrays rapid price movements becoming untethered from underlying asset value. Furthermore, by extrapolating this rate of growth into an impossible future in which the South Sea Company has enough money to purchase the entire world, the narrator mimics the wild excesses of optimism that characterized South Sea speculation and shows such rises to be manifestly unsustainable. Coming two weeks after the notice of Signior Nihilini's inflation of the opera company's stock, this South Sea postscript reinforces the sense that the public is willingly contributing to an economy of false value, consuming mindless entertainment and buying into the market's empty promises.

POSTSCRIPT.

The Stock of the South-Sea *rose fifty* per Cent. *in one Hour's Time, which, by the Year, is* 8760 l. per Cent. *and that upon the Whole, forty Millions comes to*

17,520,000,000,000.

I am confidering, at this Rate, in what time the Company may purchafe the Terraqueous Globe, Gibraltar *and* Minorca *inclufive.*

ADVERTISEMENTS.

In a few Days will be Publifh'd,

‡|‡ The State of the Cafe between the Lord-Chamberlain of His Majefty's Houfhold, and the Governor of the Royal Company of Comedians. By Sir Richard Steele.

To-Morrow will be Publifhed,

⊥ Confiderations occafion'd by the Bill for enabling the South-Sea Company to increafe their Capital Stock, &c. Sold by J. Roberts in Warwick-lane. Price 6 d.

FIGURE 3. Detail from *Theatre* 24, March 22, 1720, verso. (© The British Library Board, Burney Collection 201b)

Not only does this postscript satirize the rapid price movements characterizing speculative mania around the South Sea Company, but the notices that follow it return the reader to the parallel between the economics of the theater and public finance: an advertisement for Steele's pamphlet making his argument against the Lord Chamberlain in the Drury Lane case is followed by another for a pamphlet debating the merits of the South Sea Bill. Although the advertisements were placed by the publisher rather than by Steele himself, the juxtaposition visually reinforces the *Theatre*'s concerns. Here it is important to note that Steele was acutely aware of how readers engaged with the space dedicated to advertisements at the end of periodicals. In the *Tatler*, narrator Isaac Bickerstaff remarks:

> It is my custom in a Dearth of News to entertain my self with those Collections of Advertisements that appear at the End of all our publick Prints. These I consider as Accounts of News from the little World, in the same Manner that the foregoing Parts of the Paper are from the

great. If in one we hear that a Sovereign Prince is fled from his Capital City, in the other we hear of a Tradesman who hath shut up his Shop and run away. If in one we find the Victory of a General, in the other we see the Desertion of a private Soldier.[40]

Steele was highly attuned, then, to parallels between the events happening at different echelons of society, and he was aware of the ability of the advertisements in the "publick Prints" to bring those resonances to light. Furthermore, he saw it as part of the task of the publishing bookseller—who often took in advertisements at his shop—to construct insightful analogies through the arrangement of this section. Later in the same issue of the *Tatler*, Bickerstaff claims that "a Collection of Advertisements is a Kind of Miscellany" and that "the Genius of the Bookseller is chiefly shown in his Method of ranging and digesting these little Tracts." The juxtaposition and arrangement of these notices and their surrounding material had the potential to be both compelling and meaningful, and Steele was aware that some readers would turn to the advertisements page as a source of information, diversion, and commentary that might not otherwise make it into the body of the paper. His use of the space directly above the publishers' notices in the *Theatre* is therefore a strategic one, designed to call attention to parallels between the forms of false value circulating through financial and theatrical markets.[41]

Throughout the *Theatre* Steele evokes the specter of the unthinking crowd, suggesting that both the entertainment industry and the major joint-stock companies prey on the people's base desire for stimulation and pleasure rather than cultivating a more engaged and critical public. In *Theatre* 24 (March 23), Steele lays out the tactics used by the South Sea directors to improve the company's value artificially, and he argues that "these Appearances don't at all make the Stock worth more, but only serve to amuse the People, in order to their Undoing." The word "amuse" here signifies the public's desire for diversion and specifically ties the behavior of gullible investors to that of naïve theater or pageant spectators. Likewise, at the end of *Theatre* 20—which is mostly given over to an exposé of the South Sea Bill as a scam—Steele evokes the mindless multitude in thrall to their senses, concluding that the investment scheme "is but a gay, flaring, City Pageant, which amazes the Crowd through which it passes." The word "Crowd" signals a public that acts as one, unified by a shared sensory spectacle. As the image develops, it becomes clear that this spectacle serves to distract from the underlying instability of the system: "[W]e know *the Bearers are changed,* tho' the Show still marches on; but a boisterous Multitude from the Water-Side, a Noise of Fire, or a Cry and Throng after a Pickpocket, would be a very just Alarm to make them lay down their Burden, without staying for the Consent of their Owners." The bearers of the pageant—standing here for the holders of South Sea shares—are not only the supporters of the spectacle; they are also part of the crowd and therefore just as easy to influence and distract as the viewers they amaze. The South Sea scheme relies on the same gullibility and crowd mentality cultivated by such mindless entertainments, but it is subject to the weakness of the public on which it depends for its operation: if the bearers are spooked, they could sell off their shares and bring the whole pageant crashing down.

Steele's dark vision of the crowd in thrall to its senses finds its bleakest expression in *Theatre* 21 (March 12), in which the narrator rails against the indecency of the French comedians and gymnasts then in London. He paints the public's approbation of these performers as the fullest expression of its hunger for sensory pleasure, placing the sexually explicit French harlequinades on a continuum with the dominance of "sound" over "sense" in the Italian opera: "Sensation is to banish Reflection, as Sound is to beat down Sense." Steele jumps from the threat of mindless and indecent entertainments to the greed of speculators: "[A]s Lust is made the reigning Impulse of the Town, Avarice is the one and entire Passion of the City." He goes on to point out the similarity of the language that predominates in both spheres: "[T]hey mean emphatically their different Appetites by the same common term. *Doing* in the City is getting money, *Doing* in the Town is getting Children." In matters of entertainment and finance alike, Steele suggests, Londoners are falling prey to their basest instincts. Although the City and Town are here distinguishable social spheres, they are linked by the ascendance of appetite over rational or humane behavior. The connection is reinforced by the letters that conclude the issue—one pertaining to a jealous opera singer, the other relating a young woman's struggle to distinguish truth and lies in the assessment of South Sea stocks—both of which reveal the "violence" of the two "prevailing inclinations" in London life. Steele sees both novel entertainments and novel financial ventures threatening to overturn deliberation and manners in favor of pure, unchecked desire. Ultimately, he fears that the government's backing of endeavors like the South Sea Company and the Royal Academy of Music reveals its complicity in the creation of a thoughtless mob driven only by its passions.

The concerns Steele expresses in the *Theatre* participate in larger contemporary debates over the nature and function of crowds following the Sacheverell Riots in 1710, the Jacobite uprising in 1715, and the passage of the Riot Act that same year. In 1720, the year of the *Theatre*, historian Robert B. Shoemaker estimates that "a riot that resulted in a criminal prosecution occurred, on the average, once every other day in London."[42] Historically, mobs offered an important way for England's disenfranchised masses to exercise influence over the authorities, in part because the legitimacy of rulers' power was understood to rest on their protection of the poor and needy.[43] E. P. Thompson has argued that popular uprisings in England in the eighteenth century were expressions of "the moral economy of the poor," a set of social obligations amongst the estates that the crowd defended by rioting against economic behaviors they considered exploitive or destructive to a traditional social order.[44] We can see aspects of this moral economy in Steele's attacks on the rapaciousness of the South Sea Company, even as he takes a rather supercilious view of the crowd as a mindless multitude responding impulsively rather than rationally.

Steele's simultaneously protective and disgusted attitude towards the mob—his desire to save them from what he imagines to be their own worst impulses—reflects the complex relationship of the ruling Whigs to crowd action. Adrian Randall argues that Whig elites saw themselves as advancing a more modern and egalitarian social order through their support of City financial interests, yet they also benefited from a stratification of wealth and power that excluded the populace from politics.[45] Steele's sympathy for those being exploited by the South Sea Company and the Royal Academy of Music is not incompatible, then, with his fear of the mob. Informed by a version of the moral economy of the poor—which, despite its view from below, could be and was used to sustain a traditional, paternalistic social order—Steele's guiding mission is to create a more rational and genteel middling-class public that he imagines would act in line with his own values if given the opportunity for reasonable discussion and debate. Here, then, is a key tension in Steele's work: he believes that the public must be rational in order to take action in its own interests and that irrationality renders it passive; yet he also needs the rational bourgeois public he is cultivating to be at least somewhat malleable in order to heed his warnings and accede to his vision of how it should behave. There is no room in his theory of publics for a crowd called into being by spectacle to be politically active in ways that escape the control of the elite. That is, while his vision of the operations of crowds is necessarily darker than many have recognized, it does anticipate and correspond to an assumption at work in Habermas's theories: that the existence of a rational-critical public that can hold institutions to account is fundamentally incompatible with the kind of mass public activated by commercialized art.

Indeed, it is telling that Steele voices his concern about the role of spectacle in manipulating crowd psychology through an evocation of London street action, which was uniquely tied to theatrical and spectacular practices.[46] Due to London's population density, crowds could gather and grow spontaneously, incorporating onlookers as participants.[47] In the context of spectacles of power that took place on London's streets—feasts, parades, fireworks, effigy burnings—riots could become what Randall calls "a counter-theatre of license that matched the theatre of order and domination of the patricians."[48] Steele's parade metaphor in the *Theatre* illuminates how he understood the passivity of the mob to be conditioned by experiences of spectatorship. People who were easily, unthinkingly caught up in the opera or in a parade might be swept up in a passing riot just as easily. Yet the image of spectacular street action is also a reminder that theatricality could stimulate the creation of new counterpublics with motives and logics that did not correspond neatly to the protocols of rational-critical debate at play in the coffeehouses. When Steele dismisses such publics as passive dupes of predatory powers, he fails to see the possibility that they might be active and powerful in other ways.

Steele understood the threat posed by the opera not only in terms of its supposed delusion of the mindless public or its unstable, predatory financial model but also in terms of its competition with the kind of discursive drama that he prized as a medium of instruction for a middling-class public. Nichols clearly considered this an important context, and in his 1791 edition of the *Theatre*, he included a footnote to issue 26 excerpting a letter from one Dr. Rundle to a Mrs. Sandys: "It is said, a most excellent Comedy of Sir R. STEEL's is to be prohibited acting, lest it should draw away good company, and spoil the relish for Operas, by seducing them with sense, wit, and humour."[49] Dr. Rundle, like Steele's narrator in *Theatre* 18, opposes the "sense, wit, and humour" of dialog-driven drama to the contemporary fad for opera, which presumably lacks all of the above.

Furthermore, this quotation expresses a sense that Steele was being suppressed by a government less concerned with his actual supposed crimes against the Lord Chamberlain than with protecting its vested interest in the opera. This suspicion seems at least somewhat grounded: Newcastle was not only the Lord Chamberlain responsible for prohibiting Steele's plays from being performed onstage but was also one of the chief investors in the Royal Academy of Music.[50] Dr. Rundle's portrayal of "good company" being "seduced" by the relative pleasures of various dramatic entertainments implicitly positions Steele's didactic drama as a counterweight to government-backed opera, which appears to function (at least in part) as a way to profit from the docile masses. The next section turns to *The Conscious Lovers*, one of Steele's own dramatic offerings, to examine how that play offered an alternative to the sensual entertainment of the opera and a continuation of the commentary on speculation and spectacle begun in the *Theatre*.

The Conscious Lovers

The *Theatre* makes plain the close conceptual relationship between theatrical and financial markets during the South Sea Bubble, a relationship that sheds new light on the stakes of dramatic offerings that were successful in the aftermath of the crash. One such play was Steele's *The Conscious Lovers*, a runaway success upon its debut on November 7, 1722. The comedy's eighteen-night opening run brought in more money than any previous production at Drury Lane, and the first edition of the play text went through numerous printings and was pirated repeatedly.[51] When *The Conscious Lovers* premiered two and a half years after the *Theatre*'s run had ended, the play invited viewers to understand it within the context of its author's periodical journalism. As Nicole Horejsi notes, the play first introduces its exemplary young gentleman, Bevil Junior, reading the *Spectator* and commenting on how Addison's "charming Vision of *Mirza* . . . sets the Spirit for the Vicissitudes of the Day."[52] Many critics have seen *The Conscious Lovers* as the culmination of the mission expressed throughout Steele's periodical journalism—that of promoting the interests of the middling classes and reforming social codes defined by outdated aristocratic values.[53] Lisa Freeman suggests that *The Conscious Lovers* brought philosophy into the theater as the *Spectator* brought it into homes and coffeehouses, and James

Chandler makes a case that the printed play text works deliberately to draw the reading public to performances and shape a new kind of theatrical audience that mirrors the polite, mercantile readership of Steele's periodicals.[54]

In reading *The Conscious Lovers* as an extension of Steele's projects in the *Tatler* and the *Spectator* while according little attention to the *Theatre*, however, these studies dwell mainly on the play's treatment of class while ignoring its engagement with speculative finance. Yet the South Sea scheme and the *Theatre*'s financial polemic are vital contexts for *The Conscious Lovers* and its thematizations of class, trade, and the workings of publics. By shifting attention to the play's intertextual relationship with its more contemporaneous publication, the *Theatre*, it is possible to see how *The Conscious Lovers* engaged audiences in immediate and pressing debates about the risky speculative ventures that underwrote England's colonial trade and the rise of its middling classes.

There are several reasons to read these texts together. First, Steele was working on them at the same time: although the play did not debut until November 1722, it had been in preparation for about a decade.[55] Second, the play and periodical have in common a number of elements: both feature wealthy merchants who embody Whig ideals; both participate in Steele's project of dramatic reform; and, as I will discuss, the play's exemplary characters voice criticisms of the opera similar to those found in the *Theatre*.[56] Third, multiple instances of intertextuality exist between the periodical and the play; most strikingly, the cast of characters in the early issues of the *Theatre* closely matches the *dramatis personae* of *The Conscious Lovers*.[57] Sir John Edgar himself, the narrator of the *Theatre*, bears the original name of the character who eventually became Sir John Bevil in the play; evidence from Steele's papers suggests that he changed his character's name to Bevil sometime after 1720, perhaps because of Edgar's association with the *Theatre* and therefore with the controversy over the Drury Lane patent.[58] Sir John Edgar's son Harry has several traits in common with Bevil Junior in *The Conscious Lovers*, and in *Theatre* 3 (January 9) readers meet other characters from the play—including Mr. Sealand, Lucinda, and Charles Myrtle—in the context of their places in a proposed representative body for theater audiences.[59] For all these reasons, Loftis goes so far as to call the *Theatre* "a companion piece to the play" that allowed Steele to explore the same ideas in a different form while also generating excitement about *The Conscious Lovers* in advance of its debut.[60]

The Conscious Lovers revolves around the intended marriage between Bevil Junior, the son of a gentleman, and Lucinda, the daughter of the wealthy merchant Sealand. Bevil Junior wishes to escape the engagement so that he can marry Indiana, an English-born orphan he has supported financially since rescuing her from a series of misfortunes in France. Yet his strong sense of filial duty prevents him from defying his father's will and choosing his own wife. Lucinda, in turn, hopes to marry Bevil's friend Myrtle, while her mother conspires to wed her to Cimberton, an odious aristocratic relative. When the play opens, Sealand has learned that Bevil has been seen with Indiana, and he has postponed the marriage until he can ascertain that his prospective son-in-law is not keeping a mistress. The young people take the opportunity to shape their matches to their own ends.

It has long been recognized that Steele's play engages with economic concerns in at least two prominent ways: first, in its extended critique of the financial and libidinal motivations that often drive marriage, and second, in its direct engagement with the changing class structures of English society. The former critique is exemplified by act 3, scene 1, in which Lucinda is forced by her mother to submit to the lascivious gaze of Cimberton, who insistently figures her as breeding stock upon which he will beget his heir, uniting sexual and economic desire to the exclusion of companionship or mutual respect. Lucinda protests her treatment as a "steed at sale" (49) but is repeatedly silenced by her mother, who is as obsessed as Cimberton with bloodline—a concern that neatly collapses sexual generation and the accumulation and transfer of wealth.[61] Steele's staging of class is most obvious in the marriage of Bevil Junior to Indiana at the end of the play, following the revelation of her identity as Sealand's long-lost daughter. Their union is often read as an ideological fantasy of a happy alliance between the old landed aristocracy and the new moneyed interests.[62]

The other frequently cited example of the play's class consciousness is the exchange between Sealand and Sir John Bevil in act 4, in which the two debate the importance of genealogy and the commensurability of notions of credit and honor. Sealand famously asserts: "We Merchants are a Species of Gentry, that have grown into the World this last Century, and are as honourable, and almost as useful, as you landed Folks, that have always thought yourselves so much above us" (62–63). These scenes make plain why Laura Brown calls *The Conscious Lovers* "one of the period's preeminent expressions of bourgeois ideology" and why James Thompson calls it "the exemplary text for illustrating shifting class consciousness in drama and an attendant transition from a drama of social status to a drama of inner worth."[63] Yet beyond the play's representation of domestic class tensions, its portrayal of colonial trade reveals a more nuanced economic commentary.

The play engages with matters of international trade most forcefully through its representations of Sealand and Indiana. The identification of both characters with the Indies is clear from the beginning: Sealand is introduced as a "great *India* Merchant," and Indiana—her name itself evocative, although not revealed at first—is initially described wearing an "*Indian* mantle" at a masked ball (3, emphasis in original). Thompson and Horejsi both read Indiana, whose identity is indefinable within the system of patrilineal inheritance, as a floating or empty sign whose ambiguous relationships to multiple men dramatize the circulation of colonial goods and the difficulty of ascertaining value in a credit-based economy.[64] Horejsi further argues that Indiana's association with exotic goods evokes contemporary protests and legal prohibitions around East Indian and imitation Indian calico, which threatened England's domestic wool industry. Horejsi suggests that the figure of Indiana complicates the play's celebration of commerce and expresses "nascent imperialist guilt" over "the potentially ill-gotten fruits of the emerging empire."[65]

While I find Horejsi's reading compelling, I will here insist on the ambiguity of Indiana's "Indian"-ness. Readers know that she was born in England and that her father traded in "the Indies" when she was a child (18). Certainly, some contemporaries did associate her with the Indian subcontinent, as Horejsi does.[66] It is equally possible, however, to associate her with the West Indies. Ashley L. Cohen has argued that eighteenth-century Britons understood the Atlantic and Indian Ocean worlds to be "deeply linked—so deeply, in fact, that they shared a common name: the Indies," and she calls on scholars studying the period to recognize the extent to which these areas "form[ed] a single unit of analysis" for many English people at the time.[67] For Steele, who was writing about the operations of the South Sea Company in the *Theatre* at the same time that he was completing *The Conscious Lovers*, any reference to the "Indies" would be as likely to call to mind the Atlantic slave-trading operations of the South Sea Company as it would the trade in consumer goods operated by the East India Company. Furthermore, beginning in 1705, Steele himself held financial interests in a complex of sugar plantations on the island of Barbados inherited through his first wife, property that he entangled in a complex series of mortgages, leases, and indentures before selling it in 1708; evidence suggests that it took him years afterwards to settle all the lawsuits related to this sale.[68] Steele therefore had personal experience with the plantation economy of the West Indies and with the ongoing abstraction and mystification of the trade in enslaved people as a series of financial transactions linking the personal, domestic economies of English citizens to the operations of international markets.

Seen in light of Britain's speculative trade with the West Indies, Indiana's repeated figuration as vulnerable to kidnapping and appropriation by various predatory men takes on a new significance. Her backstory, related by Bevil Junior, is as follows: Indiana was born to "an Eminent Merchant of Bristol" named Danvers who found himself ruined and "reduced to go privately to the *Indies*" when she was still an infant (18). Six years later, having rebuilt his fortune, he sent for Indiana and her mother, who embarked for the Indies accompanied by Danvers' sister Isabella. En route their ship was commandeered and the women kidnapped by French privateers, the shock of which led to Indiana's mother's death. The French captain took Indiana and Isabella into his home in France, and he and his English wife raised the orphaned Indiana "as his own adopted Daughter" (19). However, the captain himself died after several years, leaving his estate to his brother, who "coming soon to take Possession, there found (among his other Riches) this blooming Virgin, at his Mercy" (19). When Indiana refused both his advances and his threats, he resorted to charging her for the expense undertaken by his brother in raising her, taking "her little Fortune, as his own Inheritance" (19). He was in the process of dragging her to debtor's prison when Bevil Junior rescued her by paying her debt (19–20). Bevil Junior then brought her to England, where he set her up in a house and undertook to support her financially. This is the situation when the play begins.

As this story reveals, Indiana—despite her characteristic "Indian mantle"— has never lived outside of Europe. Her sense of foreignness accrues to her through the associations of her name and belongings and through the occupations of her two father figures, the merchant and the sea captain. Born to an Englishman with a French name, raised by a French privateer and his English wife, persecuted by a French lawyer, and rescued by an English gentleman, she has been passed from hand to hand among English and French men. Like South Sea or Mississippi stock, she is a domestically circulated pointer to colonial trade, identified with and tied to an overseas economy that she herself never touches.

This simultaneous association with and distance from the Indies allows Indiana to function as a counterpart to the stereotypical figure of the white creole woman—the woman of European descent born in or having spent much of her life in the Caribbean—featured in texts like *The Jamaica Lady* (1720).[69] The titular "Jamaica lady," Bavia, is a half-English, half-Scottish woman returning to England after several years in the West Indies. Like Indiana, Bavia is given a highly detailed and romanticized backstory that emphasizes her virtue, victimization, and dependence on the kindness of strangers as she moves around the Atlantic world.[70] Unlike Indiana, however, Bavia is exposed as a sexually transgressive and dangerous figure when her original history is revealed as a lie and is supplanted by one that portrays her as greedy, lasciviousness, and fraudulent.[71] While Indiana is reclaimed into English society through marriage, Bavia is eventually banished back to the Caribbean. Melissa K. Downes and Erin Mackie both read *The Jamaica Lady* as a reflection of the anxieties over colonialism, trade, and value raised by the South Sea scheme, and Bavia as a figure akin to Lady Credit—a reflection of broader cultural anxieties about the relationships between luxury, fraud, and monstrous feminine sexuality.[72] If, as Jennifer Donahue suggests, we read Indiana as a figure of the West Indian creole, her portrayal stands in marked opposition to that of a character like Bavia; indeed, Donahue argues that the representation of Indiana serves to counter audience fears of the "otherness" of white creoles and to argue for their reintegration into English society.[73] In creating a notably less threatening version of the creole woman type, Steele refutes the economic anxieties tied up in this figure, countering the notion that foreign trade is inherently unstable and dangerous. Instead, he uses the figure of Indiana to reframe the issue. What is problematic, according to Steele, is not the international trade conducted by entities like the South Sea Company; instead, the danger lies in the susceptibility of speculative financial ventures to manipulation by predatory forces, and the cooptation of middling-class interests by the elite. To make this point, Steele emphasizes Indiana's sexual vulnerability as he shifts the locus of audience suspicion from her to Bevil Junior.

Indiana's constant circulation highlights her vulnerability, as she is orphaned, kidnapped, and subjected to sexual, economic, and legal exploitation; even her eventual salvation happens entirely at the behest of a benevolent stranger. Her aunt, Isabella, reminds Indiana of this vulnerability and warns her to be wary of Bevil Junior's motivations in maintaining her. She raises the possibility that his seeming generosity is a scam, "all Skill and

Management" (27), designed to produce a sense of obligation and attachment that will make it easier for him to seduce her. Isabella warns:

> There are, among the Destroyers of Women, the Gentle, the Generous, the Mild, the Affable, the Humble, who all, soon after their Success in their Designs, turn to the contrary of those Characters. I will own to you, Mr. *Bevil* carries his Hypocrisie the best of any Man living, but still he is a Man, and therefore a Hypocrite. . . . Trust not those, who will think the worse of you for your Confidence in them. Serpents, who lie in wait for Doves. Won't you be on your Guard against those who would betray you? Won't you doubt those who would contemn you for believing 'em? Take it from me: Fair and natural Dealing is to invite Injuries, 'tis bleating to escape Wolves who would devour you! Such is the World. (29)

While Isabella turns out to be wrong about Bevil Junior's intentions, her advice seems prudent at this point given what the audience has already learned about Indiana's previous experience with the lawyer who attempted to coerce her sexually and stole her fortune. Indiana's association with the West Indies trade allows her story of vulnerability and exploitation to evoke the recent events of the South Sea Bubble and to suggest the precariousness of the joint-stock trading companies undergirding England's colonial trade—specifically, their troubling ability to blur the lines between the agendas of the landed and moneyed interests, between the wealthy and the emergent middling classes. It is worth remembering that Bevil Junior, who seems to embody Whiggish ideals of politeness, civility, and sentiment—who reads Addison to start his day—is actually a gentleman poised to inherit from his titled father. At this point in the play, his willingness to support the economic burden of a kept mistress with none of the usual sexual *quid pro quo* of such arrangements may well seem too good to be true; indeed, it so struck many contemporary critics of the play, who were likewise skeptical of Bevil Junior's degree of filial piety. Isabella's concern that Bevil Junior's generous, mannerly persona masks a calculating and rapacious villain parallels Steele's warning in the *Theatre* that middling-class values and hopes are ripe for cooptation and exploitation by the elite.

Eventually it becomes clear that Bevil Junior represents a younger generation of gentry who actively and wholeheartedly choose a new standard of behavior, distinct from the courtly aristocratic norms of previous eras. The play highlights this shift through its repeated invocations of generational conflict. The older characters often bemoan the degraded sensibilities of the younger generation, but dramatic irony consistently undermines their perspective. For example, even as he assesses Lucinda openly as potential breeding stock, Cimberton claims that "the young Women of this Age are treated with Discourses of such a Tendency, and their Imaginations so bewilder'd in Flesh and Blood, that a Man of Reason can't talk to be understood: They have no Ideas of Happiness, but what are more gross than the Gratification of Hunger and Thirst" (46). Yet Cimberton describes himself, not the current generation of young women; the play makes it clear that he is an exceedingly lascivious figure. In the final act Sealand attempts to catch Bevil Junior with Indiana, whom Sealand assumes is the younger man's kept woman. Upon meeting Indiana, Sealand declares: "I fear'd, indeed, an unwarranted Passion here, but I did not think it was in Abuse of so worthy an Object[,] . . . but the Youth of our Age care not what Merit and Virtue they bring to Shame, so they gratify—" (78–79). Indiana interrupts him before he can describe the baser impulses young people strive so ardently to satisfy, but the implication is clear. The youth are once again associated with superficial, material, and bodily impulses. However, the audience knows that Sealand is mistaken and that Bevil Junior has no such sexual relationship with Indiana. The dramatic irony of this moment undermines nostalgic narratives of generational difference and degeneration.[74]

The notion that the younger generation of the 1720s are more sensual and corrupt than their forebears is called into question not only implicitly by the moral fortitude of the play's exemplary young people but also explicitly in an exchange between Bevil Junior and Indiana about the opera. In act 2 Bevil Junior calls on Indiana at her lodgings, and we learn that he has bought her opera tickets. They discuss two characters from the opera, Crispo and Griselda, and they debate which is more sympathetic, suggesting that well-bred young people may be able to have edifying conversations about such entertainment. Yet Indiana finds something lacking, and she laments that "all the Pleasure the best Opera gives us, is but meer Sensation—Methinks it's Pity the Mind can't have a little more Share in the Entertainment.—The Musick's certainly fine; but, in my Thoughts, there's none of your Composers come up to Old *Shakespear* and *Otway*" (34). As we have seen, the older characters in the play view Bevil Junior and Indiana's generation as lewd and mindless, a stereotype that Indiana challenges when she declares her desire for intellectual rather than sensory stimulation. Yet she herself gives voice to the idea that newly fashionable entertainments are inferior to and degenerated from the products of earlier ages ("*Shakespear* and *Otway*"). Opera, like the projections of young people described by Sealand and Cimberton, cares only for appetite.

Throughout *The Conscious Lovers,* Steele exposes the destructive trends in modern life, including the appetitive bent of new entertainments like the opera and the vulnerability of foreign trade to cooptation by elite interests. However, he simultaneously suggests that the youth have the opportunity to be more civilized than previous generations, provided they embrace the values of the rising middling classes and ferret out efforts to deploy those values for hypocritical ends. The theater, like trade, is crucial to Steele's program for advancing British society, but both institutions must be carefully guarded against predatory, libidinal forces that hide behind false promises of easy stimulation and profit. Steele believed plays like *The Conscious Lovers* could enact the kinds of reform embodied by the virtuous Bevil Junior. Indeed, Steele positioned *The Conscious Lovers* explicitly as a new breed of sentimental comedy—one that, as Horejsi puts it, "fostered fellow-feeling, rather than ridicule."[75] In doing so, he placed it at the center of a public debate over the proper contours of the comedy genre.[76]

Yet some of his contemporaries, including John Dennis, turned Steele's own arguments against him in order to cast doubt on the sincerity of Steele's reformist agenda, suggesting that it was merely a ploy to stir up controversy and attract audiences. Steele's moralizing looked to Dennis like part of an aggressive marketing campaign conducted on multiple fronts, from ensuring that the play was puffed in prominent periodicals to drumming up excitement about its characters by introducing them in the *Theatre*. In *Remarks on a Play, Call'd, The Conscious Lovers* (1723), Dennis called Steele's advertising campaign a "double Cheat" played on the town's "Pockets, and upon their Understandings," echoing Steele's own remarks in *Theatre* 18 about the "nightly succession of bubbles" who enter the opera willing to "part with their cash, as well as their understanding."[77] The remark also echoes part 1 of *The Characters and Conduct of Sir John Edgar* (1720), a rebuke of the *Theatre* commonly attributed to Dennis. That pamphlet portrays Steele as a hypocrite who hides his obsession with profit behind the façade of morality and reform. Dennis asks rhetorically of Sir John Edgar (i.e., Steele):

> Have you really a Mind to throw off the Mask at last; and to own to the World, that all those plausible Words Religion, Honour, Conscience, Justice, Benificence, Innocence, with some *Nomenclators* mean one and the same Thing; and that is, private Interest? That they are with some Persons, nothing but a sort of a conjuring Cant; a kind of a *Hocus Pocus* Language; by virtue of which, he who uses them, does all his Tricks of *Legerdemain* without being discover'd, and calls the Money out from other People's Pockets into his own?[78]

In other words, Dennis suggests, Steele merely takes the stance of the moralist in order to distract others from his true goal: stealing their money. These responses to both the *Theatre* and *The Conscious Lovers* accuse Steele of attempting to exploit the masses in much the same way that Steele himself saw the South Sea Company and the Royal Academy of Music behaving.

Dennis's attacks on Steele are significant because they demonstrate the ease with which Steele's critiques of financial and theatrical institutions could be turned against him. They make it clear that the *Theatre* and *The Conscious Lovers* are not isolated theorizations of the ways that the public can fall prey to predatory individuals and institutions; these texts are, instead, forays into a wider attempt to understand the nature of those publics—how rationally or irrationally they behave and how passive or active they are in defining and defending their own interests. These critiques help us to see once again how Steele collapses the notion of a rational public with that of an active one; if the public were not so much in thrall to sensual pleasures, Steele contends, it would not be so easily manipulated by predatory forces and institutions. Dennis, however, shows how Steele himself uses the supposedly moral and rational pleasures offered by both his periodical journalism and his drama to construct a public from which he can profit, rendering the viewing and reading publics his passive subjects even as he supposedly aims to cultivate their powers of reason and morality.

In the act of turning Steele's own arguments against him, John Dennis opens up space to question the emergent ideal of rational-critical debate as the hallmark of the bourgeois public sphere and to ask whether the sensual pleasures lambasted by Steele are necessarily productive of a passive public that participates willingly in its own destruction. The next chapter will explore a similar set of problems raised in the publicity surrounding the 1721 premiere of Colley Cibber's play *The Refusal*, which made use of the South Sea Bubble to motivate its marriage plot. As Cibber was accused of plagiarism and his interactions with the changing literary economy were compared to the very deceitful financial practices on display in his play, he found his critiques of the financial sector and the investing public turned against him—as, we have seen, was the case with his colleague and ally Steele. The plasticity and versatility of these critiques help reveal how competing visions of the public sphere were set forth in the aftermath of the South Sea Bubble. Furthermore, the portrayal of Cibber as a plagiarist—an image that had haunted his entire writing career—gained intensity in this moment, as controversies over theatrical and literary property became central to wider debates about the ways publics related to and interacted with the financial and cultural institutions that sought to channel their energies.

• 5 •

"His Title, Not His Play, We Set to Sale"

Literary Property in the Aftermath of the South Sea Bubble

Chapter 4 examined how Richard Steele's 1722 play *The Conscious Lovers* implicitly reflected concerns about the South Sea Bubble that his 1720 periodical the *Theatre* expressed more explicitly. Because the play's topical engagement with the financial crisis was relatively subtle, however, it was able to endure as a repertory staple throughout the eighteenth century. Other plays and entertainments that premiered during and immediately after the South Sea affair took on current events more directly. From 1720 to 1723 London's papers were full of advertisements for stage and fairground performances of songs and farces with names like *Four and Twenty Stock-Jobbers*, *The Broken Stock-Jobbers*, and *The Chimera; or, An Hue and Cry to Change Alley*.[1] Colley Cibber's comedy *The Refusal; or, The Ladies Philosophy* (1721), which premiered eight months after the *Theatre* ended its print run and a year and a half before *The Conscious Lovers* debuted, struck a middle ground between topical satire and evergreen comedy. It did so by presenting a standard courtship plot with an innovative twist: the young lovers' fates are tied up in an exchange of South Sea Company stock.

Cibber's play takes up several of the same concerns seen in Steele's work from the same period, theorizing the relationship between changing class structures, speculative investment, and public opinion. As associates in the management of the Theatre Royal in Drury Lane during this period, Steele and Cibber drew similar connections in their plays between financial and cultural markets, and they have often been seen as partners in their advancement of the economic interests and morally reformist tendencies of the emergent middling classes. This chapter exposes not only the similarities but also the key differences between their perspectives on the South Sea crisis. In doing so, it emphasizes the richness and heterogeneity of viewpoints that were able to flourish in the theater-finance nexus, a space that promoted debate even among relatively like-minded individuals.

In the first section I trace the two competing viewpoints *The Refusal* offers on the financial activities of fictional South Sea Company director Sir Gilbert Wrangle: on the one hand he openly practices market manipulation, yet on the other he makes compelling speeches about the ascendance of the moneyed interest in England. Most critics have understood Sir Gilbert as a character cut from the same cloth as Mr. Sealand in *The Conscious Lovers*, a straightforward mouthpiece for the rising trading classes at the center of the Whig ideological program. This common interpretation of Sir Gilbert sits uneasily, however, with *The Refusal*'s clear critique of the South Sea scheme, in which he is strongly implicated. I reconcile this tension by arguing that Sir Gilbert, far from being a "merchant hero" (as some would have it), in fact figures the ways that the financial elite have harnessed the optimism of the masses for their own purposes. In this sense, Sir Gilbert embodies the fears Steele expresses in the *Theatre* about the machinations of South Sea Company and Royal Academy directors.

However, Sir Gilbert's story interacts with the play's larger marriage plot to produce a more complex portrait of London society during the Bubble, implicating the wider public in the cultivation of an atmosphere of cutthroat competition and wild speculation that allowed elites' predatory schemes to take hold. The second section of this chapter explores how this critique emerges through *The Refusal*'s marriage plot, which uses the changing landscape of courtship to reflect on issues of tangible and intangible property, exploitation, and deception and to explore how the changing norms of market society affect familiar cultural forms. Harnessing the ire spectators might initially aim at Sir Gilbert, Cibber turns the satirical lens back on his audiences, showing the wider theatrical and investing publics to be complicit in the manipulative, competitive practices that spread from the realm of finance into other arenas of social interaction, including courtship. While Steele imagines the London public as passive victims of the South Sea Company and unthinking dupes of the Royal Academy of Music—a mindless multitude caught up in spectacle and speculation—Cibber figures the public as more active and savvy and therefore more to blame for the increasing rapacity of England's economic landscape.

Given his nuanced presentation of London society's participation in its own exploitation by the South Sea Company, it is both fitting and ironic that Cibber himself came under fire for his own relationship to the theatrical market, a relationship that his critics charged was predatory in precisely the same ways as the South Sea scheme. In the third section of this chapter, I trace the relationship of *The Refusal* to its sources and detail how Cibber's adaptation practices were maligned in the publicity for and reception of the play. Advertisements and editorial content in London's newspapers and periodicals aligned Cibber with the South Sea Company, suggesting that he too was fabricating value by placing a new name on old dramatic materials. Cibber found himself under fire from publisher Edmund Curll, just as Steele's advertising campaign for *The Conscious Lovers* allowed him to be cast by John Dennis as a market manipulator operating along the same lines as the fraudulent enterprises he decried. Curll's attacks on Cibber built a web of connections among the South Sea scheme, the business of stage adaptation, and the cutthroat world of publishing. Reading these attacks in light of the play's own financial themes sheds light on the broader conceptual problems of intangible property, speculative markets, and the abstraction of value being debated at the theater-finance nexus in the wake of the South Sea Bubble.

In returning to Cibber—whose first play, *Love's Last Shift* (1696), was the subject of chapter 1—this final chapter aims to register important changes in the conceptual interplay of theatrical and financial markets from the 1690s to the 1720s. Just as *Love's Last Shift* used the recoinage crisis to figure the changing aesthetic and ideological stakes of dramatic comedy, *The Refusal* is set in the midst of a financial crisis that reflects metadramatically on the market conditions in which the play itself was produced and received. *Love's Last Shift* reveled in its reworking of stock character types and plots, foregrounding the interplay between familiarity and novelty as a pleasure central to both the instruments of emergent financial capitalism and the repertory theater. In the epilogue to *Love's Last Shift*, as in many of the prologues and epilogues of the 1690s examined in chapter 2, the playwright was figured as a speculator trading in risky investments, bringing a newly entrepreneurial spirit to the endeavor of creating entertainment for an audience that increasingly demanded new forms of innovation and spectacle. By the 1720s, in the wake of the South Sea Bubble, new ethical concerns arose around the trade of speculative property. Adapting the repertory "stock," like trading in the stock of a flotation company, raised questions about the valuation of intangible property. The processes of abstraction at work in both theatrical and financial markets made it harder to tell whose labor had generated a commodity's value, opening up a gap that could allow individuals to wrongly profit from one another's work. In this light the playwright may be viewed less like a bold entrepreneur and more like an unscrupulous speculator, generating unwarranted excitement about supposedly new and exciting products that are in fact appropriations of others' labor. In such a system, the play asks, what kind of transparency is owed to the public, and what responsibility does that public have to recognize and resist these market mystifications?

The Refusal's South Sea Villain

The Refusal debuted in February 1721, six months after the collapse of the South Sea Bubble, and it transported its first audiences to the previous summer—the final and most feverish phase of speculation. The prologue, spoken by Cibber himself during the play's first run, promises the audience that the comedy will enact a kind of revenge on play's fictional company director, Sir Gilbert Wrangle: "[O]ur Muse's Fire (but pray protect her) / Roasts, to your Taste, a whole *South-Sea* Director."[2] This vengeful fantasy is quickly complicated, however, as Cibber tempers his promise of a public "roasting" of Sir Gilbert:

> Besides, he's painted here in Height of Power,
> Long e'er we laid such Ruin at his Door:
> When he was Levee'd, like a Statesman, by the Town,
> And thought his heap'd up Millions all his own.
> No, no; Stock's always at a Thousand here,
> He'll almost honest on the Stage appear. (iv, lines 24–29)

These lines chronicle Sir Gilbert's loss of influence, esteem, and wealth in terms that are simultaneously sincere and ironic, emphasizing that his money was never "his own" and that his power was a mere simulacrum, his "levees" a spectacle without substance. The prologue promises a similarly conflicted portrait in the play itself: since Sir Gilbert will be shown at the "Height of Power" in the months before the crash, he will appear "almost honest," frozen in the moment before his crimes are revealed. To make Sir Gilbert appear truly honest, it is implied, is beyond even the representational and imaginative power of the stage. The prologue thus prepares its audience to experience a kind of time travel that may induce a nostalgic admiration for the fantasy of what Sir Gilbert represents ("Stock's always at a Thousand here"), while equipping viewers to remain vigilant and skeptical. It also registers the rise and fall of fortunes as the ordinary, albeit calamitous, course of things—the perpetual crisis of life under emerging financial capitalism. These lines thus establish the crucial dynamic of hindsight that enables the play's simultaneous critique of the South Sea Company and its chastening of gulled investors.[3]

The play repeatedly and insistently stages Sir Gilbert's corruption, highlighting the instability of speculative market dynamics and their vulnerability to manipulation. Sir Gilbert takes bribes and arbitrarily strikes out the names of investors to make room for his friends on the subscriber lists; he even fills one such list with the names of the dead to create the artificial impression that company stocks are in high demand (10–11, 65). In the play's final scene, he admonishes his family and friends to sell their stock, a moment of insider trading that reveals his full knowledge that he has been perpetrating a scam: "And now you are part of my Family, Gentlemen, I'll tell you a Secret that concerns your Fortunes—Hark you—in one word—sell—sell out as fast as you can: for (among friends) the Game's up—ask no Questions—but, I tell you, the Jest is over—but Money down! (d'ye observe me) Money down! don't meddle for Time: for the Time's a coming, when those that buy will not be able to pay; and so the Devil take the hindmost, and Heaven bless you all together" (85). This passage makes clear that Sir Gilbert recognizes the chain-letter structure of the South Sea investment scheme, in which money from later investors is used to pay dividends to earlier investors out of the company's capital rather than from its nonexistent profits. The phrase "Devil take the hindmost" echoes Steele's epigraph to *Theatre* 27, the unattributed quotation from Horace translated as "MURRAIN take the hindmost" that follows pages of calculations demonstrating the fraudulence and unsustainability of the South Sea scheme.[4] Cibber's glancing reference to the *Theatre* links his own representation of a South Sea director to Steele's more explicit criticisms of the scheme and reinforces the company's willingness to sacrifice late-coming investors to those who had the foresight to get in early on the scam. In this moment the play offers a final unflinching look at Sir Gilbert's corruption, dismantling the "almost honest" appearance promised by the prologue.

The end of the play, the epilogue, following close on Sir Gilbert's final revelations, delivers a sharper rebuke to the company directors. The play's satire is once again linked to its temporal remove, and the audience's indulgence in this nostalgic fantasy morphs into a form of willful ignorance:

> Forgive the Muse then, if her Scenes were laid
> Before your fair Possessions were betray'd;
> She took the fitting Form, as Fame then ran,
> While a *Director* seem'd an honest Man:
> But were she from his present Form to take him,
> What a huge Gorging Monster must she make him?
> How would his Paunch with Golden Ruin swell?
> Whole Families devouring at a Meal? (vi–vii, lines 13–20)

This passage explicitly calls out as an illusion the notion that Sir Gilbert could "seem ... honest." Whereas the prologue ambiguously alluded to the "Ruin" for which the audience blamed directors like Sir Gilbert—evading the question of whether that blame was assigned justly—this epilogue unequivocally laments the "ruin" of the British people. No longer sympathetic to the downfall of the once-wealthy directors, as the prologue was, the epilogue imagines the leaders of the South Sea Company as monsters fattening themselves on the destruction of others. Not only do they consume families, but this "Goosequill Race of Rulers" bows the "Warlike Britons" as a people, threatening the very foundations of English fiscal-military might (vi, lines 6–7). The epilogue ends by bidding the honest audience members to "Enjoy the Muses Vengeance" offered by the play, effectively delivering the public punishment that the prologue attempted to defer (vii, line 38). The difference between the prologue's and epilogue's judgments of Sir Gilbert stages the temporal experience of speculation—the deferral of assessments of value into the future, at which time those values are experienced as absolute, their past indeterminacy all but forgotten. In doing so it reminds audiences of the contingency and instability of value, undermining any sense that individuals or commodities have a clearly discernible intrinsic worth.

Attention to the framing prologue and epilogue makes it clear that Sir Gilbert is a corrupted figure designed to evoke complex and shifting responses from the audience over the course of the play. Yet critics have tended to see him as a straightforward affirmation of the promarket values of Walpole's ministry and his Whig faction. Isaac Kramnick, for example, calls Sir Gilbert the "merchant hero" of the play, positioning him a figure who confirms, victoriously, "the worst fears of Bolingbroke and his group"—that the "age of gentlemen" has been replaced by an era in which moneyed interests rather than landed aristocrats hold sway over king and Parliament.[5] As evidence Kramnick cites one of Sir Gilbert's most extended commentaries on the state of finance and politics in London:

> You'll find 'tis not your Court, but City-Politicians must do the Nation's Business at last. Why, what did your Courtiers do all the two last Reigns, but borrow Money to make War? and make War to make Peace, and make Peace to make War? And then to be Bullies in one, and Bubbles in t'other? A very pretty Account truly; but we have made Money, Man: Money! Money! there's the Health, and Life-Blood of a Government: And therefore I insist upon't, that we are the wisest Citizens in *Europe*; for we have coin'd more Cash in an Hour, than the Tower of *London* in twenty Years. (42)

In this speech Sir Gilbert does indeed give voice to the most extreme views of the moneyed interest: he portrays the landed wealth of the aristocracy as a fading source of power and fantasizes that the emergent financial classes are capable of producing value out of thin air. His emphasis on the ready availability of new funds would have reinforced the landed interest's fear that the basis of the new war economy—credit-based and speculative financial instruments—was too ephemeral to provide a firm basis for the nation's finances. However, the notion that Cibber is straightforwardly approving of Sir Gilbert's extreme views—or even that we are meant to see Sir Gilbert's own actions as affirming his stated values—comes not from the play but from an *a priori* assumption of Cibber's status as propagandist for the Whig party and the moneyed interests with which it was aligned. Colin Nicholson, for instance, calls Cibber "Walpole's laureate and cultural paradigm of market morality"; Loftis likewise calls *The Refusal* and *The Conscious Lovers* "the most distinctly Whiggish comedies" of their era.[6] Viewing *The Refusal* as a "Whiggish" play in this sense relies on a view of Sir Gilbert as an overall positive figure, a view that ignores the play's crucial conclusion and epilogue; it also depends on the sincerity of speeches like the one quoted by Kramnick. Yet Sir Gilbert's appearances throughout the play give audiences ample reason to be skeptical of his promarket rhetoric.

The tension between Sir Gilbert's words and deeds is on prominent display in the discussion of honor, credit, and titles that takes place in act 3. Speaking to the young lover Frankly, Sir Gilbert defends his decision to honor a rather unorthodox contract that obliges him to give consent to a suitor he would not normally permit to court his daughter Charlotte. Sir Gilbert explains that he must honor his contracts in order to maintain his credit among other traders: "[W]e Citizens are as tender of our Credit in *Change-Alley*, as you fine Gentlemen are of your Honour at Court" (42). Frankly rejects this alignment with the values of the court, and he expresses a preference for credit as a barometer of a man's worth because it must be earned through continual performances of honesty, whereas honor is conferred as a privilege of high birth. Frankly reframes "honour" as a synonym for the honesty available to every citizen, stating that it is the "Privilege of a private Subject" to be "believ'd upon your Honour, or trusted upon your Word." Sir Gilbert likewise exclaims, "Honour's a Joke! Is not every honest Man a Man of Honour?" leaving Frankly to deliver the punch line: "Ay, but the best Joke is, that every Man of Honour is not an honest Man, Sir" (43). This exchange pits an ideal of honor, one defined by character, against the reality in which honor accrues automatically to those from powerful families.

Frankly, a witty young man and a largely positive figure in the play, appears here to agree with Sir Gilbert, an ambivalent figure at best; both men align themselves with the Whiggish position that credit and honesty are more important than birth. Yet their seeming agreement is complicated by their discussion of titles and by an exchange earlier in the play. Sir Gilbert approves of Frankly's disdain for traditional, class-based notions of honor, stating: "I see you know the World, you judge of Men by their intrinsick Value; and you're right! you're right! Titles are empty things: A wise Man will always be a wise Man, whether he has any Title or no" (42). The phrase "intrinsick Value," often linked to bullionism and offered in opposition to the kind of ephemeral or artificial value produced by credit instruments, links the valuation of individuals to the operations of the financial markets. At this point in the play, however, it has been established that Sir Gilbert himself is deeply involved in a scheme to fabricate riches, so the phrase "intrinsick Value" alerts the audience to the hypocritical disjunction between his disdain for titles as "empty" signifiers of worth and his own attempts to inflate his personal credit through dishonest manipulations of stock values that represent nonexistent wealth.

The irony of this exchange is deepened if the audience recalls an earlier conversation between Frankly and his friend Granger, in which it was established that Sir Gilbert's aversion to the nobility stems from his bitterness at having failed to purchase a title. When Granger remarks approvingly that Sir Gilbert is "no blind Admirer of a Man of Quality," Frankly explains that he "had lately a mind to be made a Lord himself: but applying to the wrong Person, it seems, he was disappointed; and ever since piques himself upon despising any Nobleman, who is not as rich as himself" (7). Sir Gilbert shuns titles not because of a deep-seated belief in their meaninglessness, but because he has been unable to buy one for himself. Granger mockingly approves, ironically calling Sir Gilbert "the right *Plebian* Spirit of *Old-England*" (7). In doing so he ridicules the false and self-serving bravado of traders like Sir Gilbert, who position themselves as advocates of a new world order only until they can successfully ensconce themselves among the elite. Finally, Granger suggests that Sir Gilbert is "counted an honest Man" despite his evident hypocrisy and foolishness. Frankly responds by damning with faint praise: "Umh! yes! well enough—a good sort of a mercantile Conscience; he is punctual in Bargains, and expects the same from others: he will neither steal, nor cheat, unless he thinks he has the Protection of the Law: then indeed, as most thriving Men do, he thinks Honour and Equity are chimerical Notions" (7). Here, Sir Gilbert's "mercantile Conscience" is revealed to center around a desire to appear honest rather than to be honest. This time, Granger gets to deliver the final blow: "That is, he bluntly professes what other People practice with more Breeding" (7). Granger's assessment collapses the perceived distinction between the landed elite and the moneyed elite replacing them. The only difference between Sir Gilbert and his social betters is that he "bluntly professes" a skepticism towards the middling-class ideal of honor that remains unstated among the nobility.

The play's recurrent concern with the definition of honor echoes *Theatre* 16, which offers a portrait of the "Man of Honour" defined by "conscious Integrity" rather than "Distinctions, Titles or Appellations." Like Cibber, Steele highlights the conceptual link between monetary and individual value, drawing out the tension between intrinsic worth and potentially empty signification: "The common Simile between Money coined, and a Man ennobled, is very just; and it is the Matter of the Metal, and not the Impression upon it, which gives it its true Value."[7] While Sir Gilbert directly mirrors Steele's sentiments, however, he is not the paragon of mercantile honor he pretends to be. In Steele's estimation, the ideal member of the new merchant aristocracy is one who "does Business with the Candour of a Gentleman, and performs his Engagements with the Exactness of a Citizen."[8] Sir Gilbert, in contrast, is manifestly dishonest and self-serving. His "mercantile Conscience" extends only so far as it preserves the appearance of honesty that directly affects his credit and therefore his ability to do business. Sir Gilbert thus represents the ability of unscrupulous and self-serving people at all levels of society to exploit Whig values for their own benefit. His identification with the South Sea Company further suggests that the company only appears to suit the aims of merchants and others trying to rise in society, while in fact preying on their hopes of mobility to benefit the privileged few. The fact that critics have taken Sir Gilbert at his word merely reinforces how easily the rhetoric of the moneyed interests could be adapted to support schemes that did not ultimately benefit most middling-class people.

While my reading complicates the conventional view of *The Refusal* as a piece of straightforward promarket propaganda, it is perfectly in keeping with the fact that the South Sea Company was a Tory company and that the effort to mitigate the damage from the crash was spearheaded by Robert Walpole, with whose Whig faction Cibber was closely aligned. As chapter 3 showed, some Whigs, like Susanna Centlivre, viewed the company's directors as Tory partisans attempting to harness the powers of new and predominantly Whig-led financial markets for their own party. Although the company drew investors from across the political spectrum—including both Walpole and Cibber—it was viewed in hindsight as a Tory effort to undermine the financial sector and public credit.[9] Taking this historical context into account, it becomes clear that Sir Gilbert is not meant to be a true embodiment of Whig ideals; rather, he is a vehicle for Cibber's critique of the ways that elites and would-be elites have turned the financial optimism of the masses to their own benefit.

In the character of Sir Gilbert, Cibber updated and combined well-known stage types. His representation as a threatening, conniving economic upstart resembles that of Sir Giles Overreach in Philip Massinger's *A New Way to Pay Old Debts* (c. 1625, 1633). His eagerness to buy a title is reminiscent of the bungling knights Jack Daw and LaFoole in Ben Jonson's *Epicœne* (1609, 1616), which satirizes the transformation of social status into a saleable commodity. Sir Gilbert's character also incorporates elements of the "cit" stereotype of early seventeenth-century city comedies and their

Restoration descendants. The crass and gullible citizen in these plays, typically a tradesman or merchant, is outwitted—and often cuckolded—by more refined aristocratic men over the course of the play. As Mark S. Dawson points out, the cit type gradually morphed in this period from a local London merchant to an international speculative investor; while the seventeenth-century cit had represented the intrusion of new commercial motives and practices on traditional social norms, Dawson argues, the eighteenth-century cit posed a threat because his allegiance to the trade and government of the City was only nominal, a front for "self-interested speculation that diverted capital from honest trade and, therefore, the public interest."[10] As the next section will show, however, Cibber's reworking of familiar dramatic materials does more than echo traditional critiques of individualism, greed, and hypocrisy; his play also chastens investors who fell for the South Sea scam. Through a highly self-aware interrogation of the mechanisms of the marriage plot under the newly speculative economic order, Cibber invites audience members to consider how they, too, engaged in competitive and predatory behavior during the height of South Sea fever.

"Is Marriage a Bubble Too?"

In act 1 of *The Refusal*, Granger utters one of the play's central questions: "[I]s Marriage a Bubble too?" (13). Granger's incredulous aside is a response to Sir Gilbert's assertion that South Sea stock prices have risen so high that he will have to allow a coxcomb to marry one of his daughters. The explanation for this unlikely situation brings together the seemingly unconnected stock and marriage markets in material ways, while also allowing Cibber to explore their more intangible connections. If marriage operates under the conditions of speculative finance, the play suggests, it is vulnerable to the same kind of corrupt self-interest that plagued the South Sea scheme.

The audience learns early in the play that Sir Gilbert's eldest daughter Sophronia, a pretender to learning and disdainer of men's authority, has sworn never to marry. Naturally, her aloofness excites the young gallant Granger, who is drawn to the thrill of conquest as much as to the convenience of marriage. Granger's friend Frankly, meanwhile, pursues the younger daughter Charlotte, who has a more limited education and a more appealing disposition than her haughty sister. The play's conventional courtship plot is complicated, however, by a financial deal Sir Gilbert has struck with Witling, an obnoxious beau recently enriched by his South Sea investments.[11] In essence Sir Gilbert has sold his right of consent for his daughters' hands in marriage as part of a bet loosely formalized as a stock transaction. The details of the deal unfold gradually over the course of the play. When South Sea shares were valued at £200, Sir Gilbert and others mocked Witling for purchasing high-priced refusals, also known as calls—essentially, time bargains in which the purchaser pays a premium for the right to buy or refuse stock at a given price on a future date.[12] Witling, seeking to defend his pride, offered a different sort of time bargain to Sir Gilbert; as Frankly explains to Charlotte: "He told an Hundred Guineas into your Father's hand; in consideration of which, (if *Witling* could prove himself worth Fifty Thousand Pound within the Year, and the *South-Sea* Stock should in that time mount to a Thousand *per Cent.* why then, and on those Conditions only) your Father was to give him the Refusal of you, or your Sister, in Marriage" (37). In the play's present (late summer 1720), Witling's net worth is £100,000 and the South Sea stock is at its high-water mark of £1,000 per share, so he issues his formal call for Charlotte's hand (17). If Sir Gilbert honors the deal, he must also settle a considerable fortune on Charlotte; having invested her portion of £3,000 in South Sea stocks when they were around par (£100), their value has now inflated ten times to £30,000 (18). If, however, Sir Gilbert reneges on the contract, he must pay a penalty to compensate Witling for the loss of Charlotte's dowry (37–38, 82).

The deal has a loophole, of course: as Frankly asks pointedly, "[H]as not the Lady herself a Right of Refusal?" (18). It turns out that Sir Gilbert has not voided his daughter's right to refuse a suitor. If she denies Witling, her father pays no penalty. He may not, however, give his consent to another suitor for the term of the contract, which is valid for another six months (38). Charlotte and Frankly, eager to marry immediately, conspire with Sir Gilbert to cozen Witling out of his contract entirely; by making him believe Charlotte loves him, they convince him to give up the contract simply to prove that she is marrying him of her own free choice. Once the contract is voided, she marries Frankly instead.

The play puns insistently on "refusal," drawing attention to the term's dual meaning: a type of time bargain struck between the investors as well as the traditional right of women to reject a suitor chosen by their parents. At the end of the play, when Witling has been duped, Frankly gloats: "No, no, my dear *Billy*, thou art no Loser at all; for you have made your

Call, you see—and now have fairly had your Refusal too." Even Witling must acknowledge that it is a good joke, admitting, "Ha! ha! that's pleasantly said however, I-gad! I can't help laughing at a good thing though, tho' I am half ready to hang myself" (84). By highlighting the term's duality, the play links the workings of new financial instruments to long-standing operations of the marriage market, revealing how the changing dynamics of high finance affect people at all levels of society. This moment points to the comedy's larger investigation of how the economics of marriage are shifting in connection with the new culture of speculative investment, as material property is rapidly replaced by immaterial, imaginative possessions—as, for example, in the case of Charlotte's dowry, the value of which has inflated by a factor of ten in less than a year.

These economic questions are foregrounded in a debate between Granger and Frankly over the nature of marriage. Frankly sees it as a companionate relationship, whereas Granger considers it an economic arrangement. Granger muses on men's inexplicable boredom with their wives: "[T]he grossest Fools have generally Sense enough to be fond of a fine House, or a good Horse, when they have bought them: They can see the Value of them, at least; and why a poor Wife should not have as fair play for one's Inclination, I can see no Reason" (2). Appalled, Frankly responds: "But what! would you have a Wife have no more Charms than a Chariot?" (2). Frankly criticizes Granger's figuration of a wife as a material possession to be valued as part of a landed gentleman's estate, highlighting the contrast between Frankly's ideal of companionate marriage and Granger's jaded view of it as financial transaction.

Yet even Granger's dispassionate view of marriage turns out to be overly idealized. Over the course of the play women's value becomes harder to fix than that of a horse or a house, and marriage is revealed to operate more like speculative financial markets than the comparatively stable market in real estate. When Charlotte stages a faux rejection of Frankly for Witling's benefit, the former plays the scorned lover: "[S]ince I find your Heart is like Stock, to be transfer'd upon a Bargain, it will be some pleasure, at least, to see the Grossness of your Choice revenge me on your Infidelity" (60). Witling extends the analogy between Charlotte's graces and stock when he requests her hand in marriage, asking: "[A]re not you willing, (as soon as the Church-Books can be open) to make a Transfer of your whole Stock of Beauty, for the conjugal Uses of your humble Servant?" (64). The allusion to the "Church-Books" is a playful reference to the South Sea Company's transfer books, which were closed for several weeks at midsummer 1720 while the company paid out dividends, halting legal transfers of stock and pushing trade in South Sea shares to the secondary market in subscriptions. The fact that the books were closed meant that all quotes at the height of the Bubble were what were known as forward prices; in other words, South Sea subscriptions were trading at the prices that shares were anticipated to command at the upcoming opening of the books, rather than at the (lower) prices they had commanded when the books were closed. This temporal displacement may have contributed to the feverish trading taking place in July 1720, when there were no daily price reports to act as a tether for speculation. The analogy thus invites the audience to think about whether Charlotte's "Stock of Beauty" is inflated by the excitement of the transaction itself—the thrill of winning a bet at the expense of another investor—rather than a realistic assessment of the commodity at the root of the transaction.

Together, these moments suggest that marriage, like the South Sea scheme, is a speculative market in which value has become abstracted from the material world; in both cases market movements reflect the public's taste for competition and gambling rather than the intrinsic value of the goods being exchanged. This spirit is nowhere more clearly represented than when Granger, having successfully wooed the resistant Sophronia, gloats: "[T]ill I was victorious, I knew not half the Value of my Conquest" (79). The play's marriage plot provides an analogy to the South Sea mania, showing how the mechanisms of social and economic exchange in London life are increasingly based on the thrill of competition and the excitement of risk taking rather than on a sober-minded assessment of value. Here, Cibber appears to share Steele's concern with the irrationality of the investing public, although he attributes it less to a weakness for sensory pleasures and more to a drive towards one-upmanship.

The play's temporal displacement further reinforces the notion that investors behave in ways that defy reason. Cibber uses dramatic irony to highlight portents of the South Sea Company's inevitable failure that were overlooked by the public. For instance, the play's characters are aware of the recent collapse of the French Mississippi scheme, which in the audience's hindsight is a clear pattern of the fate awaiting the similarly structured South Sea scheme. Sir Gilbert asks Granger, who has just returned from Paris, "[H]ow goes *Mississippi*, Man? What! do they bring their Money by

Waggon-Loads to Market still? Hay! Hah! hah! hah!" Sir Gilbert's laughter suggests that he already knows how Granger will reply: "O! all gone, good for nothing, Sir, your *South-Sea* has brought it to waste Paper" (8). Granger attributes the failure of the Mississippi scheme to market contagion: investors losing confidence in the French project have moved their money to the more promising South Sea Company. Yet the audience knows that the characters should be able to draw the connection between the two speculative bubbles. This moment implies that Londoners ignored the signs of the South Sea scheme's instability and that their investment behavior was therefore irrational. In making this suggestion, the play distributes blame for the crash: while the portrait of Sir Gilbert dramatizes the ways that some investors were hoodwinked by dishonest directors, the marriage plot highlights how other individuals were carried away by the desire to make a better bet than their neighbors. The interaction between these two plots complicates the formulation seen in texts like Steele's *Theatre* that equate irrational investment behavior with passivity and vulnerability. Cibber shows how investors could become active and witting participants in a senseless scheme, caught up in a broader culture of competition and exploitation that led them to hope they could turn the odds in their own favor. The next section will show how the reception of *The Refusal* reinforced the play's sense of Londoners' reciprocal blame for the South Sea affair and for the more predatory social dynamics the scheme reflected.

Adaptation or Fraud?

As I have argued, Cibber's reworking of familiar English dramatic types and plot elements is central to his critique of the South Sea scheme and his investigation of its implications for British culture more broadly. In addition, *The Refusal* owes a debt to a French source, Molière's *Les Femmes Savantes* (1672), from which Cibber takes his satire of educated women obsessed with classical learning and Neoplatonic ideals of love. Cibber was not the only writer of his day to adapt Molière's play: Thomas Wright had revised it as *The Female Vertuoso's* in 1693, and Centlivre had responded with *The Platonick Lady* in 1707.[13] However, a series of events in 1721 made Cibber's borrowing a topic of controversy. The contours of this controversy offer an intriguing case study in shifting conceptions of literary property in the 1720s. As Adrian Johns argues, literary piracy was associated in early eighteenth-century London with financial malfeasance, and both sets of behaviors were understood within a constellation of practices that subverted the philosophical and moral foundations of the Revolution Settlement: "If the Whig defense of 1688 rested on the principle of property—as it largely did—then piracy, like stock-jobbing, represented the weakness, amorality, ambition, and transgression that came with it."[14] At this conceptual intersection *The Refusal*'s South Sea subject matter allowed it to act as a locus for thinking about the relationship between speculative financial markets and the changing conditions of the literary marketplace.

Evidence suggests that audiences—which were reportedly quite hostile during the play's respectable, if unimpressive, six-night premiere—would have been aware of *The Refusal*'s debt to a number of sources, and they may even have considered it plagiarism.[15] In early January 1721, a month before *The Refusal*'s debut, Lincoln's Inn Fields had mounted a play by John Gay titled *No Fools Like Wits*. Although Gay's play does not survive, it was probably a revision of Wright's *The Female Vertuoso's*, mentioned above as an adaptation of *Les Femmes Savantes*. Gay likely knew about Cibber's newest play from press reports that it was then in rehearsal at Drury Lane, and he used *No Fools* to undercut the competition. According to theater historian Rodney L. Hayley, "His revision of Thomas Wright's old play, with its similar plot to Cibber's, was no doubt intended to expose Cibber as a plagiarist."[16] Bookseller and notorious pirate Edmund Curll, always ready to stoke the fires of literary rivalries if doing so would turn a profit, quickly became involved. Curll placed advertisements for a new book being sold in his shop, titled *No Fools Like Wits; or, The Female Virtuosoes*.[17] This play was attributed on the title page to Wright rather than Gay, but it bore the subtitle, "As It Was Acted at the Theatre in Lincolns-Inn-Fields," clearly linking it to Gay's adaptation. This edition was, in fact, entirely Wright's play. It was virtually identical to the first edition (1693), having the same number of pages, the same dedication, the same prologue, and the same layout. Other than the allusion to the recent performance in the title, it made no effort to represent Gay's alterations.[18] In reprinting Wright's play under the title of Gay's new version, Curll preempted Gay's attempt to accuse Cibber of plagiarism, instead positioning Gay himself as the thief.

This is not to say, however, that Curll was in any way attempting to protect Cibber from the rival house's attacks. After *The Refusal* debuted, Curll issued a new edition of *No Fools*. While the work was still attributed to Wright, it now bore the absurdly lengthy title *No Fools like Wits; or, The Female Vertuosoes. A Comedy. As It Was Acted at the Theatre in Lincolns-Inn-Fields. Or, The Refusal: or, The Ladies Philosophy. As it is Acted at the Theatre Royal in Drury-Lane.* This new book, advertised as the second edition of the earlier version, actually bore a new layout and additional prefatory materials. It featured a dedication in which Curll detailed Cibber's borrowing, including the elements he had taken from Molière, whose *Femmes Savantes* is not included in the omnibus title but has a clear presence in Curll's paratext. The epigraph, for instance, specifically mentions "Moliere's Sense," and the dedication admits that Cibber does Molière more justice than another, unnamed "reviver" (an ambiguous reference to either Wright or Gay) by using all of the characters instead of blending and condensing the cast. To reinforce the point, Curll juxtaposes the cast list from Wright's play with the "Cibberized" cast list, inviting and facilitating comparison between the play he prints and the version some readers may have seen on stage. Curll's publishing antics may account for the delayed release of Cibber's octavo, which had certainly lost its topicality by the time it was finally printed in November 1721.[19]

In his dedication, Curll mocks one unique element of the "Cibberized" play: "[Y]our bringing a *South-Sea Director* into an honest Family, is like grafting a *Crab* upon a *Pippin*."[20] Even Curll had to admit the originality of Cibber's South Sea subplot, which distinguished it from the versions by Molière, Wright, and Gay. Yet critics have long tended to see the play's setting at the height of the Bubble as incidental or superficial. Leonard R. N. Ashley, for instance, claims that "Cibber cashed in on the South Sea craze" with *The Refusal*, a reading that reduces the subplot to mere opportunism.[21] However, the advertisements around *The Refusal*'s performance, as well as the advertisements associated with Curll's manufactured controversy, reveal the importance of the South Sea connection and its conceptual significance for contemporaries. While Cibber used his South Sea subplot to highlight the company directors' dishonesty and to reveal the public's complicity in a wider culture of competitive, predatory, and risky behavior, Curll and the periodical press turned the tables on Cibber, suggesting that he himself had fraudulently manufactured value by appropriating others' property.

An advertisement in the *Daily Journal* for January 24, 1721, provides an initial illustration of how closely financial and theatrical news items were connected in the periodicals of the time (fig. 4). The excerpt contains four paragraphs: two news stories concerning developments in the investigation

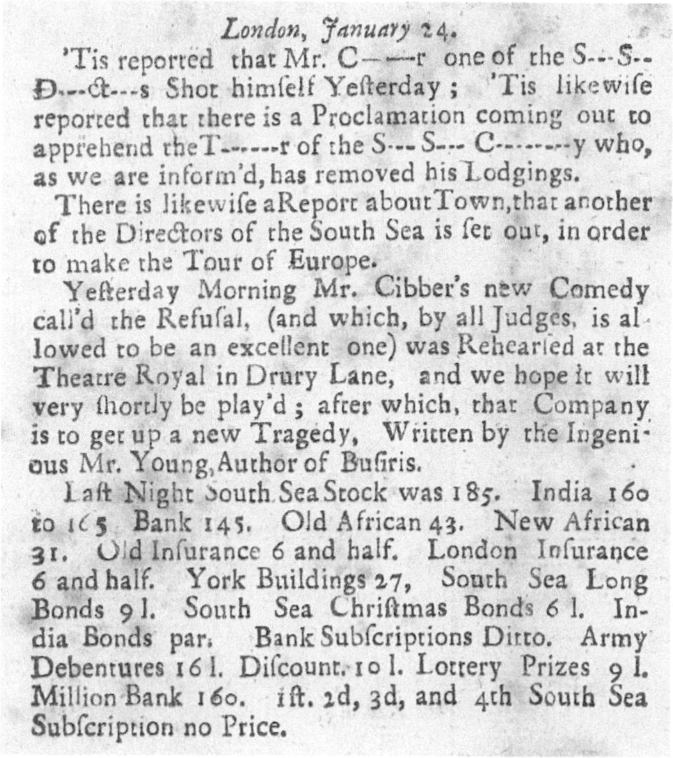

London, January 24.
'Tis reported that Mr. C——r one of the S---S--D---ct---s Shot himself Yesterday; 'Tis likewise reported that there is a Proclamation coming out to apprehend the T------r of the S---S---C--------y who, as we are inform'd, has removed his Lodgings.

There is likewise a Report about Town, that another of the Directors of the South Sea is set out, in order to make the Tour of Europe.

Yesterday Morning Mr. Cibber's new Comedy call'd the Refusal, (and which, by all Judges, is allowed to be an excellent one) was Rehearsed at the Theatre Royal in Drury Lane, and we hope it will very shortly be play'd; after which, that Company is to get up a new Tragedy, Written by the Ingenious Mr. Young, Author of Busiris.

Last Night South Sea Stock was 185. India 160 to 165. Bank 145. Old African 43. New African 31. Old Insurance 6 and half. London Insurance 6 and half. York Buildings 27. South Sea Long Bonds 9 l. South Sea Christmas Bonds 6 l. India Bonds par. Bank Subscriptions Ditto. Army Debentures 16 l. Discount. 10 l. Lottery Prizes 9 l. Million Bank 160. 1st. 2d, 3d, and 4th South Sea Subscription no Price.

FIGURE 4. Detail from *Daily Journal* 2, January 24, 1721, verso. (© The British Library Board, Burney Collection 212b)

of the South Sea Company (notably the suicide of a director and the flight of the treasurer); one advertisement drumming up anticipation for Cibber's new play *The Refusal,* currently in rehearsal; and a list of stock prices, including South Sea shares, bonds, and subscriptions. The first four subscriptions, no longer desirable commodities now that the company is no longer expected to continue growing in value, have "no Price." While company shares are still valued at £185, reflecting a sense that the company has some underlying worth, subscriptions would represent a no-longer-tenable confidence in its future. The notice about Cibber's new play, which "is allowed to be an excellent one" and which the editors "hope . . . will very shortly be play'd," stands as an anomalous piece of optimism in a visual landscape of disappointment. *The Refusal* is one commodity, at least, on which futures are trading high.

After its opening on February 14, *The Refusal* garnered less flattering attention from some papers. On February 18, Nathaniel Mist's *Weekly Journal or Saturday's Post* included a notice of the play's debut and a description of its provenance (fig. 5):

> On Tuesday Night last at the Theatre in Drury-Lane, was acted a Comedy, called the Refusal, or the Ladies Philosophy, which was stolen from a Comedy lately acted in Lincolns-Inn-Fields, called no Fools like Wits, which was stolen from a Comedy called The Female Virtuoso's, which was stolen from a Comedy of Moliere, called *Les Femmes Scavantes* [sic]. Such Authors as this Mr, D—s says are fed like Hogs in Westphalia, one is tied to the Tail of another, and the last feeds only upon the Excrements of the rest, and therefore is generally when full grown, no bigger than a Pig.

The hypotactic parallel structure of the first sentence ("called . . . which was stolen . . . called . . . which was stolen . . . called . . . which was stolen") creates the impression of an endless series of thefts stretching back continuously for fifty years. Through the repetition of the verb "stolen," this advertisement insists that Wright, Gay, and Cibber are literary criminals rather than benign adapters of their source materials. The second sentence, with its scatological humor, compares plagiarism to feeding on other writers' waste products. Like the runt pig at the back of this grotesque chain of transmission, Cibber is diminished by his diet of used dramatic materials, from which all the nutrients have already been extracted by previous generations of writers.[22]

Aside from offering a bitingly satirical take on the derivative work of professional writers—not unlike other passages one might recall from familiar Augustan texts like Pope's *Dunciad*—this hog metaphor carries additional meaning, which only becomes available by reading the other advertisements on the page. In the *Weekly Journal* of February 19, 1721, the item about *The Refusal* is found at the bottom of the left-hand column; to its right sits a description of a trial in which Mr. Barry, the recipient of South Sea shares, has been forced to make payment for them to one Mr. Holmes, his bankers having refused to do so. The notice about *The Refusal* is followed, near the top of the right-hand column, by two notes about the South Sea Company (see fig. 5). The first states that "[t]he Directors of the South-Sea Company

> hundred and thirty Charity Children of Tower Ward.
>   On Tuesday Night last at the Theatre in Drury-Lane, was acted a Comedy, called the Refusal, or the Ladies Philosophy, which was stolen from a Comedy lately acted in Lincolns--Inn-Fields, called no Fools like Wits, which was stolen from a Comedy called The Female Virtuoso's, which was stolen from a Comedy of Moliere, called *Les Femmes Scavantes*. Such Authors as this Mr. D——s says are fed like Hogs in Westphalia, one is tied to the Tail of another, and the last feeds only upon the Excrements of the rest, and therefore is generally when full grown, no bigger than a Pig.

> been dangerously ill of a Fever, is now in a fair Way of Recovery.
>   Wednesday there was a Tryal at Guildhall before the Lord Chief Justice King, between one Mr. Holmes Plaintiff, and Mr. Barry Defendant. It appeared that the Plaintiff sold the Defendant 100 l. Capital South Sea Stock which was transferred, and a Note of 500 l. on Midford and Mertins paid for the same; but the said Bankers stopping Payment before the Money was received, Holmes brought his Action against Barry for Payment of the said Note of 500 l. which the Jury confirmed, by giving the Plaintiff 500 l. Damages besides Costs of Suits.

> His Majesty's Ship the Enterprize Captain Ifco, is ordered to Portsmouth, to take General Nicholson and 100 invalid Soldiers on board for South Carolina.
>   The Directors of the South-Sea Company have continued a great many of the old Clerks in their Places.
>   The Accompt Books of the Company have been committed to the Care of Mr. Lockier.

FIGURE 5. Details from *Weekly Journal or Saturday's Post* 116, February 18, 1721, 694. (© The British Library Board, Burney Collection 207b)

have continued a great many of the old clerks in their places," and the second reports that "[t]he Accompt Books of the Company have been committed to the Care of Mr. Lockier." Taken together, these three notices reflect a complex moment in the effort to repair the damage from the South Sea scheme. Although the account books have been secured and are under investigation, the old clerks have kept their jobs, suggesting that the ranks are not being as fully purged as some members of the public might prefer. Furthermore, unfinished transactions from the Bubble year are still being resolved. The price reflected in the notice of the Guildhall trial (£500 pounds for £100 stock) means that the transaction likely took place during the September 1720 sell-off. Mr. Holmes, then, was probably already taking a significant loss by selling his stock at this rate, roughly half of its peak value during the summer months. Having parted with his stock, he was then denied payment, leaving him with an even greater loss. Although he finally received his money in February (plus damages), the process took six costly months. As these ads reveal, the process of restitution is slow and incomplete.

How do these ads relate to the criticism of *The Refusal* that appears on the same page? Recall, from chapter 4, Isaac Bickerstaff's assertion in the *Tatler* that advertisements convey "News from the little World"—items that reflect and parallel larger news stories within the body of the periodical—and that the arrangement of the ads to tell these resonant stories is an important part of the bookseller's craft. Joad Raymond, Michael Harris, and Stuart Sherman have all shown that newspapers and their advertisement sections were constructed in a way that invited readers to draw connections and construct narratives linking the seemingly disparate items juxtaposed on their pages.[23] The notice about *The Refusal* must be read not only with the play's South Sea subject matter in mind, but also in the context of advertisements elsewhere on the page detailing the slow and uneven pace of recovery from the crash. Read this way, the image of plagiarizing dramatists as hogs feeding on one another's excrement operates as a metaphor for the workings of the South Sea investment scheme, in which later investors' losses were used to pay the investors who entered earlier. It is for this reason that Steele concludes his analysis of South Sea dividends in the *Theatre* with the epigraph "Murrain take the hindmost" and that Cibber echoes this sentiment with Sir Gilbert's final speech in *The Refusal,* in which he warns his family that they should sell their stocks, or "Devil take the hindmost." Contemporaries were well aware by early 1721 that late-comers to the scheme had been the worst hit, and the government's efforts to make amends specifically worked to redistribute some of the early investors' profits to those who had bought in at the height of the Bubble. The hog metaphor suggests that literary property—like South Sea shares or the nutrients in food—is easily transferred and quickly abstracted from the source of its value. Nonetheless, its possession and transfer should be governed by ethical principles, and those who seek to profit from others' rightful property will be impoverished in their turn. Although Cibber is figured as the unfortunate hog at the back of the chain, he is not a victim; like the others before him, he "stole" his comedy. Likewise, latecomers to the South Sea Bubble may have been victims of fraud, but they too sought to make profits on the backs of others. These advertisements, then, create much the same impression as Cibber's play, knitting together the entire public in a web of responsibility for cultivating the habits of mind that allowed such great numbers to be swept up in such a predatory scheme. The *Weekly Journal* goes a step further than the play, however, by positioning dramatic adaptation itself as a form of theft that exploits long chains of transmission to abstract and obscure the source of a commodity's value, enabling the playwright to make a tenuous profit from a gullible yet complicit public.

Curll takes up a similar, albeit softer, line of attack on Cibber in advertising his second edition of *No Fools Like Wits*. In the *Post Boy* for February 9, at the bottom of an advertisement for another book, Curll writes: "Next Week will be publish'd in 8vo. the 2d Edit. Of No Fools like Wits, a Comedy; wherein will be marked the Passages which Mr. Cibber has borrow'd from Moliere in his Refusal, or the Ladies Philosophy." It is difficult to know whether Curll ever intended to produce the ambitious glosses described in this advertisement. As mentioned above, however, the edition was nothing more than a reprint of Wright's *The Female Vertuoso's*, with new paratextual materials outlining Cibber's borrowings and innovations. Hayley points to the *Post Boy* advertisement (and the attendant edition) as evidence that "Curll decided to cash in on Cibber's as well as Gay's profits."[24] As I see it, however, this and other ads placed by Curll around the same time constitute, in and of themselves, a deliberate commentary on the status of dramatic and literary property, one that works by proximity to the surrounding financial news.

Curll published the promised edition on February 25, two weeks following the *Post Boy* advertisement and five days after *The Refusal*'s initial run ended. On that day an advertisement appeared in the *Whitehall Evening Post* that worked to undermine Cibber's authority and ownership of his play (fig. 6). In the ad Curll labels Cibber first and foremost a "Comedian" rather than a playwright. The pile of titles signals, as did the item in the *Weekly Journal* for February 18, that Cibber's play is the latest in a long series of

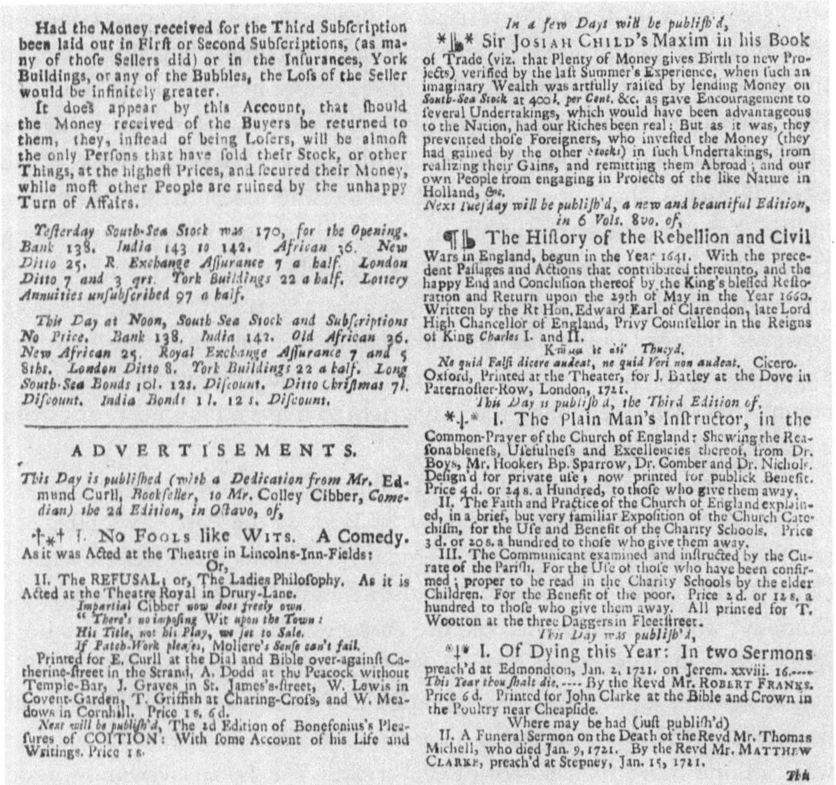

Had the Money received for the Third Subſcription been laid out in Firſt or Second Subſcriptions, (as many of thoſe Sellers did) or in the Inſurances, York Buildings, or any of the Bubbles, the Loſs of the Seller would be infinitely greater.

It does appear by this Account, that ſhould the Money received of the Buyers be returned to them, they, inſtead of being Loſers, will be almoſt the only Perſons that have ſold their Stock, or other Things, at the higheſt Prices, and ſecured their Money, while moſt other People are ruined by the unhappy Turn of Affairs.

Yeſterday South-Sea Stock was 170, for the Opening. Bank 138. India 143 to 142. African 36. New Ditto 25. R. Exchange Aſſurance 7 a half. London Ditto 7 and 3 qrs. York Buildings 22 a half. Lottery Annuities unſubſcribed 97 a half.

This Day at Noon, South Sea Stock and Subſcriptions No Price. Bank 138. India 142. Old African 36. New African 25. Royal Exchange Aſſurance 7 and 5 8ths. London Ditto 8. York Buildings 22 a half. Long South-Sea Bonds 10l. 12s. Diſcount. Ditto Chriſtmas 7l. Diſcount. India Bonds 1 l. 12 s. Diſcount.

ADVERTISEMENTS.

This Day is publiſhed (with a Dedication from Mr. Edmund Curll, *Bookſeller, to Mr.* Colley Cibber, *Comedian) the 2d Edition, in Octavo, of,*

†*† I. No Fools like Wits. A Comedy. As it was Acted at the Theatre in Lincolns-Inn-Fields:

Or,

II. The REFUSAL; or, The Ladies Philoſophy. As it is Acted at the Theatre Royal in Drury-Lane.

Impartial Cibber *now does freely own*
"*There's no impoſing* Wit *upon the Town:*
His Title, not his Play, we ſet to Sale.
If Patch-Work pleaſes, Moliere's *Senſe can't fail.*

Printed for E. Curll at the Dial and Bible over-againſt Catherine-ſtreet in the Strand, A. Dodd at the Peacock without Temple-Bar, J. Graves in St. James's-ſtreet, W. Lewis in Covent-Garden, T. Griffith at Charing-Croſs, and W. Meadows in Cornhill. Price 1 s. 6 d.

Next will be publiſh'd, The 2d Edition of Bonefonius's Pleaſures of COITION: With ſome Account of his Life and Writings. Price 1 s.

In a few Days will be publiſh'd,

‖ Sir Josiah Child's Maxim in his Book of Trade (viz. that Plenty of Money gives Birth to new Projects) verified by the laſt Summer's Experience, when ſuch an imaginary Wealth was artfully raiſed by lending Money on *South-Sea Stock* at 400 *l. per Cent.* &c. as gave Encouragement to ſeveral Undertakings, which would have been advantageous to the Nation, had our Riches been real: But as it was, they prevented thoſe Foreigners, who inveſted the Money (they had gained by the other *Stocks*) in ſuch Undertakings, from realizing their Gains, and remitting them Abroad; and our own People from engaging in Projects of the like Nature in Holland, *&c.*

Next Tueſday will be publiſh'd, a new and beautiful Edition, in 6 Vols. 8vo. of,

¶‖ The Hiſtory of the Rebellion and Civil Wars in England, begun in the Year 1641. With the precedent Paſſages and Actions that contributed thereunto, and the happy End and Concluſion thereof by the King's bleſſed Reſtoration and Return upon the 29th of May in the Year 1660. Written by the Rt Hon. Edward Earl of Clarendon, late Lord High Chancellor of England, Privy Counſellor in the Reigns of King *Charles* I. and II.

Κτῆμα ἐς ἀεὶ *Thucyd.*

Ne quid Falſi dicere audeat, ne quid Veri non audeat. Cicero.

Oxford, Printed at the Theater, for J. Batley at the Dove in Paternoſter-Row, London, 1721.

This Day is publiſh'd, the Third Edition of,

‡ I. The Plain Man's Inſtructor, in the Common-Prayer of the Church of England: Shewing the Reaſonableneſs, Uſefulneſs and Excellencies thereof, from Dr. Boys, Mr. Hooker, Bp. Sparrow, Dr. Comber and Dr. Nichols. Deſign'd for private uſe; now printed for publick Benefit. Price 4 d. or 24 s. a Hundred, to thoſe who give them away.

II. The Faith and Practice of the Church of England explained, in a brief, but very familiar Expoſition of the Church Catechiſm, for the Uſe and Benefit of the Charity Schools. Price 3 d. or 20 s. a hundred to thoſe who give them away.

III. The Communicant examined and inſtructed by the Curate of the Pariſh. For the Uſe of thoſe who have been confirmed; proper to be read in the Charity Schools by the elder Children. For the Benefit of the poor. Price 2 d. or 12 s. a hundred to thoſe who give them away. All printed for T. Wootton at the three Daggers in Fleetſtreet.

This Day was publiſh'd,

‡ I. Of Dying this Year: In two Sermons preach'd at Edmondton, Jan. 2, 1721. on Jerem. xxviii. 16.---- *This Year thou ſhalt die.* ---- By the Revd Mr. Robert Franks. Price 6 d. Printed for John Clarke at the Bible and Crown in the Poultry near Cheapſide.

Where may be had (juſt publiſh'd)

II. A Funeral Sermon on the Death of the Revd Mr. Thomas Michell, who died Jan. 9, 1721. By the Revd Mr. Matthew Clarke, preach'd at Stepney, Jan. 15, 1721.

This

FIGURE 6. *Whitehall Evening Post* 383, February 25, 1721, 3. (Harry Ransom Center, The University of Texas at Austin)

plagiarisms. Any success with which it might meet is attributed to Molière, whose "Sense can't fail"—even, the ad implies, in the hands of a hack like Cibber. Yet this advertisement also self-consciously places Curll himself within the same literary economy, positioning him and Cibber as mirror images of dishonesty. Curll admits that his edition does not reflect Cibber's actual text, gleefully drawing attention to the gap between the goods on offer and the label they bear: "His Title, not his Play, we set to Sale." It is a brazen admission; Curll here seems to be confessing to setting out a false bill of sale. He seeks to profit from Cibber's work without having acquired his content—just as Cibber, in his view, seeks to profit from a story not of his own creation. In the same way that Cibber's adaptation of his sources may be seen as superficial, Curll himself borrows and distorts Cibber's words, misquoting a line from *The Refusal*'s prologue: "There's no imposing Pleasure on a Town" becomes, in Curll's hands, "There's no imposing Wit upon the Town." Curll goes on to call Cibber's play a "Patch-Work," yet the long list of titles to his edition marks it, too, as a patchwork. Indeed, the final line of the quatrain—"If Patch-Work pleases, *Moliere's* Sense can't fail"—can easily be read as an expression of Curll's, rather than Cibber's, hopes for making money from Molière's story. In this short but dense advertisement, Curll binds "Bookseller" and "Comedian" together, showing how both are implicated in a literary economy where profit is based not on who owns a commodity or where it originates, but on who circulates it and controls the perception of its value.

Curll's ad mischievously exposes the similarities between the fraudulent economics of the theater and those of the bookshop. The advertisement page of the *Evening Post* suggests and reinforces the implicit parallels between the literary marketplace and larger speculative markets, as Curll's ad is sandwiched between complaints about the ongoing suffering caused by the South Sea scheme. Immediately preceding Curll's advertisement is a piece lamenting that the weight of the disaster has been borne unevenly by investors who bought and sold at different stages of the scheme—a theme we have already seen reflected in the *Weekly Journal*. Furthermore, Curll's ad is followed by another bookseller's ad for Sir Josiah Child's *Book of Trade*, positioned as a timely release in light of "last Summer's Experience, when such an imaginary Wealth was artfully raised by lending Money on *South-Sea Stock* at 400 *l. per Cent*, &c. as gave Encouragement to several Undertakings, which would have been advantageous to the Nation, had our Riches been real." The advertisement illustrates the danger of using the "imaginary" money created by investment in one company to fund another, as was the case for the numerous new companies that sprang up around 1720 and depended on the liquidity with which the South Sea Company was flooding markets through its low-interest loans. The devastation caused by the burst of the Bubble was so extensive in part because so many speculative investment schemes were interconnected. This advertisement again reinforces the sense that, when value is abstracted from its source via a long chain of transmission, it becomes ever more difficult to ascertain ownership, agency, or blame; instead, investors become caught up in a web of dependencies that are nearly impossible to comprehend or control.

Likewise, in the literary marketplace as envisioned by Curll, the networks of adaptation and transmission have become so convoluted that the rightful direction of profit is nearly impossible; into this gap may step any number of agents seeking to make money from others' work.

Curll explicitly signals the stakes of his edition in another advertisement for the second edition of *No Fools*, which appeared in the *Post Boy* in mid-March (fig. 7). The wording is similar to earlier advertisements, except that it switches the order of the titles—suggesting, perhaps, that by this point, Cibber's title was more recognizable than Gay's for readers—and offers a description of what Curll's dedication actually does: "[G]iving the Publick an Account of the several Changes this Play has undergone this Winter." Whereas the *Evening Post* advertisement relied on readers' knowledge of the Gay/Cibber rivalry and the relationship of their adaptations to multiple sources, this version makes no such presumption. Although the quatrain remains, allowing Curll to continue positioning himself as a chaotic and playful agent exposing the hypocrisies of the literary marketplace, he also expresses a sense of being accountable to "the Publick." Readers have a right to know where their entertainment is coming from, this advertisement suggests. This idea of the public as a collective with interests worth defending is echoed in the surrounding items, which again concern the South Sea Company. Curll's advertisement immediately follows four advertisements for recently or soon-to-be published books that allude to the South Sea affair, including one titled "A Letter to a Friend in the Country, occasion'd by a REPORT that there is a Design still forming by the late DIRECTORS of the South-Sea COMPANY, their Agents and Associates, to issue the Receipts of the Third and Fourth SUBSCRIPTIONS at 1000 l. *per Cent*. and to extort about Ten Millions more from the miserable People of GREAT-BRITAIN." The juxtaposition of these notices creates a shared sense of the role of the periodical advertisement in alerting the public to attempts to trick or defraud them, whether attempts by the theaters or the trading companies. The advertisement page acts as a bulwark against these equally untrustworthy institutions, both of which it suggests are in the business of fabricating value and imposing on readers.

In response to Gay's and Curll's attempts to cast him as a plagiarist, Cibber fought back, asserting what Joseph Loewenstein has called "possessive authorship": a proprietary relation to his own work that existed in tension with the actual market conditions of both the theater and the book

> *In a few days will be publish'd,*
> †↓† Sir Josiah Child's Maxim in his Book of Trade, viz. That Plenty of Money gives Birth to new Projects, verify'd by the last Summer's Experience, when such an imaginary Wealth was artfully raised by lending 400 per Cent. on South-Sea Stock, &c. as gave Encouragement to several Undertakings, which would have been Advantageous to the Nation, had our Riches been real: But as it was, they prevented those Foreigners, who invested the Money they had gained by other Stocks in such Undertakings, from realizing their Gains, and remitting them abroad, and our own People from engaging in Projects of the like Nature in Holland, &c.
>
> *This Day is publish'd,*
> †↓† Francis Lord Bacon; or, the Case of Private and National Corruption and Bribery, impartially consider'd. Address'd to all South-Sea Directors, Members of Parliament, Ministers of State, and Church-Dignitaries. By a True-born Englishman. Printed for J. Roberts near the Oxford-Arms in Warwick-Lane; price 1 s.
>
> *This Day is publish'd,*
> ‖¶‖ Love drain'd in the South-Sea: Or, Cymena's Epistle to the perfidious Cratander, on his Marriage to Cælia. By F. H. Gent.
>   *Oh Love! What poor Omnipotence hast Thou,*
>   *When Gold and Titles buy thee?* Dryden's Spanish Fryar.
> Sold by J. Roberts in Warwick-Lane; price 6 d.
>
> *This Day is publish'd,*
> ⁎†⁎ A Letter to a Friend in the Country, occasion'd by a REPORT that there is a Design still forming by the late DIRECTORS of the South-Sea COMPANY, their Agents and Associates, to issue the Receipts of the Third and Fourth SUBSCRIPTIONS at 1000 l. per Cent. and to extort about Ten Millions more from the miserable People of GREAT-BRITAIN. With some OBSERVATIONS on the present State of Affairs at Home and Abroad. By EUSTACE BUDGELL Esq; Printed for J. Roberts near the Oxford-Arms in Warwick-Lane.
>
> *This Day is publish'd the 2d Edition of*
> ⁎↓⁎ I. The REFUSAL: Or, The Ladies Philosophy. A Comedy. As Acted at the Theatre-Royal in Drury-Lane: Or,
>   II. No FOOLS like WITS: Or, The Female Vertuoses. As Acted at the Theatre in Lincolns-Inn-Fields.
>   *Impartial Cibber now does freely own,*
>   *There's no imposing Wit upon the Town;*
>   *His Title, not his Play we set to Sale:*
>   *If Patch-Work pleases, Moliere's Sense can't fail.*
> With a Dedication to Mr. Cibber, giving the Publick an Account of the several Changes this Play has undergone this Winter. By E. Curll. Printed for E. Curll at the Dial and Bible over-against Katharine-street in the Strand; price 1 s. 6 d. Where may be had, just publish'd, the 3d Edition, price 2 s. 6 d. of

FIGURE 7. Detail from *Post Boy* 4935, March 11, 1721, verso. (© The British Library Board, Burney Collection 209b)

trade.[25] After its opening week of performances, *The Refusal* was published twice in the same year: first in Cibber's collected *Plays*, which was delivered to subscribers on July 1, 1721; and again in an octavo that was issued twice in November (one run dated 1721, the other dated 1722).[26] When the octavo edition was released, advertisements in London papers emphasized the play's authenticity and originality. The *Post Boy* for November 11, for instance, included a publication notice that asserted that the play had been "acted at the Theatre Royal in Drury-Lane," was "Written by Mr. Cibber," and included "the Original Prologue and Epilogue." The advertisement thus tied the edition closely to the performance event of the preceding February, whereas Curll's edition bore the name of Cibber's play while containing a script from the 1690s. More importantly, the phrase "Written by Mr. Cibber"—as opposed to possible alternative formulations like "revised and improved by Mr. Cibber from Molière" or "taken from the French, with additions by Mr. Cibber"—positions him unequivocally as the author, a clear push against the perception of *The Refusal* as plagiarized. Cibber's authorial presence is further underscored by a final note that his collected *Works* are available from the same booksellers, a reminder that he is a sufficiently important and prolific author to have two volumes of plays printed on expensive paper for high-end consumers.

Cibber's self-protective maneuvers and Curll's accusations regarding *The Refusal* stand at the intersection of changing notions of dramatic authorship and originality, as plays came to be seen more like the property of their writers and less like malleable raw materials owned by the theaters.[27] The reuse of existing plots, characters, and themes was, of course, central to the practices of the commercial theaters, which had traditionally held play texts as stage properties like costumes or sets. Following the Restoration these practices had begun to come under scrutiny; while writers like Dryden defended the position of the dramatist as one who adapts and improves cultural inheritance for modern tastes, others, like critic Gerard Langbaine, blasted such playwrights as patch-workers and plagiarists. Paulina Kewes finds that by the early eighteenth century, playwrights felt increasingly compelled to acknowledge their debts to sources. Laura J. Rosenthal points to Cibber's *Richard III* (1700), the printed text of which clearly delineates Shakespeare's original lines from Cibber's revisions and additions, as evidence that adaptation became a uniquely self-conscious genre at this time.[28]

While a growing sense of playwrights as owners was taking hold in the theaters, the Act of Anne in 1710 was the first piece of legislation to recognize authors as potential proprietors of their own work, capable of holding copyright. While in practice most authors continued to sell their copyright to booksellers in perpetuity, individual writers were understood to have a kind of intangible property in their work, and plagiarism and piracy were increasingly viewed as violations of this natural right.[29] Mark Rose argues that literary property at this time was conceptualized on the model of the landed estate, as evidenced by the discourses of paternity, theft, and inheritance surrounding proprietary authorship.[30] Dramatic writing sat uneasily with emergent theories of ownership founded on Lockean theories of possessive individualism, however, because writing for the stage had historically been openly, self-consciously derivative. Yet land was not the only model for thinking about the kind of property that inhered in literary and dramatic works. Financial markets offered an alternative analogy, one perhaps better suited to the nature of dramatic writing. Like the speculative property represented by stocks and derivatives, plays were risky and intangible investments—and, like financial instruments, adapted plays founded their value on others' abstracted and mystified labor. Intangible property, whether a South Sea share or a copyright, alienated the value of a commodity from the original labor that had produced it, opening up a gap that could be exploited by those who wished to profit from others' work.

Given this conceptual relationship between theatrical adaptation and speculative finance, the issues raised by the South Sea Bubble took on new implications for the stage. The market crash had made visible the vulnerability of intangible property to manipulation, and for many it had revealed the predatory impulses at the heart of financial capitalism and the entertainment industry alike. Curll exposed Cibber's play as an attempt to profit from the work of Molière, Wright, and perhaps also Gay, and he suggested that Cibber as an adapter had not performed sufficient work to ascribe his own name and title to the play. In putting Cibber's title on Wright's play, Curll essentially performed the same act of which he accused Cibber: appropriating the efforts of others for his own financial benefit. Yet Curll's advertisements for *No Fools Like Wits* reveal that he is fully aware of the irony of his position—a known pirate policing the boundaries of literary property and originality. By placing himself within a web of culpability and revealing theatrical adaptation to be a kind of reproduction not unlike that he practices with his pirated editions, Curll in these notices undermines the very notion of literary or cultural ownership, strengthening his own position as someone who operates at the boundaries of authors' rights to their work.

Far from being a minor skirmish between two notorious figures of the Augustan literary world, the clash between Edmund Curll and Colley Cibber over *The Refusal* illustrates how contemporaries theorized the nature of literary and dramatic property in the wake of events that profoundly shook Londoners' understandings of the workings of markets. As does Cibber in *The Refusal*, Curll represents everyone as complicit in a system of predatory, speculative behavior. Unlike Cibber, however, Curll does not seem driven by a desire to reform the public or help it see the error of its ways. Instead, he works to normalize a view of property as intangible, abstracted, and vulnerable to appropriation; this, he suggests, is simply the way of the world. Yet running through Curll's advertisements is a new thread of argument that the public—however rational or irrational it may be, however active or passive in its own destruction—has a fundamental right to understand the mystified operations of new speculative markets. Curll is interested not in reform but in transparency: as long as the abstraction of labor from value is made visible, members of the public can make their own decisions about when and how to invest in the latest speculative scheme or dubious dramatic adaptation. Curll, then, imagines a public that exerts agency while still behaving in ways that appear irrational or self-destructive; unlike Steele, Curll does not see the embrace of irrational, speculative market dynamics as a sign of the public's passivity. In some ways Curll engages the kind of mass public theorized by Michael Warner, one that understands itself in relation to commercialized entertainment markets rather than in terms of a Habermasian assembly engaged in rational-critical debate. As the coda to this book will explore, Curll's vision prefigures new public formations that took shape in subsequent decades, enabling an active mass public to lay claim to rights of transparency and access that did not fit neatly within the Enlightenment institutions of civil society and Lockean property rights.

• CODA •

The Theater-Finance Nexus in Later Eighteenth-Century London

This book has traced the development of the theater-finance nexus across the late seventeenth and early eighteenth century, showing how that nexus enabled Londoners to theorize their city's emerging public spheres. During the 1690s the growth of a newly powerful financial sector undermined traditional repositories of economic value, including specie and land. The recoinage crisis foregrounded the importance of faith and credit in securing even the seemingly intrinsic value of currency. Prologues and epilogues of the period, as well as plays like Colley Cibber's *Love's Last Shift*, used these financial developments as a metaphorical lens through which to examine the effects of public feeling on not only economic but also cultural and aesthetic value. The playwrights and actors behind these pieces recognized the theater as a speculative enterprise like the stock market—an arena in which companies competed for profits by courting public favor that could control the value of intangible, abstract commodities. As the career of Susanna Centlivre reveals, this speculative environment created new possibilities for women's participation in public life, even as it made room for exploitive behaviors that undermined its egalitarian potential.

Analogies between Drury Lane and Exchange Alley took on new urgency during the South Sea crisis of 1720 and in its aftermath. Richard Steele used his periodical the *Theatre* to urge caution toward the South Sea Company and the Royal Academy of Music alike. Steele warned that the opera house—like the joint-stock companies from which it took its corporate structure—allowed elites to harness the imaginative power of spectacle and speculation in order to lure the masses into spending money against their own interests. During the same period, Cibber's South Sea play distributed blame somewhat differently. *The Refusal* exposed the dishonesty of its director character but also suggested that the fraudulent investment scheme was able to flourish only because London provided a competitive atmosphere in which members of the public strove to profit from one another's losses. Cibber's play was subsequently attacked as plagiarism in a satirical print battle that highlighted the exploitive operations of the theatrical and print marketplaces, likening each of these cultural arenas to the predatory South Sea Company.

All these texts reflect a shared understanding of the nascent financial sector and the patent playhouses as deeply interconnected institutions that, when considered together, shed new light on the operations of publics more broadly. The plays, framing pieces, periodicals, advertisements, reviews, poems, and images I have examined throughout this book revolve around a set of central questions: Is the public a rational, discerning body passing ethical and aesthetic judgment on matters of common concern, such as entertainments and investment opportunities? Or is it fundamentally irrational, driven by sensual appetites and consumerist desires? Do the irrational elements of crowd behavior render the masses passive dupes, vulnerable to exploitation by elites who wish to coopt their energies? Or might the collectives called into being through shared speculation claim their own forms of agency? Under what conditions, and according to what rules, can these collectives hold public institutions accountable?

Many of the writers featured in this book expressed varying degrees of trepidation about the possibility that publics operate according to the rules of economic markets, particularly the speculative logics of financial capitalism. Thinkers like Steele endorsed a proto-Habermasian ideal of rational-critical debate, one that "took place in principle without regard to all preexisting social and political rank and in accord with universal rules," producing "results that . . . lay claim to being in accord with reason" rather than individual or partisan interests. Even as he gives voice to this claim, however, Habermas recognizes it as an ideological fiction. In reality, the eighteenth-century public sphere was formed by "private persons whose autonomy [was] based on ownership of private property" because property rights were historically one of the first checks on monarchical power that helped to secure individual freedoms.[1] As a result of the identification of private personhood with property ownership, the concept of "public opinion" became an engine through which "the interest of the class, via critical public debate, could assume the appearance of the general interest."[2] In other words, the protocols of rational-critical debate disguised the perspectives of socially dominant groups as the results of pure reason. Steele, Cibber, and many of their contemporaries turned this engine, even as they also hinted at the problems and paradoxes inherent in such an understanding of what it meant to participate in the public sphere.

Yet, as I have shown, another model of associational politics emerged in the theater-finance nexus in this period, one that anticipated understandings of mass culture developed by theorists like Michael Warner in the context of late twentieth-century American culture. This model recognized that the theater, as a form of mass culture, had the potential to foster counterpublics in opposition to the fiction of a single, unified public whose opinions supposedly reflected the results of collective reasoning. Because the entertainment industry was understood in terms of financial markets, theatrical media foregrounded the economic relationships among members of the public, emphasizing dynamics of self-interest, risk taking, and interdependence. In doing so they exposed the ways that market forces, at least as much as rational-critical debate, shaped public opinion—thereby creating space for those disqualified from participation in the bourgeois public sphere due to their inability to conform to gendered and classed standards of reason.[3] Furthermore, the speculative market relations activated in the theatrical public sphere stood in contradistinction to the modes of property ownership that served as a barrier to full participation in the bourgeois public sphere. Nonpropertied producers and consumers of dramatic entertainment could still spectate and speculate in the theater in ways that challenged normative ideals of participation in public life.

This coda briefly considers one instance in which the theater-finance nexus enabled a counterpublic to form and to assert itself against the silencing and exclusionary operations of rational-critical debate: the Half-Price Riots of 1763. These crowd actions occurred in response to the suspension of the longstanding discount on admissions to shows after the third act of the mainpiece. Defenders of the theater managers and their new policy portrayed the protesters as irrational and ungentlemanlike, incapable of engaging in the kind of reasoned deliberation that they argued should define all public debate. These writers attempted to shut the protesters out of the public sphere, insisting that their gender, class, and national identities prevented them from engaging in a disinterested exchange of ideas over matters of common concern. The protesters' supposed irrationality was also bound up with their disrespect for the property rights of the theater managers and shareholders, a disrespect implicitly grounded in their own lack of property. While the theater managers and their defenders appealed to property rights, however, the rioters asserted a different kind of economic power—one bound up with their rights as participants in a dynamic, speculative theatrical market. The protesters made it clear that they could convey or withhold approval in the form of ticket sales, but they also defied the suggestion that they should merely boycott the theaters. Instead, they insisted that the theater was a public institution that owed transparency and accountability to all its consumers. In making this case, they rhetorically positioned the entire theatergoing public as shareholders whose fundamental right to participation in the theatrical market rivaled the property rights of the owners and shareholders.

The Half-Price Rots were precipitated by anger over the monopolistic practices of the patent theaters. While David Garrick's Drury Lane and John Beard's Covent Garden were theoretically in competition, in practice they "functioned like a modern cartel," colluding to control ticket prices across the market.[4] In January 1763 they apparently decided to try to end the practice of admitting theatergoers at half price following the third act of the mainpiece. In the days leading up to January 25, Drury Lane advertised a performance of *Two Gentlemen of Verona,* specifying in the playbills that all tickets would cost full price. In response, critic Thaddeus Fitzpatrick distributed a pamphlet in coffeehouses and taverns across London that called on the public to oppose these changes. That evening the audience at Drury Lane refused to allow the performance to go forward; when Garrick came onstage to address the crowd in his capacity as manager, it erupted. The *London Magazine* described the action vividly: "The ladies withdrawing, the benches were torn up, the glass lustres were broke and thrown on the stage, and a total confusion ensued, which prevented the play from going on; and about nine the house was cleared, the money being returned."[5] According to the same source, the audience at Covent Garden that evening succeeded in securing a promise from Beard to continue offering half-price tickets, and so the show was allowed to go on. Other accounts, including by Beard himself, deny that any such concession was made.[6] The next day a piece apparently placed by Garrick in the *Public Advertiser* asked for a few days to come up with a "full and satisfactory Answer" to the rioters' demands; that night, however, faced with another angry audience gathered at Drury Lane, Garrick too conceded.[7]

An uneasy truce held for the month that followed, during which no full-price-only performances were advertised. When Beard advertised the February 24 performance of the opera *Artaxerxes* at full price, however, Fitzpatrick again called for protest.[8] The audience summoned Beard onstage at the opening of that evening's show and called for him to commit immediately to half-price admissions going forward, but he refused to speak on behalf of the other proprietors without first consulting them. The *London Magazine, or Gentleman's Monthly Intelligencer* for February 1763 reported:

> From six in the evening until past-nine, there were several messages and speeches passed, but none that the audience thought satisfactory[.] . . . For want of this point being determined, at about half an hour past nine, the audience grew so exasperated, that the benches of the second gallery, the fore part of it, the seats in the boxes, the glasses, and every thing else that could be come at, were pulled to pieces.
> The stage was crowded with the audience, that left the boxes and pit.[9]

The same piece stated that the demonstrations resulted in several injuries and at least £100 worth of damages; other sources estimated damages as high as £2,000.[10] At least four and perhaps as many as sixteen of the protesters were arrested.[11] The theaters were closed for the next six nights, while print battles over the matter raged in London's daily and weekly papers. On March 1, Beard conceded to the crowd's demands, placing an announcement in several major papers that the Covent Garden proprietors had authorized him to maintain the same prices as those to which Garrick had agreed.[12] Two nights later the theaters reopened, and the audience at Covent Garden once again halted the show until Beard had agreed to drop charges against those in custody.[13] Even after this resolution was reached, the disturbances remained a topic of conversation throughout the spring of 1763, inspiring satirical ballads, librettos, odes, and engravings.

As Heather McPherson has argued, print debates about these events suggest "an awareness that pressing cultural and political issues about the theater and its public were at stake."[14] Fitzpatrick's handbills frame the uprisings as defenses of the public's prerogative to assemble and to make known its will, and at least one contemporary account describes a leader of the Drury Lane riot—probably Fitzpatrick—standing in the middle of the pit and announcing to Garrick, "I call on you in the name of the public."[15] The theater managers and their defenders agreed that these events provided a window onto the makeup and rightful conduct of the public, even as they rejected the rioters' claims to represent that public. The anonymous writer of the pamphlet *An Appeal to the Public in Behalf of the Manager* (1763) asks rhetorically whether the rioters' demands really represent the "general voice of the public, or the partial and prejudiced sentiments of a few."[16] Likewise, the pamphlet *Theatrical Disquisitions: or, A Review of the Late Riot at Drury-Lane Theatre* complains that "the public are imposed on, by the specious pretences, those rioters of the 25th and 26th of January made to public spiritedness and justice."[17] A notice apparently placed by Garrick and Beard in the *Public Advertiser* for February 25—the day after the riot at Covent Garden—attempts to minimize the organizers of the disturbance by calling them "a particular Set of Persons (contrary to the general Sense of the Audience)" and accusing them of acting "in violation of that Decorum which is due to all public Assemblies."[18] In each of these texts, defenders of the theater management deny that the rioters are the representative body they claim to be.

Writers who sided with Garrick and Beard distinguished Fitzpatrick and his followers from an imagined "real" public by accusing the rioters of acting based on self-interest rather than impartial, dispassionate reason. The February 25 *Public Advertiser* piece mentioned above states that the new price increase is considered justified by "many disinterested Persons."[19] *An Appeal to the Public in Behalf of the Manager* echoes this point, insisting that the need to charge full price at new productions "must appear evident to the unbiassed and impartial" (6). The writer also questions "the impartiality of the conductor of this *irregular regulation*" (9)—Fitzpatrick—and ironically praises his handbill's "elegance of diction . . . consistency, impartiality, and truth" (21). In Beard's published concession, he recounts his experience of the February riot at Covent Garden in the third person: "[W]hen He was called upon the Stage, [he] would have humbly offered such Reasons as, had they been calmly and dispassionately heard, might possibly have prevented the Violence which ensued: In this He was continually prevented by an incessant and clamorous Demand of a general and decisive YES or NO."[20] In presenting his own case, Beard distinguishes between the kind of "calm" and "dispassionate" public exchange that he considers desirable, and the "incessant," "clamorous" crowd that shapes its own terms of debate.

This representation of the rioters as unwilling to engage in reasonable debate occurs throughout printed defenses of Garrick and Beard's conduct. The writer of the pamphlet *Three Original Letters to a Friend in the Country, on the Cause and Manner of the Late Riot at the Theatre-Royal in Drury-Lane*—who claims to be an eyewitness and "dispassionate spectator"—laments that if the protestors had given the managers an opportunity to defend themselves, "an *explanation* would at least have been attempted; and if their fallacy and weakness of argument had been discovered, then the author of the printed paper might have led on his complainants with a good grace—but they wanted neither *explanation* or *grace* before their entertainment, and so fell to without ceremony."[21] The writer of *Theatrical Disquisitions* describes the January riot at Drury Lane in strikingly similar terms, emphasizing the rioters' short-circuiting of what should have been a disinterested exchange of ideas: "[W]hen Mr. Garrick would have explained to them, *why* the difference [in prices] was made, and politely asked, as a *favour*, that they would allow him *but a few words*, they refused. . . . Had they heard him, 'tis possible, *they* would not have suffered themselves to be convinced; but every impartial and equitable hearer must have given it in the present manager's favour" (25–26). To reinforce this point, the writer momentarily brackets the rectitude of the crowd's demands, instead taking issue with their mode of expressing their discontent: "Had all their claims been as just as they were the reverse, what kind of pretence had they to do more than *speak* those claims, and hear them objected to, and if not satisfactorily answered, to refuse, by absenting themselves, any encouragement to what might appear an imposition?" (29). In other words, the rioters should have operated according to the accepted protocols of public debate, resorting to a boycott of the theater if they found the managers' response unacceptable. Notably, this limitation on theatrical consumers' recourse requires them to "absent themselves" from a significant public sphere in order to express their displeasure. The parameters of acceptable debate, in this case, work to exclude certain kinds of voices and interests from public life.

The same pamphlet marginalizes Fitzpatrick and his followers based not only on their means of expression but also on their class status, distinguishing them from the ideal of the English gentleman who understands implicitly the norms of participation in public debate. While ascribing the status of a

"Lady" to "her" self, the pamphleteer refers to Fitzpatrick as an "ungentle man" (4). The writer paints Fitzpatrick's followers as a "hired party of *waiters* from *taverns, footmen, orange-sellers,* and, in short, the *lowest, poorest desperate rabble,* that could be found" (34). A piece titled "Concerning the Disturbance at the Play-Houses" that appeared in the March 1 issue of the *Theatrical Review* lambasts the "unthinking multitude" who follow Fitzpatrick, while sketching unflattering satirical portraits of the riot organizers as middling-class professionals with pretentions to rise above their station.[22]

Accounts like these also attempt to undermine the riot organizers and participants by drawing attention to their ethnicity and adherence to norms of masculinity. Fitzpatrick's Irishness is a central point in printed criticisms of the riots. The "Lady" of *Theatrical Disquisitions* insinuates that the riot organizers' foreignness disqualifies them from leading this kind of public action: "It seems, they think themselves *authorized* to *pull a house down*, if their *countrymen* (I beg pardon, I mean *Englishmen,* for I believe neither of these men are *English*) cannot perform" (35). *An Appeal to the Public in Behalf of the Manager* reproduces the handbill that touched off the riots, then rephrases it mockingly "in the true *Kilkenny* dialect" (14), pointing to the pamphlet's diction as a telltale sign that the author is "Fizgig" (16). The satirical sketch of Fitzpatrick in the *Theatrical Review* calls him "Fizgig Fitzbully, of the county of Tipperary, Esq," emphasizing his Irish origins (116). The same sketch endorses Garrick's "Fribbleriad" (1761) as a portrait of Fitzpatrick's effeminacy and insists that his gender performance disqualifies him from representing the theatrical public: "A CITY I have ever heard spoken of in the *feminine* gender; *the Town* in the *masculine;* how then can the He-She Hero of the Fribbleriad have the assurance to call *itself* the representative of the latter?" (116). After this point, the writer insistently uses the pronoun "it" to refer to Fitzpatrick. As Leslie Ritchie has argued, attacks like these on Fitzpatrick's masculinity took part in broader debates over what it meant to be a "gentleman."[23] Her findings help to explain why—despite the fact that Fitzpatrick was well educated and in possession of a "moderate income left him by his father"—these pamphlets and periodical accounts emphasize his nationality and gender performance as well as the lower-class status of his fellow rioters, in order to call into question his claims to gentility.[24]

As I have argued, antirioter texts suggest that the agitators are beneath the status of gentlemen and therefore unaware of the unspoken rules upon which full participation in the public sphere is premised. One of those unspoken rules is the sanctity of private property rights. Drawing on Lockean notions of property ownership and its relationship to the state, defenses of the theater managers emphasize that English law protects their persons and their property against the violence of their fellow citizens. The notice placed by the managers in the *Public Advertiser* on February 25 condemns the rioters for advancing their ends "by means subversive of private Property." Beard's March 1 concession likewise underscores this point, claiming that "[a]s *Manager* only, and *Trustee* for other Proprietors, he thought himself totally unimpowered to resign up their Rights by so sudden and concise a Conveyance; and as the Point in Dispute was an essential Matter of Property, conceived their Concurrence absolutely necessary to any Determination on his Part."[25] While Beard insists here on his inability to promise away the Covent Garden shareholders' rights—and refers to them as "Proprietors," emphasizing their property in the theater—at least some defenders of Garrick focused on the damages he had sustained personally during the riots at Drury Lane. The writer of *Theatrical Disquisitions,* for example, asks indignantly, "[H]ow did they [the rioters] presume to destroy a man's private property, which they did, to near the amount of two hundred pounds?" (29). The writer further recounts how the protesters denied Garrick his request to defend the price increases and in so doing "refused that gentleman . . . the privilege which is claimed by the *culprit* at the *bar,* a right to *plead* in his own cause, and in defence of his own property" (25-26). If, as Habermas argues, state-guaranteed private property ownership was the foundation for notions of personhood that underpinned the eighteenth-century bourgeois public sphere, then accounts like these attempt to disqualify the rioters from that sphere by framing their actions as violations of this fundamental right.

While those of the managers' party emphasized the state's role in protecting theatrical proprietors against the destruction of their property, the rioters' defenders reframed this dynamic. The piece "Concerning the Disturbance" in the *Theatrical Review* acknowledges: "'Tis undoubtedly hard that the managers should suffer in their property; but is it not equally hard that the publick should suffer in theirs? And that a hundred people or more, must every night be obliged to pay three shillings for a part of an amusement, which they formerly could obtain for eighteen pence?" (111). Having established that the "publick" possesses "property" in theatrical amusements, the writer then equates an increase in prices to theft: "An attempt upon the pockets of the publick, is surely as criminal as an injury to the property of the manager" (111). To reinforce this perspective, the writer includes a letter signed by one "Barnaby Flog," who insists that "[t]he intention of the royal patent, for the establishment of the theatre, was not to enrich an individual or two, but to entertain the public; and the more general this entertainment can be made, the nearer it comes to the views of the government in allowing it," concluding that the price increase was wrong because it "prevented the entertainment from being general" (109). The writer thus responds to the managers' claims that their property has been violated by arguing that the theater is a kind of public commons that the managers have attempted to enclose.

The fictitious *A Dialogue in the Green-Room upon a Disturbance in the Pit,* often attributed to Fitzpatrick, takes the point further, satirizing and subverting the notion that the theater operates according to notions of property at all. The Manager and actor characters—stand-ins for Garrick and his company—hide backstage during the riot, protesting vehemently the violation of their property rights and lamenting that "a man's property shou'd be as well secured in a theatre, as in the funds, or a landed estate."[26] The bad faith of this analogy is revealed, however, when Lord Foppington suggests that the Manager should threaten to retire if rioters do not disband, noting that if they call his bluff he can always stage a comeback and raise prices on audiences eager to see his return. The Manager calculates his individual earnings in this scenario, a combination of his actor salary, profits from three benefit performances, his share as a manager, and the copy money from his scripts. The litany of his sources of income makes it clear that he profits wildly from his position as manager, which allows him to privilege plays and performances that enrich him personally (17–18). While he privatizes the theater's profits, however, he socializes the losses that occur from his decisions: when the Manager voices the fear that the scheme is too risky, Coadjutor reminds him, "[Y]ou'd share your dividend, if this money went among our profits, so that you wou'd not lose it all" (18). Even as they rhetorically frame property in the theater as akin to land ownership, then, adherents of the Manager attempt to benefit from the ways in which theatrical property is fundamentally speculative.

Pushing against the analogy between theatrical management and land ownership, Fitzpatrick and his followers conceptualized the theater instead as a dynamic market in which values fluctuated based on a public opinion that could be marshalled and asserted through force. Hence, when the

Manager in *Green-Room* realizes that he will have to refund all the evening's tickets, he admits that taking half price would have been a better deal than making nothing at all (23). By this admission he concedes that the audience can use their power as consumers to control prices. Yet the writer also insists that theatergoers should not be limited to withholding their ticket money as their sole form of resistance: "It is in vain to urge they are not compelled to pay, nor partake of the diversion; as every Englishman has an undoubted right, not only to amuse himself in any lawful manner, but also to prevent every kind of innovation, every sort of infraction introduced by individuals, for their private emolument, to the detriment of the community" (ii–iii). The dispute over ticket prices stands in for the larger principle that access to spaces of shared cultural experience is a fundamental right that should not be privatized.

Defenders of the riots were insistent in linking the public's right to hold the theater management accountable to the idea of the theaters as a public financial engine. Fitzpatrick—or a pseudo-Fitzpatrick using his sign-off, "An enemy to imposition"—placed a notice in the *Public Ledger* for February 25 demanding a detailed accounting of the expenses associated with the production of *Artaxerxes*. The extraordinarily detailed questionnaire includes tables of performer salaries and questions such as "Whether they [the Covent Garden managers] have not purchased the dresses used in this opera of Dr. Arne for one hundred and forty pounds, being less than half the original cost?" and "Whether in stating the account of their expences, they can with the least appearance of candour, charge the salaries of Seignor Tenducii and Paretio, solely to the night of performing Artaxerxes? And whether there be any merit in reserving those performers for that single purpose?"[27] In challenging the managers' assertions that extraordinary production expenses necessitate higher admission prices, this piece demands financial transparency—much as Steele had once demanded that the South Sea Company open its ledgers to investors. Four decades later it is not just the actual shareholders but the entire public that has a role in assessing whether the theater is spending its income wisely and setting prices appropriately. Against the managers' attempt to claim private property in the theater and exploit these public spaces for individual gain, then, Fitzpatrick and his followers insisted that the theatrical public sphere operated according to the rules of the financial markets rather than the traditional laws of property. These rules enabled citizens to organize against powerful interests to defend their right to full economic, social, and political participation in public life.

Fitzpatrick attempted to assemble a counterpublic using the market logic of mass culture and then to transmute it rhetorically into "the" public from which he and his followers had been excluded. The handbill distributed at coffeehouses on January 25 ends with a postscript explaining that it is necessary to use this medium because "all communication with the public, by the channel of News-papers, is cut off, through the influence of *one of the Theatrical Managers;* who has found means to lay that restraint upon the liberty of the Press, which no MINISTER OF STATE has hitherto been able to effect in this country."[28] Fitzpatrick frames the theater as a space of public assembly that must remain free in order to challenge attempts to encroach on the exercise of freedoms in other arenas of public debate, such as the news media. The handbill distributed on February 24 calling for the Covent Garden riot insists that additional agitation is needed to reinforce the gains made at Drury Lane on behalf of the public as a whole: "It now therefore behooves you, Gentlemen, to enforce your decisions, and convince the Directors of Covent-Garden Playhouse, that a point once determined by the tribunal of the Public, must and shall for ever remain a law, subject to no Alteration, but by their own authority."[29] In *A Dialogue in the Green-Room*, the opening address, "To the Reader," likewise insists on the public's role in governing cultural and political institutions: "From time immemorial the regulation of the stage has been thought the just right and prerogative of the public, by the most rational and equitable title. . . . As Englishmen, it is our duty, and what we owe ourselves and posterity, to be tenacious of our rights and privileges" (i). Texts like these position the rioters as defenders of a broader political right to hold institutions accountable, which is in turn imagined as a right intrinsic to English liberty.

I have suggested that the 1763 Half-Price Riots illustrate how the theater-finance nexus, as an early space of mass culture, had counterpublic-forming potential. A group of people excluded from the protocols of rational-critical debate asserted an alternative logic in which the relation of the public to the theater was understood to be fundamentally commercial. This counterpublic successfully compelled the managers to maintain half-price admissions, even for expensive productions, through a show of economic force: the destruction of property, the denial of an evening's worth of ticket sales, and the insistence that audience members had a role in overseeing the theaters' finances and setting the market value of its offerings. This is arguably the dark side of the public sphere that Steele and many of his contemporaries feared: it demonstrates that a counterpublic can hold other publics and institutions hostage to its will through force. From another perspective, however, this incident can be seen as the story of a group of people asserting their right not to be priced out of public spaces and shared cultural experiences. Whereas Steele worried that speculative markets would be coopted by the wealthy, Fitzpatrick insisted that they were uniquely equipped to allow consumers to resist elite power.

The Half-Price Riots were not an isolated incident; rather, they drew on a common set of practices for political and cultural intervention. Harry William Pedicord counts at least seven major theatrical disturbances between 1743 and 1776, and George Winchester Stone estimates that the patent houses had to redecorate about once per decade due to audience destruction of property.[30] Indeed, the contentious relationship between institutional theaters and their publics persisted into the nineteenth century; the rhetoric on both sides of the Old Price Wars in 1809 bears significant traces of the discourses surrounding the Half-Price Riots.[31] The political import of crowd actions like these, in the period that saw the Gordon Riots and the French Revolution, has long been clear to historians.[32] What has not yet been recognized is the extent to which Fitzpatrick and his followers framed their right to be part of the theatrical public sphere in terms of their status as consumers and their understanding of the theater as a space that operated according to the rules of speculative markets rather than traditional Lockean property rights. The theater-finance nexus I have traced throughout this book thus offers scholars a powerful new tool to reframe our understanding of the relationship between stock markets and the entertainment industry—and of the very nature of public formation in eighteenth-century England.

NOTES

INTRODUCTION

1. The orations were published in a four-page leaflet titled *The Entertainment Perform'd at the Theatre-Royal in Dorset-Garden, at Drawing the Lottery call'd The Wheel of Fortune*. Its publication was advertised in *Post Man* 529 (October 20–22, 1698).
2. Murphy, "Lotteries in the 1690s."
3. The satirical pamphlet *The Wheel of Fortune: or, Nothing for a Penny* states that "[a] Boy at each Wheel / Stood ready to feel / If her Ladiship *Fortune* was kind" (8). These lines are consistent with Murphy's observation that children were often used to draw prizes in lotteries of the 1690s, as their innocence was thought to allay fears of cheating ("Lotteries in the 1690s," 243).
4. *Wheel of Fortune; or, a Thousand Pounds for a Penny*.
5. Dickson introduced this widely used term in the landmark 1967 study *The Financial Revolution in England*. Dickson's dates remain contested; see, for example, Roseveare, *Financial Revolution, 1660–1760*.
6. Stone, "Making of a Repertory"; see also Ritchie and Sabor, *Shakespeare in the Eighteenth Century*. My approach to repertory, revival, and adaptation is indebted to the work of Joseph Roach, Marvin Carlson, and Diana Taylor; see especially the theorizations of performance in relation to cultural memory and historical imagination in Roach, *Cities of the Dead*; Carlson, *Haunted Stage*; and Taylor, *Archive and the Repertoire*.
7. Howard, for example, reads the Royal Exchange in Thomas Heywood's *If You Know Not Me You Know Nobody* (1605) as a figure of the tension between London's economic past and present. See *Theater of a City*, 50–51.
8. "Speculation, n.," *Oxford English Dictionary Online*. As Knight points out, attempts to profit from short-term price fluctuations were not theorized as a distinct set of speculative behaviors until the late eighteenth century,

but speculative practices had been recognized and, in many cases, condemned in many parts of the ancient, medieval, and early modern worlds ("Speculation").

9. Agnew, *Worlds Apart*, x–xi.
10. In *Raving at Usurers*, Codr traces a distinct but related "ethics of uncertainty" in early modern economic discourses, arguing that behaviors perceived as risky or irrational from the perspective of financial capitalism could also be seen as part of a religious, moral, and spiritual tradition that rejected the certain profits of usury; see 1–8, 28–29. On the early history of political economy, see Hutchinson, *Before Adam Smith*.
11. *Entertainment Perform'd*, 4.
12. Pocock, *Virtue, Commerce, and History*, 114; Ingrassia, *Authorship, Commerce, and Gender*, 20, 30; De Goede, *Virtue, Fortune and Faith*, 25–34; Codr, *Raving at Usurers*, 8–19. On Porter, see *London Stage, 1660–1800*, part 1, 504; and Danchin, *Prologues and Epilogues of the Restoration*, 5:xxi, 6:531–41.
13. For examples from history, see Parsons, *Power of the Financial Press*; Wennerlind, *Casualties of Credit*; and Murphy, *Origins of English Financial Markets*. For examples from literary studies, see Genovese, *Problem of Profit*; Ingrassia, *Authorship, Commerce, and Gender*; Finn, *Character of Credit*; Lynch, *Economy of Character*; Roxburgh, *Representing Public Credit*; Sherman, *Finance and Fictionality*; J. Thompson, *Models of Value*; Brantlinger, *Fictions of State*; Brown, *Fables of Modernity*; and Nicholson, *Writing and the Rise of Finance*. For a critique of Thompson, Sherman, and Brantlinger, see Mitchell, "'Beings that Have Existence.'"
14. L. Hughes, *Drama's Patrons*, 154–88; Pedicord, "Changing Audience"; Dharwadker, "Restoration Drama and Social Class."
15. On the cultural centrality of the theater during this period, see Worrall, *Celebrity, Performance, Reception*, 1; and O'Brien, *Harlequin Britain*, xix.
16. Theater entrepreneur and political economist Charles Davenant, for instance, wrote: "Of all Beings that have Existence only in the Minds of Men, nothing is more fantastical and nice than Credit; 'tis never to be forc'd; it hangs upon Opinion; it depends upon our Passions of Hope and Fear; it comes many times unsought for, and often goes away without Reason; and when once lost, is hardly to be quite recover'd" (*Discourses on the Publick Revenues*, 38).
17. Foundational studies in the New Economic Criticism include Shell, *Economy of Literature* (1978) and *Money, Language, and Thought* (1982); Michaels, *Gold Standard and the Logic of Naturalism* (1987); and Goux, *Symbolic Economies* (1990). This loose set of approaches was formalized

as a movement with the publication of Martha Woodmansee and Mark Osteen's collection *New Economic Criticism* in 1999. Work in this vein came under fire for its adherence to Marxist theory at the expense of historical and textual specificity; see Schmidgen, "Robinson Crusoe, Enumeration, and the Mercantile Fetish" (2001), and Hoxby, *Mammon's Music* (2002), 7. More recent studies have paid greater attention to the specifics of markets and their representations at particular places and times; see, for example, Schmidgen, *Eighteenth-Century Fiction* (2002); Poovey, *Genres of the Credit Economy* (2008); and O'Brien, *Literature Incorporated* (2016). In their introduction to the *Routledge Companion to Literature and Economics* (2019), Chihara and Seybold identify a current strain of "econo-literary criticism" that succeeds and moves beyond both Marxist literary criticism and the New Economic Criticism; this new work pays "rigorous attention to the disciplinary vocabulary, methodological assumptions, and intellectual history of economics" while also resisting the "prevailing disciplinary hegemony" of that field (2–3). Adelman and Packham likewise view current scholarship in the field as moving into a post–New Economic Criticism phase, one in which "political economy is studied as part of the history of knowledge formation and discipline building, bringing into relief the relationship between discourses, knowledge, and the disciplines, but in a way which enables a return to questions of genre, literature and writing, as well as cultural and literary history" (introduction to *Political Economy*, 3).
18. See Gallagher, *Nobody's Story*; Johns, *Piracy*; McDowell, *Women of Grub Street*; Rosenthal, *Playwrights and Plagiarists*; and Mandell, *Misogynous Economies*.
19. See Bruster, *Drama and the Market*; Forman, *Tragicomic Redemptions*; Leinwand, *Theatre, Finance, and Society*; Ingram, *Idioms of Self-Interest*; Aaron, *Global Economics*; Sullivan, *Rhetoric of Credit*; and Wawso, "Crises of Credit."
20. On the economics of the eighteenth-century theater, see Kewes, *Authorship and Appropriation*; Hume, "Economics of Culture"; and Maguire, *Regicide and Restoration*, chapter 4. On the discursive interchange between political economy and the theater, see Peters, "Novelty"; J. Thompson, "'Sure I have seen that face before'"; and Kroll, *Restoration Drama*.
21. Habermas, *Structural Transformation of the Public Sphere*. For the continued influence of Habermas's thinking in early modern studies, see Raymond's introduction to *News, Newspapers, and Society*; Lake and Pincus, "Rethinking the Public Sphere"; Lake and Pincus, *Politics of the Public Sphere*; McKeon, *Secret History of Domesticity*, 44–48, 56–75; and McKeon, "Parsing Habermas's 'Bourgeois Public Sphere.'"

22. See Fraser, "Rethinking the Public Sphere"; Benhabib, "Deliberative Rationality"; and Meehan, *Feminists Read Habermas*.
23. M. Warner, *Publics and Counterpublics*.
24. M. Warner, "Mass Public," 387.
25. Moody and O'Quinn note that "the dynamic interactions between performance and print in eighteenth-century Britain helped to generate many features of what we now recognize as mass culture," although they do not further expand on this point (preface to *Cambridge Companion to British Theatre, 1730–1830*, xiii).
26. M. Warner, "Mass Public," 379; see also M. Warner, *Letters of the Republic*. The more recent collection *Social Networks in the Long Eighteenth Century* likewise centers "coffeehouses, intellectual and literary salons, and print media" as the key sites of public formation in this period (see Baird, "Social Networks," 3).
27. Drawing on Michael Warner, I use the term "mass culture" to refer to a set of materials produced for widespread consumption that form a common set of referents for a significant portion of the population ("Mass Public," 386). The texts and performances I examine demonstrate an acute awareness of mass culture as an emergent construct. I do not, however, intend to suggest that all members of London society had equal access to materials like plays and periodicals. While members of the middling classes gained increasing access to cultural products over the long eighteenth century, they remained "extremely costly" for such people in the earlier part of the period (Baldyga, "Tasteful Publics," 46).
28. As Freeman notes in *Antitheatricality and the Body Public*, "Theater has long been distinguished from other representational media . . . by its capacity to conduct a kind of sociological survey as it gathers together in a *public* space, both onstage and in the audience, persons from a cross-section of society to compose, however temporarily, a site of imaginary affiliation" (3). Dillon likewise emphasizes the importance of embodiment to the public-forming and political potential of the eighteenth-century playhouse: "The theatre in the Anglo-Atlantic world of the eighteenth century thus achieved political force not simply or even primarily in terms of the subject matter of plays enacted on stage, but in terms of the force of the bodies that were gathered together in public at the theatre and the representational strategies that were deployed to give meaning to that collection of bodies" (*New World Drama*, 40–41). The centrality of "liveness" to performance theory can be traced to the influence of Phelan's *Unmarked* (1993).
29. In their introduction to a special issue of *Eighteenth-Century Fiction* on "Georgian Theatre in an Information Age: Media, Performance,

Sociability" (2015), O'Quinn and Russell insist that eighteenth-century theater "was a multi-layered performance event, occurring on stage and in the auditorium, but also ... mediated through the print public sphere," and they call for further research on "the complex intermedial relations endemic to theatrical culture," and on "the ways in which theatrical experience is embedded in the mediascape of London" (337, 340). The growing importance of intermedial approaches to long-eighteenth-century studies is further attested to by the fall 2018 special issue of *Restoration* on "The Intermedia Restoration"; in the introduction Trudell explains that the term "intermedia" emphasizes "the extensive collaboration and competition among media"—written, oral, visual, and embodied—in the final decades of the seventeenth century (5).

30. For scholarship that has begun to examine the cultural functions of these materials, see Balme, "Playbills and the Theatrical Public Sphere"; Solomon, *Prologues and Epilogues*; T. Stern, *Documents of Performance*; and Ennis and Slagle, *Prologues, Epilogues, Curtain-Raisers, and Afterpieces*. On the interplay of print and performance cultures, see Peters, *Theatre of the Book*; Sherman, "'General Entertainment of My Life'" and "Garrick among Media"; Frank, *Gender, Theatre and the Origins of Criticism*; and Prescott, *Reviewing Shakespeare*. For case studies that combine an intermedial approach to theater with an attention to the textured temporality of theatrical revival and adaptation, see Depledge, "Playbills, Prologues, and Playbooks"; Straub, "Newspaper 'Trial'"; and Cogswell and Lake, "Buckingham Does the Globe."
31. Muldrew, *Economy of Obligation*; Valenze, *Social Life of Money*.
32. Wennerlind, *Casualties of Credit*, 17–43.
33. Milhous, "Company Management," 2–6.
34. Maus, *Inwardness and Theater*; Kitch, "Character of Credit."
35. Lake and Pincus, "Rethinking the Public Sphere," 282.
36. See Wennerlind, *Casualties of Credit*, especially chapter 2.
37. Dickson, *Financial Revolution*, 43–45; Carruthers, *City of Capital*, 122–23; Murphy, *Origins of English Financial Markets*, 55.
38. Private performances continued to flourish in Royalist circles while the public theaters were closed; see D. Randall, *Winter Fruit*.
39. Langhans, "The Theatres," 35.
40. Mihous, "Company Management," 2.
41. Langhans, "The Theatres," 37–40.
42. Milhous, "Company Management," 6.
43. O'Brien, *Harlequin Britain*, 46.
44. Milhous, "Company Management," 6, 13.

45. Ibid., 7.
46. Milhous, "Company Management," 3–9; "Killigrew and Davenant Patents." See also J. P. Vander Motten, s.v. "Killigrew, Thomas (1612–1683)"; and R.O. Bucholz, s.v. "Killigrew, Charles (1655–1724/5)," in *Oxford Dictionary of National Biography*, online edition.
47. J. Powell, *Restoration Theatre Production*, 180.
48. The authoritative account of this period is Milhous's *Thomas Betterton* (1979).
49. Milhous, "Company Management," 8.
50. Ibid., 9.
51. On the Revolution Settlement and its relationship to broader political and economic shifts, see Pincus, *1688*; and Deringer, "Finding the Money."
52. I draw here on North and Weingast's well-known thesis that the political settlement of 1688–9, in reassigning control of state finances to Parliament, raised the English government's credit by assuring creditors of the state's commitment to uphold property rights ("Constitutions and Commitment"). This thesis has been challenged; see Coffman, Leonard, and Neal, *Questioning Credible Commitment*.
53. Defoe, *Essay upon Projects*, 1. See also Alff, *Wreckage of Intentions*, 2–5; and Murphy, *Origins of English Financial Markets*, 10–38.
54. Owen, preface to *Companion to Restoration Drama*, xii. See also Dharwadker, "Restoration Drama and Social Class," 145.
55. Pedicord, "Changing Audience," 240–42. I take the phrase "the middling sort" from Hunt's important study of that name. As Hunt notes: "The terms *middling sort, middling classes, trading classes,* and *commercial classes* are used in this study—as they were used in the eighteenth century—more or less interchangeably to refer to shopkeepers, manufacturers, better-off independent artisans, civil servants, professionals, lesser merchants, and the like. These people were beneath the gentry but above the level of the laboring classes; most of them worked for a living, although a growing number lived wholly or partially on rent income and other investments" (15). My use of terms like "middling sort" and "middling classes" also serves as a reminder that the category of the "middle class," as used today, was still emergent in the eighteenth century.
56. Nussbaum, *Rival Queens*, 132.
57. Pedicord describes how theater seating corresponded to social class: "Persons of quality [sat] in the front and side-boxes; the pit and first gallery [were] occupied by wealthy tradesmen, their wives and families; the upper gallery [was] occupied by 'the Mob' at a shilling apiece" ("Changing Audience," 243). Hume approximates the prices of theater tickets during the

Restoration in today's terms: "Carolean prices were 4s for a box seat, 2s 6d for a place in the pit, 1s 6d for the first gallery, 1s for the second. If we assume as a very rough approximation a multiplier in the vicinity of 200 to 300 times these sums to get a modern equivalent, then a box seat was £40–60, a pit seat was £25–37.50, first gallery £15–22.50, second gallery £10–15" ("Theatre as Property," 20).
58. Hoppit, "Financial Crises."
59. Zimmerman, Panic!, 13.
60. Throughout this study, I use the terms "publisher" and "bookseller" largely interchangeably; there was a great deal of overlap in the financing, printing, distributing, and retailing of books throughout the early modern period, and the same individuals often performed multiple roles. See Belanger, "Publishers and Writers," 8; and Raven, Business of Books, 4–5.
61. On the problematic category of "crisis" itself, see Klein, Shock Doctrine; Berlant, Cruel Optimism, 7–11; Roitman, Anti-Crisis; Bjerg, Making Money; Chun, Updating to Remain, 2–3; and McClanahan, Dead Pledges. On continuities between eighteenth- and twenty-first-century financial capitalism, see Baucom, Specters of the Atlantic.

1. "VIRTUE IS AS MUCH DEBASED AS OUR MONEY"

1. Jonson, Workes, 5. The date of the play's first performance is on page 1.
2. Dryden, Of Dramatick Poesie, 66.
3. On the relationship between city comedy and economic concerns, see Kitch, "Character of Credit"; Wawso, "Crises of Credit"; and Forman, "Marked Angels."
4. Waddell, "Politics of Economic Distress," 325.
5. Combe defines sentiment as the "'touch within' producing . . . empathy and mutual good-will towards our fellow being," but he notes that the term was ambiguous in the eighteenth century and was not used to describe dramatic genres until much later ("Rakes, Wives, and Merchants," 300–2). Love's Last Shift was long seen as an early sentimental comedy; see, for instance, Fone, "'Love's Last Shift' and Sentimental Comedy." Hume rejects the idea that 1690s saw the advent of a newly sentimental comedic genre, but he does see Cibber's play as part of a transition from hard to humane comedy (Development of English Drama, 382, 411–12). Gollapudi (Moral Reform in Comedy and Culture) and McGirr (Partial Histories) have called for a reevaluation of plays like Love's Last Shift as part of a wave of reform comedies rather than a sentimental turn, noting that these plays retain a satiric edge not found in later plays.

6. Potter, "Colley Cibber," 153.
7. See, for example, Parnell, "Equivocation"; Drougge, "Cibber's 'Genteel Comedy'"; Hughes, "Cibber and Vanbrugh," 303n18; and Brown, *English Dramatic Form*, 110–17.
8. Fone, "'Love's Last Shift' and Sentimental Comedy," 13; Gollapudi, *Moral Reform*, 1; Drougge, "Cibber's 'Genteel Comedy,'" 65.
9. Koon and Gollapudi both argue that reading *Love's Last Shift* as a performance text renders Loveless's fifth-act conversion more believable, while McGirr defends Cibber's comedies as "dramatically coherent and expertly crafted" plays that simply failed to align with later critical tastes. Koon, *Colley Cibber*, 28; Gollapudi, *Moral Reform*, 32–34; McGirr, "Rethinking Reform Comedies," 386.
10. Langbaine, *Lives and Characters*, 20. Although Charles Gildon is not named on the title page, he is thought to have completed and extended the work after Langbaine's death in 1692, making him the likely source of these remarks. See Sambrook, s.v. "Gildon, Charles (c. 1665–1724), Writer," in *Oxford Dictionary of National Biography*, online edition.
11. Peters, "The Novelty," 170.
12. [Defoe], *Essay upon Projects*, 1–2.
13. Although the controversy surrounding Collier's *Short View of the Immorality and Profaneness of the English Stage* (1698) was still in the future, movements like the Societies for the Reformation of Manners had already begun to call for curbing the sexual and moral excesses of the theater (Gollapudi, *Moral Reform*, 8–10, 19–20).
14. Cibber reprised the role of Sir Novelty, freshly ennobled as Lord Foppington, in Vanbrugh's *The Relapse* (1697) and again in his own *The Careless Husband* (1704). In 1727 James Moore Smythe's *The Rival Modes* (1727) featured Cibber as Lord Foppington—now with a new title, the Earl of Late Airs. See Staves, "Few Kind Words," 416–17.
15. See, for example, McGirr, *Partial Histories*.
16. Finke, "Virtue in Fashion," 174.
17. Larkin, "Great Recoinage."
18. Ibid. See also Quinn, "Gold, Silver, and the Glorious Revolution." For the changing value of the gold guinea in the 1690s, see Sargent and Velde, *Big Problem of Small Change*, 278.
19. The key pamphlets from this debate are [Locke], *Some Considerations of the Consequences of the Lowering of Interest, and Raising the Value of Money* (1692); [Lowndes], *Report Containing an Essay for the Amendment of the Silver Coins* (1695); and Locke, *Further Considerations* (1695). For examinations of Locke's economic thought, see O'Brien, *Literature Incorporated*,

28–63; Kelly, introduction to *Locke on Money*, 1:1–121; and Caffentzis, *Clipped Coins*. For a reexamination of the recoinage debate as a proxy for larger political struggles, see Kleer, *Money, Politics, and Power*. On the natural-philosophical dimensions of the recoinage debates, see Smith, "'Foundation in Nature.'"
20. Wennerlind, *Casualties of Credit*, 128–33. For more on the factors leading to the recoinage as well as the process itself, see Li, *Great Recoinage*; and Sargent and Velde, *Big Problem of Small Change*, 261–90.
21. Larkin, "Great Recoinage," 112–14.
22. Ibid., 113.
23. Quoted in Horwitz, *Parliament, Policy, and Politics*, 180. For a detailed examination of how the economic hardships of the 1690s were experienced and politicized by the so-called "common people," see Waddell, "Politics of Economic Distress."
24. Cibber, *Love's Last Shift* (1696), 7. Further citations from this source are given parenthetically in the text.
25. Caffentzis, *Clipped Coins*, 38–39.
26. Cibber, *Plays Written by Mr. Cibber*, 1:7.
27. For more on the changes that Cibber introduced to the 1721 edition, which is the basis for most modern critical editions, see MacMillan, "Text of *Love's Last Shift*."
28. Cibber, *Love's Last Shift*, in *Restoration Drama*, ed. Womersley, 559n26.
29. On the relationship between monetary theory and comedic marriage plots in this period, see J. Thompson, "'Sure I have seen that face before.'" For a more comprehensive discussion of how the changing financial system affected broader cultural notions of value, see Peters, "The Bank, the Press."
30. Pasanek notes: "On almost all eighteenth-century British coinage, along with an impression of a monarch's head appears the inscription 'DEI GRATIA' or 'DG.' As an indication of divine right, the 'DEI GRATIA' may be read as an assurance that a king's position (and his coinage) is secured 'by the grace of God'" (*Metaphors of Mind*, 54).
31. Larkin, "Great Recoinage," 86–87.
32. Evelyn, *Diary*, 5:228–30.
33. For more on the Societies for the Reformation of Manners, see Hunt, *Middling Sort*, 101–24.
34. See Evelyn, *Diary*, entries for December 22, 1695; January 12, 1696; February 2, 1696; February 26, 1696; May 24, 1696; June 11, 1696; August 9, 1696; August 16, 1696; August 23, 1696; and January 31, 1697.
35. Wennerlind, *Casualties of Credit*, 134–35.
36. Murphy, *Origins of English Financial Markets*, 15–16, 25.

37. Ibid., 14–15; see also Wennerlind, *Casualties of Credit*, 94.
38. Murphy, *Origins of English Financial Markets*, 10–11.
39. Ibid., 12. See also Dickson, *Financial Revolution*, 29.
40. Murphy, *Origins of English Financial Markets*, 17–18.
41. Defoe, *Essay upon Projects*, 1–2.
42. Dickson, *Financial Revolution*, 48–49; see also Carruthers, *City of Capital*, 75–76.
43. Dickson, *Financial Revolution*, 497.
44. Ibid., 486.
45. Murphy, *Origins of English Financial Markets*, 77–79.
46. Staves, "Few Kind Words," 425–28; Straub, *Sexual Suspects*, 57–59.
47. Rosenthal, *Playwrights and Plagiarists*, 202; Pocock, *Virtue, Commerce, and History*, 112–13.
48. Koon, *Colley Cibber*, 26; Brown, *English Dramatic Form*, 113.
49. Potter, "Colley Cibber," 158.
50. Langbaine, *Lives and Characters*, 20. On the authorship of this source, see note 10 above.
51. Potter, "Colley Cibber," 159.
52. Gollapudi, *Moral Reform*, 25.
53. The text notes that the speaker, Miss Cross, played Cupid in the masque at the end of the fifth act.
54. This question is answered cynically in Vanbrugh's sequel, *The Relapse* (1697).

2. RECOINING THE REPERTORY

1. *London Stage, 1660–1800*, part 1, 449.
2. *Comparison between the Two Stages*, sometimes attributed to Charles Gildon (see Wells, "Eighteenth-Century Attribution").
3. [Norton], *Pausanias*, A3r.
4. Evelyn, *Diary*, 5:209.
5. *Comparison between the Two Stages*, A3v–A4r, A4r.
6. Ibid., A4r–A4v.
7. Cibber, *Apology*, 58.
8. Solomon, *Prologues and Epilogues*; and T. Stern, *Documents of Performance*. See also Schneider, *Framing Text*; and Bruster and Weimann, *Prologues to Shakespeare's Theatre*. On the marginalization of framing materials vis-à-vis mainpieces, see Scott, "Events and Texts," 227–28, as well as Ennis and Slagle's introduction to *Prologues, Epilogues, Curtain-Raisers, and Afterpieces*, 13.

9. Solomon, *Prologues and Epilogues*, 2. The twentieth century saw the publication of several surveys and collections of prologues and epilogues to seventeenth- and eighteenth-century plays: Danchin, *Prologues and Epilogues of the Restoration* and *Prologues and Epilogues of the Eighteenth Century*; Wiley, *Rare Prologues and Epilogues*; and Knapp, *Prologues and Epilogues of the Eighteenth Century*. Despite the existence of such collections, however, these pieces remain an undertheorized and underused archive.
10. Milhous and Hume lament the difficulty of dating play performances before 1705, when the playhouse managers began placing advertisements regularly in the daily papers; see "Dating Play Premieres," 374.
11. Danchin finds nineteen pieces per season from 1690 to 1694, then thirty-three in 1695, fifty-six in 1696, and forty-seven in 1697; the number of pieces drops back into the thirties for the final years of the decade. The fluctuation in available materials therefore appears to be the effect of a temporary increase in output around the mid-1690s rather than a gradual increase in textual survival over time.
12. Danchin, *Prologues and Epilogues of the Restoration*, 5:xii.
13. On the topicality of these pieces, see Ennis and Slagle, introduction to *Prologues, Epilogues, Curtain-Raisers*, 20; Thorson, "Dialogue"; and Nadj, "'Free Zones of Speech.'"
14. Kewes, *Authorship and Appropriation*, 40.
15. Ennis and Slagle, introduction to *Prologues, Epilogues, Curtain-Raisers*, 19.
16. Bruster and Weimann, *Prologues to Shakespeare's Theatre*, 10; Danchin, "Prologues and Epilogues as Evidence," 126–27.
17. T. Stern, *Documents of Performance*, 81.
18. Ibid., 86.
19. Ibid., 84, 81; see also Kewes, *Authorship and Appropriation*, 40; and Powell, *Restoration Theatre Production*, 16. As Solomon cautions, however, "Scholars still differ over whether prologues and epilogues usually were performed on a play's first night, first three nights, or entire first run" (*Prologues and Epilogues*, 16).
20. Bruster and Weimann, *Prologues to Shakespeare's Theatre*, 13.
21. T. Stern, *Documents of Performance*, 113–15.
22. Bruster and Weimann, *Prologues to Shakespeare's Theatre*, 19–20.
23. Danchin, "Prologues and Epilogues as Evidence," 127; Milling, "'For Without Vanity,'" 62–63.
24. T. Stern, *Documents of Performance*, 115–17.
25. Kewes, *Authorship and Appropriation*, 25–26.
26. Ibid., 20.

27. Peters, "The Bank, the Press," 367.
28. Bruster and Weimann, *Prologues to Shakespeare's Theatre*, 49; see also Agnew, *Worlds Apart*.
29. Swenson, "'Soldier Is Her Darling Character.'"
30. McCallum, "Cozening the Pit."
31. On these interconnections, see also Depledge, "Playbills, Prologues, and Playbooks"; and Russell, *Women, Sociability and Theatre*, 125–35.
32. On the composition and circulation of framing pieces separately from mainpieces, see Stern, *Documents of Performance*, 98–99, 110–11; Milling, "'For Without Vanity,'" 62; Knapp, *Prologues and Epilogues*, v, 4, 8; and Danchin, "David Garrick," and "Unidentified Items," 446. Conversely, Solomon highlights the formal and thematic links between stage orations and mainpieces ("Tragic Play, Bawdy Epilogue?") and calls for a two-fold methodology that treats prologues and epilogues both "as performances that shaped the audience's reception of the play, and as material artifacts published in a variety of formats before and after the play's premiere." This binocular approach attends to the different ways these pieces would resonate depending on their proximity to a mainpiece (*Prologues and Epilogues*, 6–7). Coppola discusses the tension between mainpieces and epilogues that "disturb a complacent interpretation of the performance" they follow (*Theater of Experiment*, 179). Schneider provides a taxonomy of the different functions prologues and epilogues could have in their circulation separately from the play as well as alongside it in performance (*Framing Text*, 6).
33. Li, *Great Recoinage*, 116–24; Dickson, *Financial Revolution*, 367, 367n4; Larkin, "Great Recoinage," 112–13; Caffentzis, *Clipped Coins*, 38–39; and Jones, *War and Economy*, 22.
34. Gould, *The Rival Sisters*, A4r, lines 20–25. Further citations from this source are taken from the same page and are given parenthetically in text.
35. Dryden, *Husband His Own Cuckold*, A6r, lines 26–27.
36. Ibid., lines 30–31.
37. Harris, *City Bride*, A3v, lines 14–19.
38. Ibid., A4r, lines 34–35.
39. Behn, *Younger Brother*, A6r, lines 33, 34–40.
40. *Timoleon*, A4v, lines 9–10.
41. Ibid., lines 15–19.
42. Ibid., lines 25–29. "Tom's" may refer to Tom's Coffee House, which was located in Covent Garden and frequented by theater-goers; see Hibbert, Weinreb, Keay, and Keay, *London Encyclopædia*, 919; Richardson, *Annals of London*, 169; and Cowan, *Social Life of Coffee*, 108–9, 250.
43. Scot, *Unhappy Kindness*, A2r.

44. Lowerre, *Music and Musicians*, 2.
45. See O'Brien, *Harlequin Britain*, xvii–xix, 41–49.
46. *Comparison between the Two Stages*, 7.
47. Danchin, *Prologues and Epilogues of the Restoration*, 5:177, 197.
48. Settle, *Philaster*, A4r, lines 11–13. Francis Beaumont (who died in 1616) is listed as the primary author of this text in the English Short Title Catalogue, but the dedication is signed by its adapter, Settle. Mentions of the Catalogue below are given as ESTC.
49. Ibid., lines 20–21, 26.
50. Fletcher, *Bonduca*, A2v. On the unnamed adapter, see the note "To the Reader," A3v.
51. Ibid., A4r, lines 2, 5, 3. Further citations from this source are taken from the same page, and line numbers are given parenthetically in text.
52. *Comparison between the Two Stages*, 15.
53. Filmer, *Unnatural Brother*, A2r.
54. Ibid., A2v.
55. Ravenscroft, *Anatomist*, A3v, lines 1, 3–6.
56. On the continuities between early Stuart court masques and operatic spectacles in the later seventeenth-century public theaters, see Lewcock, *Sir William Davenant*.
57. Ravenscroft, *Anatomist*, A3v, lines 11–14.
58. Ibid., lines 15–18. On the reference to *Brutus of Alba*, see Danchin, *Prologues and Epilogues of the Restoration*, 6:334.
59. Filmer, *Unnatural Brother*, A3v, lines 1–2. Further citations from this source are taken from the same page, and line numbers are given parenthetically in text.
60. [Drake], *Sham Lawyer*, A2r, lines 1–6. Further citations from this source are taken from the same page, and line numbers are given parenthetically in text.

3. WOMEN AT THE THEATER-FINANCE NEXUS

1. "South Sea Bubble" is an anachronistic term that was coined in the 1771 *Encyclopedia Britannica* (Hoppit, "Myths of the South Sea Bubble," 163). Contemporaries were more likely to refer to the inflation and crash of the South Sea Company's stock value as the "South Sea scheme," while they used "the Bubble year" to refer to the explosion of flotation companies that occurred simultaneously. I use the term "South Sea Bubble" to encapsulate the interrelated speculative energies that captured London's imagination in that moment.

2. Centlivre also wrote two afterpieces not licensed for performance: *The Humours of Elections* and *The Wife Well Manag'd* (1715). On Centlivre's position at a transitional moment in the theater, see Lock, *Susanna Centlivre*, 26; and Pearson, *Prostituted Muse*, 203.
3. On celebrity, see Lock, *Susanna Centlivre*, 13. In *Tatler* 15 (May 14, 1709) and *Tatler* 19 (May 24, 1709), Steele puffs *The Busie Body*, and he again recommends *The Wonder* in the *Lover* for April 27, 1714; on his gendered and arguably backhanded praise for Centlivre, see O'Brien, introduction to *The Wonder*, 10–11. In *Female Tatler* 69 (December 12–14, 1709), the narrator, Mrs. Crackenthorpe, claims to have received a visit from Centlivre, whom she characterizes as irate at the actors' unfair treatment of her scripts. This piece apparently caused problems between Centlivre and the actors, and she insisted in the published preface to her next play that it was a false report (*Man's Bewitch'd*, A4v–A5v). The authorship of the *Female Tatler* is much debated; some scholars even posit that Centlivre herself became involved in writing for the periodical at a later date. For a review of the relevant literature on this topic, see M. Powell, *Performing Authorship*, 242–43n21. On the sale of Centlivre's portraits in 1720, see Bowyer, *Celebrated Mrs. Centlivre*, 232.
4. On her parties, see the *Flying Post* 3813 (June 23, 1716), as well as the *Weekly Journal or British Gazetteer* for June 7, 1718. For Pope's allusions to Centlivre, see, *Dunciad, Variorum*, 60, and *A Further Account*, 12. The moniker "the cook's wife" refers to her marriage to Joseph Centlivre, Yeoman of the Mouth to Queen Anne and then to King George I. For more on Pope's contentious relationship with Centlivre, see Bowyer, *Celebrated Mrs. Centlivre*, 192–93.
5. On the identification of Centlivre with Clinket, see Lock, *Susanna Centlivre*, 30; Bowyer, *Celebrated Mrs. Centlivre*, 197–206; Sherburn, "Fortunes and Misfortunes," 95–97; Hammond, *Professional Imaginative Writing*, 203; Connor, "Heirs," 259–60; and Rosenthal, *Playwrights and Plagiarists*, 205. On the identification of Centlivre as the mantua-maker in the 1716 and 1720 keys to Manley's text, see Manley, *New Atalantis*, ed. Rosalind Ballaster, 383n224; and Jerrold and Jerrold, *Five Queer Women*, 163–64.
6. *Letter from the Dead Thomas Brown to the Living Heraclitus*, 10; Duncombe, *Feminiad*, 15; see also Sutherland, "Progress of Error," 177.
7. On Centlivre's friendship with Oldfield, see Egerton [Curll], *Faithful Memoirs*, 58–59. On Centlivre's literary circles, see Lock, *Susanna Centlivre*, 19–21; and Bowyer, *Celebrated Mrs. Centlivre*, 229–30.
8. The earliest biographies of Centlivre appear in [Jacob], *Poetical Register*, 1:31–34; Whincop, *Scanderbeg*, 185–92; Chetwood, *British Theatre*, 140–41; and [Baker], *Companion to the Play-House*, 2:E3v–E5r. On the

discrepancies among the early accounts of Centlivre's life, see Sutherland, "Progress of Error"; and O'Brien, introduction to *The Wonder*, 19, 23. The movement of elements from these biographies into popular discourse is evidenced by the address "To the World" that appears in *Works of the Celebrated Mrs. Centlivre*, vii–xii, and by the "Life of Mrs. Susanna Centlivre" published in the *Court Miscellany, or, Ladies New Magazine* for August 1765.

9. Collins calculates that Centlivre's plays were performed 1,227 times between 1700 and 1800 and that *The Busie Body* (1709) and *A Bold Stroke for a Wife* (1718) were the two most popular woman-authored plays of the eighteenth century ("Centlivre v. Hardwicke," 179). Stanton calculates popularity based on the number of years a play was produced over the long eighteenth century; by that metric Centlivre secures the top three spots among woman-authored plays: *Busie Body* (staged during eighty-seven years), *Bold Stroke* (seventy-five), and *The Wonder* (fifty-three) ("'This New-Found Path Attempting,'" 333).

10. O'Brien, "Busy Bodies," 185–86; Gieger, "Susanna Centlivre," 83.

11. See Rosenthal, *Playwrights and Plagiarists*, 233–41; M. Anderson, *Female Playwrights*, 109–38; and Hammond, "Is There a Whig Canon?"

12. O'Brien, "Busy Bodies"; Davis, "Dramatizing the Sexual Contract"; Airey, "'I Must Vary Shapes,'" 94; Milling, "'Gotham Election.'"

13. Feminist attempts to recover Centlivre's work include Pearson, *Prostituted Muse*; Cotton, *Women Playwrights*, 122–49; Rubik, *Early Women Dramatists*, 93–112; and Kreis-Schinck, *Women, Writing, and the Theater*.

14. Bratton, "Reading the Intertheatrical," 10. Copeland and Pearson have likewise called for approaches to Centlivre's work that move beyond the terms of literary analysis to consider the conditions of stage production; see Pearson, *Susanna Centlivre*, xii–xiii; and Copeland, *Staging Gender*, 10, 17n9.

15. The first documented performance of *The Gamester* was on February 22, 1705, but Burling argues that it may have debuted in January or early February (*Checklist*, 174). The premiere of *The Basset Table* is recorded on November 20 of the same year (*London Stage, 1660–1800*, part 2, 1:107).

16. Molesworth, *Chance and the Eighteenth-Century Novel*, 23–25, 61–62.

17. Venden Herrell, "Luck Be a Lady Tonight"; Wallace, "A Modest Defence"; Tierney-Hynes, "Emotional Economies"; Rigamonti and Carraro, "Women at Stake"; Warren, "Gender and Genre."

18. [Centlivre], *The Gamester*, 6.

19. [Centlivre], *The Basset-Table*, 7.

20. As Molesworth points out, prior to the success of Hoyle's card-playing manuals in the 1740s, "gambling was almost synonymous with cheating" in most people's minds (*Chance and the Eighteenth-Century Novel*, 68).

21. *London Stage, 1660–1800*, part 2, 2:xl.
22. See *Post Man* 1101 (March 11, 1703); and *Smith v. Betterton*, 1705 (National Archives, ref. no. C 5/337/72); *Smith v. Syderfin*, 1704 (National Archives, ref. no. C 8/597/28); *Smith v. Lord Hervey*, 1704 (National Archives, ref. no. C 8/599/74); *Smith v. Skipwith*, 1704 (National Archives, ref. no. C 8/599/77). https://discovery.nationalarchives.gov.uk.
23. *Lunatick*, A3r–A3v.
24. *Diverting Post* 1 (October 28, 1704) and 25 (April 14, 1705).
25. [Gildon], *Post-Boy*, 343. The dedication is signed "C. G." (A3v), which the English Short Title Catalogue glosses as Charles Gildon (ESTC T57329). Further citations from *Post-Boy* are given parenthetically in the text.
26. Papers (Bound) of Miscellaneous Nature, UK National Archives LC 7/3, fol. 179–180, transcribed in Milhous and Hume, *Coke's Theatrical Papers*, 9–11.
27. *To the Right Honourable the Earl of Kent*, recto.
28. Ibid., verso.
29. See, for example, the poem "The Player's Litany" in *Diverting Post* 26 (April 21, 1705).
30. *To the Right Honourable the Earl of Kent*, recto; names of signatories appear on verso.
31. [Centlivre], *The Gamester*, 33–35.
32. M. Anderson, *Female Playwrights*, 114.
33. Mrs. Topknot's concern that Valere's debt stands in the way of the fulfillment of her daughter's marriage contract also anticipates a petition from Charles Killigrew to Queen Anne in 1709 protesting that the silencing of the theater was jeopardizing the value of his shares in the company, on which his pending marriage settlement rested ("Charles Killigrew, Master of the Revels: Petitions to Qu. Anne and the Lord Chamberlain: 1709 and n.d.," Papers Relating to the Patent of Drury Lane Theatre, British Library Additional Manuscript 20726, fol. 16–17). Killigrew's petition states that "the said shares of the profitts of Acting and of the said rent being att the time of your pet[itione]rs Marriage generally look't upon to be of good value, was a considerable part of the Settlement made by him on his Wife and their issues." Another petition by the patentees and investors in the Drury Lane company likewise suggests the interrelation of theatrical and domestic finances: "[I]n Confidence of the said Letters Patents, and the Inheritance thereby Granted, to them [the shareholders], and their Heires, and through the long, and quiet Enjoyment thereof, many Purchases Mortgages, and Settlements on Wives and Children have been made" ("Francis North, 2nd

Baron Guilford: Petition to Qu. Anne: 1709 / John Hervey, 1st Earl of Bristol: Petition to Qu. Anne: 1709," Papers Relating to the Patent of Drury Lane Theatre, British Library Additional Manuscript 20726, fol. 22).
34. [Centlivre], *The Gamester*, 28.
35. [Centlivre], *Basset-Table*, 48–49.
36. *Daily Courant* 1123 (November 19, 1705).
37. Nicoll points to these back-to-back performances as evidence that "*The Basset-Table* was regarded by contemporaries as a kind of companion play to *The Gamester*" (*History of English Drama*, 2:196n1).
38. Oney, "Women Playwrights," 306–7.
39. Milhous and Hume, *Coke's Theatrical Papers*, 5.
40. See "Henry Grey, Marquis; afterwards Duke, of Kent, Lord Chamberlain: Order as to theatres: 1707," Papers Relating to the Patent of Drury Lane Theatre, British Library Additional Manuscript 20726, fol. 36; and Lord Chamberlain's Department: Miscellaneous Records, Warrant Books: General, UK National Archives LC 5/154, 299–300.
41. Avery, "Some New Prologues and Epilogues," 466.
42. See Milhous and Hume, *Coke's Theatrical Papers*, 136; and Papers (Bound) of Miscellaneous Nature, UK National Archives LC 7/3, fol. 33.
43. Milhous and Hume, *Coke's Theatrical Papers*, 143–44; *Tatler* 93 (July 4, 1710).
44. Milhous and Hume, *Coke's Theatrical Papers*, 147.
45. Whincop, *Scanderbeg*, 190. This book includes a dramatic catalog frequently attributed to John Mottley; see J. M. Rigg, "Mottley, John (1692–1750)" in *Oxford Dictionary of National Biography*, online edition. This account should be approached with skepticism, given the fairytale-like account of Centlivre's youth that precedes the discussion of her plays.
46. *Daily Courant* 2356 (May 13, 1709).
47. Whincop, *Scanderbeg*, 190.
48. *London Stage, 1660–1800*, part 2, records performances on October 11, 13, and 15, which are advertised in the *Daily Courant*; Burney records another on October 14 but does not name his source. See Burney's *Theatrical Register*, British Library General Reference Collection 938.a.9.
49. *Daily Courant* 2484 (October 10, 1709) and 2485 (October 11, 1709).
50. *Daily Courant* 2486 (October 12, 1709), 2487 (October 13, 1709), 2488 (October 14, 1709), and 2489 (October 15, 1709).
51. Centlivre, *The Busie Body*, 3. Further citations from this source are given parenthetically in the text.
52. Both Pearson and Copeland have discussed Miranda's complex negotiations of feminine agency through her incognita persona and through

her refusal to speak in the "dumb show" scene; see Copeland, *Staging Gender*, 103–4; and Pearson, *Prostituted Muse*, 218. Neither, however, links Miranda to Centlivre's own negotiations of agency.

53. Gallagher, *Nobody's Story*, xiii–xv.
54. Gavin, *Invention of English Criticism*, 81–85.
55. *Tatler* 15 (May 14, 1709).
56. *Tatler* 19 (May 24, 1709).
57. *Female Tatler* 41 (October 10, 1709). The issue must have been published at least a few days later than its date suggests, since it refers to *The Busie Body* (which had not yet debuted on October 10) as "successful."
58. [Centlivre], *Stolen Heiress*, A4r.
59. Caldwell, *Popular Plays*, 17.
60. Bowyer, *Celebrated Mrs. Centlivre*, 42.
61. Rosenthal, *Playwrights and Plagiarists*, 211n11.
62. [Centlivre], *Platonick Lady*, A2v. In contrast to Centlivre's claim of her play having been "play'd at least a hundred times," *London Stage, 1660–1800*, part 2 records nine performances of *Love's Contrivance* before 1707, as well as two performances of only its final act.
63. [Centlivre], *Platonick Lady*, A2r.
64. *Daily Courant* 363 (June 16, 1703).
65. While we cannot know who placed such advertisements, it is difficult to imagine who besides Centlivre would have an interest in exposing the misleading initials in such a fashion. The advertising pages of London's daily and weekly papers were a regular staging ground for contests over the circulation of Centlivre's name and identity. After her play *The Artifice* (1722) was attacked in a pamphlet called *A Monthly Packet of Advices from Parnassus* (British Library General Reference Collection 517.g.42), an advertisement signed by Centlivre appeared in the *Daily Journal* for November 7, 1722, defending the play against the attack. On November 22 another advertisement signed by Centlivre appeared in the *St. James Journal* (which had puffed *The Artifice* twice, on September 20 and October 4), claiming that the earlier ad was placed by her Jacobite rivals to surreptitiously promote the pamphlet attack (179). In addition, want ads for missing items to be returned to her appear in the *Evening Post* 1532 (May 28, 1719), *Daily Journal* 312 (January 22, 1722), and *Daily Post* 728 (January 29, 1722); the last two, however, are more likely satirical, as they advertise that Centlivre has lost "several Bills in a Bundle together, drawn by Scotch Officers, late in the Service of the States-General upon their Agents in the Hague"—materials Centlivre would have been unlikely to possess in the first place.

66. *Daily Courant* 5082 (February 3, 1718).
67. M. Anderson, *Female Playwrights*, 109. On women's participation in the stock markets, see Staves, *Married Women's Separate Property*, and "Investments, Votes, and Bribes"; Ingrassia, *Authorship, Commerce, and Gender*, 30–37; and Froide, *Silent Partners*.
68. Airey, like Anderson, interprets Lovely's inability to control her own fate as a reflection of contract theory's failure to guarantee women's liberty ("'I Must Vary Shapes,'" 94). Davis complicates this reading by arguing that performance serves as an alternative means for women like Lovely to exert agency in marriage ("Dramatizing the Sexual Contract," 532). Swenson reads Lovely as a figure for the playwright rather than for the actress, emphasizing how her reliance on a good actor (Fainwell) thematizes interdependence and mutual desire within the playhouse ("'Soldier Is Her Darling Character'").
69. [Centlivre], *Bold Stroke*, 4. Further citations from this source are given parenthetically in the text.
70. O'Brien, "Busy Bodies," 185; Tierney-Hynes, "Emotional Economies," 97; Coppola, *Theater of Experiment*, 109–12.
71. Freeman examines how Fainwell achieves his goals by exploiting his access to "exclusively male taverns and coffeehouses" and by treating Lovely as a commodity (*Character's Theater*, 155).
72. Wennerlind, *Casualties of Credit*, 167–68, 197–201; Carruthers, *City of Capital*, 79, 152. Public creditors may have felt obligated to exchange their bonds for South Sea stock, since it was not clear whether the government had a plan for making payments on the unconverted debt (Dale, *First Crash*, 46–48).
73. Brewer, *Sinews of Power*, 125, 207. Although the South Sea Company is now best remembered for financial malfeasance, other major joint-stock companies of the day also took on public debt in return for trade privileges; see Murphy, *Origins of English Financial Markets*, 217; Wennerlind, *Casualties of Credit*, 199; and Carruthers, *City of Capital*, 14.
74. On the *Asiento*, see Paul, *South Sea Bubble*, 39–42. Dale claims that slave trading operations never mattered to the company's stock price (*First Crash*, 50). However, a search of Emory University's website Voyages: The Trans-Atlantic Slave Trade Database (www.slavevoyages.org) returns statistics for forty-one voyages between 1714 and 1719 on ships owned by the South Sea Company with the outcome "delivered slaves for the original owners." These ships transported a total of 13,951 kidnapped and enslaved people from the Gold Coast, the Bight of Benin, West Central Africa, and

St. Helena; of those, 11,235 survived the trip and were sold in Jamaica, Barbados, Río de la Plata, St. Kitts, Antigua, and the broader Spanish Circum-Caribbean.

75. Wennerlind, *Casualties of Credit*, 232–34; Neal, *Rise of Financial Capitalism*, 96; Dickson, *Financial Revolution*, 88–89.
76. The 1719 and 1720 expansions of the South Sea Company were also influenced by Scottish exile John Law's system for reforming French finance, which included engrafting the French national debt onto a private monopoly trading company, the Mississippi Company. On the relationship between the Mississippi and South Sea schemes, see Wennerlind, *Casualties of Credit*, 232; Dickson, *Financial Revolution*, 94; and Garber, *Famous First Bubbles*, 109. For more on Law's system, see Neal, *Rise of Financial Capitalism*, 73–76.
77. Wennerlind, *Casualties of Credit*, 234; Dickson, *Financial Revolution*, 96–104, 110.
78. Dickson explains this necessity: "If, for example, the whole £31m. of subscribable debts were exchanged for £15.5m. new South Sea Stock valued at [£]200, the South Sea Company would be entitled to increase its nominal capital by £31m., but would only be obliged to assign £15.5m. of this to the public creditors. It could sell the other £15.5m. at the highest possible price. Its profit would come from the difference between the proceeds of this sale and the sum payable to the government" (*Financial Revolution*, 101). In Dickson's scenario the South Sea Company would absorb the £31 million in outstanding government annuities by doling out £15.5 million in company stock, valued speculatively at double its face value, to annuity holders. The government would still owe the company £31 million, which was essentially refinanced at a lower interest rate than the government would have owed to the annuitants. Because it was expecting the full £31 million from the government, the company would then be considered to possess a capital stock of £31 million. However, it would be considered only to have "sold" half of its stock, the £15.5 million assigned to the former annuitants. It would still be able to sell the remaining £15.5 million of new stock at market prices. Neal, Dale, and Garber all caution that the excess share price would not, in fact, produce profit for the company; rather, it would create capital stock that could be used to undertake profitable trade and salvage operations and would generate cash flow that could be used to make loans at interest to shareholders (Neal, *Rise of Financial Capitalism*, 110; Dale, *First Crash*, 80–81; Garber, *Famous First Bubbles*, 111). The company's colonial trade opportunities remained suspended, however, closing off the former avenue of reinvestment.

79. Dickson, *Financial Revolution*, 141.
80. Garber suggests another reason the money subscriptions were held early: to raise funds to pay out the free stock options offered to Members of Parliament and other government officials as bribes (*Famous First Bubbles*, 115). The company also engaged in further manipulations to pump liquidity into the stock market. As the share price rose, the company made credit readily available and eased the terms of payment, allowing subscribers to pay over the course of several "call" dates months apart. These terms encouraged people to purchase subscriptions they could pay off over time or transfer to another investor before the payments came due (Neal, *Rise of Financial Capitalism*, 101; Dickson, *Financial Revolution*, 123–26, 144; Dale, *First Crash*, 100). In addition, the company likely was purchasing its own stock illegally to keep cash in the market (Nicholson, *Writing and the Rise of Finance*, 62). Against the view that these practices were deliberately inflationary, Kleer posits that they simply represented an attempt to keep share prices high enough to give the company time to complete its debt-to-equity swaps and avoid paying a fine for the unconverted debt ("Riding a Wave," 277).
81. Dale, *First Crash*, 81–82.
82. Garber, *Famous First Bubbles*, 121.
83. Dickson, *Financial Revolution*, 153, 159. The causes of the crash probably included Parliament's increased scrutiny of unscrupulous financial behavior under the Bubble Act passed in June; the diversion of foreign investments into the Amsterdam and Hamburg bubbles in late summer; and the September collapse of the South Sea Company's lender, the Sword Blade Company (Neal, *Rise of Financial Capitalism*, 106–12; Dickson, *Financial Revolution*, 148–52; Garber, *Famous First Bubbles*, 119). For more on the Sword Blade Company, see Dale, *First Crash*, 43; Carruthers, *City of Capital*, 153, and Sandra Sherman, *Finance and Fictionality*, 20.
84. Dale, *First Crash*, 142–48.
85. Ibid., 149–52; Dickson, *Financial Revolution*, 118–23, 171–75; Murphy, *Origins of English Financial Markets*, 219. While historians continue to debate the extent to which the company's financial machinations in the spring and summer of 1720 constituted deliberate fraud or mere mismanagement, most agree that an inner circle of directors was responsible for the most egregious market manipulations.
86. W. A. Speck and Matthew Kilburn, s.v. "Promoters of the South Sea Bubble," in *Oxford Dictionary of National Biography*, online edition.
87. Staves, "Investments, Votes, and Bribes," 268. Bowyer mentions that Alexander Pope likewise received stock from Craggs and that Nicholas Amherst published a poem requesting stock from John Blunt (*Celebrated*

Mrs. Centlivre, 226). Interestingly, Centlivre dedicated the published edition of her unacted farces, *The Humours of Elections* and *The Wife Well Manag'd*, to Craggs in 1715, but she did not turn to him again as the addressee of her 1720 poem.

88. Staves, "Investments, Votes, and Bribes," 267.
89. M. Anderson, *Female Playwrights*, 111.
90. O'Brien, introduction to *The Wonder*, 19.
91. Tierney-Hynes similarly describes the poem as one that "paints a picture of her own marriage to Joseph Centlivre, by all accounts a happy one" ("Emotional Economies," 83), while Lock calls it "public in occasion but largely personal in content," featuring "playful glimpses of life in the modest Centlivre household" (*Susanna Centlivre*, 129). Rosenthal's and Cotton's readings of the poem are more alert to the performativity of the authorial persona, but nonetheless they both treat it as a sincere request for South Sea shares (Rosenthal, *Playwrights and Plagiarists*, 215–18; Cotton, *Women Playwrights*, 129).
92. Centlivre, *A Woman's Case*, 1. Further citations from this source are given parenthetically in the text.
93. Bowyer, *Celebrated Mrs. Centlivre*, 167, 168n20.
94. Minutes of "Proceedings" of the Court of Directors of the South Sea Company "in vertue of ye Act. to encrease the S[outh] S[ea] Capital. 1720," British Library Additional Manuscript 25579, 13. Further citations from this source are given parenthetically in the text. In all quotations from this manuscript, superscript letters have been silently lowered.
95. As Bowyer points out, "If Joy [sic] did make her a gift, she was very unkind to mention 'A *Quondam South-Sea* Director' among the varieties of living dead in *The Artifice*, Act V" (*Celebrated Mrs. Centlivre*, 229n16).
96. The scheduled March 17 performance of *Volpone* was advertised in *Daily Courant* 5741 (March 16, 1720). The next day, however, the same paper ran an advertisement reading, "By His Majesty's Command. For the Benefit of the Author. By His Majesty's Company of Comedians. AT the Theatre Royal in Drury-Lane, this present Thursday, being the 17th of March, will be presented, A Comedy call'd the Busie-Body. With Entertainments of Dancing" (*Daily Courant* 5742). *Volpone* resumed the next evening (*Daily Courant* 5743).
97. Centlivre, *Woman's Case*, 2. She also published an eight-page panegyric to King George I himself on his accession (*A Poem. Humbly Presented to His Most Sacred Majesty*).
98. Although a publication date for the poem cannot be ascertained from other advertising or from the Stationer's Register, additional evidence for

an early 1720 publication comes from the fact that Defoe praised *A Woman's Case* in the *Mercurius Politicus* in July (Bowyer, *Celebrated Mrs. Centlivre*, 229).

99. *Miscellaneous Collection of Poems*, 1:175–84. The collection contains two other poems by Centlivre: "An Epistle to the King of Sweden, from a Lady of England" (2:73–79) and "Letter on the Receipt of a Present of Cyder" (1:131–32).
100. *Miscellaneous Collection of Poems*, 2:147–58. The poem was first printed in 1721, although an excerpt appears in a satirical print from the previous year titled *The Bubbler's Medley*. In London the poem was published in both quarto (ESTC N15168) and octavo (ESTC T29755), and in Dublin in octavo (ESTC N32830). It is attributed to Jonathan Swift in the ESTC entries for all three. The Dublin octavo begins with an advertisement that reads: "The Subject of the following POEM, is the *South-Sea;* It is ascribed to a great Name, but whether truly or no, I shall not presume to determine" (A1v). The version published in the miscellany appears to be based on that in the Dublin edition, as it includes two verses not found in the London editions; see page 5 of the Dublin octavo, and page 149 of the miscellany. For a recent analysis of the poem, see Wilkinson, "'Visionary Scene,'" 40–44. Further citations from this source are given parenthetically in the text.
101. Rosenthal, *Playwrights and Plagiarists*.
102. Connor glosses these lines: "The first that took coach and had often took T[arse? (penis)] / Was the fam'd Mrs B[arry] with P[i]x at her A[rse]" ("Heirs," 111).
103. Sutherland notes that several contemporary sources alluded to Centlivre having a squint or an irregularity on her eyelid ("Progress of Error," 176–77).
104. *Players Turn'd Academicks*, 3.
105. Anderson, "Innocence and Artifice," 362. The story is supported by bookseller Bernard Lintot's memo book, which on May 14, 1703, notes, "Paid Mrs. Knight for Love's Contrivance." He apparently paid the same sum to Centlivre herself for *The Busie Body* on May 14, 1709. The sum of £10 was a relatively low fee compared to what Lintot was paying other authors and printers for their plays. For example, it appears that Cibber's first comedy, *Love's Last Shift*, was also worth £10, based on the fact that Lintot paid £3 4s 6d for one-third share in 1701; by 1718, however, Cibber was able to command £105 for *The Nonjuror*. In 1722 Lintot paid fellow bookseller Jacob Tonson £70 for one-half share in Steele's *The Conscious Lovers*, suggesting the copyright was valued at £140 in total (Nichols, *Literary Anecdotes*, 8:294–95, 303).

4. DEFRAUDING THE PUBLIC

1. In *Literature Incorporated*, John O'Brien draws some of the same conclusions I have reached about the links between the *Theatre*, *The Conscious Lovers*, and the South Sea Bubble (95–103). While our accounts differ in several key ways, his study reinforces my sense of the significance and interrelatedness of these materials.
2. Mackay's *Extraordinary Popular Delusions and the Madness of Crowds* (1841) secured the Bubble's status as an exemplar of the vulnerability of market psychology to fits of insanity. His title suggests how the South Sea crisis has been understood to reflect not only on investment behavior but also on the broader danger of crowds.
3. Dale cites eighteenth-century methods of stock evaluation and specific warnings by contemporaries like Archibald Hutcheson as evidence that investors had every reason to anticipate the instability of the scheme (*First Crash* 82–88, 160–61, 180–82). Hoppit likewise points to the extensive Parliamentary debates and the warnings issued by Steele in his numerous periodicals as proof that the worst was thinkable ("Myths of the South Sea Bubble," 146–48).
4. O'Brien discusses the status of the South Sea Bubble for these different schools of economic theory in *Literature Incorporated*, 17–18. Mary Poovey explores the ongoing significance today of eighteenth-century ideas about investors as "rational, self-maximizing agents who can model risk in probabilistic terms" ("From the South Sea Bubble," 205).
5. Paul, *South Sea Bubble*, 5. Like Paul, Kleer combines cliometric methods and insights from behavioral economics in order to complicate the common view of the company's actions as purely fraudulent; see "'The folly of particulars'" and "Riding a Wave."
6. Although Charles Ponzi's infamous scheme postdates the South Sea Bubble by two centuries, the analogy is apt; the *Oxford English Dictionary Online* defines a Ponzi scheme as "a form of fraud in which belief in the success of a non-existent enterprise is fostered by payment of quick returns to first investors using money invested by others; any system which operates on the principle of using the investments of later contributors to pay early contributors" (s.v. "Ponzi scheme, *n.*"). On the possibility that investors in the South Sea Company understood this to be the nature of the scheme, see Garber, *Famous First Bubbles*, 89–90.
7. Historians have tended to refer to pamphlets, periodicals, poems, and broadsides to support their respective positions on London's stock market

in 1720, with limited recourse to playhouse productions or to the theatrical press. Since the mid-1990s, several scholars have examined literary texts surrounding the Bubble, but their investigations have tended to focus on the novel, rather than drama or the theater, as the primary locus of tropological engagement with speculative finance. See Nicholson, *Writing and the Rise of Finance;* Sherman, *Finance and Fictionality;* Ingrassia, *Authorship, Commerce, and Gender;* Stratmann, *Myths of Speculation;* and Poovey, *Genres of the Credit Economy.*

8. Brewer, *Sinews of Power,* 192.
9. Peters, *Theatre of the Book,* 244.
10. Ibid., 247.
11. Cowan, "Mr. Spectator," 350–52.
12. Habermas, *Structural Transformation of the Public Sphere.* On Steele and the role of the "moral weeklies," see especially 41–42.
13. M. Warner, *Publics and Counterpublics,* 99.
14. Ibid., 106. See Cowan, "Mr. Spectator"; and Mackie, *Market à la Mode.*
15. See M. Warner, "Mass Public," as well as my discussion of mass culture and the bourgeois public sphere in the introduction to this book.
16. *Post Boy* 4760 (January 28, 1720).
17. Nichols, ed., *Theatre, by Sir Richard Steele* (1791).
18. See advertisements in *Daily Post* 174 (April 22, 1720) and 175 (April 23, 1720). The ads themselves might even be satirical reflections of a nonexistent performance, as Genest states that the farce was never acted (*Some Account of the English Stage* 3:43). Blanchard refers to the stage oration supposedly written by Steele as "A Recorded Prologue not Found" (*Occasional Verse of Richard Steele,* 116).
19. From the beginning the veil is thin and often lifted. In issue 8 (January 26), Sir John takes up the defense of the "injured knight," printing an open letter from Steele to the Duke of Newcastle. In issue 11 (February 6), Sir John responds to *The Characters and Conduct of Sir John Edgar,* which exposes Steele as the author of the *Theatre;* Sir John winkingly refuses this identification in the same breath that he passionately defends the use of aliases. In issue 14 (February 16), Sir John relates a visit to Steele's house. In issue 17 (February 27), Sir John claims to have been reading Steele's pamphlets and offers a detailed summary and endorsement of their arguments. By March Sir John as a character has virtually disappeared, and in the final issue (April 5), Steele admits what readers had undoubtedly realized—that Sir John was a fictional persona—and promises to print a comedy featuring the character soon. That comedy

was *The Conscious Lovers*, in which Sir John Edgar appeared reincarnated as Sir John Bevil.
20. Loftis, *Richard Steele's* The Theatre, xxv.
21. Loftis, *Steele at Drury Lane*, 121–22, 126–27, 131.
22. Ibid., 127–29.
23. Ibid., 136–54.
24. For a review of the investment mechanisms involved in the South Sea scheme, see chapter 3, esp. pp. 108–10 and 218n78.
25. Issue 27 is missing from the British Library's Burney Collection and corresponding database. Here, spelling, capitalization, and punctuation are reproduced from Nichols, ed., *Theatre, by Sir Richard Steele*, 198–209.
26. Hume, "Sponsorship of Opera"; Milhous and Hume, *Coke's Theatrical Papers*, xxii–xxiii. The account of the Royal Academy that follows draws from Hume as well as from McGeary, *Politics of Opera*, 63–72; and Knapp, "Handel," 149–50. See also Deutsch, *Handel*, 91.
27. Hume, "Sponsorship of Opera," 432.
28. McGeary, *Politics of Opera*, 65.
29. Hume, "Sponsorship of Opera," 432.
30. McGeary, *Politics of Opera*, 63.
31. Knapp, "Handel," 150. McGeary cites another contemporary source that links the two companies: a letter from Guiseppe Riva, an Italian diplomatic secretary, to his friend Agostino Steffani in March 1721. Riva writes: "The Royal Academy of Music has succeeded in becoming a kind of South Sea Company. Everything went marvellously well at the beginning, but as it progressed the devil entered and sowed discord among the singers, subscribers and directors. The parties have started making insulting remarks to each other, and everyone has been carried away by mad passion" (*Politics of Opera*, 70).
32. McGeary, *Politics of Opera*, 1. For more on contemporary opinion of the opera, see the introduction to LaRue, *Handel and His Singers*.
33. Cibber, *Apology*, 299–300.
34. See, for example, *Tatler* 4 (April 19, 1709), presumed to be written by Steele, as well as *Spectator* 5 (March 6, 1711), 18 (March 21, 1711), 29 (April 3, 1711), and 31 (April 5, 1711), all attributed to Addison.
35. According to *London Stage, 1660–1800*, *Volpone* was performed at least once per season from 1700 to 1720, apart from the 1701–2 and 1717–18 seasons. At the time of *Theatre* 18's publication (March 1, 1720), the most recent performances had been in October 1718, but the play was performed twice at Drury Lane in March 1720. See chapter 3 for a discussion

of the rescheduling of *Volpone* to accommodate a command performance of Centlivre's *Busie Body*.

36. Katharine Eisaman Maus, introduction to *Volpone*, in Bevington et al., *English Renaissance Drama*, 674.

37. The name Volpone was already a byword for greedy and exploitive behavior in the theatrical world, having circulated for years in association with theater manager Christopher Rich. *Female Tatler* 37 (September 30, 1709), for instance, referred to "Volpone's" attempts to "humble" the "Rebellious" actors through pay deductions, while playwright William Congreve remarked in a 1706 letter about the lead actors' "desertion" of Drury Lane for the Haymarket that "Mr. Rich complains and rails like Volpone when counterplotted by Mosca" (Congreve, *Letters and Documents*, 43).

38. Deutsch reproduces the faux advertisement discussed here, noting that Steele's "were, of course, ironical remarks, comparing the 'Academy of Music' with the doubtful South Sea Company, and their precarious shares with the dangerous ones of the latter" (*Handel*, 100). McGeary cites a similar notice from the *Weekly Journal* stating that opera stock will fall if internal dissentions continue; he points out that such ads are necessarily facetious, as "the Academy shares are not known to have been traded" (*Politics of Opera*, 311n53). For published notices of the affairs of the Royal Academy prior to *Theatre* 18, see, for example, the *Original Weekly Journal* for May 17, 1719, p. 1562; and *London Gazette* 5787 (October 6, 1719), 5796 (November 7, 1719), 5800 (November 21, 1719), 5805 (December 8, 1719), 5807 (December 15, 1719), 5815 (January 12, 1720), and 5820 (January 30, 1720). The announcement of General Court meetings and calls on subscribers in the *Gazette*, the official government journal, reflects the close ties between the Royal Academy and the state; the *Gazette* was also one of the venues (along with the *Daily Courant* and the *Evening Post*) in which the Court of Directors of the South Sea Company placed their official notices.

39. Deutsch notes that in addition to Nicolini, the fictitious name also evokes Benedetto, another singer who gave a concert on March 11 (*Handel*, 101). For more on Steele's tangles with the castrati of the Royal Academy, see Burden, *London Opera Observed*, 1:53–57.

40. *Tatler* 224 (September 14, 1710).

41. The practice of including satirical pseudo-advertisements above the paid ones did not originate with the *Theatre*; it was common, for instance, in both the *Tatler* and the *Female Tatler*.

42. Shoemaker, "London 'Mob,'" 276.

43. Walter, *Crowds and Popular Politics*, 10.

44. E. P. Thompson, "Moral Economy."
45. A. Randall, *Riotous Assemblies*, 10.
46. Munro, *Figure of the Crowd*.
47. Shoemaker, "London 'Mob,'" 281–82.
48. Randall et al., "Markets, Market Culture, and Popular Protest," 23.
49. Nichols, ed., *Theatre, by Sir Richard Steele*, 197. The source of the letter is not cited, but it likely comes from a published collection of exemplary correspondence.
50. Loftis, *Steele at Drury Lane*, 132.
51. Ibid., 193–95; Kenny, *Plays of Richard Steele*, 290, 293.
52. Steele, *Conscious Lovers*, 13; Horejsi, "(Re)Valuing the 'Foreign Trinket,'" 29; cf. *Spectator* 159 (September 1, 1711; incorrectly numbered 160 in original printing). Further citations from *The Conscious Lovers* are given parenthetically in the text.
53. Wolfram, "'I Am My Master's Servant.'"
54. Freeman, *Character's Theater*, 197; Chandler, "Moving Accidents," 157–63.
55. Loftis presents evidence that Steele had the idea for *The Conscious Lovers* sometime between 1710 and 1713, finished drafting the play in winter 1719–20, and then continued to revise it for another two years (*Steele at Drury Lane*, 184–90).
56. Loftis, introduction to *Richard Steele's The Theatre*, xx–xxi, and *Steele at Drury Lane*, 183–84.
57. Stuart Sherman, "'General Entertainment of My Life,'" 369–70.
58. Loftis, *Steele at Drury Lane*, 191.
59. Loftis, introduction to *Richard Steele's The Theatre*, xix–xx. On the political and class implications of this crossover moment, see also Wilson, "Bevil's Eyes," 509; and Dawson, *Gentility*, 36. For more connections between the *Theatre* and *The Conscious Lovers*, see Kenny, *Plays of Richard Steele*, 279–80.
60. Loftis, introduction to *Richard Steele's The Theatre*, xxi.
61. See Wilson, "Bevil's Eyes," 505–6; and Freeman, *Character's Theater*, 214–15.
62. For arguments in this vein, see Horejsi, "(Re)Valuing the 'Foreign Trinket,'" 23; Wilson, "Bevil's Eyes," 501–2, 516n27; Wolfram, "'I Am My Master's Servant,'" 457–58; and Canfield, "Shifting Tropes," 220.
63. Brown, *English Dramatic Form*, 170; J. Thompson, "'Sure I have seen that face before,'" 295.
64. J. Thompson, "'Sure I have seen that face before,'" 295; Horejsi, "(Re)Valuing the 'Foreign Trinket,'" 13–14.
65. Horejsi, "(Re)Valuing the 'Foreign Trinket,'" 12.
66. See, for example, Dennis, *Remarks on a Play*, 28.

67. Cohen, "Global Indies," 9.
68. Blanchard, "Steele's West Indian Plantation"; Owen and Cooke, "Addison vs. Steele."
69. Bauer explains that while the term "creole" today refers to "a 'black' person or a person of mixed racial heritage," prior to the nineteenth century it referred more often to "settlers of European ancestry born in the Americas" ("Hemispheric Genealogies of 'Race,'" 40). As Bauer shows, the figure of the creole was a locus of anxiety about whiteness as an emergent racial category, as racial identity was understood to be influenced not only by ancestry but also by climate.
70. *Jamaica Lady*, 11–20.
71. Ibid., 52–74.
72. M. Downes, "Ladies of Ill-Repute"; Mackie, "Jamaican Ladies." See also Barash, "Character of Difference."
73. Donahue, "Bringing the Other into View."
74. On the play's treatment of generational conflict and genealogy as they relate metadramatically to its program for reforming comedy, see Hynes, "Richard Steele."
75. Horejsi, "(Re)Valuing the 'Foreign Trinket,'" 11.
76. See Wilson, "Bevil's Eyes," 499. Bernbaum argues that *Love's Last Shift* (1696) was the first "sentimental comedy," but *The Conscious Lovers* marked an important moment in the form's development, particularly its alignment with classical models; see *Drama of Sensibility*, 26 and *passim*. Loftis contends that *The Conscious Lovers* was not the first of its kind but the lightning rod that brought proponents of the new style into open conflict with supporters of laughing or satirical comedy (*Steele at Drury Lane*, 195–213). I am persuaded by Loftis's insight that Steele's contribution was not a particular innovation in dramatic form but rather the synergy he created between the play and his journalism to simultaneously embody his theory of comedy and articulate it, thereby creating the conditions for his play's reception and theorization.
77. Dennis, *Remarks on a Play*, A5r.
78. [Dennis], *Characters and Conduct*, 16–17.

5. "HIS TITLE, NOT HIS PLAY, WE SET TO SALE"

1. A performance of *The Committee* at Lincoln's Inn Fields on May 3, 1720, was accompanied by "a Comick Scene by Mr. Harper, mimicking a drunken Man, in which he will perform the Song of *Four and Twenty Stock-Jobbers*" (*Daily Post* 182 [May 2, 1720]). The routine seems to have

been repeated on May 10, 11, 12, and 24 and revived at Harper's benefits the following season (*Daily Post* 188–91 [May 9–12, 1720], 201 [May 24, 1720], 306 [September 23, 1720], 497 [May 4, 1721]). An anonymous farce called *The Broken Stock-Jobbers: Or, Work for the Bailiffs* was published in 1720 and acted at the Booth in Bird-Cage Alley, Southwark, in October (*Daily Post* 320 [October 10, 1720]). Lincoln's Inn Fields advertised three performances of a one-act farce titled *The Chimera; or, An Hue and Cry to Change Alley* on January 19, 20, and 21, 1721 (*Daily Post* 407–9). February 1722 saw three performances at Lincoln's Inn Fields of a song alternately titled "South Sea Ballad" or "Song of South-Sea," sung by Mr. Aston, each time accompanied by a pantomime titled *The Magician; or, Harlequin a Director* (*Daily Post* 739 [February 10, 1722], 751 [February 24, 1721], and 752 [February 26, 1722]). As late as summer 1723, Drury Lane debuted a two-act farce called *It Shou'd Have Come Sooner; Being the Historick, Satyrick, Tragic, Comic Humours of Exchange-Alley* (*Daily Courant* 6793 [July 30, 1723] and 6795 [August 1, 1723]). In addition, several topical plays on the Bubble were published but apparently not performed. These included two scripts attributed to sometime Drury Lane prompter and publisher of both the *Theatre* and *The Refusal*, William Rufus Chetwood: *South-Sea, or, The Biters Bit* and *The Stock-Jobbers, or, The Humours of Exchange Alley*.
2. Cibber, *The Refusal* (1721), iv, lines 20–21. Further citations from this source are given parenthetically in the text.
3. My reading of the play as a satire of directors and investors alike reconciles two seemingly opposed positions taken by critics of the play. Helene Koon views *The Refusal* as Cibber's personal "revenge" for his South Sea losses, claiming that he "faced ruin" when the bubble burst (*Colley Cibber*, 98–100). Hayley, on the other hand, argues that Cibber embedded an extended satiric dig at the Scriblerus circle into the first scene of *The Refusal*, triumphantly mocking his enemies for losing money in the South Sea Bubble ("Scriblerians," 452). I read Cibber's critique as being more nuanced than either Koon or Hayley suggests, insofar as it implicates both agents and victims of the scheme in the disaster.
4. Steele, *Theatre* 27 (April 2, 1720).
5. Kramnick, *Bolingbroke and His Circle*, 200.
6. Nicholson, *Writing and the Rise of Finance*, 10; Loftis, *Politics of Drama*, 83. After George I's accession in 1714, Drury Lane's management associated itself with the Whigs and the Hanoverians, and, after 1720, with Walpole, while simultaneously trying to cast Lincoln's Inn Fields as Tory

and anti-Walpole and therefore disloyal or even Jacobite (Loftis, *Politics of Drama*, 63; see also Peck, "Anne Oldfield's Lady Townly," 400).
7. Steele, *Theatre* 16 (February 23, 1720).
8. Steele, *Theatre* 3 (January 9, 1720).
9. Dawson claims that Sir Gilbert's name would have linked him in audience members' minds to Sir Gilbert Heathcote, a powerful Whig financier who played a pivotal role in dismantling the Tory South Sea Company after the bubble burst (*Gentility*, 83). The ambiguous connections invited by the name and by Sir Gilbert's own speeches underline the ease with which financial elites could cross boundaries of political party and class, using rhetorical appeals to disguise their true affiliations and motives.
10. Dawson, *Gentility*, 83.
11. Rosenthal explores how Witling embodies contemporary anxieties about participation in the market as a feminizing activity; see *Playwrights and Plagiarists*, 200–201.
12. On calls and refusals, see Dale, *First Crash*, 28.
13. On Cibber's engagement with Centlivre, see Rosenthal, *Playwrights and Plagiarists*, 226–27; and Pearson, *Prostituted Muse*, 213–14. While *The Platonick Lady* is often mentioned by critics as a possible source for *The Refusal*, Coppola instead reads Cibber's play in conversation with Centlivre's *The Bassett Table*, which (like Wright's *Female Vertuoso's*) features a woman scientist rather than the Platonic she-philosopher type taken from Molière (*Theater of Experiment*, 159–63).
14. Johns, *Piracy*, 44–45.
15. Whincop, *Scanderbeg*, 197; Genest, *Some Account of the English Stage*, 3:49.
16. Hayley, "'Swingeing' of Cibber," 293. Hayley elsewhere places the appearance of *No Fools Like Wits* in the context of Cibber's longstanding rivalry with the Scriblerians, including Gay: "Just as Curll was to reprint Wright's earlier adaptation of the Molière play (*Female Virtuosos*, 1693) in an effort to expose Cibber's plagiarism of *Les Femmes Sçavantes*, so Gay (we can surmise), hearing that Cibber was to produce a play using the Molière source, dashed off an adaptation for the rival theatre to forestall his enemy" ("Scriblerians," 457).
17. *Post Boy*, January 14 and 19, 1721, cited in Hayley, "'Swingeing' of Cibber," 293, 293n15.
18. Wright, *No Fools Like Wits; or, the Female Virtuosoes: A Comedy. As It Is Acted at the Theatre in Lincolns-Inn-Fields* (1721); cf. Wright, *The Female Vertuoso's. A Comedy: As It Is Acted at the Queen's Theatre, by Their Majesties Servants* (1693).

19. Hayley, "'Swingeing' of Cibber," 296.
20. Wright, *No Fools Like Wits* (2nd ed.), 3–4.
21. Ashley, *Colley Cibber*, 71. The author of the dramatic catalogue appended to Whincop's *Scanderbeg* (frequently attributed to John Mottley; see 215n45, above) similarly reduces the subplot to a topical gesture, noting only that the play was performed "at the Time of the fatal *South-Sea* Scheme, and one of the *South-Sea* Directors is a Character in the Play" (196).
22. Peters identifies a strikingly similar metaphor in John Denham's prefatory verse to the 1647 folio edition of Beaumont and Fletcher's works. Denham describes plagiarists and pirates as "hounds" feeding on the corpses of the dead playwrights: "Which first their Braines, and then their Bellies fed, / And from their excrements new Poets bred" (*Theatre of the Book*, 227–28). As Peters points out, Denham's poem moves quickly and seamlessly between scatological and economic figurations of plagiarism, staking overlapping claims for the play author's rights in a legal and commercial environment where such claims were considered tenuous.
23. Raymond, "The Newspaper"; M. Harris, "Timely Notices"; Stuart Sherman, "'General Entertainment.'"
24. Hayley, "'Swingeing' of Cibber," 293.
25. See Loewenstein, *Ben Jonson* and *The Author's Due*.
26. Hayley, "Scriblerians," 457n6, and "'Swingeing' of Cibber," 290–91. Hayley points to bibliographic evidence that the octavo was set first but that its publication was delayed because of the controversy surrounding its performance.
27. It is important to note that some playwrights had asserted a kind of proprietary authorship over their plays much earlier; see, for instance, Donaldson, "'Fripperie of Wit.'" Nonetheless, scholarly consensus holds that Jonson's attitude towards his works was anomalous for his time.
28. Kewes, *Authorship and Appropriation*, 32–129, esp. 57 and 93–95; Peters, *Theatre of the Book*, 219–36; Rosenthal, *Playwrights and Plagiarists*, 166.
29. See Rose, *Authors and Owners*; Belanger, "Publishers and Writers"; Woodmansee, *Author, Art, and the Market*; Kewes, *Authorship and Appropriation* and *Plagiarism*; Greene, *Trouble with Ownership*; and Maruca, *Work of Print*. While the law protected copyright holders (whether authors or booksellers) against the reproduction of whole works, there were no statutory prohibitions against the borrowing of individual elements of a text; see Stern, "Creating a Public Domain." For case studies, see Judge, "Kidnapped and Counterfeit."
30. Rose, *Authors and Owners*, 7.

CODA

1. Habermas, *Structural Transformation of the Public Sphere*, 54–55.
2. Ibid., 88.
3. Feminist interlocutors of Habermas have stressed that participation in rational-critical debate is premised implicitly on the ability to bracket one's identity position, a privilege unequally accorded to white, propertied men in the eighteenth century. See Fraser, "Rethinking the Public Sphere"; and Meehan, *Feminists Read Habermas*.
4. McPherson, "Theatrical Riots," 240. For other overviews of the Half-Price Riots, see Burden, *London Opera Observed*, 1:233–37; and Whitty, "Half-Price Riots."
5. "Theatrical Squabble," *London Magazine, or, Gentleman's Monthly Intelligencer* 32 (January 1763), 7.
6. See Beard, *Case Concerning the Late Disturbance at Covent Garden Theatre*. This pamphlet reproduced a notice that originally ran in several periodicals, including the *St. James Chronicle* and *London Chronicle* on March 1 and the *Public Advertiser* on March 3.
7. *Public Advertiser* 8809 (January 26, 1763); on the authorship of this notice, see McPherson, "Theatrical Riots," 242.
8. See Whitty, "Half-Price Riots," 30.
9. "A Second Theatrical Disturbance," *London Magazine, or, Gentleman's Monthly Intelligencer* 32 (February 1763), 57.
10. *Public Advertiser* 8836 (February 26, 1763).
11. Notices in the *London Evening Post* and *Public Advertiser* for February 26, 1763, state that four people were "committed to the Gatehouse by Sir John Fielding"; the *Gentleman's Magazine* for February 1763 reports the same number. The *Derby Mercury* for March 4, 1763, collating reports dated February 26, estimates "fifteen or sixteen Persons in Custody." My thanks to Fiona Ritchie for helping to locate the latter source.
12. Beard, *Case Concerning the Late Disturbance*.
13. *Historical and Succinct Account*, 39.
14. McPherson, "Theatrical Riots," 244.
15. *Historical and Succinct Account*, 11.
16. *Appeal to the Public*, 38. Further citations from this source are given parenthetically in the text.
17. *Theatrical Disquisitions*, 19. Burden places the publication of this piece in the early part of March (*London Opera Observed*, 1:235). Further citations from this source are given parenthetically in the text. Due to an error in the ESTC

metadata not corrected until after its ingestion into Eighteenth-Century Collections Online, electronic retrieval of this item (ESTC T50023) may require that the title be entered as "Theatrical Disquistions [sic]".

18. *Public Advertiser* 8835 (February 25, 1763).
19. Ibid.
20. Beard, *Case Concerning the Late Disturbance*, 2.
21. *Three Original Letters*, 10, 9, Burney Collection of Theatrical Materials, British Library General Reference Collection 938.e.26; accessed via microfilm, Mic.C.11853.
22. "Concerning the Disturbance," 113. Further citations from this source are given parenthetically in the text.
23. L. Ritchie, "Garrick's *Male-Coquette.*"
24. Davies, *Memoirs of the Life of David Garrick*, 2:15, quoted in L. Ritchie, "Garrick's *Male-Coquette*," 166.
25. Beard, *Case Concerning the Late Disturbance*.
26. *Dialogue in the Green-Room*, 6, 13–14, 29–30. Further citations from this source are given parenthetically in the text. On the attribution to Fitzpatrick, see McPherson, "Theatrical Riots," 244.
27. *Historical and Succinct Account*, 26, 27.
28. Ibid., 9. On Garrick's influence over the newspaper industry, see Stuart Sherman, "Garrick among Media"; and L. Ritchie, *David Garrick*, 44–71.
29. "To the Frequenters of the Theatres," reproduced in *London Chronicle* 962 (February 26, 1763) and in *Historical and Succinct Account* (with slightly different capitalization and formatting), 21.
30. Stone, "Making of a Repertory," 190.
31. Hadley, *Melodramatic Tactics*, 34–76.
32. Gilmour, *Riot, Rising, and Revolution*, 16.

BIBLIOGRAPHY

AUTHOR'S NOTE: Many primary texts were accessed in digital facsimile through the databases Early English Books Online (EEBO), Eighteenth-Century Collections Online (ECCO), and Seventeenth and Eighteenth Century Burney Newspapers Collection (BN). EEBO and ECCO metadata derives from the English Short Title Catalogue (ESTC). The database that maintains the primary texts cited below is indicated by its acronym at the end of the entry. Inferred or conjectured author names, places of publication, and dates are enclosed in brackets.

Aaron, Melissa D. *Global Economics: A History of the Theater Business, the Chamberlain's/King's Men, and Their Plays, 1599–1642*. Newark: University of Delaware Press, 2005.

Adelman, Richard, and Catherine Packham. "Introduction: The Formation of Political Economy as a Knowledge Practice." In *Political Economy, Literature, and the Formation of Knowledge, 1720–1850*, edited by Richard Adelman and Catherine Packham, 1–20. New York: Routledge, 2018.

Agnew, Jean-Christophe. *Worlds Apart: The Market and the Theater in Anglo-American Thought, 1550–1750*. Cambridge: Cambridge University Press, 1986.

Airey, Jennifer L. "'I Must Vary Shapes as Often as a Player': Susanna Centlivre and the Liberty of the British Stage." *Restoration and Eighteenth-Century Theatre Research* 28.1 (2013): 45–62.

Alff, David. *The Wreckage of Intentions: Projects in British Culture, 1660–1730*. Philadelphia: University of Pennsylvania Press, 2017.

Anderson, Benedict. *Imagined Communities: Reflections on the Origin and Spread of Nationalism*. London: Verso, 1983.

Anderson, Misty G. *Female Playwrights and Eighteenth-Century Comedy: Negotiating Marriage on the London Stage*. New York: Palgrave, 2002.

Anderson, Misty G. "The Scottish Play: Nationalism, Masculinity, and the Georgian Afterlife of *The Wonder: A Woman Keeps a Secret.*" *Eighteenth-Century Fiction* 27.3–4 (2015): 451–78.

Anderson, Paul Bunyan. "Innocence and Artifice, or, Mrs. Centlivre and *The Female Tatler.*" *Philological Quarterly* 16 (1937): 358–75.

An Appeal to the Public in Behalf of the Manager. London, 1763. ECCO.

Ashley, Leonard R. N. *Colley Cibber.* New York: Twayne, 1965.

Avery, Emmett L. "Some New Prologues and Epilogues, 1704–1708." *Studies in English Literature* 5.3 (1965): 455–67.

Baines, Paul, and Pat Rogers. *Edmund Curll: Bookseller.* Oxford: Oxford University Press, 2007.

Baird, Ileana. "Social Networks in the Long Eighteenth Century: The Public Sphere Revisited." In *Social Networks in the Long Eighteenth Century: Clubs, Literary Salons, Textual Coteries*, edited by Ileana Baird, 1–28. Newcastle upon Tyne: Cambridge Scholars Publishing, 2014.

[Baker, David Erskine.] *The Companion to the Play-House: or, an Historical Account of All the Dramatic Writers (and Their Works) That Have Appeared in Great Britain and Ireland, From the Commencement of our Theatrical Exhibitions, Down to the Present Year.* 2 vols. London, 1764. ECCO.

Baldyga, Natalya. "Tasteful Publics and Public Tastes: Theatre Criticism and the Construction of Community in Eighteenth-Century London." In *Public Theatres and Theatre Publics*, edited by Robert B. Shimko and Sara Freeman, 42–53. Newcastle upon Tyne: Cambridge Scholars Publishing, 2012.

Balme, Christopher. "Playbills and the Theatrical Public Sphere." In *Representing the Past: Essays in Performance Historiography*, edited by Charlotte M. Canning and Thomas Postlewait, 37–62. Iowa City: University of Iowa Press, 2010.

Barash, Carol. "The Character of Difference: The Creole Woman as Cultural Mediator in Narratives about Jamaica." *Eighteenth-Century Studies* 23.4 (1990): 406–24.

Baucom, Ian. *Specters of the Atlantic: Finance Capital, Slavery, and the Philosophy of History.* Durham, NC: Duke University Press, 2005.

Bauer, Ralph. "The Hemispheric Genealogies of 'Race': Creolization and the Cultural Geography of Colonial Difference across the Eighteenth-Century Americas." In *Hemispheric American Studies*, edited by Caroline Field Levander and Robert S. Levine, 36–56. New Brunswick, NJ: Rutgers University Press, 2007.

Beard, John. *The Case Concerning the Late Disturbance at Covent Garden Theatre, Fairly Stated and Submitted to the Sense of the Public in General.* [London, 1763.] ECCO.

Behn, Aphra. *The Younger Brother: Or, The Amorous Jilt. A Comedy, Acted at the Theatre Royal, by His Majesty's Servants.* London, 1696. EEBO.

Belanger, Terry. "Publishers and Writers in Eighteenth-Century England." In *Books and Their Readers in Eighteenth-Century England*, edited by Isabel Rivers, 5–25. Leicester, UK: Leicester University Press, 1982.

Benhabib, Seyla. "Deliberative Rationality and Models of Democratic Legitimacy." *Constellations* 1 (1994): 26–52.

Berlant, Lauren. *Cruel Optimism*. Durham, NC: Duke University Press, 2011.

Bernbaum, Ernest. *The Drama of Sensibility: A Sketch of the History of English Sentimental Comedy and Domestic Tragedy, 1696–1780*. Gloucester, MA: P. Smith, 1958.

Bevington, David, Lars Engle, Katharine Eisaman Maus, and Eric Rasmussen, eds. *English Renaissance Drama: A Norton Anthology*. New York: Norton, 2002.

Bjerg, Ole. *Making Money: The Philosophy of Crisis Capitalism*. London: Verso, 2014.

Blanchard, Rae. *The Occasional Verse of Richard Steele*. Oxford: Clarendon, 1952.

Blanchard, Rae. "Richard Steele's West Indian Plantation." *Modern Philology* 39.3 (1942): 281–85.

Bowyer, John Wilson. *The Celebrated Mrs. Centlivre*. Durham, NC: Duke University Press, 1952.

Brantlinger, Patrick. *Fictions of State: Culture and Credit in Britain, 1694–1994*. Ithaca, NY: Cornell University Press, 1996.

Bratton, Jacky. "Reading the Intertheatrical, or, The Mysterious Disappearance of Susanna Centlivre." In *Women, Theatre and Performance: New Histories, New Historiographies*, edited by Maggie B. Gale and Viv Gardner, 7–24. Manchester: Manchester University Press, 2000.

Brewer, John. *The Sinews of Power: War, Money, and the English State, 1688–1783*. London: Unwin Hyman, 1989.

Brown, Laura. *English Dramatic Form, 1660–1760: An Essay in Generic History*. New Haven, CT: Yale University Press, 1981.

Brown, Laura. *Fables of Modernity: Literature and Culture in the Eighteenth Century*. Ithaca, NY: Cornell University Press, 2003.

Bruster, Douglas. *Drama and the Market in the Age of Shakespeare*. Cambridge: Cambridge University Press, 1992.

Bruster, Douglas, and Robert Weimann. *Prologues to Shakespeare's Theatre: Performance and Liminality in Early Modern Drama*. Abingdon, UK: Routledge, 2004. Electronic edition, Taylor and Francis Group, 2005.

The Bubbler's Medley, or a Sketch of the Times Being Europes Memorial for the Year 1720. London, 1720. British Museum.

Burden, Michael, ed. *London Opera Observed, 1711–1844.* 5 vols. London: Pickering and Chatto, 2013.

Burling, William J. *A Checklist of New Plays and Entertainments on the London Stage, 1700–1737.* Rutherford, NJ: Farleigh Dickson University Press, 1993.

Butler, Douglas R. "Plot and Politics in Susanna Centlivre's *A Bold Stroke for a Wife.*" In *Curtain Calls: British and American Women and the Theater, 1660–1820,* edited by Mary Anne Schofield and Cecelia Macheski, 357–70. Athens: Ohio State University Press, 1991.

Butler, Martin. *Theatre and Crisis, 1632–1642.* Cambridge: Cambridge University Press, 1984.

Caffentzis, Constantine George. *Clipped Coins, Abused Words, and Civil Government: John Locke's Philosophy of Money.* New York: Autonomedia, 1989.

Caldwell, Tanya M., ed. *Popular Plays by Women in the Restoration and Eighteenth Century.* Petersborough, Ontario: Broadview, 2011.

Canfield, J. Douglas. "Shifting Tropes of Ideology in English Serious Drama, Late Stuart to Early Georgian." In *Cultural Readings of Restoration and Eighteenth-Century English Theater,* edited by J. Douglas Canfield and Deborah C. Payne, 195–227. Athens: University of George Press, 1995.

Carlson, Marvin. *The Haunted Stage: The Theatre as Memory Machine.* Ann Arbor: University of Michigan Press, 2001.

Carruthers, Bruce G. *City of Capital: Politics and Markets in the English Financial Revolution.* Princeton, NJ: Princeton University Press, 1996.

Centlivre, Susanna. *The Busie Body: A Comedy. As It Is Acted at the Theatre-Royal in Drury-Lane, By Her Majesty's Servants.* London, [1709]. ECCO.

Centlivre, Susanna. *The Man's Bewitch'd; or, The Devil to Do about Her.* London, [1709]. ECCO.

Centlivre, Susanna. *A Poem. Humbly Presented to His Most Sacred Majesty George, King of Great Britain, France, and Ireland. Upon his Accession to the Throne.* London, 1715. ECCO.

Centlivre, Susanna. *A Woman's Case: In An Epistle to Charles Joye, Esq; Deputy-Governor of the South-Sea.* London, 1720. ECCO.

Centlivre, Susanna. *The Works of the Celebrated Mrs. Centlivre.* 3 vols. London, 1761. ECCO.

[Centlivre, Susanna.] *The Basset-Table. A Comedy. As It Is Acted at the Theatre-Royal in Drury-Lane, by Her Majesty's Servants.* London, 1706. ECCO.

[Centlivre, Susanna.] *A Bold Stroke for a Wife: A Comedy; As it is Acted at the Theatre in Little Lincoln's-Inn-Fields.* London, 1718. ECCO.

[Centlivre, Susanna.] *The Gamester: A Comedy. As It Is Acted at the New-Theatre in Lincolns-Inn-Fields, by Her Majesty's Servants.* London, 1705. ECCO.

[Centlivre, Susanna.] *The Humours of Elections. And A Cure for Cuckoldom: or the Wife Well Manag'd. Two Farces*. London, 1715. ECCO.
[Centlivre, Susanna.] *Love's Contrivance, or, Le Medecin Malgre Lui. A Comedy. As It Is Acted at the Theatre Royal in Drury-Lane*. London, 1703. ECCO.
[Centlivre, Susanna.] *The Platonick Lady. A Comedy. As It Is Acted at the Queens Theatre in the Hay-Market*. London, 1707. ECCO.
[Centlivre, Susanna.] *The Stolen Heiress or The Salamanca Doctor Outplotted. A Comedy. As It Is Acted at the New Theatre in Lincolns-Inn-Fields. By Her Majesties Servants*. London, [1703]. ECCO.
Chandler, James. "Moving Accidents: The Emergence of Sentimental Probability." In *The Age of Cultural Revolutions: Britain and France, 1750–1820*, edited by Colin Jones and Dror Wahrman, 137–65. Berkeley: University of California Press, 2002.
Chetwood, William Rufus. *The British Theatre. Containing the Lives of the English Dramatic Poets; with an Account of All Their Plays*. Dublin, 1750. ECCO.
[Chetwood, William Rufus.] *South-Sea; or, The Biters Bit. A Tragi-Comi-Pastoral Farce. Humbly Offer'd to the Reading of an Honest Director*. London, 1720. ECCO.
[Chetwood, William Rufus.] *The Stock-Jobbers: Or, The Humours of Exchange-Alley. A Comedy, of Three Acts*. London, 1720. ECCO.
Chico, Tita. "Gimcrack's Legacy: Sex, Wealth, and the Theater of Experimental Philosophy." *Comparative Drama* 42.1 (2008): 29–49.
Chihara, Michelle, and Matt Seybold. Introduction to *The Routledge Companion to Literature and Economics*, edited by Matt Seybold and Michelle Chihara, 1–12. London: Routledge, 2019.
Chun, Wendy Hui Kyong. *Updating to Remain the Same: Habitual New Media*. Cambridge, MA: MIT Press, 2016.
Cibber, Colley. *An Apology for the Life of Mr. Colley Cibber, Comedian, and Late Patentee of the Theatre-Royal. With an Historical View of the Stage during His Own Time*. London, 1740. ECCO.
Cibber, Colley. *The Careless Husband. A Comedy. As It Is Acted at the Theatre Royal, by Her Majesty's Servants*. London, 1705. ECCO.
Cibber, Colley. *The Lady's Last Stake, or, The Wife's Resentment*. London, [1707]. ECCO.
Cibber, Colley. *Love's Last Shift; or, The Fool in Fashion. A Comedy. As It Is Acted at the Theatre Royal, by His Majesty's Servants*. London, 1696. EEBO.
Cibber, Colley. *Love's Last Shift; or, The Fool in Fashion*. In *Restoration Drama: An Anthology*, edited by David Womersley, 553–93. Malden, MA: Blackwell, 2000.
Cibber, Colley. *Plays Written by Mr. Cibber*. 2 vols. London, 1721. ECCO.

Cibber, Colley. *The Refusal; or, The Ladies Philosophy: A Comedy. Acted at the Theatre-Royal, by His Majesty's Servants*. London, 1721. ECCO.
Codr, Dwight. *Raving at Usurers: Anti-Finance and the Ethics of Uncertainty in England, 1690–1750*. Charlottesville: University of Virginia Press, 2016.
Coffman, D'Maris, Adrian Leonard, and Larry Neal, eds. *Questioning Credible Commitment: Perspectives on the Rise of Financial Capitalism*. Cambridge: Cambridge University Press, 2013.
Cogswell, Thomas, and Peter Lake. "Buckingham Does the Globe: *Henry VIII* and the Politics of Popularity in the 1620s." *Shakespeare Quarterly* 60 (2009): 253–78.
Cohen, Ashley L. "The Global Indies: Historicizing Oceanic Metageographies." *Comparative Literature* 69.1 (2017): 7–15.
Collier, Jeremy. *A Short View of the Immorality, and Profaneness of the English Stage, Together with the Sense of Antiquity upon this Argument*. London, 1698. EEBO.
Collins, Margo. "Centlivre v. Hardwicke: Susannah Centlivre's Plays and the Marriage Act of 1753." *Comparative Drama* 33.2 (1999): 179–98.
Combe, Kirk. "Rakes, Wives, and Merchants: Shifts from the Satirical to the Sentimental." In *A Companion to Restoration Drama*, edited by Susan J. Owen, 291–308. Oxford: Blackwell, 2001.
A Comparison between the Two Stages, with an Examen of The Generous Conqueror; and Some Critical Remarks on The Funeral, or Grief Alamode, The False Friend, Tamerlane and Others. In Dialogue. London, 1702. ECCO.
"Concerning the Disturbance at the Play-Houses." In *The Theatrical Review; or, Annals of the Drama*, vol. 1, 108–17. London, 1763. ECCO.
Congreve, William. *William Congreve: Letters and Documents*. Edited by John C. Hodges. New York: Harcourt, Brace & World, 1964.
Connor, Margarette. "Heirs to 'Astrea's vacant throne': Behn's Influence on Trotter, Pix, Manley, and Centlivre." PhD diss., City University of New York, 1995.
Copeland, Nancy. *Staging Gender in Behn and Centlivre: Women's Comedy and the Theatre*. Aldershot, UK: Ashgate, 2004.
Coppola, Al. *The Theater of Experiment: Staging Natural Philosophy in Eighteenth-Century Britain*. Oxford: Oxford University Press, 2016.
Cotton, Nancy. *Women Playwrights in England, c. 1363–1750*. Lewisburg, PA: Bucknell University Press, 1980.
Cowan, Brian. "Mr. Spectator and the Coffeehouse Public Sphere." *Eighteenth-Century Studies* 37 (2004): 345–66.
Cowan, Brian. *The Social Life of Coffee: The Emergence of the British Coffeehouse*. New Haven, CT: Yale University Press, 2005.

Crosthwaite, Paul, Peter Knight, and Nicky Marsh. "Economic Criticism." *The Year's Work in Critical and Cultural Theory* 23 (2015): 108–33.
Crosthwaite, Paul, Peter Knight, and Nicky Marsh. *Show Me the Money: The Image of Finance, 1700 to the Present.* Manchester: Manchester University Press, 2014.
Dale, Richard. *The First Crash: Lessons from the South Sea Bubble.* Princeton, NJ: Princeton University Press, 2004.
Danchin, Pierre. "David Garrick et les prologues et épilogues: Evolution et disparition d'un sous-genre littéraire." *Recherches Anglaises et Nord-Américaines* 35 (2002): 7–13.
Danchin, Pierre. "Prologues and Epilogues as Evidence of Changing Taste on the Eighteenth-Century English Stage." In *Historical and Cultural Contexts of Linguistic and Literary Phenomena,* edited by G. D. Killam, 126–36. Guelph: University of Guelph, 1989.
Danchin, Pierre. *The Prologues and Epilogues of the Eighteenth Century: A Complete Edition.* 8 vols. Nancy, France: Presses Universitaires de Nancy, 1990–2001.
Danchin, Pierre. *The Prologues and Epilogues of the Restoration, 1660–1700.* 7 vols. Nancy, France: Publications Université de Nancy II, 1981–84.
Danchin, Pierre. "Unidentified Items in the Larpent Collection: Addresses, Prologues, and Epilogues." *Huntington Library Quarterly* 64 (2001): 445–67.
[Davenant, Charles.] *Discourses on the Publick Revenues and on the Trade of England.* London, 1698. EEBO.
Davies, Thomas. *Memoirs of the Life of David Garrick, Esq. Interspersed with Characters and Anecdotes of His Theatrical Contemporaries. The Whole Forming a History of the Stage, Which Includes a Period of Thirty-Six Years.* 2 vols. London, 1780. ECCO.
Davis, Vivian. "Dramatizing the Sexual Contract: Congreve and Centlivre." *Studies in English Literature, 1500–1900* 51.3 (2011): 519–43.
Dawson, Mark S. *Gentility and the Comic Theatre of Late Stuart London.* Cambridge: Cambridge University Press, 2005.
Dean, Ann C. *The Talk of the Town: Figurative Publics in Eighteenth-Century Britain.* Lewisburg, PA: Bucknell University Press, 2007.
[Defoe, Daniel.] *An Essay upon Projects.* London, 1697. EEBO.
De Goede, Marieke. *Virtue, Fortune, and Faith: A Genealogy of Finance.* Minneapolis: University of Minnesota Press, 2005.
Dennis, John. *Remarks on a Play, Call'd, The Conscious Lovers, a Comedy.* London, 1723. ECCO.
[Dennis, John.] *The Characters and Conduct of Sir John Edgar, Call'd by Himself Sole Monarch of the Stage in Drury-Lane; and His Three Deputy-Governors. In Two Letters to Sir John Edgar.* London, 1720. ECCO.

[Dennis, John.] *A Defense of Sir Fopling Flutter. A Comedy Written by Sir George Etherege. In Which Defence is Shewn, That Sir Fopling, That Merry Knight, Was Rightly Compos'd by the Knight His Father, to Answer the Ends of Comedy; and That He Has Been Barbarously and Scurrilously Attack'd by the Knight His Brother, in the 65th Spectator. By Which It Appears, That the Latter Knight Knows Nothing of the Nature of Comedy.* London, 1722. ECCO.

Depledge, Emma Lesley. "Playbills, Prologues, and Playbooks: Selling Shakespeare Adaptations, 1678–82." *Philological Quarterly* 91 (2012): 305–30.

Deringer, William Peter. "Finding the Money: Public Accounting, Political Arithmetic, and Probability in the 1690s." *Journal of British Studies* 52 (2013): 638–68.

Deutsch, Otto Erich. *Handel: A Documentary Biography.* New York: Norton, 1955.

Dharwadker, Aparna. "Restoration Drama and Social Class." In *A Companion to Restoration Drama*, edited by Susan J. Owen, 140–60. Oxford: Blackwell Publishers, 2001.

A Dialogue in the Green-Room upon a Disturbance in the Pit. London, 1763. ECCO.

Dick, Alexander. *Romanticism and the Gold Standard: Money, Literature and Economic Debate in Britain, 1790–1830.* Basingstoke, UK: Palgrave Macmillan, 2013.

Dickson, P. G. M. *The Financial Revolution in England: A Study in the Development of Public Credit, 1688–1756.* London: St. Martin's Press, 1967.

Dillon, Elizabeth Maddock. *New World Drama: The Performative Commons in the Atlantic World, 1649–1849.* Durham, NC: Duke University Press, 2014.

Donahue, Jennifer. "Bringing the Other into View: Confronting the West Indian Creole in the *Conscious Lovers* and the *West Indian.*" *Restoration and Eighteenth-Century Theatre Research* 26 (2011): 41–56.

Donaldson, Ian. "'The Fripperie of Wit': Jonson and Plagiarism." In *Plagiarism in Early Modern England*, edited by Paulina Kewes, 119–33. New York: Palgrave Macmillan, 2003.

Downes, John. *Roscius Anglicanus, or, an Historical Review of the Stage: After It Had Been Suppres'd by Means of the Late Unhappy Civil War, Begun in 1641, Till the Time of King Charles the II's Restoration in May 1660. Giving an Account of Its Rise Again; of the Times and Places the Governours of Both the Companies First Erected Their Theatres.* London, 1708. ECCO.

Downes, Melissa K. "Ladies of Ill-Repute: The South Sea Bubble, the Caribbean, and *The Jamaica Lady.*" *Studies in Eighteenth-Century Culture* 33 (2004): 23–48.

[Drake, James, and John Fletcher.] *The Sham Lawyer, or, The Lucky Extravagant. As It Was Damnably Acted at the Theatre-Royal in Drury-Lane.* London, 1697. EEBO.

Drougge, Helga. "Colley Cibber's 'Genteel Comedy': *Love's Last Shift* and *The Careless Husband*." *Studia Neophilologica* 54 (1982): 61–79.
Dryden, John. *Of Dramatick Poesie, an Essay*. London, 1668. EEBO.
Dryden, John Jr. *The Husband His Own Cuckold. A Comedy. As It Is Acted at the Theater in Little Lincolns-Inn-Fields, by His Majesty's Servants*. London, 1696. EEBO.
Duncombe, John. *The Feminiad: A Poem*. London, 1754. ECCO.
Egerton, William [Edmund Curll]. *Faithful Memoirs of the Life, Amours and Performances of That Justly Celebrated, and Most Eminent Actress of Her Time, Mrs. Anne Oldfield. Interspersed with Several Other Dramatical Memoirs*. London, 1731. ECCO.
Ennis, Daniel J., and Judith Bailey Slagle, eds. *Prologues, Epilogues, Curtain-Raisers, and Afterpieces: The Rest of the Eighteenth-Century London Stage*. Newark: University of Delaware Press, 2007.
The Entertainment Perform'd at the Theatre-Royal in Dorset-Garden, at Drawing the Lottery call'd The Wheel of Fortune: Being the Speeches Addrest to the Spectators, as Prologues and Epilogues. London, 1698. EEBO.
Evelyn, John. *The Diary of John Evelyn*. Vol. 5, *Kalendarium, 1690–1706*, edited by E. S. De Beer. London: Oxford University Press, 1955.
Fawcett, Julia H. "The Overexpressive Celebrity and the Deformed King: Recasting the Spectacle as Subject in Colley Cibber's *Richard III*." *PMLA* 126 (2011): 950–65.
Fawcett, Julia H. *Spectacular Disappearances: Celebrity and Privacy, 1696–1801*. Ann Arbor: University of Michigan Press, 2016.
Filmer, Edward. *The Unnatural Brother: A Tragedy. As It Was Acted by His Majesty's Servants, at the Theatre in Little Lincoln's-Inn-Fields*. London, 1697. EEBO.
Finke, Laurie. "Virtue in Fashion: The Fate of Women in the Comedies of Cibber and Vanbrugh." In *From Renaissance to Restoration: Metamorphoses of the Drama*, edited by Robert Markley and Laurie Finke, 154–79. Cleveland, OH: Bellflower, 1984.
Finn, Margot C. *The Character of Credit: Personal Debt in English Culture, 1740–1914*. Cambridge: Cambridge University Press, 2003.
Fletcher, John. *Bonduca, or, The British Heroine, a Tragedy. Acted at the Theatre Royal. By His Majesty's Servants. With a New Entertainment of Musick, Vocal and Instrumental*. London, 1696. EEBO.
Fone, B. R. S. "'Love's Last Shift' and Sentimental Comedy." *Restoration and Eighteenth-Century Theatre Research* 9 (1970): 11–23.
Forman, Valerie. "Marked Angels: Counterfeits, Commodities, and *The Roaring Girl*." *Renaissance Quarterly* 54 (2001): 1531–60.

Forman, Valerie. *Tragicomic Redemptions: Global Economics and the Early Modern English Stage*. Philadelphia: University of Pennsylvania Press, 2008.
Frank, Marcie. *Gender, Theatre, and the Origins of Criticism from Dryden to Manley*. Cambridge: Cambridge University Press, 2003.
Fraser, Nancy. "Rethinking the Public Sphere: A Contribution to the Critique of Actually Existing Democracy." In *Habermas and the Public Sphere*, edited by Craig Calhoun, 109–42. Cambridge, MA: MIT Press, 1992.
Freeman, Lisa A. *Antitheatricality and the Body Public*. Philadelphia: University of Pennsylvania Press, 2016.
Freeman, Lisa A. *Character's Theater: Genre and Identity on the Eighteenth-Century English Stage*. Philadelphia: University of Pennsylvania Press, 2002.
Froide, Amy M. *Silent Partners: Women as Public Investors during Britain's Financial Revolution, 1690–1750*. Oxford: Oxford University Press, 2017.
Gallagher, Catherine. *The Body Economic: Life, Death, and Sensation in Political Economy and the Victorian Novel*. Princeton, NJ: Princeton University Press, 2006.
Gallagher, Catherine. *Nobody's Story: The Vanishing Acts of Women Writers in the Marketplace, 1670–1820*. Berkeley: University of California Press, 1994.
Garber, Peter M. *Famous First Bubbles: The Fundamentals of Early Manias*. Cambridge, MA: MIT Press, 2000.
[Garrick, David.] "Fitzgig's Triumph." In *The Poetical Works of David Garrick, Esq. Now First Collected into Two Volumes. With Explanatory Notes*, vol. 2, 492–99. Edited by George Kearsley. London, 1785. ECCO.
Gavin, Michael. *The Invention of English Criticism: 1650–1760*. Cambridge: Cambridge University Press, 2015.
Genest, John. *Some Account of the English Stage: From the Restoration in 1660 to 1830*. 10 vols. Bath, UK: H. E. Carrington, 1832. HathiTrust Digital Library.
Genovese, Michael. *The Problem of Profit: Finance and Feeling in Eighteenth-Century British Literature*. Charlottesville: University of Virginia Press, 2019.
Gieger, Jason Curtis. "Susanna Centlivre, Sir George Etherege, and the Invention of the Restoration Comedy of Manners, 1880–1940." *Restoration and Eighteenth-Century Theatre Research* 17.1 (2012): 75–95.
[Gildon, Charles.] *The Post-Boy Robb'd of His Mail: or, The Pacquet Broke Open. Consisting of Letters of Love and Gallantry, and All Miscellaneous Subjects: In Which Are Discover'd the Vertues, Vices, Follies, Humours and Intrigues of Mankind*. 1705. 2nd ed., London, 1706. ECCO.
Gilmour, Ian. *Riot, Rising, and Revolution: Governance and Violence in Eighteenth-Century England*. London: Pimlico, 1993.

Glaisyer, Natasha. "'A Due Circulation in the Veins of the Publick': Imagining Credit in Late Seventeenth- and Early Eighteenth-Century England." *The Eighteenth Century: Theory and Interpretation* 46.3 (2005): 277–97.

Gollapudi, Aparna. *Moral Reform in Comedy and Culture, 1696–1747.* Farnham, UK: Ashgate, 2011.

Gould, Robert. *The Rival Sisters, or, The Violence of Love, a Tragedy. As It Is Acted at the Theatre-Royal, by His Majesty's Servants.* London, 1696. EEBO.

Goux, Jean-Joseph. *Symbolic Economies: After Marx and Freud.* Ithaca, NY: Cornell University Press, 1990.

Greene, Jody. *The Trouble with Ownership: Literary Property and Authorial Liability in England, 1660–1730.* Philadelphia: University of Pennsylvania Press, 2005.

Habermas, Jürgen. *The Structural Transformation of the Public Sphere: An Inquiry into a Category of Bourgeois Society.* 1962. Translated by Thomas Burger and Frederick Lawrence. Cambridge, MA: MIT Press, 1989.

Hadley, Elaine. *Melodramatic Tactics: Theatricalized Dissent in the English Marketplace, 1800–1885.* Stanford, CA: Stanford University Press, 1995.

[Hammond, Anthony.] *A Modest Apology. Occasion'd by the Late Unhappy Turn of Affairs, with Relation to Public Credit.* London, 1721. ECCO.

Hammond, Brean S. "Is There a Whig Canon? The Case of Susanna Centlivre." *Women's Writing* 7.3 (2000): 373–90.

Hammond, Brean S. *Professional Imaginative Writing in England, 1670–1740: "Hackney for Bread."* Oxford: Clarendon, 1997.

Harris, Joseph. *The City Bride: Or, The Merry Cuckold. A Comedy. Acted at the New Theatre, in Little Lincolns Inn-Fields. By His Majesty's Servants.* London, 1696. EEBO.

Harris, Michael. "Timely Notices: The Uses of Advertising and Its Relationship to News during the Late Seventeenth Century." In *News, Newspapers, and Society in Early Modern Britain*, edited by Joad Raymond, 141–56. London: Frank Cass, 1999.

Harris, Tim. "Perceptions of the Crowd in Later Stuart London." In *Imagining Early Modern London: Perceptions and Portrayals of the City from Stow to Strype, 1598–1720*, edited by J. F. Merritt, 250–72. Cambridge: Cambridge University Press, 2001.

Hayley, R. L. "The 'Swingeing' of Cibber: The Suppression of the First Edition of *The Refusal.*" *Studies in Bibliography* 28 (1975): 290–97.

Hayley, R. L. "The Scriblerians and the South Sea Bubble: A Hit by Cibber." *Review of English Studies* 24 (1973): 452–58.

Hibbert, Christopher, Ben Weinreb, John Keay, and Julia Keay, eds. *The London Encyclopædia.* 3rd ed. London: Macmillan, 1983, 2008.

An Historical and Succinct Account of the Late Riots at the Theatres of Drury-Lane and Covent-Garden. Interspersed with the Principal Letters and Advertisements that Have Been Published on Each Side of the Question. London, 1763. ECCO.

Hogarth, William. *An Emblematical Print on the South Sea Scheme.* London, 1721. In *Engravings by Hogarth*, edited by Sean Shesgreen. New York: Dover, 1973.

Hogarth, William. *The Lottery.* London, 1724. Metropolitan Museum of Art, New York.

Hoppit, Julian. "Financial Crises in Eighteenth-Century England." *Economic History Review* 39 (1986): 39–58.

Hoppit, Julian. "The Myths of the South Sea Bubble." *Transactions of the Royal Historical Society* 12 (2002): 141–65.

Horejsi, Nicole. "(Re)Valuing the 'Foreign Trinket': Sentimentalizing the Language of Economics in Steele's *Conscious Lovers.*" *Restoration and Eighteenth-Century Theatre Research* 18 (2003): 11–36.

Horwitz, Henry. *Parliament, Policy, and Politics in the Reign of William III.* Manchester, UK: Manchester University Press, 1977.

Hotson, Leslie. *The Commonwealth and Restoration Stage.* Cambridge, MA: Harvard University Press, 1928.

Howard, Jean E. *Theater of a City: The Places of London Comedy, 1598–1642.* Philadelphia: University of Pennsylvania Press, 2007.

Hoxby, Blair. *Mammon's Music: Literature and Economics in the Age of Milton.* New Haven, CT: Yale University Press, 2002.

Hughes, Derek. "Cibber and Vanbrugh: Language, Place, and Social Order in *Love's Last Shift.*" *Comparative Drama* 20 (1986–87): 287–304.

Hughes, Leo. *The Drama's Patrons: A Study of the Eighteenth-Century London Audience.* Austin: University of Texas Press, 1971.

Hume, Robert D. "Before the Bard: 'Shakespeare' in Early Eighteenth-Century London." *English Literary History* 64 (1997): 41–75.

Hume, Robert D. *The Development of English Drama in the Late Seventeenth Century.* Oxford: Clarendon Press, 1976.

Hume, Robert D. "The Economics of Culture in London, 1660–1740." *Huntington Library Quarterly* 69 (2006): 487–533.

Hume, Robert D. "Securing a Repertory: Plays on the London Stage, 1660–5." In *Poetry and Drama, 1570–1700: Essays in Honour of Harold F. Brooks*, edited by Antony Coleman and Anton Hammond, 156–72. London: Methuen, 1981.

Hume, Robert D. "The Sponsorship of Opera in London, 1704–1720." *Modern Philology* 85 (1988): 420–32.

Hume, Robert D. "Theatre as Property in Eighteenth-Century London." *Journal for Eighteenth-Century Studies* 31 (2008): 17–46.
Hunt, Margaret R. *The Middling Sort: Commerce, Gender, and the Family in England, 1680–1780*. Berkeley: University of California Press, 1996.
Hutchinson, T. W. *Before Adam Smith: The Emergence of Political Economy, 1662–1776*. Oxford: Blackwell, 1988.
Hynes, Peter. "Richard Steele and the Genealogy of Sentimental Drama: A Reading of *The Conscious Lovers*." *Papers on Language and Literature* 40 (2004): 142–66.
Ingram, Jill Philips. *Idioms of Self-Interest: Credit, Identity, and Property in Early Modern English Literature*. New York: Routledge, 2006.
Ingrassia, Catherine. *Authorship, Commerce, and Gender in Early Eighteenth-Century England: A Culture of Paper Credit*. New York: Cambridge University Press, 1998.
[Jacob, Giles.] *The Poetical Register: Or, the Lives and Characters of the English Dramatick Poets. With an Account of their Writings*. 2 vols. London, 1719. ECCO.
The Jamaica Lady: or, The Life of Bavia. Containing an Account of Her Intrigues, Cheats, Amours in England, Jamaica, and the Royal Navy. A Pleasant Relation of the Amours of the Officers of a Fourth Rate Man of War with Their Female Passengers, in a Voyage from Jamaica to England. London, 1720. ECCO.
Jerrold, Walter, and Clare Jerrold. *Five Queer Women*. London: Brentano's, 1929.
Johns, Adrian. *The Nature of the Book: Print and Knowledge in the Making*. Chicago: University of Chicago Press, 1998.
Johns, Adrian. *Piracy: The Intellectual Property Wars from Gutenberg to Gates*. Chicago: University of Chicago Press, 2010.
Jones, D. W. *War and Economy in the Age of William III and Marlborough*. Oxford: Basil Blackwell, 1988.
Jonson, Ben. *The Workes of Beniamin Ionson*. London, 1616. EEBO.
Judge, Elizabeth F. "Kidnapped and Counterfeit Characters: Eighteenth-Century Fan Fiction, Copyright Law, and the Custody of Fictional Characters." In *Originality and Intellectual Property in the French and English Enlightenment*, edited by Reginald McGinnis, 22–68. New York: Routledge, 2009.
Kelly, Patrick Hyde. *Locke on Money*. 2 vols. Oxford: Clarendon, 1991.
Kenny, Shirley Strum, ed. *The Plays of Richard Steele*. Oxford: Clarendon, 1971.
Kewes, Paulina. *Authorship and Appropriation: Writing for the Stage in England, 1660–1710*. Oxford: Clarendon, 1998.

Kewes, Paulina, ed. *Plagiarism in Early Modern England*. New York: Palgrave Macmillan, 2003.

"The Killigrew and Davenant Patents." In *Survey of London*. Vol. 35, *The Theatre Royal, Drury Lane, and the Royal Opera House, Covent Garden*, edited by F. H. W. Sheppard, 1–8. London: London County Council, 1970.

Kitch, Aaron. "The Character of Credit and the Problem of Belief in Middleton's City Comedies." *Studies in English Literature* 47 (2007): 403–26.

Kleer, Richard A. "'The folly of particulars': The Political Economy of the South Sea Bubble." *Financial History Review* 19.2 (2012): 175–97.

Kleer, Richard A. *Money, Politics, and Power: Banking and Public Finance in Wartime England, 1694–96*. Abingdon, UK: Routledge, 2017.

Kleer, Richard A. "Riding a Wave: The Company's Role in the South Sea Bubble." *Economic History Review* 68.1 (February 2015): 264–85.

Klein, Naomi. *The Shock Doctrine: The Rise of Disaster Capitalism*. New York: Picador, 2007.

Knapp, J. Merrill. "Handel, the Royal Academy of Music, and Its First Opera Season in London (1720)." *Musical Quarterly* 45 (1959): 145–67.

Knapp, Mary E. *Prologues and Epilogues of the Eighteenth Century*. New Haven, CT: Yale University Press, 1961.

Knight, Peter. "Speculation." In *The Routledge Companion to Literature and Economics*, edited by Matt Seybold and Michelle Chihara, 346–56. London: Routledge, 2019.

Koon, Helene. *Colley Cibber: A Biography*. Lexington: University Press of Kentucky, 1986.

Kramnick, Isaac. *Bolingbroke and His Circle: The Politics of Nostalgia in the Age of Walpole*. Cambridge, MA: Harvard University Press, 1968.

Kreis-Schinck, Annette. *Women, Writing, and the Theater in the Early Modern Period: The Plays of Aphra Behn and Susanne Centlivre*. Madison, NJ: Farleigh Dickson University Press, 2001.

Kroll, Richard. *Restoration Drama and "The Circle of Commerce": Tragicomedy, Politics, and Trade in the Seventeenth Century*. Cambridge: Cambridge University Press, 2007.

Lake, Peter, and Stephen Pincus, eds. *The Politics of the Public Sphere in Early Modern England*. Manchester: Manchester University Press, 2007.

Lake, Peter, and Stephen Pincus. "Rethinking the Public Sphere in Early Modern England." *Journal of British Studies* 45 (2006): 270–92.

Landreth, David. *The Face of Mammon: The Matter of Money in English Renaissance Literature*. Oxford: Oxford University Press, 2012.

Langbaine, Gerard. *The Lives and Characters of the English Dramatick Poets. Also an Exact Account of All the Plays that Were Ever Yet Printed in the English*

Tongue, Their Double Titles, the Places Where Acted, the Dates When Printed, and the Persons to Whom Dedicated, With Remarks and Observations on Most of the Said Plays. London, 1699. EEBO.

Langhans, Edward A. "The Theatres." In *The London Theatre World, 1660–1800*, edited by Robert D. Hume, 35–65. Carbondale: Southern Illinois University Press, 1980.

Larkin, Charles James. "The Great Recoinage of 1696: Charles Davenant and Monetary Theory." In *Money and Political Economy in the Enlightenment*, edited by Daniel Carey, 83–116. Oxford: Voltaire Foundation, 2014.

LaRue, C. Steven. *Handel and His Singers: The Creation of the Royal Academy Operas, 1720–28*. Oxford: Clarendon, 1995.

Leinwand, Theodore B. *Theatre, Finance, and Society in Early Modern England*. Cambridge: Cambridge University Press, 1999.

A Letter from the Dead Thomas Brown to the Living Heraclitus: With Heraclitus Ridens, His Answer. To Which is Added, the Last Will and Testament of Mr. Thomas Brown, Archi-Poet & Celeberrimi. Wherein Are Inserted the Several Legacies He Bequeathed to the Poets that Survive Him. London, 1704. British Library via Google Books.

Lewcock, Dawn. *Sir William Davenant, the Court Masque, and the English Seventeenth-Century Scenic Stage, c. 1605–1700*. Amherst, NY: Cambria Press, 2008.

Li, Ming-Hsun. *The Great Recoinage of 1696–9*. London: Weidenfeld and Nicolson, 1963.

"Life of Mrs. Susanna Centlivre." In *The Court Miscellany, or, Ladies New Magazine*, 57–61. London, 1765. ECCO.

Lock, F. P. *Susanna Centlivre*. Boston: Twayne, 1979.

Locke, John. *Further Considerations Concerning Raising the Value of Money. Wherein Mr. Lowndes's Arguments for It in His Late Report Concerning an Essay for the Amendment of the Silver Coins, are Particularly Examined*. London, 1695. EEBO.

[Locke, John.] *Some Considerations of the Consequences of the Lowering of Interest, and Raising the Value of Money. In A Letter to a Member of Parliament*. London, 1692. EEBO.

Loewenstein, Joseph. *The Author's Due: Printing and the Prehistory of Copyright*. Chicago: University of Chicago Press, 2010.

Loewenstein, Joseph. *Ben Jonson and Possessive Authorship*. Cambridge: Cambridge University Press, 2002.

Loftis, John Clyde. *The Politics of Drama in Augustan England*. Oxford: Clarendon Press, 1963.

Loftis, John Clyde, ed. *Richard Steele's* The Theatre. Oxford: Clarendon Press, 1962.

Loftis, John Clyde. *Steele at Drury Lane*. Berkeley: University of California Press, 1952.

The London Stage, 1660–1800: A Calendar of Plays, Entertainments and Afterpieces, Together with Casts, Box-Receipts and Contemporary Comment. Compiled from the Playbills, Newspapers and Theatrical Diaries of the Period. Part 1, 1660–1700, edited by William Van Lennep; part 2, 1700–29 (2 vols.), edited by Emmett L. Avery; part 3, 1729–47 (2 vols.), edited by Arthur H. Scouten; part 4, 1747–76 (3 vols.), edited by George Winchester Stone Jr.; part 5, 1776–1800 (3 vols.), edited by Charles Beecher Hogan. Carbondale: Southern Illinois University Press, 1965–68.

Lord Chamberlain's Department: Miscellaneous Records. Warrant Books: General. 1704–9. National Archives. Kew, UK.

Lowerre, Kathryn. *Music and Musicians on the London Stage, 1695–1705*. Farnham, UK: Ashgate, 2009.

[Lowndes, William.] *A Report Containing an Essay for the Amendment of the Silver Coins*. London, 1695. EEBO.

The Lunatick. A Comedy. Dedicated to the Three Ruling B—S at the New-House in Lincolns-Inn-Fields. London, 1705. ECCO.

Lynch, Deidre Shauna. *The Economy of Character: Novels, Market Culture, and the Business of Inner Meaning*. Chicago: University of Chicago Press, 1998.

Mackay, Charles. *Memoirs of Extraordinary Popular Delusions and the Madness of Crowds*. London: National Illustrated Library, 1852. Originally published as *Memoirs of Extraordinary Popular Delusions*, London: Richard Bentley, 1841.

Mackie, Erin. "Jamaican Ladies and Tropical Charms." *ARIEL: A Review of Literature* 37 (2006): 189–220.

Mackie, Erin. *Market à la Mode: Fashion, Commodity, and Gender in* The Tatler *and* The Spectator. Baltimore: Johns Hopkins University Press, 1997.

MacMillan, Dougald. "The Text of *Love's Last Shift*." *Modern Language Notes* 46 (1931): 518–19.

Maguire, Nancy Klein. *Regicide and Restoration: English Tragicomedy, 1660–1671*. Cambridge: Cambridge University Press, 1992.

Mandell, Laura. *Misogynous Economies: The Business of Literature in Eighteenth-Century Britain*. Lexington: University Press of Kentucky, 1999.

Manley, Delarivier. *The New Atalantis*. Edited by Rosalind Ballaster. London: Pickering and Chatto, 1991; Penguin, 1992.

Maruca, Lisa. *The Work of Print: Authorship and the English Text Trades, 1660–1760*. Seattle: University of Washington Press, 2007.

Maus, Katharine Eisaman. *Inwardness and Theater in the English Renaissance*. Chicago: University of Chicago Press, 1995.

McCallum, Paul. "Cozening the Pit: Prologues, Epilogues, and Poetic Authority in Restoration England." In *Prologues, Epilogues, Curtain-Raisers, and Afterpieces: The Rest of the Eighteenth-Century London Stage*, edited by Daniel J. Ennis and Judith Bailey Slagle, 33–69. Newark: University of Delaware Press, 2007.

McClanahan, Annie. *Dead Pledges: Debt, Crisis, and Twenty-First-Century Culture*. Stanford, CA: Stanford University Press, 2016.

McDowell, Paula. *The Women of Grub Street: Press, Politics, and Gender in the London Literary Marketplace, 1678–1730*. Oxford: Clarendon Press, 1998.

McGeary, Thomas. *The Politics of Opera in Handel's Britain*. Cambridge: Cambridge University Press, 2013.

McGirr, Elaine. *Partial Histories: A Reappraisal of Colley Cibber*. London: Palgrave Macmillan, 2016.

McGirr, Elaine. "Rethinking Reform Comedies: Colley Cibber's Desiring Women." *Eighteenth-Century Studies* 46 (2013): 385–97.

McKeon, Michael. "Parsing Habermas's 'Bourgeois Public Sphere.'" *Criticism* 46 (2004): 273–77.

McKeon, Michael. *The Secret History of Domesticity: Public, Private, and the Division of Knowledge*. Baltimore: Johns Hopkins University Press, 2005.

McPherson, Heather. "Theatrical Riots and Cultural Politics in Eighteenth-Century London." *Eighteenth Century: Theory and Interpretation* (2002): 236–52.

Meehan, Johanna, ed. *Feminists Read Habermas: Gendering the Subject of Discourse*. London: Routledge, 1995.

Michaels, Walter Benn. *The Gold Standard and the Logic of Naturalism: American Literature at the Turn of the Century*. Berkeley: University of California Press, 1987.

Milhous, Judith. "Company Management." In *The London Theatre World, 1660–1800*, edited by Robert D. Hume, 1–34. Carbondale: Southern Illinois University Press, 1980.

Milhous, Judith. *Thomas Betterton and the Management of Lincoln's Inn Fields, 1695–1708*. Carbondale: Southern Illinois University Press, 1979.

Milhous, Judith, and Robert Hume. "Dating Play Premieres from Publication Data, 1660–1700." *Harvard Library Bulletin* 22 (1974): 374–405.

Milhous, Judith, and Robert Hume. *A Register of English Theatrical Documents 1660–1737*. Carbondale: Southern Illinois University Press, 1991.

Milhous, Judith, and Robert Hume. *Vice Chamberlain Coke's Theatrical Papers, 1706–1715*. Carbondale: Southern Illinois University Press, 1982.

Milling, Jane. "'For Without Vanity, I'm Better Known': Restoration Actors and Metatheatre on the London Stage." *Theatre Survey* 52 (2011): 59–82.

Milling, Jane. "'A Gotham Election': Women and Performance Politics." *Restoration and Eighteenth-Century Theatre Research* 21.2 (2006): 74–89.
Minutes of "Proceedings" of the Court of Directors of the South Sea Company "in vertue of ye Act. to encrease the S[outh] S[ea] Capital. 1720." British Library. London.
A Miscellaneous Collection of Poems, Songs and Epigrams. By Several Hands. Publish'd by T. M. Gent. 2 vols. Dublin, 1721.
Mitchell, Robert. "'Beings that Have Existence Only in Ye Minds of Men': State Finance and the Origins of Collective Imagination." *The Eighteenth Century* 49 (2008): 117–39.
Molesworth, Jessie. *Chance and the Eighteenth-Century Novel: Realism, Probability, Magic.* Cambridge: Cambridge University Press, 2010.
A Monthly Packet of Advices from Parnassus, Establish'd by Apollo's Express Authority, and Sent to England. London, 1723. British Library. London.
Moody, Jane, and Daniel O'Quinn. Preface to *The Cambridge Companion to British Theatre, 1730–1830*, edited by Jane Moody and Daniel O'Quinn, xiii–xvi. Cambridge: Cambridge University Press, 2007.
Muldrew, Craig. *The Economy of Obligation: The Culture of Credit and Social Relations in Early Modern England.* Basingstoke, UK: Macmillan, 1998.
Munro, Ian. *The Figure of the Crowd in Early Modern London: The City and Its Double.* New York: Palgrave Macmillan, 2005.
Murphy, Anne L. "Lotteries in the 1690s: Investment or Gamble?" *Financial History Review* 12 (2005): 227–46.
Murphy, Anne L. *The Origins of English Financial Markets: Investment and Speculation before the South Sea Bubble.* Cambridge: Cambridge University Press, 2009.
Nadj, Julijana. "'Free Zones of Speech': Multiple Functions of Aphra Behn's Dramatic Prologues and Epilogues." In *Funktionen von Literatur: Theoretische Grundlagen und Modellinterpretationen*, edited by Marion Gymnich and Ansgar Nünning, 143–56. Trier: Wissenschaftlicher Verlag Trier, 2005.
Neal, Larry. *The Rise of Financial Capitalism: International Capital Markets in the Age of Reason.* Cambridge: Cambridge University Press, 1990.
Nicoll, Allardyce. *A History of English Drama 1660–1900.* 7 vols. 3rd ed. Cambridge: Cambridge University Press, 1952.
Nichols, John. *Literary Anecdotes of the Eighteenth Century, Comprizing Biographical Memoirs of William Bowyer, Printer, F. S. A. and Many of His Learned Friends; An Incidental View of the Progress and Advancement of Literature in This Kingdom During the Last Century; and Biographical Anecdotes of a Considerable Number of Eminent Writers and Ingenious Artists.* 9 vols. London, 1814.

Nichols, John, ed. *The Theatre, by Sir Richard Steele; to Which Are Added, The Anti-Theatre; The Character of Sir John Edgar; Steele's Case with the Lord Chamberlain; The Crisis of Property, with the Sequel, Two Pasquins, &c. &c. Illustrated with Literary and Historical Anecdotes by John Nichols.* London, 1791. ECCO.

Nicholson, Colin. *Writing and the Rise of Finance: Capital Satires of the Early Eighteenth Century.* Cambridge: Cambridge University Press, 1994.

North, Douglass C., and Barry R. Weingast. "Constitutions and Commitment: The Evolution of Institutions Governing Public Choice in Seventeenth-Century England." *Journal of Economic History* 49 (1989): 803–32.

[Norton, Richard.] *Pausanias, The Betrayer of His Country. A Tragedy, Acted at the Theatre Royal, By His Majesties Servants.* London, 1696. EEBO.

Nussbaum, Felicity. *Rival Queens: Actresses, Performance, and the Eighteenth-Century British Theater.* Philadelphia: University of Pennsylvania Press, 2010.

O'Brien, John. "Busy Bodies: The Plots of Susanna Centlivre." In *Eighteenth-Century Genre and Culture: Serious Reflections on Occasional Form: Essays in Honor of J. Paul Hunter,* edited by Dennis Todd and Cynthia Wall, 170–83. Newark: University of Delaware Press, 2001.

O'Brien, John. *Harlequin Britain: Pantomime and Entertainment, 1690–1760.* Baltimore: Johns Hopkins University Press, 2004.

O'Brien, John. Introduction to *The Wonder: A Woman Keeps a Secret,* by Susanna Centlivre, 9–28. Petersborough, Ontario: Broadview, 2004.

O'Brien, John. *Literature Incorporated: The Cultural Unconscious of the Business Corporation, 1650–1850.* Chicago: University of Chicago Press, 2016.

Oney, Jay Edward. "Women Playwrights during the Struggle for Control of the London Theatre, 1695–1710." PhD diss., Ohio State University, Columbus, 1996.

O'Quinn, Daniel, and Gillian Russell. Introduction to "Georgian Theatre in an Information Age: Media, Performance, Sociability," *Eighteenth-Century Fiction* 27 (2015): 337–40.

Owen, John, and Arthur L. Cooke. "Addison vs. Steele, 1708." *PMLA* 68.1 (1953): 313–20.

Owen, Susan J., ed. *A Companion to Restoration Drama.* Oxford: Blackwell Publishers, 2001.

Papers (Bound) of Miscellaneous Nature, Concerning Applications for Licences; Grants and Renewals of the Same; Notifications of Management Appointments in Theatres; Complaints, Including Abuses of Licence and Unlicensed Performances, Contents of Plays and Behaviour at Performances; Playbills; Surveys of Buildings and Building Works; Patents and Petitions. 1673/4–1797. National Archives. Kew, UK.

Papers Relating to the Patent of Drury Lane Theatre, etc. British Library. London.

Parnell, Paul E. "Equivocation in Cibber's 'Love's Last Shift.'" *Studies in Philology* 57 (1960): 519–34.

Parsons, Wayne. *The Power of the Financial Press: Journalism and Economic Opinion in Britain and America.* Aldershot, UK: Edward Elgar, 1989.

Pasanek, Brad. *Metaphors of Mind: An Eighteenth-Century Dictionary.* Baltimore: Johns Hopkins University Press, 2015.

Paul, Helen J. *The South Sea Bubble: An Economic History of Its Origins and Consequences.* London: Routledge, 2010.

Pearson, Jacqueline. *The Prostituted Muse: Images of Women and Women Dramatists, 1642–1737.* New York: St. Martin's, 1989.

Pearson, Jacqueline, ed. *Susanna Centlivre.* Vol. 3 of *Eighteenth-Century Women Playwrights.* Series editor Derek Hughes. London: Pickering and Chatto, 2001.

Peck, James. "Anne Oldfield's Lady Townly: Consumption, Credit, and the Whig Hegemony of the 1720s." *Theatre Journal* 49 (1997): 397–416.

Pedicord, Harry William. "The Changing Audience." In *The London Theatre World, 1660–1800,* edited by Robert D. Hume, 236–52. Carbondale: Southern Illinois University Press, 1980.

Peters, J. S. "The Bank, the Press and the 'Return of Nature': On Currency, Credit, and Literary Property in the 1690s." In *Early Modern Conceptions of Property,* edited by John Brewer and Susan Staves, 365–88. London: Routledge, 1995.

Peters, J. S. "The Novelty; or, Print, Money, Fashion, Getting, Spending, and Glut." In *Cultural Readings of Restoration and Eighteenth-Century English Theater,* edited by J. Douglas Canfield and Deborah C. Payne, 169–94. Athens: University of Georgia Press, 1995.

Peters, Julie Stone. *Theatre of the Book, 1480–1880: Print, Text, and Performance in Europe.* Oxford: Oxford University Press, 2000.

Phelan, Peggy. *Unmarked: The Politics of Performance.* London: Routledge, 1993.

Pincus, Steven. "Shadwell's Dramatic Trimming." In *Religion, Literature, and Politics in Post-Reformation England, 1540–1688,* edited by Donna B. Hamilton and Richard Strier, 253–74. Cambridge: Cambridge University Press, 1996.

Pincus, Steven. *1688: The First Modern Revolution.* New Haven, CT: Yale University Press, 2009.

The Players Turn'd Academicks: or, A Description (in Merry Metre) of Their Translation from the Theatre in Little Lincoln's-Inn Fields, to the Tennis-Court in Oxford. London, 1703. ECCO.

Pocock, J. G. A. *Virtue, Commerce, and History: Essays on Political Thought and History, Chiefly in the Eighteenth Century*. Cambridge: Cambridge University Press, 1985.

Poovey, Mary. "From the South Sea Bubble to Modern Finance: The Legacy of Two Eighteenth-Century Economic Ideas." In *Political Economy, Literature, and the Formation of Knowledge, 1720–1850*, edited by Richard Adelman and Catherine Packham, 205–19. New York: Routledge, 2018.

Poovey, Mary. *Genres of the Credit Economy: Mediating Value in Eighteenth- and Nineteenth-Century Britain*. Chicago: University of Chicago Press, 2008.

[Pope, Alexander.] *The Dunciad, in Four Books. Printed According to the Complete Copy Found in the Year 1742. With the Prolegomena of Scriblerus, and Notes Variorum*. London, 1743. ECCO.

[Pope, Alexander.] *The Dunciad, Variorum, with the Prolegomena of Scriblerus*. London, 1729. ECCO.

[Pope, Alexander.] *A Further Account of the Most Deplorable Condition of Mr. Edmund Curll. Since His Being Poison'd on the 28th of March. To Be Publish'd Weekly*. London, 1716. ECCO.

Potter, Lois. "Colley Cibber: The Fop as Hero." In *Augustan Worlds*, edited by J. C. Hilson, M. M. B. Jones, and J. R. Watson, 153–64. Leicester, UK: Leicester University Press, 1978.

Powell, Jocelyn. *Restoration Theatre Production*. London: Routledge and Kegan Paul, 1984.

Powell, Manushag. *Performing Authorship in Eighteenth-Century English Periodicals*. Lewisburg, PA: Bucknell University Press, 2012.

Prescott, Paul. *Reviewing Shakespeare: Journalism and Performance from the Eighteenth Century to the Present*. Cambridge: Cambridge University Press, 2013.

Prologue Design'd for the Last New Farce, Call'd, The Fool's Expectation: Or, The Wheel of Fortune. Acted at the Theatre Royal in Dorset Gardens. London, 1698. EEBO.

Quinn, Steven. "Gold, Silver, and the Glorious Revolution: Arbitrage between Bills of Exchange and Bullion." *Economic History Review* 49 (1996): 473–90.

Randall, Adrian. *Riotous Assemblies: Popular Protest in Hanoverian England*. Oxford: Oxford University Press, 2006.

Randall, Adrian, Andrew Charlesworth, Richard Sheldon, and David Walsh. "Markets, Market Culture and Popular Protest in Eighteenth-Century Britain and Ireland." In *Markets, Market Culture, and Popular Protest in*

Eighteenth-Century Britain and Ireland, edited by Adrian Randall and Andrew Charlesworth, 1–24. Liverpool: Liverpool University Press, 1996.

Randall, Dale B. J. *Winter Fruit: English Drama, 1642–1660*. Lexington: University of Kentucky Press, 1995.

Raven, James. *The Business of Books: Booksellers and the English Book Trade, 1450–1850*. New Haven, CT: Yale University Press, 2007.

Ravenscroft, Edward. *The Anatomist: Or, The Sham Doctor. Written by Mr. Ravenscroft. With The Loves of Mars and Venus. A Play Set to Music. Written by Mr. Motteux. As They Are Acted Together at the New Theatre, in Little Lincolns-Inn-Fields*. London, 1697. EEBO.

Raymond, Joad. "Introduction: Newspapers, Forgeries, and Histories." In *News, Newspapers, and Society in Early Modern Britain*, edited by Joad Raymond, 1–11. London: Frank Cass, 1999.

Raymond, Joad. "The Newspaper, Public Opinion, and the Public Sphere in the Seventeenth Century." In *News, Newspapers, and Society in Early Modern Britain*, edited by Joad Raymond, 109–40. London: Frank Cass, 1999.

Richardson, John. *The Annals of London: A Year-by-Year Record of a Thousand Years of History*. Berkeley: University of California Press, 2000.

Rigamonti, Antonella, and Laura Favero Carraro. "Women at Stake: The Self-Assertive Potential of Gambling in Susanna Centlivre's *The Basset Table*." *Restoration and Eighteenth-Century Theatre Research* 16.2 (2001): 53–62.

Ritchie, Fiona, and Peter Sabor, eds. *Shakespeare in the Eighteenth Century*. Cambridge: Cambridge University Press, 2012.

Ritchie, Leslie. *David Garrick and the Mediation of Celebrity*. Cambridge: Cambridge University Press, 2019.

Ritchie, Leslie. "Garrick's *Male-Coquette* and Theatrical Masculinities." In *Refiguring the Coquette: Essays on Culture and Coquetry*, 164–98. Edited by Yael Rachel Schlick and Shelley King. Lewisburg, PA: Bucknell University Press, 2008.

Roach, Joseph. "Afterword: What Now?" *Eighteenth-Century Fiction* 27 (2015): 731–34.

Roach, Joseph. *Cities of the Dead: Circum-Atlantic Performance*. New York: Columbia University Press, 1996.

Roach, Joseph. *It*. Ann Arbor: University of Michigan Press, 2007.

Roitman, Janet. *Anti-Crisis*. Durham: Duke University Press, 2013.

Rose, Mark. *Authors and Owners: The Invention of Copyright*. Cambridge, MA: Harvard University Press, 1993.

Rosenthal, Laura J. *Playwrights and Plagiarists in Early Modern England: Gender, Authorship, Literary Property*. Ithaca: Cornell University Press, 1996.

Roseveare, Henry. *The Financial Revolution, 1660–1760.* London: Longman, 1991.

Rowlinson, Matthew. *Real Money and Romanticism.* Cambridge: Cambridge University Press, 2013.

Roxburgh, Natalie. *Representing Public Credit: Credible Commitment, Fiction, and the Rise of the Financial Subject.* Abingdon: Routledge, 2016.

Rubik, Margarete. *Early Women Dramatists, 1550–1800.* Basingstoke, UK: MacMillan, 1998.

Russell, Gillian. *Women, Sociability, and Theatre in Georgian London.* Cambridge: Cambridge University Press, 2007.

Sargent, Thomas J., and François R. Velde. *The Big Problem of Small Change.* Princeton, NJ: Princeton University Press, 2002.

Schabas, Margaret. *The Natural Origins of Economics.* Chicago: University of Chicago Press, 2005.

Schabas, Margaret, and Neil De Marchi, eds. *Oeconomies in the Age of Newton.* Durham, NC: Duke University Press, 2003.

Schmidgen, Wolfram. *Eighteenth-Century Fiction and the Law of Property.* Cambridge: Cambridge University Press, 2002.

Schmidgen, Wolfram. "Robinson Crusoe, Enumeration, and the Mercantile Fetish." *Eighteenth-Century Studies* 35 (2001): 19–39.

Schneider, Brian W. *The Framing Text in Early Modern English Drama: "Whining" Prologues and "Armed" Epilogues.* Farnham, UK: Ashgate, 2011.

Scot, Mr. *The Unhappy Kindness: or A Fruitless Revenge. A Tragedy, As It Is Acted at the Theatre Royal.* London, 1697. EEBO.

Scott, Amy. "Events and Texts: The Prologues and Epilogues of the Arbury Plays." *Early Theatre: A Journal Associated with the Records of Early English Drama* 14 (2011): 227–28.

Settle, Elkanah. *Philaster: Or, Love Lies a Bleeding. A Tragi-Comedy. As It Is Now Acted at His Majesty's Theatre Royal. Revis'd, and the Two Last Acts New Written.* London, 1695. EEBO.

Shadwell, Thomas. *The Volunteers, or, The Stock Jobbers. A Comedy, As It Is Acted by Their Majesties Servants, at the Theatre Royal.* London, 1693. EEBO.

Shell, Mark. *The Economy of Literature.* Baltimore: Johns Hopkins University Press, 1978.

Shell, Mark. *Money, Language, and Thought: Literary and Philosophical Economies from the Medieval to the Modern Era.* Berkeley: University of California Press, 1982.

Sherburn, George, ed. *The Correspondence of Alexander Pope.* Oxford: Oxford University Press, 1956.

Sherburn, George. "The Fortunes and Misfortunes of *Three Hours after Marriage.*" *Modern Philology* 24 (1925): 91–109.
Sherman, Sandra. *Finance and Fictionality in the Early Eighteenth Century: Accounting for Defoe.* Cambridge: Cambridge University Press, 2005.
Sherman, Stuart. "Garrick among Media: The 'Now Performer' Navigates the News." *PMLA* 126 (2011): 966–82.
Sherman, Stuart. "'The General Entertainment of My Life': The *Tatler,* The *Spectator,* and the Quidnunc's Cure." *Eighteenth-Century Fiction* 27 (2015): 343–71.
Shimko, Robert B., and Sara Freeman. "Introduction: Theatre, Performance, and the Public Sphere." In *Public Theatres and Theatre Publics,* edited by Robert B. Shimko and Sara Freeman, 1–21. Newcastle upon Tyne: Cambridge Scholars Publishing, 2012.
Shoemaker, Robert B. "The London 'Mob' in the Early Eighteenth Century." *Journal of British Studies* 26 (1987): 273–304.
Smith, Courtney Weiss. "A 'Foundation in Nature': New Economic Criticism and the Problem of Money in 1690s England." *Eighteenth Century* 53 (2012): 209–28.
Smythe, James Moore. *The Rival Modes. A Comedy. As it is Acted by His Majesty's Company of Comedians, at the Theatre-Royal in Drury-Lane.* London, 1727. ECCO.
Solomon, Diana. *Prologues and Epilogues of Restoration Theater: Gender and Comedy, Performance and Print.* Newark: University of Delaware Press, 2013.
Solomon, Diana. "Tragic Play, Bawdy Epilogue?" In *Prologues, Epilogues, Curtain-Raisers, and Afterpieces,* edited by Daniel J. Ennis and Judith Baily Slagle, 155–78. Newark: University of Delaware Press, 2007.
Stanton, Judith Phillips. "'This New-Found Path Attempting': Women Dramatists in England, 1660–1800." In *Curtain Calls: British and American Women and the Theater, 1660–1820,* edited by Mary Anne Schofield and Cecilia Macheski, 325–54. Athens: Ohio University Press, 1991.
Stathas, Thalia. "A Critical Edition of Three Plays by Susanna Centlivre." PhD diss., Stanford University, Stanford, California, 1965.
Staves, Susan. "A Few Kind Words for the Fop." *Studies in English Literature, 1500–1900* 22 (1982): 413–28.
Staves, Susan. "Investments, Votes, and Bribes: Women as Shareholders in the Chartered National Companies." In *Women Writers and the Early Modern British Political Tradition,* edited by Hilda Smith, 259–78. Cambridge: Cambridge University Press, 1998.
Staves, Susan. *Married Women's Separate Property in England, 1660–1833.* Cambridge, MA: Harvard University Press, 1990.

Steele, Richard. *The Conscious Lovers. A Comedy. As it is Acted at the Theatre Royal in Drury-Lane, by His Majesty's Servants*. London, 1723 [1722]. ECCO.
Steele, Richard. *The Crisis of Property: An Argument Proving That the Annuitants for Ninety-Nine Years, As Such, Are Not in the Condition of Other Subjects of Great Britain, but by Compact with the Legislature Are Exempt from Any New Direction Relating to the Said Estates*. London, 1720. ECCO.
Steele, Richard. *A Nation A Family: Being the Sequel of The Crisis of Property: Or, A Plan for the Improvement of the South-Sea Proposal*. London, 1720. ECCO.
Stern, Simon. "Creating a Public Domain in Eighteenth-Century England." *Oxford Handbooks Online*. Oxford: Oxford University Press, 2015. DOI: 10.1093/oxfordhb/9780199935338.013.39.
Stern, Tiffany. *Documents of Performance in Early Modern England*. Cambridge: Cambridge University Press, 2012.
Stone, George Winchester. "The Making of a Repertory." In *The London Theatre World, 1660–1800*, edited by Robert D. Hume, 181–209. Carbondale: Southern Illinois University Press, 1980.
Stratmann, Silke. *Myths of Speculation: The South Sea Bubble and Eighteenth-Century English Literature*. Munich: Fink, 2000.
Straub, Kristina. "The Newspaper 'Trial' of Charles Macklin's Macbeth and the Theatre as Juridical Public Sphere." *Eighteenth-Century Fiction* 27 (2015): 395–418.
Straub, Kristina. *Sexual Suspects: Eighteenth-Century Players and Sexual Ideology*. Princeton, NJ: Princeton University Press, 1992.
Strauss, Ralph. *The Unspeakable Curll: Being Some Account of Edmund Curll, Bookseller; To Which Is Added a Full List of His Books*. New York: Augustus M. Kelley, 1927, 1970.
Sullivan, Ceri. *The Rhetoric of Credit: Merchants in Early Modern Writing*. Madison, NJ: Farleigh Dickson University Press, 2002.
Sutherland, James R. "The Progress of Error: Mrs. Centlivre and the Biographers." *Review of English Studies* 18.70 (1942): 167–182.
Swenson, Rivka. "'A Soldier Is Her Darling Character': Susanna Centlivre, Desire, Difference, and Disguise." *Journal of Narrative Theory* 37.1 (2007): 65–86.
[Swift, Jonathan.] *The Bubble: A Poem*. London, 1721. ECCO.
Taylor, Diana. *The Archive and the Repertoire: Performing Cultural Memory in the Americas*. Durham, NC: Duke University Press, 2003.
Theatrical Disquisitions: or, A Review of the Late Riot at Drury-Lane Theatre, on the 25th and 26th of January, with an Impartial Examen of the Profession and Professors of the Drama; Some Few Hints on the Prerogatives of an Audience,

and, a Short Appendix, Relative to a More Flagrant Disturbance Committed at Covent-Garden Theatre, on Thursday the 24th of February. London, 1763. ECCO.

Thompson, E. P. "The Moral Economy of the English Crowd." *Past and Present* 1 (1971): 76–136.

Thompson, James. *Models of Value: Eighteenth-Century Political Economy and the Novel.* Durham, NC: Duke University Press, 1996.

Thompson, James. "'Sure I have seen that face before': Representation and Value in Eighteenth-Century Drama." In *Cultural Readings of Restoration and Eighteenth-Century English Theater*, edited by J. Douglas Canfield and Deborah C. Payne, 281–308. Athens: University of George Press, 1995.

Thorson, James. "The Dialogue between the Stage and the Audience: Prologues and Epilogues in the Era of the Popish Plot." In *Compendious Conversations: The Method of Dialogue in the Early Enlightenment*, edited by Kevin L. Cope, 331–45. Frankfurt, Germany: Peter Lang, 1992.

Three Original Letters to a Friend in the Country, on the Cause and Manner of the Late Riot at the Theatre-Royal in Drury-Lane. London, 1763. British Library. London.

Tierney-Hynes, Rebecca. "Emotional Economies: Centlivre's Comic Ends." *Studies in Eighteenth-Century Culture* 45 (2016): 83–106.

Timoleon: Or, The Revolution. A Tragi-Comedy. London, 1697. EEBO.

To the Right Honourable the Earl of Kent; Lord Chamberlain of Her Majesty's Household. The Humble Petition of the Comedians Acting at the Theatre Royal in Drury Lane. [London, 1705.] ECCO.

Trudell, Scott A. "Introduction: The Intermedia Restoration." *Restoration: Studies in English Literary Culture, 1660–1700* 42.2 (2018): 3–11.

Valenze, Deborah. *The Social Life of Money in the English Past.* Cambridge: Cambridge University Press, 2006.

Vanbrugh, John. *The Relapse; or, Virtue in Danger: Being the Sequel of The Fool in Fashion, a Comedy. Acted at the Theatre-Royal in Drury-Lane.* [London], 1697. EEBO.

Venden Herrell, Lu Ann. "Luck Be a Lady Tonight, or at Least Make Me a Gentleman: Economic Anxiety in Susanna Centlivre's *The Gamester* and *The Basset Table*." *Studies in the Literary Imagination* 32.2 (1999): 45–61.

Waddell, Brodie. "The Politics of Economic Distress in the Aftermath of the Glorious Revolution, 1689–1702." *English Historical Review* 130 (2015): 318–51.

Wallace, Beth Kowaleski. "A Modest Defence of Gaming Women." *Studies in Eighteenth-Century Culture* 31 (2002): 21–39.

Walter, John. *Crowds and Popular Politics in Early Modern England.* Manchester: Manchester University Press, 2006.

Warner, Michael. *The Letters of the Republic: Publication and the Public Sphere in Eighteenth-Century America.* Cambridge, MA: Harvard University Press, 1990.

Warner, Michael. "The Mass Public and the Mass Subject." In *Habermas and the Public Sphere,* edited by Craig Calhoun, 377–401. Cambridge, MA: MIT Press, 1992.

Warner, Michael. *Publics and Counterpublics.* New York: Zone, 2002.

Warner, William B. *Licensing Entertainment: The Elevation of Novel Reading in Britain, 1684–1750.* Berkeley: University of California Press, 1998.

Warren, Victoria. "Gender and Genre in Susanna Centlivre's *The Gamester* and *The Basset Table.*" *Studies in English Literature* 43.3 (2003): 605–24.

Wawso, Richard. "Crises of Credit: Monetary and Erotic Economies in the Jacobean Theatre." In *Plotting Early Modern London: New Essays on Jacobean City Comedy,* edited by Dieter Mehl, Angela Stock, and Anne-Julia Zwierlein, 55–74. Burlington, VT: Ashgate, 2004.

Wells, Staring B. "An Eighteenth-Century Attribution." *Journal of English and Germanic Philology* 38 (1939): 233–46.

Wennerlind, Carl. *Casualties of Credit: The English Financial Revolution, 1620–1720.* Cambridge, MA: Harvard University Press, 2011.

The Wheel of Fortune; or, a Thousand Pounds for a Penny. With the Permission of Authority. Being a Fair Adventure to All Persons, and a Vast Return of Profit to the Fortunate. [London, 1698.] EEBO.

The Wheel of Fortune: or, Nothing for a Penny. Being Remarks on the Dawing [sic] the Penny-Lottery, at the Theatre-Royal, in Dorset-Garden, With the Characters of Some of the Honorable Trustees, and All Due Acknowledgments Paid to His Honour the Undertaker. London, 1698. EEBO.

Whincop, Thomas. *Scanderbeg: or, Love and Liberty. A Tragedy. Written by the Late Thomas Whincop, Esq. To Which Are Added a List of All the Dramatic Authors, With Some Account of Their Lives; and of All the Dramatic Pieces Ever Published in the English Language, to the Year 1747.* London, 1747. ECCO.

Whitty, John C. "The Half-Price Riots of 1763." *Theatre Notebook* 24 (1969): 25–32.

Wiley, Autrey Nell. *Rare Prologues and Epilogues, 1642–1700.* London: G. Allen and Unwin, 1940.

Wilkinson, Claire. "'The Visionary Scene Was Lost in Air': Conceptualizing Finance after the South Sea Bubble." In *Political Economy, Literature, and the Formation of Knowledge, 1720–1850,* edited by Richard Adelman and Catherine Packham, 23–50. New York: Routledge, 2018.

Wilson, Brett D. "Bevil's Eyes: or, How Crying at *The Conscious Lovers* Could Save Britain." *Eighteenth-Century Studies* 45 (2012): 497–518.

Wolfram, Nathalie. "'I Am My Master's Servant for Hire': Contract and Identity in Richard Steele's *The Conscious Lovers*." *The Eighteenth Century* 53 (2012): 455-72.
Woodmansee, Martha. *The Author, Art, and the Market: Rereading the History of Aesthetics*. New York: Columbia University Press, 1994.
Woodmansee, Martha, and Mark Osteen, eds. *The New Economic Criticism: Studies at the Intersection of Literature and Economics*. London: Routledge, 1999.
Worrall, David. *Celebrity, Performance, Reception: British Georgian Theatre as Social Assemblage*. Cambridge: Cambridge University Press, 2013.
Wright, Thomas. *The Female Vertuoso's. A Comedy: As It Is Acted at the Queen's Theatre, by Their Majesties Servants*. London, 1693. EEBO.
Wright, Thomas. *No Fools Like Wits; or, The Female Virtuosoes: A Comedy. As It Is Acted at the Theatre in Lincolns-Inn-Fields*. London, 1721. ECCO.
Wright, Thomas. *No Fools Like Wits: or, The Female Vertuosoes. A Comedy. As It Was Acted at the Theatre in Lincolns-Inn-Fields. Or, The Refusal: or, The Ladies Philosophy. As It Is Acted at the Theatre Royal in Drury-Lane*. 2nd ed. London, 1721. ECCO.
Zimmerman, David A. *Panic! Markets, Crises, and Crowds in American Fiction*. Chapel Hill: University of North Carolina Press, 2006.

PRIMARY SOURCE NEWSPAPERS AND PERIODICALS

AUTHOR'S NOTE: The periodicals in this list were accessed through the database Seventeenth and Eighteenth Century Burney Newspapers Collection, unless otherwise noted.

Daily Courant. London, 1702-35.
Daily Journal. London, 1721-37.
Daily Post. London, 1719-46.
Diverting Post. London, 1704-6.
Derby Mercury. London, 1732-1900. British Newspaper Archive.
Evening Post. London, 1706.
Female Tatler. London, 1709-10. Eighteenth-Century Journals.
Flying Post. London, 1695-1731.
Gentleman's Magazine: and Historical Chronicle. London, 1731-1907. HathiTrust Digital Library.
London Chronicle. London, 1757-1823.
London Evening Post. 1727-1806.

London Gazette. London, 1666–present.
London Magazine, or, Gentleman's Monthly Intelligencer. London, 1732–85. HathiTrust Digital Library.
Lover. London, 1714.
Original Weekly Journal. London, 1715–20.
Post Boy. London, 1695–1728.
Post Man and the Historical Account. London, 1695–1730.
Public Advertiser. London, 1752–94.
Spectator. London, 1711–12.
St. James Chronicle or the British Evening Post. London, 1761–1822.
St. James's Journal. London, 1722–23.
Tatler. London, 1709–10.
Theatre. London, 1720.
Weekly Journal or British Gazetteer. London, 1715–30.
Weekly Journal, or Saturday's Post. London, 1716–25.
Whitehall Evening Post. London, 1718–39. Eighteenth-Century Journals.

INDEX

abstraction: association of, with speculation and speculative markets, 4, 97; as characteristic of commodities, 3, 118, 159, 177, 185; as characteristic of financial instruments, 3, 81, 97, 106–7, 109, 169, 176, 179; as characteristic of values or ideals, 88, 111; as conceptual problem, 20, 158; embrace of, 108; of identity, 98; of labor, 159, 183, 184; of property, 106–7, 176, 184; of the slave trade, 149

accountability, 4; of institutions, 6, 7, 85, 135, 144, 180, 186, 188, 195, 196; of monarchs, 11

accounting, 86, 130, 175, 195

acting shares. *See* profit shares

Act of Anne, 183. *See also* Anne, Queen; copyright; Parliament, Acts of

Act to Restore Publick Credit, 110. *See also* Parliament, Acts of

actors: ages of, 15, 53, 63–65, 74; as celebrities, 53; compensation of, 3, 12, 86, 194; competition between, 15; economic dependencies of, 52, 55, 58, 67, 89–90; hiring and firing of, 11; literary representations of, 106, 118–19, 194, 217n68; as managers, 102; movement between companies, 54, 88, 94, 96, 225n37; as playwrights, 27, 53; relationships with audiences, 53, 55, 57–58, 71, 84–85; relationships with management, 12, 45, 48, 85, 89, 94, 225n37; relationships with playwrights, 53, 54, 55, 60, 81, 93, 95, 118–19, 212n3; sexuality of, 5, 63, 119; as shareholders in theater companies, 12, 48; as speakers of prologues and epilogues, 53, 58, 185. *See also names of individual actors*

Actors' Company, 15, 46, 63, 65, 74

Actors' Rebellion, 12, 15, 45–46, 63, 79, 85

adaptation, 199n6, 203n30; as analogous to recoinage, 44, 69–75; as fraud, 18, 158, 170–84; of dramatic types, 41; of French drama, 66, 170–84, 229n16; of Tudor and early Stuart drama, 3, 16, 63–66, 69–75, 211n48, 211n50

Addison, Joseph, 7, 126–27, 145, 151, 224n34, 227n68. See also *Spectator*; *Tatler*

adventurers, 1, 13, 48, 105, 108, 117, 118–19, 131

adventurer's shares. *See* profit shares

advertisements: as criticism, 18, 174, 177–80, 184, 216n65; in dialogue with one another, 18, 172–77, 180; as evidence of authorship, 99–102, 216n65, 221n100; as evidence of market penetration, 128; as evidence of publication date, 220–21n98; for joint-stock companies, 115–16, 137–38, 225n38; for lottery drawings, 1, 199n1; for

advertisements (*continued*)
  missing items, 216n65; as "News from the little World," 140–41, 176; as part of theatrical media landscape, 8–9, 17, 186; for performances, 92, 95–96, 100, 107, 128, 156, 172, 173, 188, 189, 209n10, 215n48, 220n96, 223n18, 227–28n1; for portraits, 80; portrayed as dishonest, 153, 158; for publications, 100, 101–2, 171–72, 177–82, 183. *See also* mock advertisements
afterpieces, 16, 212
agrarianism, 9
Anatomist, The (Ravenscroft): as adaptation of *Crispin Médecin* (Hauteroche), 66; prologue to, 66–68
Ancients and Moderns, battle between, 25
Anglo-Dutch Wars, 10
Anne, Queen, 13, 108, 111, 112, 113, 212n4, 214–15n33. *See also* Act of Anne
annuities, 37, 70; engraftment by South Sea Company, 109–10, 115, 130, 218n78
anonymity: as authorial strategy, 99–102, 216n65; of nondramatic texts, 80, 117, 190, 192; of plays, 60, 64, 227–28n1
antifeminism, 80. *See also* feminism
Anti-Theatre, 128
Apology for the Life of Mr. Colley Cibber, An. See under Cibber, Colley
Appeal to the Public in Behalf of the Managers, An, 190, 192
arbitrage, 29, 33, 34, 56
Arbuthnot, John, 80. *See also* Scriblerians
archives, 9, 125, 128, 50–55, 209n9. *See also* British Library; National Archives (UK)
aristocracy: dramatic representations of, 145, 147, 151, 162, 166; influence on Restoration theater, 15, 24, 41; involvement with Royal Academy of Music, 132–33. *See also* elite; nobility; upper classes
Arne, Thomas, 195
Artaxerxes (Arne), 189, 195

Artifice, The. See under Centlivre, Susanna
Asiento, 109, 130, 217–18n74. *See also* plantation economy; slavery; South Sea Company; West Indies
Astrea (goddess), 1
Astrea (pseudonym). *See* Behn, Aphra
authors: compensation of, 52, 53–54, 220n96, 221n105; intellectual property rights of, 54, 182–84, 230n22, 230n29; representations of, 53. *See also* authorship; playwrights
authorship: attributive, 69, 87, 95, 117, 132, 153, 171, 194, 208n2, 211n48, 212n3, 215n45, 221n100, 223n19, 224n34, 227–28n1, 230n21; dramatic, 53, 182; gendered negotiations of, 82, 83, 97, 99–102, 119; possessive, 180–81; professionalization of, 6; proprietary, 182–83, 230n27. *See also* anonymity

bankers, 34, 50, 54, 73, 130, 131, 174. *See also* goldsmith bankers
Bank of England: bills issued by, 60, 71; dramatic references to, 34–35, 59, 69–72; establishment of, 13, 14, 29, 38, 79; rivalry with Land Bank, 72; run on, 30, 35; Whig leadership of, 108. *See also* bankers; banks; national debt; paper credit; public credit
bankruptcy, 70, 72. *See also* debt
banks, 36, 69–70, 72. *See also* bankers; Bank of England
Barbados, 148, 217–18n74. *See also* West Indies
Barry, Elizabeth, 45, 86, 118–19
Basset Table, The. See under Centlivre, Susanna
Beard, John, 188–91, 193
Beaumont, Francis, 63, 211n48, 230n22
behavioral economics, 125, 222n5
Behn, Aphra, 24, 59, 80, 99. *See also Rover, The; Younger Brother, The*
Benedetto (Benedetto Marcello), 225n39

benefit performances: for actors, 86, 94, 194, 227–28n1; for authors, 52, 54, 95, 116, 220n96
Betterton, Thomas: as author of *The Vintner Trick'd*, 65; as leader of Actors' Rebellion, 12, 45–47; as manager of Lincoln's Inn Fields, 63–64, 85–87, 92–93, 118; as party to lawsuit, 214n22; as prologue speaker, 66–67
Bickerstaff, Isaac (pseudonym), 140–41, 176. *See also* Addison, Joseph; Steele, Richard; Swift, Jonathan; *Tatler*
Bickerstaff's Burying, A. *See under* Centlivre, Susanna
Bills of Exchange, 10, 29, 71. *See also* paper credit
Bold Stroke for a Wife, A. *See under* Centlivre, Susanna
bonds, 104, 108, 173, 217n72
Bonduca, or, the British Heroine (Fletcher), 64–65
booksellers: as copyright holders, 182–83, 230n29; as publishers of periodicals, 127–28, 137; as publishers of plays, 101, 182; role in placing advertisements, 137, 139–41, 176, 179; use of term, 205n60. *See also* Chetwood, William Rufus; Curll, Edmund; Lintot, Bernard
boom-bust cycles, 2, 13, 16, 36
Booth, Barton, 102, 129–30
bourgeois public sphere, 6–8, 124, 126–27, 143–44, 154, 186–88, 192–93, 201n21. *See also* Habermas, Jürgen; rational-critical debate
Boyer, Abel, 80
Bracegirdle, Anne: as epilogue speaker, 58–59; as manager of Lincoln's Inn Fields, 86; as participant in Actors' Rebellion, 45
bribery, 37–38, 47, 85, 134, 160, 219n80
British East India Company. *See* East India Company
British Library, 114, 214–15n33, 215n40, 215n48, 216n65, 220n94, 232n21

Broken Stock-Jobbers, The, 156, 227–28n1
Brutus of Alba, 67
"Bubble, The" (Swift), 117
Bubble Act (1720), 219n83. *See also* Parliament, Acts of
Bubbler's Medley, The, 221n100
bubbles (economic phenomena), 2, 125, 166, 170. *See also* Mississippi Bubble; South Sea Bubble
bubbles (gullible persons), 84, 136–38, 154, 162
Bubble year (1720), 82, 120, 123, 175, 211n1
building shares, 11–12
bullion, 26, 29, 31, 33, 34, 73. *See also* gold; silver
bullionism, 35, 38, 163
Burney, Frances, 99
Busie Body, The. *See under* Centlivre, Susanna

calls, 133, 167–68, 219n80, 225n38, 229n12. *See also* refusals; time bargains
Canary Islands, 12
capitalism: development of, 2–4, 9, 48, 158, 205n61; individualism of, 106; irrationality of, 39; predatory impulses of, 183; rejection of, 200n10; speculative logics of, 186; as state of perpetual crisis, 19, 160
Careless Husband, The (Cibber). *See under* Cibber, Colley
Caribbean, 36, 105, 150, 217–18n74. *See also* Barbados; Jamaica; West Indies
celebrity, 9, 53, 56, 80, 82, 212n3
censorship, 54. *See also* licensing; Master of Revels
Centlivre, Joseph, 81, 110–14, 116, 212n4, 220n91
Centlivre, Susanna: biographical accounts of, 80–81, 212–13n8; celebrity of, 80–81, 212n3; connections with Richard Steele, 112; exclusion from canon and feminist recovery of, 81–82, 213n13;

Centlivre, Susanna (*continued*)
gendered discrimination against, 95, 101; marriage to Joseph Centlivre, 81, 212n4; place in repertory, 16, 81, 213n9; political beliefs, 16, 80, 81, 84, 103, 106, 108, 110, 111–14, 116; satirical representations of, 80, 118–19, 216n65. Works of: *The Artifice,* 216n65, 220n95; *The Basset Table,* 82–84, 91–93, 95, 103, 104, 119, 213n15, 215n37, 229n13; *A Bickerstaff's Burying,* 96–97; *A Bold Stroke for a Wife,* 17, 83, 102–8, 119–20, 213n9; *The Busie Body,* 16, 83, 93–103, 107, 116, 119, 212n3, 213n9, 216n57, 220n96, 221n105, 224–25n35; *The Cruel Gift,* 103; *The Gamester,* 16, 82–85, 89–90, 92–93, 95, 96, 101, 102, 103, 104, 117, 119, 213n15, 215n37; *The Humours of Elections,* 212n2, 219–20n87; *Love's Contrivance,* 101–2, 119, 216n62, 221n105; *The Man's Bewitch'd,* 96–97, 212n3; *Marplot,* 96–97; *The Platonick Lady,* 101, 170, 229n13; *A Poem. Humbly Presented to His Most Sacred Majesty,* 220n97; *The Stolen Heiress,* 100; "Upon the Bells ringing at St. Martins in the Fields," 113; *The Wife Well Manag'd,* 212n2, 219–20n87; *A Woman's Case,* 17, 83, 103, 108, 110–18, 119–20, 123, 220–21n98; *The Wonder,* 102, 116, 212n3, 213n9
chain-letter scheme, 110, 160, 176. See also Ponzi scheme
Chancery Court, 85–86, 214n22
Change-Alley. See Exchange Alley
Characters and Conduct of Sir John Edgar, The (Dennis, attrib.), 153–54, 223n19
character types, 25, 158, 165, 170; cit, 42, 57, 61, 73, 165–66; creole woman, 150, 227n69; fop, 26, 27, 37, 39–41, 105, 194, 206n14; rake, 24, 41–43; virtuoso, 105, 170, 229n13
Charles II, King, 13
Chetwood, William Rufus, 127, 212n8, 227–28n1
Chimera, The, 156, 227–28n1

chocolate houses, 98–99. See also coffeehouses
Cibber, Colley: as accused plagiarist, 155, 171–72, 174, 177–83, 186; as actor, 27, 40, 68, 159, 177; connections with Richard Steele, 18, 129, 156, 160, 164, 169, 176, 187; connections with Susanna Centlivre, 229n13; influenced by George Etherege, 40; losses in the South Sea Bubble, 228n3; management of Drury Lane, 102, 129–30; political views, 18, 162, 165; reputation for opportunism, 25, 172, 230n21; rivalry with Scriblerians, 24, 228n3, 229n16; silencing of, 129–30; treatment in twentieth-century criticism, 24, 27. Works of: *An Apology for the Life of Mr. Colley Cibber,* 47–48, 134; *The Careless Husband,* 206n14; *Love's Last Shift,* 15, 24–44, 45, 49, 68, 72, 74–75, 158, 185, 205n5, 206n9, 207n27, 221n105, 227n76; *The Nonjuror,* 221n105; *Plays Written by Mr. Cibber* (1721), 31, 181–82, 207n27; *The Refusal,* 18, 155, 156–84, 186, 227–28n1, 228n3, 229n13; *Richard III* (adapted from Shakespeare), 182; *Ximena,* 129
cit. See under character types
City, the (historic core of London), 61, 141, 162, 166, 192; as metonym for London financial sector, 35, 73, 105, 106, 108, 142, 143
City Bride, The (Harris, attrib.), 59
city comedy, 23, 205n3
civil wars. See English civil wars
class: of audiences, 5, 14, 19, 24, 42, 73, 74, 91, 202n27, 204–5n57; as basis of access to public life, 123, 187–88, 191–92; as basis of power, 82, 93; changing structures of, 3, 84, 147, 156; dramatic representations of, 40–43, 90, 146–48, 163–65; naturalization of, 91, 143–44. See also aristocracy; elites; gentry; lower classes; middling classes; nobility; upper classes; workers

clipping. *See under* currency
coffeehouses: as gendered spaces, 103, 217n71; Jonathan's, 103–4; as sites for distribution of printed materials, 145, 188; as sites of financial trading, 62, 104–5; as sites of public formation and debate, 4, 6, 8, 19, 28, 44, 126–27, 144, 202n26; Tom's, 61, 201n42. *See also* chocolate houses
coins. *See* currency
collective action, 127, 186
Collier, Jeremy, 206n13
Collier, William, 94, 97
colonialism: dramatic representations of, 106, 148–51; relationship to trade, 18, 124, 146, 218n78. *See also* Caribbean; Dutch East India Company; East India Company; East Indies; New East India Company; slavery; South Sea Company; West Indies
comedy: changing sensibilities of, 24, 26–27, 43, 45, 49, 158, 227n74; features of, 44, 58; subject matter of, 23, 31. *See also* city comedy; marriage plot; sentimental comedy
Comical Revenge, The (Etherege), 95
command performances, 116, 220n96, 224–25n35
Committee, The (Howard), 227–28n1
Committee of Secrecy, 110
commodification: of cultural products, 6, 7, 40, 61, 92–93, 118, 173; of non-English people, 106; of social status, 156; of women, 28, 38–39, 97–99, 102, 107, 119, 217. *See also* commodities
commodities: coins as, 31, 33; speculation in, 3, 34, 36–39; stock subscriptions as, 173; theater shares as, 13; valuation of, 3, 4, 31, 36–39, 50, 67, 119, 159, 161, 169, 177, 179, 183, 185. *See also* commodification
Commonwealth, 54. *See also* Cromwell, Oliver; English civil wars; Interregnum, the

Comparison between the Two Stages, A, 46–47, 63, 65
Congreve, William, 86, 225n37; *Love for Love*, 40; *The Old Batchelor*, 40
Conscious Lovers, The (Steele). *See under* Steele, Richard
Continent, the (mainland Europe), 29, 132, 133
contracts: echoes of, in prologues and epilogues, 55; for marriage, 90, 103, 214n33; between playwrights and theater companies, 54; representation of, in *The Refusal*, 163, 167; right of women to enter into, 81, 103, 108, 110–11, 118; threatened by proposed theater merger, 88
contract theory, 81, 217n68. *See also* Locke, John
"Cooper's Hill" (Denham), 132
copyright, 119, 182–83, 221n105, 230n29. *See also* Act of Anne; booksellers; piracy
counterfeiting. *See under* currency
counterpublics, 7–8, 19, 144, 187, 196–97
court performances, 54, 133, 211n56
Covent Garden Theatre. *See* Theatre Royal Covent Garden
Craggs, James, the younger, 110, 219–20n87
Credit (goddess), 5
credit: availability of, 70, 108, 219n80; of Bank of England, 14–15, 71; as basis for currency, 2, 185; as basis for financial markets, 5, 13, 126; dependence of trades and institutions on, 54, 59; disingenuous criticism of, 60–61, 70–71, 72; ephemerality of, 5, 162, 163, 200n16; instruments of, 10, 35, 70, 162, 163; in Jacobean comedy, 23; personal, 10, 23, 38, 87, 106, 147, 163, 165; shift to, 10, 14, 35, 38, 79. *See also* bankruptcy; Credit (goddess); credit economy; debt; financial instruments; Lady Credit; national credit; paper credit; public credit

credit economy, 36, 60, 79, 148. *See also* credit
creole woman. *See under* character types
crisis: perpetual, as condition of financial capitalism, 19–20, 160; as problematic category, 205n61; recoinage as, 23, 26, 28–31, 33, 49, 56, 58, 75, 158, 185; South Sea Bubble as, 120, 124–26, 156–57, 158, 185, 222n2; as structuring device for this book, 14–20. *See also* Exclusion Crisis
Crisis of Property, The. *See under* Steele, Richard
Crispin Médicin (Hauteroche), 66
criticism: anti-opera, 133–34; of *Love's Last Shift*, 24–25, 40; as object of study, 62–63, 76; as part of theatrical media landscape, 3, 8–9, 79; perceived as low-quality, 47; reflective of middling-class values, 13–14. *See also* critics
critics: as brokers of public opinion, 16, 50, 62, 68, 70–71, 76; literary representations of, 65; as targets of prologues and epilogues, 52, 54–62. *See also Comparison between the Two Stages, A*; criticism; Fitzpatrick, Thaddeus; Gildon, Charles; Langbaine, Gerard
Cromwell, Oliver, 10. *See also* Commonwealth; English civil wars; Interregnum, the
Cross, Letitia, 96, 208n53
crowd action, 143–44, 187, 197. *See also* collective action; riots
crowds: armed, 94; behavior of, 17; "Dull," 57; irrationality of, 124, 125, 141–44, 186, 222n2; in the theater, 1, 8, 134, 188–89, 191. *See also* counterpublics; crowd action; publics; riots
Cruel Gift, The. *See under* Centlivre, Susanna
Cupid (goddess), 42, 208n53
Curll, Edmund, 18, 80, 158, 171–72, 177–84, 212n7, 229n16

currency: analogized to dramatic wit, 56–60, 67–70, 72–73; clipping and counterfeiting of, 10, 15, 29–30, 33, 34, 56–57, 59, 67; relationship to credit economy, 2, 60; shortages of, 10, 49, 50; unstable value of, 31, 34–36, 43–44, 58, 67, 185. *See also* arbitrage; bullion; gold; recoinage; silver

Daily Courant, 92, 95, 101–2, 115–16, 215n48, 220n96, 225n38
Daily Journal, 172–73, 216n65
Dante (Dante Alighieri), 70
Davenant, Alexander, 12
Davenant, Charles, 12, 200n16
Davenant, William, 11–12, 85, 129, 211n56
debt: in *A Bold Stroke for a Wife* (Centlivre), 104–5, 107; in *The Conscious Lovers* (Steele), 149; demonization of, 70, 86, 118; as figure for theatrical relationships, 59, 73–74; as formal structure, 6; in *The Gamester* (Centlivre), 89–90, 214–15n33; growing importance to English economy, 79; as interpersonal arrangement, 10. *See also* credit; interest (financial); national debt; usury
Defoe, Daniel: connections with Centlivre, 80, 220–21n98; *An Essay upon Projects*, 13, 26, 36, 37; as writer of "polite" periodicals, 126
Denham, John, 132, 230n22
Dennis, John, 153–54, 158
dialogism, 16, 28, 44, 50, 76, 111
Dialogue in the Green Room, A (Fitzpatrick, attrib.), 194–96
disguise: in *A Bold Stroke for a Wife* (Centlivre), 104–7; in *Love's Last Shift* (Cibber), 24; in *The Busie Body* (Centlivre), 98
disinterestedness, 188, 190, 191. *See also* interest (concept)
Diverting Post, 84, 87, 214n29
Doggett, Thomas (actor), 95, 96

Drake, James, 69
Drury Lane Theatre. *See* Theatre Royal Drury Lane
Dryden, John, 23, 25, 182
Dryden, John, Jr., 58
Duke's Company, 11–12, 46
Dunciad (Pope), 24, 80, 174, 212n4
Duncombe, John, 80
duopolies, 46–48, 79. *See also* monopolies
D'Urfey, Thomas, 56
Dutch Courtesan, The (Marston), 65
Dutch East India Company, 36. *See also* colonialism; East India Company; East Indies; global Indies; New East India Company

East India Company: corruption scandal and loss of monopoly, 38, 46–48; dramatic allusions to, 18, 104, 105; origins of, 10, 36; Whig leadership of, 108, 128–29. *See also* colonialism; Dutch East India Company; East Indies; global Indies; New East India Company
East Indies, 48, 148. *See also* Dutch East India Company; East India Company; global Indies; New East India Company
economics: cultural attitudes toward, 5; of marriage, 27, 31, 97, 168; of opera, 135; relationships with literature, 6, 200–201n17; of theater, 3, 25, 52, 84, 103, 140, 179, 201n20; tropology of, 4. *See also* behavioral economics; New Economic Criticism; political economy
Edgeworth, Maria, 99
Egerton, Sarah Fyge, 80
elite: cultural, 17, 19; economic, 17, 18, 76, 120, 164; financial, 157, 229n9; masculine, 102, 120, 123. *See also* class
Elizabeth I, Queen, 9–10, 23, 33, 52–53, 57, 72

English civil wars, 10, 54, 80, 126. *See also* Cromwell, Oliver; Interregnum, the; Restoration, the
English monarchy: borrowing power of, 11, 13, 14; checks on, 186; control over theaters, 10, 11; representation on coins, 207n30; Restoration of, 11. *See also* Hanoverian Dynasty; Stuart Dynasty; Tudor Dynasty; *and names of individual monarchs*
English opera. *See* semi-opera
Enlightenment, the, 6–7, 184
entertainment industry, 19, 75, 124, 134, 141, 183, 187, 197
entrepreneurialism, 15, 48, 49, 75; of playwrights, 53–54, 74, 80, 158–59. *See also* virtuoso (opera entrepreneur)
entrepreneurs: greed of, 88, 89; theater, 80, 91, 200
ephemerality, 5, 97, 98, 162, 163
Epicœne (Jonson), 165
epilogues: to *The Gamester* (Centlivre), 84–85, 117; to *The Husband His Own Cuckold* (Dryden Jr.), 58–59; to *Love's Last Shift* (Cibber), 42–44, 74, 158; to *The Refusal* (Cibber), 161–62, 182; to *The Rival Sisters* (Gould), 56–58; to *The Wheel of Fortune*, 5; to *The Younger Brother* (Behn), 59–60, 67. *See also* prologues and epilogues
Essay upon Projects, An (Defoe), 26
Estcourt, Richard (actor), 96
Etherege, George: *The Comical Revenge*, 95; *The Man of Mode*, 40
ethnicity, 7, 106, 192
Evelyn, John, 34, 46
Evening Post, 115, 216n65, 225n38, 231n11
Every Man in His Humor (Jonson), 23
Exchange Alley, 3, 13, 103, 185, 227–28n1; referred to as Change Alley, 156, 163. *See also* Jonathan's; Royal Exchange; stock exchange; stock market
Exchequer, the, 10, 108, 115, 130
Exclusion Crisis, 126

270   INDEX

experts, 3, 16, 36, 50, 58, 62, 71, 76
exploitation: class-based, 18, 19, 124, 136, 143, 151, 154, 186; culture of, 103, 117, 125, 157, 170; dramatic adaptation as, 177, 183, 186; gender-based, 98, 150–51, 217n71; in financial markets, 70, 106–7, 114, 125, 185–86; in gambling, 84; political, 165; in the South Sea scheme, 18, 117, 143, 154, 158, 186; in the theater, 12, 60, 87, 103, 108, 195, 225n37

farce, 66, 67, 128, 156, 219–20n87, 223n18, 227–28n1
Farquhar, George, 80
Female Tatler, 80, 100, 212n3, 216n57, 225n37, 225n41
Female Vertuoso's, The (Wright), 170–72, 174, 177, 229n13
Feminiad (Duncombe), 80
femininity, 99, 150. *See also* feminization; gender; masculinity; masculinization
feminization: of the commercial theater, 82; of men, through market participation, 5, 106, 229n11; of the "nag" figure, 110. *See also* femininity; gender; masculinity; masculinization
feminism, 7, 81, 82, 202n22, 213n13, 231n3. *See also* antifeminism
Filmer, Edward, 65–69
financial capitalism. *See under* capitalism
financial instruments. *See* annuities; Bills of Exchange; bonds; calls; futures; refusals; securities; stocks; time bargains
financial revolution, 2, 9, 28, 79, 82, 199n5
Fitzpatrick, Thaddeus, 188–97
Fletcher, John, 46, 51, 63–65, 69, 72–74, 230n22
Flying Post, 113, 212n4
fop. *See under* character types
Fortuna, 1, 5
Four and Twenty Stock-Jobbers, 156, 227–28n1

France: dramatic allusions to, 71, 105, 106, 147, 149; as home country of performers in London, 142; King of, 104; war with (*see* Nine Years' War). *See also* French drama; French Revolution; Mississippi Bubble; Mississippi Company
fraud: dramatic adaptation as, 172, 179, 180; gendered anxieties about, 150; Ponzi scheme as, 222n6; South Sea Bubble as, 125, 130–32, 134, 137, 158, 160, 177, 180, 186, 219n85, 222n5
freedom: exercise of, 196; individual, 186; of movement, 98; from romantic entanglement, 38; of the stage, 47. *See also* liberty; rights
French drama, 66, 170, 182. *See also* Hauteroche, Noël Lebreton de; Molière
French Revolution, 197
"Fribbleriad, The" (Garrick), 192
futures, 4, 98. *See also* calls; commodities; refusals; speculation; time bargains

gambling: in "The Bubble" (Swift), 117; eighteenth-century views on, 213n20; in *The Gamester* and *The Basset Table* (Centlivre), 16, 83–85, 89–91, 104, 119; on lottery tickets, 37; in the *Theatre* (Steele), 131
Gamester, The. *See under* Centlivre, Susanna
Garrick, David, 188–94, 232n28
Gay, John: investment in South Sea Company, 110; *No Fools Like Wits*, 171–72, 174, 177, 180, 183, 229n16; *Three Hours after Marriage*, 80. *See also* Scriblerians
gender: and authorship, 81–82, 99–102, 212n3; exclusion based on, 16, 80, 187–88; and financial markets, 5, 81, 93, 111, 123; and gambling, 83; and makeup of theatrical audiences, 14, 19, 42; performance of, 192; power based on, 82; roles, changes to, 3, 84, 111; as theme of comedy, 31, 33; as topic

of periodical journalism, 127. *See also* femininity; feminization; masculinity; masculinization; women
generational conflict: between Actors' Company and Patent Company, 15, 65; in *The Conscious Lovers* (Steele), 151–53, 227n74; in *Love's Last Shift* (Cibber), 25, 33–34
genre: debates about, 14; experimentation with, 62; reworking of, 3, 15, 25, 26, 27, 68; as subject of literary criticism, 200–201n17, 205n5; unevenness of, 24, 27, 43. *See also* comedy; farce; masque; pantomime; semi-opera; tragedy
gentry, 89, 106, 147, 151, 204n55. *See also* class; elite; upper classes
George I, King: accession of, 220n97, 228–29n6; approval of South Sea Company expansion, 109; birthday of, 80; command performances for, 116; household of, 212n4; sponsorship of Royal Academy of Music, 132
George II, King: as electoral prince, 111, 116
Gildon, Charles: attributed works, 87, 206n10, 208n2, 214n25
global Indies, 148. *See also* East Indies; West Indies
Glorious Revolution. *See* Revolution Settlement
goddesses. *See* Astrea; Credit; Cupid; Fortuna; Luxury; Wantonness
gold, 29–32, 34, 49, 56–57, 60, 69, 113, 161, 206n18. *See also* arbitrage; bullion; currency
goldsmith bankers, 10, 29, 35, 36, 62
Gordon Riots, 197
Gould, Robert, 56–58
Great Fire of London, 10
Great Recoinage. *See* recoinage
Great Stop of the Exchequer, 10–11. *See also* Exchequer, the
greed: of cit character type, 166; of entrepreneurs, 88–89; of fictional characters, 90, 97, 150; of speculators, 83–84, 142; of theater managers, 45, 86; "Volpone" as byword for, 225n37
Gwynn, Nell, 41

Habermas, Jürgen, 6–7, 124, 126, 144, 184, 186, 193, 201n21, 231n3. *See also* bourgeois public sphere; rational-critical debate
Half-Price Riots, 18–19, 187–97, 231n4
Hammond, Anthony, 80
Hanoverian Dynasty, 13, 83, 108, 116, 228n6. *See also* George I, King; George II, King
Harlequinade, 71, 74, 142, 227–28n1. *See also* pantomime
Harley, Robert, 108, 113–14
Harris, Joseph, *The City Bride* (attrib.), 59
Hauteroche, Noël Lebreton de, 66
Haymarket Theatre: as home of united acting company, 88, 94, 225n37; opening of, as Queen's Theatre, 85–87, 91; as opera house, 94, 105–6, 132; performances of Centlivre's plays at, 91–93, 95–96; renaming as King's Theatre, 105; shareholders in, 87–89; as venue for subscription masquerades, 105
Haywood, Eliza, 80
headpieces. *See* prologues
Heidegger, John James, 105–6
Heywood, Thomas, 199n7
Hill, Aaron, 94
Hogarth, William, 1–2, 83
Hollow Sword-Blade Bank. *See* Sword-Blade Bank
honor, 90–91, 147, 163–65
Horace, 132, 160
Horden, Hildebrand, 64
House of Commons, 113–14. *See also* Parliament
House of Hanover. *See* Hanoverian Dynasty
Howard, Robert, *The Committee*, 227–28n1

Humours of Elections, The. See under Centlivre, Susanna
Husband His Own Cuckold, The (Dryden, John Jr.), 58–59

If You Know Not Me You Know Nobody (Heywood), 199n7
Indian subcontinent, 148. *See also* Dutch East India Company; East India Company; New East India Company
individualism, 166, 183
Inferno (Dante), 70
inflation: of consumer goods, 43–44; of money, 30–33, 49, 56, 69–70; of stock prices, 131, 139, 163, 167, 211n1, 219n80; of the value of women, 26, 38, 43, 168, 169
innovation: as cultural obsession, 36, 44, 48; dramatic and theatrical, 3, 50, 62, 65, 73, 76, 156, 158, 177, 227n76; financial, 13, 25; as private good, 195; with respect to speculation, 15, 39, 75, 132; sources of, 16, 47; unpredictability of, 37. *See also* novelty
interest (concept): collective, 8, 91; commercial, 6; public, defense of, 154; public, diversion of capital from 166; private, cooptation of public interest by, 8, 17, 82, 105–6, 111–12, 114–16, 118, 123; private, exploitation of others in pursuit of, 103, 124; private, as source of investment in culture, 85, 89; of shareholders in theatrical companies, 11–12, 45, 88, 89, 145. *See also* disinterestedness; landed interest; moneyed interest; self-interest
interest (financial), 10, 35, 109, 130, 131, 179, 218n78. *See also* usury
intermediality, 9, 202–3n29, 203n30
Interregnum, the, 10, 11, 53. *See also* Cromwell, Oliver; English civil wars
intertheatricality, 82

irony: in *An Appeal to the Public*, 190; in media coverage of *The Refusal* (Cibber), 18, 183; in *The Refusal* (Cibber), 152, 159, 164, 169; in the *Theatre* (Steele), 124, 135, 225n38; in *A Woman's Case* (Centlivre), 116
irrationality: of markets, 4, 39, 81, 139, 170, 184, 200n10; of opera, 133–34; of publics, 7–8, 17–18, 125, 127, 132, 143, 154, 169, 184, 186, 187–88. *See also* reason
It Should Have Come Sooner, 227–28n1

Jacobean drama. *See* Stuart drama
Jacobean period, 23, 72, 74. *See also* James I, King
Jacobitism, 143, 216n65, 228–29n6
Jamaica, 217–18n74. *See also* Caribbean; West Indies
Jamaica Lady, The, 150
James I, King, 9, 33
James II, King, 13
joint-stock companies: assumption of public debt by, 217n73; origins of, 13, 26, 36; perceptions of, as predatory, 141; relationship to colonial trade, 18, 124, 151; similarities to theater companies, 9, 13, 46–48, 53, 61–62, 74, 83, 132–33, 185–86; speculation in, 83–84. *See also* Dutch East India Company; East India Company; Mississippi Company; New East India Company; Royal Academy of Music; South Sea Company
jointures, 98. *See also* marriage
Jonathan's (coffeehouse), 103–4
Jonson, Ben, 23, 46, 57, 138, 165, 205n1, 230n27
Joye, Charles, 103, 108, 110–12

Killigrew, Charles, 12, 214–15n33
Killigrew, Thomas, 11–12, 85, 128
King's Company, 11–12, 46
King's Theatre. *See* Haymarket Theatre

Knight, Frances, 119, 221n105
Kynaston, Edward, 45

labor: of actors, 48; exploitation of, 61, 159; of fops, 40–41; mystification of, 183–84; of poets, 111. *See also* laborers
laborers, 6–7, 71, 86, 204n55. *See also* labor; workers
Lady Credit, 150. *See also* credit
Lady's Last Stake. See under Cibber, Colley
land: mortgages on, 72, 149; ownership of, as analogy for literary property, 183, 194; speculation in, 4; as traditional repository of wealth, 14, 185. *See also* landed interest
Land Bank, 72
landed interest, 124, 147, 151, 162, 164, 168. *See also* land; moneyed interest
Langbaine, Gerard, 182, 206n10
Law, John, 218n76
Lennox, Charlotte, 99
Les Femmes Savantes (Molière), 170–72, 174, 177–79, 182–83, 229n16
Letter from the Dead Thomas Brown to the Living Heraclitus, A, 80
liberty: English, 196; political, 111; of the press, 196; for women, 103, 217n68. *See also* freedom; rights
licensing: of financial operations, 13, 36; of theater, 11, 12, 85, 94, 129–30, 212n2. *See also* censorship; Licensing Act; Lord Chamberlain's office; Master of Revels
Licensing Act, 47. *See also* Parliament, Acts of
Lincoln's Inn Fields Theatre: as home of Actors' Company, 12, 15, 45–46, 63–65; loyalty of Mary Pix to, 93; management of, 86; plays performed at, 92, 103, 128, 171–72, 174, 227–28n1; political alignment of, 228–29n6; prologues and epilogues performed at, 5, 58–59, 66, 84–85; vacancy and reopening of, 89, 93–94, 102
Lintot, Bernard, 221n105
Lives and Characters of the English Dramatick Poets (Langbaine), 24–25, 206n10
Locke, John: involvement in recoinage debates, 206–7n19; theories, 81, 183, 184, 193, 197. *See also* contract theory; Enlightenment, the; property; recoinage; rights
London Magazine, 188, 189
Lord Chamberlain's office: licenses granted by, 12; orders by, 94; petitions to, 88, 89, 214n33; power struggle with Drury Lane management, 129–30, 140, 144–45, 223n19
Loss of the City, 108
lotteries: allusions to, in *The Busie Body* (Centlivre), 104; Hogarth's views of, 1–2, 83; role in financial revolution, 2, 26, 36; role in public finance, 2, 13, 37, 70; use of children to draw tickets, 199n3. *See also* Lottery Orders (1710); Wheel of Fortune
Lottery Orders (1710), 109
Louis XIV, King: death of, 104
Love for Love (Congreve), 40
Lover. See under Steele, Richard
Love's Contrivance. See under Centlivre, Susanna
Love's Last Shift. See under Cibber, Colley
lower classes, 86, 90, 91, 192; as "common people," 30. *See also* laborers; moral economy of the poor; workers
Lowndes, William, 29, 206n19
Lunatick, The, 86, 88
Luxury (goddess), 5

Magician, The, 227–28n1
mainpieces: discounted admission following third act of, 18, 187–88; generic experimentation in, 62; relation of, to prologues and epilogues, 50–52, 55, 208n8, 210n32

managers (theatrical): compensation of, 3, 194; conflicts with Lord Chamberlain's office, 129–30; economic interdependencies of, 52; fictional representations of, 118, 194–95; negative perceptions of, 85–86, 88, 91, 225n37; relationship to newspaper industry, 196, 209n10; relationship to shareholders, 12, 45, 49, 85–86, 193; relationship to theatrical patents, 11; role in selecting play scripts, 14, 46, 54, 194; role in setting admission prices, 18–19, 187–89, 190–91, 195, 196; women as, 5. *See also names of individual managers*

Manley, Delarivier, 80, 99, 212n5

Man of Mode, The (Etherege), 40

Marplot. See under Centlivre, Susanna

Man's Bewitch'd, The, See under Centlivre, Susanna

marriage: arranged, 109; companionate, 168; compared to a bubble, 166; contracts pertaining to, 88–90, 103, 167–68, 214–15n33; economics of, 27–28, 31, 91, 97–98, 168; gender roles within, 110–11, 217n68; infidelity within, 42–43. *See also* jointures; marriage plot

marriage plot, 207n29; in *The Busie Body*, 91, 97–99; in *The Conscious Lovers*, 124, 147, 150; in *The Gamester*, 90; in *The Refusal*, 154–55, 157, 166–70

Marston, John, 65

Mary II, Queen: accession of, 2; public mourning for, 37–38, 46; reign of, with William III, 13, 23, 36

masculinity, lack of: 5, 106, 110, 133–34, 192, 229n11; of the bourgeois public sphere, 8, 127; of the elite, 102, 119–20, 123. *See also* femininity; feminization; gender; masculinization

masculinization: of Romantic discourses, 82; of spaces, 83, 103. *See also* femininity; feminization; gender; masculinity

masquerade balls, 105

masques, 66, 208n53, 211n56

mass culture, 3, 6–8, 55, 187, 196, 202n25, 202n27

Massinger, Philip, 69, 165

mass media, 7

mass public, 7–8, 17, 19, 55, 120, 127, 144, 184

Master of Revels, 11, 129. *See also* censorship; licensing; Lord Chamberlain's office

media: collaboration and competition among, 202–3n29; news, 19, 196; print, 7, 91, 202n26; representational, 28; theatrical, 3, 5, 8–9, 17, 20, 126, 187. *See also* intermediality; mass culture; mass media; mediation

mediation, 8–9, 51, 55, 63, 202–3n29. *See also* media; intermediality

mercantilism, 9

mergers, 3, 12, 85–89, 93

metatheatricality, 28, 43, 80, 81, 106

middling classes: access to cultural products, 202n27; exploitation of, 18, 120, 123–24, 150–51, 165; growing power of, 4, 15, 17, 43, 49, 58, 75, 146; influence on theater, 13–14, 24, 42, 73–75; as members of bourgeois public sphere, 143–44; participation in gambling, 91; perceived dishonesty of, 60; playwrights as members of, 40–41, 80; as social climbers, 192; use of term, 204n55; values of, 15, 17, 19, 27, 42, 75–76, 145, 153, 156, 164. *See also* class; moneyed interest

milling. *See under* currency

Mills, John, 96

mint, the, 29, 33, 34, 56, 59, 67, 73. *See also* bullion; currency; gold; recoinage; silver

Mississippi Bubble, 169–70. *See also* Mississippi Company

Mississippi Company, 149, 169–70, 218n76

Mist, Nathaniel, 18, 174

mobs. *See* collective action; crowd action; crowds; riots
mock advertisements, 124, 137, 139–40, 216n65, 223n18, 225n38, 226n41
modernity: economic, of England, 3, 6; perceived, of Whig social order, 143. *See also* Ancients and Moderns
Molière (Jean-Baptiste Poquelin), 170–79, 183, 229n13, 229n16
monetary theory, 207n29
moneyed interest, 124, 147, 151, 157, 162, 164–65
monopolies: as "the Devil," 114; held by East India Company, 38, 46–47; held by Haymarket Theatre, 94; held by Mississippi Company, 218n76; held by patent companies on licensed theater in London, 11–12, 14, 15, 45, 46, 48, 86, 188; held by South Sea Company, 108–9; trading privileges associated with, 13. *See also* duopolies
moral economy of the poor, 143
mortgages, 11, 72, 148, 214–15n33. *See also* contracts; credit; debt; interest (financial); land; property
Mottley, John, 95, 215n45, 230n21
Murrain, 132, 160, 176

Nation A Family, A. See under Steele, Richard
National Archives (UK), 214n22, 214n26, 215n40, 215n42
national credit, 10, 13, 108, 204; personification of, 2. *See also* credit; national debt; public credit
national debt: of England, establishment of, 2, 10–11, 13, 38; of England, restructuring of, 13, 108–9, 114–15, 217nn72–73, 218n78; of France, restructuring of, 218n76. *See also* national credit; public credit
New Atalantis, The (Manley), 80, 212n5
New East India Company, 46–48. *See also* colonialism; Dutch East India Company; East India Company; East Indies; global Indies
New Economic Criticism, 6, 200–201n17
New Theatre. *See* Lincoln's Inn Fields Theatre
New Way to Pay Old Debts, A (Massinger), 165
Newcastle, Duke of, 129–30, 145, 223n19. *See also* Lord Chamberlain's office
newspapers: advertising in (*see* advertisements); as venue for public formation, 126; juxtaposition of economic and entertainment news in, 9, 17, 18, 84, 126; growth of, 25, 126; influence of David Garrick on, 232n28; *See also* periodical press; *and names of individual newspapers*
Nicolini (Nicola Grimaldi), 139, 225n39
Nine Years' War, 14, 23, 29, 36–37, 58
nobility: criticisms of, 90–91, 163–64; fictional members of, 206n14; influence of, on Restoration theaters, 12; members of, as theatrical patrons, 10, 86–87, 89, 129, 132–33. *See also* aristocracy; elite; upper classes
No Fools Like Wits (Gay), 171–72, 174, 229n16
No Fools Like Wits (Wright), 171–72, 177, 180, 183, 229n16
Norton, Richard: as benefactor of Drury Lane, 94; *Pausanius* (attrib.), 46
nostalgia, 3, 31–32, 33, 38, 57, 63, 65–67, 152, 160–61
novels, 5, 222–23n7
novelty: as cultural obsession, 15, 25, 44, 49; in *Love's Last Shift*, 24–27, 36–39, 42–44, 45, 158; myth of, 19–20; as selling feature of plays, 46, 62–66, 73, 74–75, 95–96

Of Dramatick Poesy (Dryden, John), 23
Old Batchelor, The (Congreve), 40
Oldfield, Anne, 80, 212n7
Old Price Wars, 197

opera: conventional critiques of, 133–34, 224n32; critiques of, in prologues and epilogues, 64–66, 71, 74; critiques of, in *The Conscious Lovers*, 152–53; critiques of, in the *Theatre*, 128, 134–39, 142, 144, 153, 185–86; government support for, 145; monopoly on, held by Haymarket Theatre, 94; relationship to masque, 66, 211n56; speculative financing of, 17, 124, 128, 132–33, 224n31, 225n38. *See also Artaxerxes*; Benedetto; *Brutus of Alba*; Nicolini; Royal Academy of Music; semi-opera; virtuoso (opera entrepreneur)
Otway, Thomas, 152–53

Pack, George, 95–96
pamphlets: as object of study, 5, 28, 222–23n7; related to drama, 153–54, 216n65; related to Half-Price riots, 188–92, 231n6; related to recoinage debates, 29–30, 206–7n19; related to South Sea Bubble, 110, 130, 140, 223–24n19; related to Wheel of Fortune lottery, 199n3. *See also names of individual pamphlets*
pantomime, 49–50, 62, 73, 227–28n1. *See also* Harlequinade
paper credit, 71, 130. *See also* Bills of Exchange; credit
Parliament: corruption within, 38, 113, 219n80; debates within, over Peerage Bill, 129; debates within, over recoinage, 15, 29–30, 34; debates within, over South Sea Bill, 128, 130, 140, 141; elections for, 134; influence over, 162; partisanship within, 108, 113, 129–30, 165; responsibility for national debt, 11, 13, 204n52; role in administration of lotteries and annuities, 37, 70; role in regulation of joint-stock companies, 38, 46; role in South Sea crisis, 108, 109, 114–15, 128, 165, 222n3. *See also* House of Commons; House of Lords; Parliament, Acts of; Tory Party; Whig Party
Parliament, Acts of: Act of Anne, 182; Act to Encrease the South Sea Capital, 115, 220n94; Act to Restore Publick Credit, 110; Bubble Act, 219n83; Licensing Act, 47; Recoinage Act, 30; Riot Act, 143
Patent Company, 15–16, 46, 63–65, 68, 85, 88
patents: boom in, during 1690s, 13, 36; theatrical, granted to Killigrew and Davenant, 11–13, 85, 129, 194; theatrical, granted to Royal Academy, 133; theatrical, held by Richard Steel, 17, 129–30, 146; theatrical, treatment as property, 19, 47–48, 87–88, 214–15n33. *See also* monopolies; Patent Company
patronage: rejection of, 132–33; solicitation of, 54, 81, 110–11; as source of cultural influence, 15, 75; of the theater, 13, 83, 86–87
Pausanius (Norton, attrib.), 46
performance studies, 8, 202n28
periodical press: centrality of, to theater-finance nexus, 3, 9, 17; representation in, of the South Sea Bubble, 120, 125–26, 172; rise of, 17, 25; role of, in public formation, 6, 28, 44, 126. *See also* newspapers
Philaster (Settle), 64, 72, 211n48
piracy: literary, 145, 170–71, 182–83, 230n22; maritime, 149. *See also* copyright; plagiarism; publication rights
Pix, Mary, 80, 93, 118–19
plagiarism: *The Refusal* (Cibber) as, 18, 155, 170–84, 186, 229n16; scatological figurations of, 174–77, 230n22. *See also* copyright; piracy; publication rights
Platonick Lady, The. See under Centlivre, Susanna
plaudite, 52
playbills, 9, 71–72, 188, 203n30
players. *See* actors
Players Turn'd Academicks, The, 118

playhouses. *See* theaters
playing companies: establishment in London, 10–12, 81; as owners of plays, 54; relationships with audiences, 50; relationships with playwrights, 52, 54, 96. *See also* actors; managers (theatrical); theaters
plays. *See titles of specific plays*
playwrights: class identity of, 41, 57, 58, 74; collusion with management, 86; compensation of, 3, 52–54, 110–11, 119, 182–83, 221n105; intellectual property of, 54, 119, 180–83, 230n22, 230n27, 230n29; metatheatrical representations of, 27, 40–41, 53, 217n68; overabundance of, 47, 60, 69–70; as plagiarists (*see* plagiarism); relationships with audiences and critics, 27, 43, 52–59; as speculative investors, 27, 40–41, 53–54, 72–74, 107–8, 158–59; women as, 5, 80–82, 93, 99–102, 118–19, 213n9; as writers of prologues and epilogues, 53. *See also names of individual playwrights*
political economy: Charles Davenant as practitioner of, 200n16; disciplinary formation of, 4, 10, 200n10; discursive interchange with theater, 201n20; as object of study, 200–201n17
Ponzi scheme, 110, 222n6. *See also* chain-letter scheme; fraud
Pope, Alexander, 24, 80, 174, 212n4, 219–20n87. *See also* Scriblerians
Poquelin, Jean-Baptiste. *See* Molière
Porter, Miss, 5, 200n12
Post Boy, 127–28, 177, 180–82
Post-Boy Robb'd of His Mail, The (Gildon, attrib.), 87–89, 214n25
Powell, George, 64
profit shares, 11–12, 48, 85–86, 88, 214–15n33. *See also* building shares
projecting, 26, 38, 48. *See also* Projecting Age; projectors; projects
Projecting Age, 13, 36. *See also* projecting; projectors; projects

projectors, 39, 87. *See also* projecting; Projecting Age; projects
projects, 26, 49, 58, 74, 87, 116, 136, 170. *See also* Projecting Age; projecting; projectors
prologues: to *The Anatomist* (Ravenscroft), 66–68; to *Bonduca* (Fletcher), 64–65; to *The Busie Body* (Centlivre), 100; to *The City Bride* (Harris, attrib.), 59; to *Every Man in His Humor* (Jonson), 23; to *The Gamester* (Centlivre), 84–85; *Henry V* (Shakespeare), 52; to *Love's Last Shift* (Cibber), 40–41, 72, 74; to *Pausanius*, (Norton, attrib.), 46; to *Philaster* (Settle), 64, 72; to *The Refusal* (Cibber), 159–61, 178–79, 182; to *The Sham Lawyer* (Drake), 50, 69–75; to *The Stolen Heiress* (Centlivre), 100; to *The Theatre*, 128, 223n18; to *Timoleon*, 60–62, 70; to *The Unnatural Brother* (Filmer), 67–69
prologues and epilogues: authorship of, 53–54, 85; delivery of, 5, 53, 63; dialogism of, 16, 50; as evidence of literary circles, 80; as marketing devices, 8, 52, 55, 63; as object of study, 50–55, 62–63, 76, 203n30, 208n8, 209n9; publication of, 8, 15, 45, 51, 84, 94, 100; relationship to mainpiece, 51, 55, 210n32; representations of audiences in, 8, 14, 52, 54–55, from 1690s, 56–69, 74–76, 209n11; topicality of, 15, 49, 51, 55, 209n13, 209n19. *See also* epilogues; prologues
property: destruction of, 18–19, 189, 193, 196, 197; intangible, 118, 157, 158–59, 168, 182–84; intellectual, 6, 99; literary, 155, 170–71, 176–77, 182–84; mobility of, 81, 98; relationship to bourgeois public sphere, 6–7, 186–87, 193; theater patent as, 87; women as, 27–28, 97–98, 106–7. *See also Crisis of Property, The* (Steele); Lock, John; property rights

278   INDEX

property rights, 19, 184, 188, 192–95, 197, 204n52
Public Advertiser, 188–89, 190–91, 193, 231n6, 231n7, 231n11
public credit, 35, 83, 108–10, 115, 130, 165, 217nn72–73, 218n78. *See also* national credit; public finance
public finance, 13, 35, 37–38, 49, 70, 79, 103, 118, 140. *See also* public credit
public good, 17, 80, 82, 87–88, 91, 111–12, 114–16, 118. *See also* public interest; publics
public interest, 8, 115, 166. *See also* interest (concept); publics
Public Ledger, 195
public opinion: anxiety around, 49, 75; deployment of, as threat, 99; failure to influence, 131; indicators of, 5, 51; influence on institutions, 4; influence on the theater, 3, 12, 49, 69, 194; influence on value, 4, 15, 26, 29, 36, 67, 75, 101; power of, 19, 44, 45, 49, 62, 124; shaping of, by the elite, 19; shaping of, by experts, 3, 16, 50, 58, 61, 62; shaping of, by financial interests, 17–18, 61, 116, 134; shaping of, by market forces, 187; shaping of, by unknown agents, 45. *See also* bourgeois public sphere; public good; public interest; publics; public sphere
publics: agency or passivity of, 19, 127, 134, 144, 154, 157, 184; competing views of, 50, 123–24; complicity of, 172, 177; dark side of, 17–18, 197; diversity of, 3; emergence or formation of, 4, 6, 8, 16, 18, 52, 74, 125, 126–27, 134, 184, 185, 197, 202n26; investing, 18, 125–26, 155, 157, 169; power of, 8, 17, 76; rationality or irrationality of, 7, 8, 49, 125–26, 127, 132, 134, 143, 154, 184, 186–88; reconfiguration of, 20; rhetorical construction of, 86, 119–20, 126, 154, 180, 190–91, 196; theatrical, 7–8, 9, 18, 19, 28, 34, 44, 49, 52, 54–55, 59, 82, 145–46, 157, 185–97, 202n28, 202–3n29; vulnerability of, 6, 125, 127, 132, 135, 141–42, 144, 154, 157, 177. *See also* bourgeois public sphere; collective; counterpublics; crowds; public credit; public finance; public good; public opinion; public spheres; riots
publishers. *See* booksellers

Queen's Theatre. *See* Haymarket Theatre; *see also* Congreve, William; Heidegger, John James; Vanbrugh, John

race, 7, 106, 227n69. *See also* colonialism; creole woman; ethnicity; plantation economy; slavery; whiteness
rake. *See under* character types
rational-critical debate, 7–8, 19, 126–27, 144, 154, 184, 186–87, 196, 231n3. *See also* bourgeois public sphere; Habermas, Jürgen
Ravenscroft, Edward, 66
reason: cultivation of, 124, 127, 154; emphasis on, in political economy, 4; as ideological fiction, 186–87, 190; invocations of, in the *Theater*, 136–37; man of, 152; rational-critical debate
recoinage: causes of, 23, 29–30, 207n20; debates over, 29–30, 206–7n19; economic crisis triggered by, 30; Recoinage Act, 30; relationship to reform movements, 34; representation of, in *Love's Last Shift*, 25–36, 38, 44, 45, 68, 158, 185; representation of, in prologues and epilogues, 45, 49–50, 56–62, 72–73, 75, 185; as structuring device for this book, 14–16. *See also* currency
Recoinage Act, 30. *See also* Parliament, Acts of
reform: of currency, 34, 36, 48; of dramatic genres, 25–27, 49, 74–75; of French finance, 218; of as overarching concern in post-1688 society, 28, 34; rakes, 15, 24, 39, 90, 205n5; of social

and cultural mores, 41–43, 145, 146, 153, 156, 227. *See also* Societies for the Reformation of Manners
refusal, right of: to marriage, 106, 167–68; to new plays, 54
refusals, 167–68, 229n12. *See also* calls; time bargains
Refusal, The. See under Cibber, Colley
Relapse, The (Vanbrugh), 24, 206n14, 208n54
Remarks on a Play, Call'd, The Conscious Lovers (Dennis), 153–54, 226n66
repertory: audience influence on, 14; fops in, 27, 37, 40, 41; mediation of, in prologues and epilogues, 55; production rights to, 46; staples of, 16, 24, 156; theoretical approaches to, 199n6; updating of, 16, 25, 27, 63, 65, 68, 69, 74, 159. *See also* adaptation; repertory theater
repertory theater, 3, 158. *See also* repertory
Restoration, the: economic and cultural history of, 10; as impetus for reopening of theaters, 11; periodization of, 6; sexual licentiousness of, 32–33, 41, 74; values of, 25. *See also* English civil wars; Restoration theater
Restoration theater: class dynamics of, 5, 12, 13, 41; comedy of, 15, 24, 37, 40, 43, 73, 74, 165; continuities and changes from prewar theater, 9, 23, 53, 182; financial operations of, 11–12, 46, 54, 204–5n57; star actors of, 41, 63, 74. *See also* Restoration, the
reviews, 8–9, 17, 46, 60, 186. *See also* criticism
revivals: compared to renewal of fashion trends, 26–27, 39, 40; glut of, 49–50, 56; prologues and epilogues to, 51, 52; of Restoration drama, 95, 172; of songs, 227–28n1; theorizations of, 199n6, 203n30; of Tudor and early Stuart drama, 3, 63–65, 69, 73, 75, 116. *See also* repertory

revolution. *See* financial revolution; French Revolution; Revolution Settlement
Revolution Settlement, 2, 11, 13, 23, 28, 41, 43, 170–71, 204n51, 204n52
Rich, Christopher, 12, 45, 85–90, 94, 102, 225n37
Richard III (Shakespeare), adaptation of. *See under* Cibber, Colley
rights: of authors, 182–83, 230n22; of the public, 184, 188, 196; of theater patentees, 46, 129; of women, 16. *See also* copyright; property rights
Riot Act. *See under* Parliament, Acts of; *see also* riots
riots: against Aaron Hill's management of Drury Lane, 94; as expressions of moral economy of the poor, 143; as spectacle, 144; as way to influence theatrical offerings, 13–14. *See also* Gordon Riots; Half-Price Riots; Old Price Wars; Riot Act; Sacheverell Riots
Rival Modes, The (Smythe), 206n14
Rival Sisters, The (Gould), 56–58
Roberts, James, 127
Rover, The (Behn), 24
Rowe, Nicholas, 80
Royal Academy of Music: castrati of, 139, 225n39; critiques of, by Richard Steele, 17, 123–24, 128–29, 133–45, 185–86; establishment of, 105–6, 132–33; published notices of, 225n38
Royal Exchange, 199n7. *See also* Exchange Alley

Sacheverell Riots, 143
satire: in advertisements, 139–40, 174, 186, 216n65, 225n41; antifeminist, 80, 118–19, 170; Augustan, 47; of Italian opera, in *Theatre*, 132, 135–37; of lotteries, 1–2, 199n3; as object of study, 5; in pamphlets, 189, 192, 194; partisan political, 80; in poetry, 87, 118–19; in prologues and epilogues, 55, 67, 157; of the Scriblerus circle, 228n3; of the

280 INDEX

satire (continued)
   South Sea company, 159–61, 221n100, 228n3; in stage comedy, 15, 73, 74, 156, 165, 205n5; of the *Theatre*, 128, 223n18; in visual culture, 1–2, 221n100
science, 25, 229n13. *See also* Ancients and Moderns; Enlightenment, the; virtuoso (character type)
Scott, Mr.: *The Unhappy Kindness* (attrib.), 62
Scriblerians, 228n3, 229n16. *See also* Arbuthnot, John; Gay, John; Pope, Alexander; Swift, Jonathan
securities, 2, 13, 36, 107
self-interest, 16, 76, 80, 87–88, 166, 187, 190
semi-opera, 1, 49–50, 62, 64, 134
sentiment, 151, 205n5. *See also* sentimental comedy
sentimental comedy, 15, 24, 27, 153, 205n5, 227n76. *See also* comedy; sentiment
Settle, Elkanah, 64, 211n48
Shakespeare, William, 46, 51, 152–53; *Henry V*, 52; *Richard III*, 182; *Two Gentlemen of Verona*, 188
Sham Lawyer, The (Drake), 50, 69–75
silver: Bank of England reserves of, 14, 35, 72; debasement of, 68; recoinage of, 15, 28–30, 33–34, 59, 206–7n19; shortage of, 49, 56. *See also* arbitrage; bullion; currency; recoinage
singers, 86, 133, 139, 142, 224n31, 225n39. *See also* Benedetto; Nicolini; opera; Royal Academy of Music
Sir Richard Steele. *See* Steele, Richard
Sir William Davenant. *See* Davenant, William
Skipwith, Thomas, 12, 214n22
slavery, 106, 108–9, 130, 148–49, 217–18n74. *See also Asiento*; colonialism; plantation economy; South Sea Company
Smythe, James Moore, 206n14

Societies for the Reformation of Manners, 34, 206n13, 207n33. *See also* reform
South-Sea, or, The Biters Bit (Chetwood, attrib.), 227–28n1
South Sea Bill, 128, 130, 140, 141. *See also* Parliament; South Sea Bubble; South Sea Company
South Sea Bubble: Bubble Act, 219n83; causes of crash, 219n83; as chain-letter scheme, 110, 160, 176, 222n6; origins of, 109–10, 217n72, 218n78; rationality of, 124–25, 222n2, 222nn4–5; relationship to Mississippi Bubble, 169–70, 218n76; symbolic dimension of, 126; use of term, 211n1. *See also* South Sea Bill; South Sea Bubble, literary responses to; South Sea Company
South Sea Bubble, literary responses to, 156, 227–28n1. *See also* Centlivre, Susanna, *A Woman's Case*; Cibber, Colley, *The Refusal*; Steele, Richard, *Theatre*; Swift, Jonathan, "The Bubble"
South Sea Company: chartering of, 108; engraftment of public debt, 108–9, 217n73, 218n76, 218n78; involvement in slave trade, 106, 108–9, 130, 217–18n74; minutes of Court of Directors of, 114–16; notices published by, 115–16, 225n38; relationship to Tory Party, 108, 111–14, 128–29, 165, 229n9; transfer books of, 168–69. *See also* South Sea Bubble; South Sea Bubble, literary responses to
Spanish Curate, The (Fletcher and Massinger), 69
spectacle: as means of deluding masses, 17, 120, 124, 157, 185–86; as means of updating repertory, 49, 63, 65, 68, 69, 74, 76; opera and semi-opera as, 1, 17, 124, 128, 132, 145, 211n56; post-1695 rise of, 50, 62–63, 66–68; public demand for, 64, 69, 139, 158; South Sea bubble as, 159; street action as, 141–42, 144

Spectator (Addison and Steele): mockery of opera in, 134, 224n34; product placement for, in *The Conscious Lovers*, 145, 226n52; as public-forming text, 7, 126–27, 146

spectatorship, 144

speculation: anxiety around, 75; collective-forming potential of, 186; dangers of, 17–18, 84, 124, 157, 185; definition of, 4, 199–200n8; emasculating effects of, 5; embrace of, 82, 93; greed as motivation for, 83–84, 166; homology with operations of literature, 6; pleasures of, 84, 120; rise of, 36, 79; similarity to gambling, 104; as source of innovation and risk, 15, 75; temporality of, 161. *See also* speculative manias

speculative manias, 37, 110, 125, 132, 140, 222n2

Stanhope-Sunderland ministry, 129–30

Steele, Richard: as lover of controversy, 128; as plantation owner, 148–49; political career, 123, 129; professional connections with Centlivre, 80, 112, 116, 212n3; role in advent of bourgeois public sphere, 126–27, 186; tangles with castrati, 225n39; as theater patentee, 129–30. Works of: *The Conscious Lovers*, 18, 124, 145–55, 156, 157, 158, 162, 221n105, 222n1, 223–24n19, 226n55, 226n59, 227n76; *The Crisis of Property*, 130; *Lover*, 80, 212n3; *A Nation A Family*, 130; the *Theatre*, 17–18, 112, 123–24, 126–46, 148, 151, 153–54, 156, 157, 160, 176, 186–87. *See also Spectator; Tatler*

stock exchange, 16, 34, 106, 107

stockjobbers, 30, 50, 62, 73, 104. *See also Broken Stock-Jobbers, The; Four and Twenty Stock-Jobbers; Stock-Jobbers, The*

Stock-Jobbers, The (Chetwood, attrib.), 227–28n1

stockjobbing, 13, 119, 131, 171. *See also* stockjobbers

stock market: audience attunement to, 28; connections to theater economics, 9, 11, 103, 124, 137, 185, 197; development of, 9, 36; dynamics of, 37, 104–5, 219; similarity of, to gambling, 83, 167; similarity of, to marriage market, 166; women's participation in, 217n67. *See also* financial instruments; joint-stock companies; securities; stock exchange; stockjobbers; stockjobbing; stocks

stocks: in the Bank of England, 30, 35; expertise in, 50; insider trading of, 104, 160; in the Mississippi Company, 149; in new plays and playwrights, 41, 72, 183; prices of, 115, 131, 137, 139, 166, 173; repertory plays compared to, 158–59; in Royal Academy of Music, 136–39, 225n38; sell-offs of, 108, 176; in the South Sea Company, 104, 108–11, 114–16, 130–31, 138, 139, 141, 142, 149, 156, 159, 160, 166–67, 169, 175–76, 179, 211, 217n72, 217n74, 218n78, 219n80, 219–20n87; speculation in, 4; use as bribes, 46–47, 219n80; value of, 39, 43, 109, 137, 139, 163, 222n3; women as, 26, 107, 168. *See also* joint-stock companies; stock exchange; stockjobbers; stockjobbing; stock market

Stolen Heiress, The. See under Centlivre, Susanna

Stop of the Exchequer, 10–11. *See also* Exchequer, the

Stuart, Anne. *See* Anne, Queen

Stuart drama, 3, 9, 15–16, 23, 64, 72–74, 211. *See also* Stuart Dynasty

Stuart Dynasty, 11. *See also* Anne, Queen; Charles I, King; Charles II, King; James I, King; James II King; Restoration, the

subscriptions: for the Bank of England, 38; for masquerade balls, 105; for printed books, 116–17, 181; for the Royal Academy of Music, 132–33, 224n31, 225n38; for the South Sea

subscriptions (*continued*)
  Company, 109–10, 114, 115, 130, 160, 169, 173, 180, 219n80; for theatrical performances, 86; for Vanbrugh's Haymarket Theatre, 86–89, 91
Swift, Jonathan, 25; "The Bubble," 117, 221n100. *See also* Scriblerians; *Tatler*
Swiney, Owen, 94
Sword-Blade Company, 104, 219n83

tailpieces. *See* epilogues
Tatler (Addison, Steele, and Swift): allusions to Centlivre in, 80, 99–100, 212n3; as exemplary public-forming text, 126–27, 146; inclusion of satirical advertisements, 225n41; mockery of opera, 134, 224n34; reflections on advertisements as "News from the Little World," 140–41, 176; reporting on theatrical riots, 94
theater-finance nexus: archival contours of, 17, 23, 50, 55, 125; definition of, 4; historical development of, 9, 19, 27; as new locus of inquiry, 6, 197; as site for debate about economics, 44, 62, 158; as site for debate about publics, 8, 17, 18, 19, 50, 79–80, 123, 124, 126, 156–57, 185; as site for formation of counterpublics, 187, 196
theaters: similarities to joint-stock companies, 3, 4, 9, 11, 13, 46–48, 49, 53, 82, 180; as sites of public formation, 4, 8, 9, 19, 202n28. *See also names of specific theaters*
Theatre. See under Steele, Richard
Theatre Royal Covent Garden, 188–90, 193, 195–96
Theatre Royal Drury Lane: construction of, 11; management of, 89, 94, 97, 129–30, 156, 188, 225n37, 228–29n6; Patent Company residency at, 15, 63–65, 68, 72, 85; patent to, 85, 87–88, 129–30, 140, 146, 194; plays performed at, 24, 46, 50, 56, 59, 62, 64, 67, 69, 92, 95, 102–3, 116, 145, 171, 174, 188, 220n96, 224–25n35, 227–28n1; prompter at, 87, 227–28n1; riots at, 94, 188–91, 193; shareholders in, 85–86, 88, 214–15n33; silencing of, 94–96, 129–30
Theatrical Disquisitions, 190–93, 231–32n17
theatrical managers. *See* managers, theatrical
Theatrical Review, 192–94
Thirty Years' War, 10
Three Hours after Marriage (Pope, Gay, Arbuthnot), 80
Three Original Letters to a Friend in the Country, 191–92
ticket prices: for lotteries, 37; for theatrical performances, 11, 47, 50, 60, 188, 195, 204–5n57. *See also* Half-Price Riots
time bargains, 167. *See also* calls; refusals
Timoleon, 60–62, 70
Tom's (coffeehouse), 61, 201n42
Tory Party: satirists associated with, 80, 108; ties to Lincoln's Inn Fields, 228–29n6; ties to the South Sea Company, 108, 111–14, 116, 128–29, 165, 229n9. *See also* Parliament; Whig Party
Tragedie of Bonduca, The (Fletcher), 64–65
tragedy, 23, 27
Treaty of Utrecht, 108–9, 113
Trotter, Catherine, 80
Tudor drama, 3, 15–16. *See also* Elizabeth, Queen
Two Gentlemen of Verona (Shakespeare), 188

Unhappy Kindness, The (Scott, attrib.), 62
United Company: breakup of, 49, 51, 62, 63; monopoly held by, 12, 45, 47–48; reestablishment of, 85–89, 93–94. *See also* Actors' Rebellion; mergers; monopolies
Unnatural Brother, The (Filmer), 65–66, 67–69

"Upon the Bells ringing at St. Martins in the Fields." *See under* Centlivre, Susanna
upper classes: cultural power of, 15, 75; interests of, 91, 124, 151, 186–87; involvement in gambling, 90; support for masquerade balls, 105; wealth of, 86. *See also* aristocracy; class; elite; landed interest; nobility
usury, 60–61, 200n10. *See also* interest (financial)

value: abstraction of, 4, 36, 109–10, 139, 158, 159, 169, 176–77, 179, 183, 184; of advertisements, 128; contingency and instability of, 26, 29, 30–33, 35, 36, 119, 161; of copyrights, 183, 221n105; cultural notions of, 207n29; of currency, 15–16, 26, 28–34, 38, 49, 56, 57, 59, 68–70, 206n18; dependence on public opinion, 3–4, 15, 29, 35–39, 40, 67, 75, 179, 185, 194; depersonalization of, 4; determination of, 50, 58, 148; fabrication of, 16, 18, 25, 61, 76, 141, 158, 162, 163, 172, 180; failure to produce, 59, 61; manipulation of, 58; of monopolies, 47; of novelty, 25, 37, 39, 43–44; of opera, 128, 137, 139; perception as absolute, 161; perception as intrinsic, 33, 36, 38, 60, 68, 163–64, 169, 185; of plays, 16, 68, 101, 118, 194, 196–97; of property, 168; of South Sea stock, 109, 110, 130–32, 139, 141, 150, 163, 167, 173, 175–76, 183, 218n78; of theater tickets, 60; traditional repositories of, 185; of United Company shares, 214n33; of women, 30, 32–33, 38–39, 43, 168–69
values: abstract, 88; aristocratic, 145; of the court, 163; of humane comedy, 26; of the middling classes, 17, 19, 73, 75–76, 124, 151, 153; moral, 34; prewar, 73–74; of the Restoration, 25; of the theater, 69; of the Whig party, 104, 162–63, 165

Vanbrugh, John: *The Relapse*, 24, 206n14, 208n54; as theater entrepreneur, 86–88, 90, 94
Verbruggen, John, 56
Vintner Trick'd, The (Betterton), 65
virtuoso (character type). *See under* character types
virtuoso (opera entrepreneur), 136–37
VOC. *See* Dutch East India Company
Volpone (Jonson): allusions to, 126, 225n37; eighteenth-century performances of, 116, 220n96, 224–25n35

Walpole, Robert, 129–30, 161–62, 165, 228–29n6
Wantonness (goddess), 2
wardship, 97, 104
wars. *See* Anglo-Dutch Wars; English civil wars, Nine Years' War; Thirty Years' War
Weekly Journal or British Gazetteer, 202n4
Weekly Journal, or Saturday's Post, 174–79; 225n38
West Indies, 18, 106, 108–9, 148–51. *See also* Barbados; Caribbean; creole woman; global Indies; *Jamaica Lady, The*; plantation economy; slavery; South Sea Company
Wheel of Fortune, 1, 4, 199n1. *See also* lotteries
Whig Party: alignment with major financial companies, 108, 129, 165; association with managers of Drury Lane Theatre, 129, 161–62, 165, 228n6; Centlivre as member of, 16, 80, 81, 103–4, 106, 108, 110–14, 165; economic ideology of, 157, 161–63, 171; ideals of, 146, 151, 165; involvement in South Sea scheme, 111–12, 113, 116, 162, 229n9; opposition to plays, 84; relationship to crowd action, 143; war debt incurred by, 108. *See also* Parliament; Tory Party; Walpole, Robert
Whitehall Evening Post, 177–79

whiteness, 8, 150, 227, 231. *See also* ethnicity; race
Wife Well Manag'd, The. See under Centlivre, Susanna
Wilks, Robert: conflict with Centlivre, 95, 100; management of Drury Lane, 102, 129, 130; role in *The Busie Body* (Centlivre), 96
William of Orange. *See* William III, King
William III, King, 2, 13, 23–24, 36, 58
Wiseman, Jane, 80
wit, 50, 56–61, 67–72, 87, 98, 99, 144, 179
Wit without Money (Fletcher), 69
Woman's Case, A. See under Centlivre, Susanna
women: as actors, 5, 9, 42, 63, 119; as audience members, 42; as contractual and financial agents, 5, 81, 97, 103, 108, 110–11, 118, 217n67; education of, 170; exclusion from public life, 6–7, 16–17, 80, 81, 83, 119, 185; as gamblers, 84; keeping of, 32, 41, 152; liberty of, 217; rights of, 16, 167; as scientists, 229n13; as theater managers, 5; value of, 30–32, 38–39, 43, 168; as vehicles of exchange, 27–28, 97–98, 107; as writers, 5, 80–83, 93, 95, 99–102, 119, 213n9. *See also* creole woman; femininity; feminism; gender
Wonder, The. See under Centlivre, Susanna
workers, 48, 88, 89. *See also* labor; laborers; lower classes; middling classes
Wright, Thomas, 170–74, 183

Ximena. See under Cibber, Colley

Younger Brother, The (Behn), 59, 67

zero-sum game, 85, 104, 117

www.ingramcontent.com/pod-product-compliance
Lightning Source LLC
Chambersburg PA
CBHW021348300426
44114CB00012B/1130